Jeff Chandler

Jeff Chandler

Film, Record, Radio, Television and Theater Performances

Jeff Wells

McFarland & Company, Inc., Publishers
Jefferson, North Carolina, and London

Photographs provided by Photofest unless otherwise noted.

LIBRARY OF CONGRESS CATALOGUING-IN-PUBLICATION DATA

Wells, Jeff, 1955–
Jeff Chandler : film, record, radio, television
and theater performances / Jeff Wells.
p.   cm.
Includes bibliographical references and index.

ISBN 978-0-7864-2001-8
softcover : 50# alkaline paper ∞

1. Chandler, Jeff, 1918–1961—Performances. I. Title.
PN2287.C475W45   2005   791.4302'8'092—dc22   2004025785

British Library cataloguing data are available

©2005 Jeff Wells. All rights reserved

*No part of this book may be reproduced or transmitted in any form
or by any means, electronic or mechanical, including photocopying
or recording, or by any information storage and retrieval system,
without permission in writing from the publisher.*

On the cover: Jeff Chandler in a Columbia Pictures publicity pose;
background: Anne Baxter and Chandler in *The Spoilers* (1955)

Manufactured in the United States of America

*McFarland & Company, Inc., Publishers
Box 611, Jefferson, North Carolina 28640
www.mcfarlandpub.com*

To the cast and crew of the motion picture,
radio, television and music industries who worked with
and provided support for Jeff Chandler.

Acknowledgments

I would like to thank the following institutions and their representatives for their invaluable assistance: Jeannette Berard and Klaudia Englund, American Radio Archives, Thousand Oaks Library; Julie L. Graham, Arts Special Collections, Young Research Library, University of California, Los Angeles; Department of Special Collections, Young Research Library, University of California, Los Angeles; Doheny Memorial Library, University of Southern California; Dennis Roverato, Family Theater; Los Angeles Central Library; Caroline Sisneros, Louis B. Mayer Library, the American Film Institute; Margaret Herrick Library, Academy of Motion Picture Arts and Sciences; New York State Archives; Ron Wolf and director-actor Ken Greenwald, Pacific Pioneer Broadcasters; Santa Monica Public Library Periodicals Department; Valerie Yaros, Screen Actors Guild; Ned Comstock, Universal Studios Collection, USC Cinema-Television Library; Warner Bros. Collection, USC; Dave Smith, the Walt Disney Archives.

My thanks to the actors, fans, family members, and others who allowed themselves to be quoted or interviewed, including Anne Milman Briscoe and Jerome Kurshan of the Class of 1935, Erasmus Hall High School; Rita Gam; Peter Graves and his publicist, Sandy Brokaw; Arline Gray; Will Hutchins; Elaine Margo; Kim Novak and her manager, Sue Cameron; Bob Rains; William Reynolds; Ed Shevelew and his son, Jon; Henry Silva; Angela von Mizener; Esther Williams and her assistant, Deborah Joseph.

I would also like to extend thanks to Kim Moses, Fred G. Haseney, L. Ron Hubbard, June Rosenberry, Kevin Connelly and Jerry Rzepecki—friend and muse.

Table of Contents

Acknowledgments
vi

Preface
1

From Flatbush to Filmland
5

The Films
39

Recordings (Music and Spoken Word)
123

Radio
131

Television
191

Theater
197

Notes
199

Bibliography
209

Index
211

Preface

In 1952, Marilyn Monroe was the hottest thing in town, with marquees billing her over such stars as Ginger Rogers and Cary Grant. 20th Century–Fox had upped her loan-out price to over $100,000, and expected to raise it another $100,000 when she completed *Gentlemen Prefer Blondes*.[1]

That same year, when 20th tried to borrow Jeff Chandler (who had previously worked at that studio in *Broken Arrow*, *Two Flags West*, and *Bird of Paradise*) from Universal-International for *The Robe*, all U-I asked for in return were the services of Marilyn Monroe.[2] That was their idea of a fair trade — which tells us a lot about Jeff Chandler.

Though he was clearly a major figure in motion pictures by 1952, Chandler started his career in Hollywood on radio in 1946. His first starring role was in *The Private Practice of Dr. Dana* in 1947.

That same year, Jeff made the transition from radio to film, and worked for, among others, Universal-International, 20th Century–Fox, United Artists and Allied Artists. He also wrote music, sharing writing credits with film composers William Lava and Henry Mancini. As if he weren't working hard enough, his first five years on film were concurrent with his work on *Our Miss Brooks*, a weekly radio series broadcast live from Hollywood that almost always required his services no matter his location.

Per *Variety*'s yearly report of the top-grossing films, Chandler was involved in the production of 27 box-office champions for ten consecutive years beginning in 1949. On the silver screen, Chandler starred and costarred with many of the biggest, the best and the brightest stars in Hollywood including Joan Crawford, Susan Hayward, James Stewart, Lana Turner, Orson Welles and Loretta Young.

At the peak of Chandler's career, tragedy struck. In 1961, Chandler injured his back while filming *Merrill's Marauders*. Shortly thereafter, he entered the hospital for surgery to correct a ruptured disk. Five weeks and four operations later, he was dead.

Preface

Despite his once tremendous popularity, Jeff Chandler is not widely remembered today. This book puts him before the public once again, in the hope that his contributions to entertainment might earn their due recognition.

This book opens with a biography of Chandler, then covers his entire professional life with detailed listings of his every work in film, radio, television, music, and spoken-word recordings. Information on his film work includes credit and cast lists, synopses, behind-the-scenes details, reviews, and comments by Chandler's fans, costars and coworkers. The sections on his work on television and theater include similar information. Information on his radio work covers nearly five hundred episodes on nearly sixty radio programs, offering the program and episode name, date, episode number and credits. The section on music and spoken word also includes the songs that Chandler wrote, cowrote and performed.

My research on Jeff Chandler began at the Margaret Herrick Library of the Academy of Motion Picture Arts and Sciences in Beverly Hills. Their non-circulating library offered a biography of Jeff Chandler composed mostly of newspaper clippings, studio biographies and press releases. I researched the library's movie production files, pressbooks and showman's manuals for nearly all of Chandler's films. Through the assistance of the Screen Actors Guild, I was able to speak with many of the actors who worked with Chandler, including Rita Gam, Peter Graves, Will Hutchins, Kim Novak, William Reynolds, Henry Silva, and Esther Williams.

From all these sources I began building the entries on Jeff Chandler's films, including advertising lines, credits, cast, behind-the-scenes details and reviews. At the Herrick Library's Special Collections Department, I read the scripts and listened to Chandler "As Broadcast" on *The Lux Radio Theatre*. Visits to their Periodicals Department afforded research of *Boxoffice*, *The Hollywood Reporter* and *Movie Life*.

Through the Herrick Library, I also found the Warner Bros. and the Universal Studios Collections at the USC Cinema-Television Library. After reviewing the daily production logs as well as the promotion and publicity files for more than 35 films, I added to, among other sections, the reviews and behind-the-scenes details of the film entries.

The Santa Monica Public Library Periodicals Department houses a collection of fifty years of bound *Photoplay* magazines. Reading the issues from Jeff Chandler's peak years made me all the more certain of his contribution to the history of Hollywood. The Cinema-Television Library at USC allowed research of *Variety*, *The Billboard* and *TV Guide*, which afforded more information on Chandler's television and recording career.

Research into Chandler's radio career proved somewhat more difficult. I obtained good information from the *Family Theater* on Sunset Boulevard in Hollywood (within walking distance of Chandler's mid–1950s home in the Fairfax Dis-

Preface

trict and NBC Radio City). *Family Theater* houses the tapes and scripts for all of Chandler's appearances on that radio program. My research stalled, however, until I located the largest private collection of recorded radio programs on tapes, discs and scripts at the Pacific Pioneer Broadcasters in Hollywood, California.

Radio logs list three known existing episodes for *Dr. Dana*. *Radio Spirits* writes that the episode of December 21, 1947 — "The Sophia Howard Case" — is the "earliest known existing episode from this CBS daytime drama."[3] But the Pacific Pioneer Broadcasters — located in the basement of a bank at the corner of Sunset and Vine where NBC Radio City once stood — houses 63 of the 68 original recordings of *Dr. Dana*. The American Radio Archives, housed in the Special Collections Department at the Grant R. Brimhall Library in Thousand Oaks, California, houses 67 of the 68 scripts of *Dr. Dana*; most labeled "As Broadcast," beginning with episode number one, June 1, 1947. Thanks to these sources, this book offers titles and dates aired of *Dr. Dana*, as well as the most complete list known to exist of the cast and crew for this radio series. Valuable resources researched at Pacific Pioneer Broadcasters include a complete set of bound volumes of *Radio Life* magazine.

A survey of radio logs for the radio series *Our Miss Brooks* revealed that 68 percent of its episodes are unknown or missing. Yet the American Radio Archives houses all of the scripts for *Our Miss Brooks*, labeled "As Broadcast," for the years Chandler was contracted by CBS (1947 to 1953). Hence this book is able to offer titles and dates aired of *Our Miss Brooks* — even for the few episodes that Chandler didn't appear in — as well as the most complete list known to exist of the cast and crew for the first five years of this radio series.

Jeff Chandler is a career chronicle and biography of a hard-working entertainer — an actor, lyricist and vocalist who experienced an unfortunate, unnecessary and untimely death — in the last vestige of Hollywood glamour and style.

From Flatbush to Filmland

Jeff Chandler was born as Ira Grossel in Brooklyn, New York, on December 15, 1918. He was the only child of Phillip and Anna Grossel, who married January 1, 1918, in New York. Anna's father, Max Shapiro, came to the United States in 1906 from Vilna, Russia, the year after the Russo-Japanese War. Max came first in order to set up a butcher shop and home for his orthodox Jewish family. In 1908, his relatives arrived: Sarah, his wife; Charles and George, their sons; and daughters Lillian, Sophie, Laura, and Anna.[1] Relocating to America was an opportune decision: occupied by German forces during both World Wars, Vilna's large Jewish population would be virtually exterminated during World War II.

The fourth of five children to parents of Austrian descent, Phillip Grossel was born in New York City in 1896. After eight years of school, Phillip set out on his own, and in 1916, he began a ten-year association as a buyer for the Royal Dress Company on Broadway in New York City.[2]

At three years of age, when his parents divorced, Ira and his mother moved in with her parents and Sophie. With an increase in women workers in 1921 brought on by the aftermath of war, Anna found employment as both a factory worker and a practical nurse. Ira's cousin, Elaine Margo, later remembered, "Ira had a disturbed childhood, being the product of a divorce with 'divorce' being a dirty word in those days, and it caused great upheaval. Everyone had an opinion on how he should be raised."[3]

Max wanted Ira to become a Rabbi; Ira, however dreamed of being an actor. At four years of age, he loved to entertain the family, sometimes doing imitations of Groucho Marx. "Being an artistic and sensitive child," says Elaine Margo. "Ira grew up introspectively and quietly among the family, always sort of within himself. He was warm and friendly, but always one step back from being congenial and outgoing, although he had all the attributes."[4]

Jeff Chandler

Ira attended grade school at Public School 181, on New York Avenue in Brooklyn. Ira had a passion for acting, but he didn't know how to go about pursuing it. One day, a teacher gave him a small part in a play to perform in class. During the performance, he used a pointer in the place of a sword, causing his classmates to laugh at his foolishness, except for one girl who sat staring with wide, green eyes filled with wonder. She knew precisely how he felt, she told him, because one day she was going to perform on Broadway. Her name: Edythe Marrener, who would later be known as the ravishing and talented actress Susan Hayward.

In 1930, Phillip Grossel became sales manager for Mayfair Fabrics on 7th Avenue in New York City, and Max purchased a two-story house on East 37th Street in Brooklyn. Ira, his grandparents, Anna, and Anna's sister Sophie lived upstairs; downstairs lived Ira's uncle George, his wife, Shirley, and their children, Paul and Elaine. "Being Ira's junior by seven years, my recollections are of a handsome, sensitive, intelligent cousin who I adored," Elaine recalled. "As we grew older, I admired him because of his positive approach to a difficult life."[5]

During the 1920s, the Jewish population in Brooklyn—many the sons and daughters of earlier immigrants—increased by 250 percent. Ira graduated from Public School 181 in the Class of 1931, shortly before his grandfather died of cancer. Upon entering Erasmus Hall High School, on Flatbush Avenue in Brooklyn, Ira was only a 12-year-old. But all the students were young, having been skipped through grade school because theirs was crowded.[6]

First pony ride for eight-year-old Ira Grossel (Jeff Chandler) in Brooklyn, New York, 1926.

From Flatbush to Filmland

Left: Thirteen-year-old Ira Grossel (Jeff Chandler) and his mother, Anna, 1931.

Below: Ira Grossell (Jeff Chandler) with his mother's relatives in 1931. ***Standing (from the left)***: Ira; uncle George Shapiro; aunt Sophie Shapiro; uncle Charles Shapiro; aunt Laura Shapiro Robbins; Laura's husband, Charles Robbins; Lillian and Joseph's daughter, Kitty Paris Schildkraut; Lillian's husband, Joseph Paris; Lillian and Joseph's son, Leonard Paris. ***Sitting***: aunt Shirley Shapiro; grandfather Max Shapiro; in front of Max: Shirley and George's daughter, Elaine Shapiro Margo; grandmother Sarah Shapiro; on Sarah's lap: Shirley and George's son, Paul Shapiro; aunt Lillian Shapiro Paris; in front of Lillian: Lillian and Joseph's daughter, Gloria Paris; mother, Anna Grossel. (Both photographs Elaine Margo).

Jeff Chandler

Ira's IQ more than met the high standards of Erasmus Hall, a prime institution and the only high school in Brooklyn with a campus situated on acres of land. The teachers there were university-educated, with some holding Ph.D.s from Oxford, Yale and Columbia. An appointment to a teaching position at Erasmus Hall, one of America's oldest and most famous academies, was a prize. They couldn't afford to teach in a college because, relatively speaking, teachers in New York City were far better paid.[7] Few institutions, if any, can equal Erasmus Hall's roster of notable alumni. Their graduates include Baseball Hall of Famer Waite Hoyt, Class of 1916; actor Eli Wallach, Class of 1932; journalist-television celebrity Dorothy Kilgallen, Class of 1932; and playwright-lyricist-screenwriter Betty Comden, Class of 1933.

By the time he was 15, Ira's hair had already started turning into a pepper-and-salt combination. As a sophomore, he played baseball and football. Some of the big football games, such as those against Manual Training High School, were played out at Ebbets Field. Ira was a respected member of a group that was considered elite, not for money or family connections, but for scholarship.[8]

Max's death, coupled with the Great Depression, forced Anna to open a candy store complete with soda fountain, where she also sold newspapers, magazines, and the like. Erasmus Hall was on double sessions, the first session going from eight o'clock in the morning to one o'clock in the afternoon. After adjusting his school schedule, Ira left Erasmus Hall daily at noon in order to help his mother in the store. As a result, his grades and activities suffered. "That's why," he once explained, "I couldn't join the Footlighters, a dramatic club."[9]

The first year he worked in the candy store, Ira ended that school semester a child. In previous years, Ira's family had vacationed in the Catskill Mountains as had some of their neighbors. But that summer holiday came and went, and Ira entered the next grade as a tall, overweight young adult.

In 1934, a business known as the Metropolitan Restaurant and Cafeteria Owners Association opened on Broadway in New York City, with Ira's father, Phillip, in charge.[10] Disbarred lawyer and friend Sam Furstenberg had given Phillip his job, but on October 25, Furstenberg walked out without an explanation and never came back.

Actually, the Metropolitan Restaurant and Cafeteria Owners Association was created by Arthur "Dutch Schultz" Flegenheimer, notorious underworld gangster of the prohibition era. The association launched a reign of terror in the food industry. Some of the most famous restaurants in the city, primarily those along Broadway, were coerced into joining the association for sums between $1,000 and $50,000. Penalties, such as stench bombs and picket lines, forced many owners to pay initiation fees and certain weekly sums for "protection."[11]

Gangland racketeering prevailed not only in Manhattan and Newark but in Brooklyn as well. Two notable gangsters ruled and died on the streets of that city:

From Flatbush to Filmland

racketeer Frankie Yale, shot down on 44th Street in the summer of 1928, and his successor, rum-runner Charles "Vannie" Higgins, shot down on Union Street four years later. Caught in between 44th and Union streets: Erasmus Hall High School.

For the Class of 1935, Erasmus Hall had two graduations, one in January and the other in June; Ira participated in the latter. The Yearbook Committee composed a memorable phrase for each senior in *The Arch*, the school's yearbook. The one for Ira read: "He doesn't fear dark shadows, why should he?"

That year, Special Prosecutor Thomas E. Dewey launched an investigation into charges of racketeering suspected of the Metropolitan Restaurant and Cafeteria Owners Association. When Phillip Grossel failed to produce its books, the court sentenced him to fifteen days in the Tombs, otherwise known as the Manhattan House of Detention for Men, on Centre Street in New York City. Released on October 22, 1935, Phillip turned the books over to the court by the next day; early that morning, the gangland killing spree began.[12]

At 1:15 A.M., police found the mutilated body of racket chief Louis "Pretty" Amberg in a burning car near the navy yard in Brooklyn. At 10:30 P.M. in Newark, gunmen shot down Dutch Schultz and three of his henchmen; within 24 hours, they died from their wounds. Ninety minutes after the Newark assault, gunmen shot down Schultz's chief lieutenant, Martin "Marty" Krompler, and an associate in Manhattan.[13]

With information that the violence in Brooklyn, Manhattan and Newark had come as the result of an order made by a rival gang leader, police began their search for the infamous gangster Charles "Lucky" Luciano. Schultz's death ended a haul that J. Edgar Hoover, the director of the FBI, estimated at $6 million a year.[14]

Ira watched his plans to play football at Cornell University fade as the candy store failed and the family lost its savings. Anna met Max Shrevelew, the owner of a grocery store and ice cream parlor in Long Branch, New Jersey. They married and moved to the seaside resort, where Max also rented bungalows during the summer months.[15] With his mother in good hands, Ira moved into an inexpensive room in Manhattan.

In October 1936, 14 men (along with the Metropolitan Restaurant and Cafeteria Owners Association) were indicted. Nine were arrested, including Phillip Grossel; his bail was $50,000. Careful estimates proved that about 90 percent of the best-known restaurants in New York had knuckled down to the racket.[16] Popular eating establishments affected included the Brass Rail, Brighton Cafeterias and Tip-Toe Inns.

Phillip's duties of the association called for him, in part, to get applications signed by prospective members as well as an affidavit-like document that stated they hadn't been coerced or threatened by any means into joining. In one case, Phillip gave a new member a tour of the association's offices. The suite included a meeting room equipped with a bar, where Phillip, in a genial mood, shared a drink with the new member. In another case, Phillip demanded initiation fees from a reluctant prospect who found one of his restaurants picketed; once the fees were paid, however, a single telephone call from Phillip ended the picket line.[17]

The racket trial began in January 1937. Phillip testified that a few days after Sam Furstenberg walked out of the Metropolitan Restaurant and Cafeteria Owners Association in October 1934, Jules Martin telephoned and told him, "I want you to know that I'm running the place. You will pay me a certain amount of money or your members will suffer the consequences." When Phillip said he would resign, Martin threatened his family. "Your wife just gave birth to a baby, didn't she? You'd like to see that baby again?" Phillip had taken a new wife, Maril, in 1932 and had a second family to provide for. "You just do as you're told," Martin told him, "Or your body will be found in the river and something will happen to the rest of your family."[18]

Nearly all of the money paid into the Metropolitan Restaurant and Cafeteria Owners Association was turned over to Jules Martin and Sam Krantz, a fugitive when the trial took place. Martin's murder in March 1935 led the authorities to the Metropolitan Restaurant and Cafeteria Owners Association. Among the captured documents were two photographs of restaurant owner and former heavyweight champion Jack Dempsey shaking hands and signing his contract with two of the smiling racketeers, Paul N. Coulcher and Phillip Grossel.[19]

The racket trial marked the first time in U.S. history that a complete industrial racket had been placed on trial. On March 25, 1937, seven defendants were convicted of all charges; the court found Phillip guilty of one count of conspiracy, four of attempted extortion and 15 of extortion. The value of the money involved, from crimes for which Phillip denied his guilt, surpassed a quarter of a million dollars. Phillip had begun those criminal acts in 1932, the year his 13-year-old son received his bar mitzvah and completed his eighth year of school. Now he was facing a maximum possible sentence of 258 years.

Supreme Court Justice Phillip J. McCook who in 1936 sentenced Charles "Lucky" Luciano to prison for 30 to 50 years, sent 41-year-old Phillip Grossel "up the river." On April 9, 1937, Phillip began a ten-to-fifteen year prison sentence in Sing Sing, prisoner number 93295; eligibility for parole: September 25, 1943.[20]

Meanwhile, Ira worked various jobs, attended an art course and later did commercial art illustrations for a catalog. A friend, aware of Ira's dramatic ambitions, suggested Ira attend an audition at the Feagin School of Dramatic Art.

By 1929, the Feagin School, located at Carnegie Hall in Manhattan, had trained Broadway and Hollywood talent such as actor-comedian Jimmy Savo; by 1936, Susan Hayward and Priscilla Lane. By 1939, the school had relocated within walking distance of Carnegie Hall. That year, 21-year-old Ira did a cold reading, playing the part of the youngster Richard from Eugene O'Neill's, *Ah! Wilderness*, and was awarded a scholarship. "That wasn't too difficult," Ira recalled. "They had so many girls enrolled and not enough men. I did some heavy work with scenery, some cleaning up, and got my tuition in return."[21]

Ira did get kicked out of Feagin, but that was because he had already secured a paying job with the Millpond Playhouse, in Roslyn, Long Island. Ira worked his way from behind the curtain to the front, making his professional debut on October 30, 1940, as Hector, commander of the Trojan Army, in Christopher Morley's play *The Trojan Horse*. Other members of the cast included Gordon MacRae (later a popular singing star in Hollywood), Sheila Margo Stephens (the future Mrs. Gordon MacRae), and Jack Chakrin (later known as actor Jack Carter). *Life* published an early photo of Ira in an article on the play as did Random House in their publication of Morley's book. *Life's* photo presented Ira dressed in a tunic, playing outdoor tennis between rehearsals, and Random House showed him with other cast members sitting on the stage.

At Millpond, Ira developed a friendship with Bill Bryan, whom Ira called "my brother."[22] In the spring of 1941, they moved to Elgin, Illinois, where Bill's uncle had a popular restaurant. They converted a large barn on his uncle's property into a theater and started their own stock company. Bill directed the productions, while Ira acted and designed the sets.

Marjorie Hoshelle was born as Marjorie Leah Hoshell in Chicago, Illinois, on January 7, 1918. Her parents, Norman and Leah Hoshell, divorced when she was a child. A willowy, green-eyed redhead, Marjorie acted at Calumet High School and into her second year at Elmhurst College, when she quit school in order to devote all her time to acting. Her goal: to become a great stage star. In 1938, she began her dramatic training at Chicago's Goodman Theatre, receiving her Bachelor of Fine Arts degree three years later as well as a scholarship for post-graduate work. Early on, she added an "e" to the end of "Hoshell" to make certain that people pronounced it correctly.[23]

In the summer of 1941, Ira dated Jean Sincere, an aspiring actress and a friend of Marjorie's. When Ira met Marjorie, however, they had little time to talk. On December 7, 1941, Japan bombed Pearl Harbor, and the U.S. entered World War II. Ira and Bill enlisted in the Army and remained a team while stationed at Ft. Riley, Kansas. Between 1941 and 1943, Ira experienced service in the cavalry and anti-aircraft units.

On April 16, 1942, the Goodman Theatre opened their eleventh season with William Shakespeare's *Romeo and Juliet*. Marjorie Hoshelle starred as Juliet. Peter Auerbach, a Warner Bros. talent scout, saw the performance and offered her a screen test. Marjorie arrived in Hollywood on June 7, took her screen test three weeks later, and on July 6, became a contract player with Warner Bros.

Two days after her twenty-fifth birthday, Warner Bros. gave Marjorie a 25 percent increase in salary. On November 5, 1943, MCA Artists represented the actress; the next day, Warner Bros. released *Find the Blackmailer* (1943), which marked her Hollywood debut. "The film," reported *Film Daily*, "introduces a newcomer named Marjorie Hoshelle, who has a healthy quality about her and performs nicely."[24]

Marjorie appeared in five films released in 1943, including *Air Force* and *Princess O'Rourke*. Actress Olivia de Havilland starred in the latter, one of her last at any film studio for the better part of two years because of legal difficulties and contract disputes with Warner Bros. Between 1943 and 1945, Ira attended officer candidate school, becoming a first lieutenant of infantry, and served in the Aleutian Islands. In 1944, Marjorie appeared in three films, and Miss de Havilland, out of work and restless, toured with the USO in order to stay in the public eye. When Miss de Havilland entertained the troops in the Aleutians during a hospital tour, the Army assigned Ira as her official escort.

On July 1, 1944, Warner Bros. chose not to renew Marjorie's contract. She had plans to wed Peter Auerbach, but when their marriage plans fell apart, she decided to audition for parts on the stage and visit Jean Sincere, who by this time lived in New York. With Ft. Benning, Georgia, as his next assignment, Ira spent a couple of weeks visiting family in New Jersey. Ira called on Jean, but with their romance on the wane, they soon parted, and Ira began to date Marjorie. After his holiday, Ira reported to duty, Marjorie returned to the West Coast, and the two often exchanged letters.

In 1945, the Army assigned Ira to Ft. Ord, California. He expected to report next to the South Pacific, but on August 14, 1945, Japan surrendered unconditionally, ending World War II. The next day, on a short leave from the service, Ira visited Marjorie, the only person he knew in Hollywood. With the news of peace and a part for Marjorie in Monogram's *Black Market Babies* (1945), they had plenty to celebrate. Marjorie soon made her first appearance in the *Academy Players Directory* after signing with the Salkow Agency, then representing such actors as Jane Wyman, Ronald Reagan and Charles Coburn.

When he had a weekend pass, Ira visited Marjorie and new friends in Hollywood, working on getting into the movies. One day, Ira recorded impersonations and straight readings for a few friends just for laughs. One of those friends took the recording to agent Leavis Green of MCA, who in turn submitted it to Mervyn LeRoy Productions, then starting preparations for the film *The Robe*, at that time to be released through Warner Bros. As a result, Ira interviewed with Mervyn LeRoy, who asked to see him again after his discharge from the Army.

At Green's suggestion, Ira scheduled an appointment with Billy Gordon, then casting for Hunt Stromberg. They were looking for a new leading man to play opposite Hedy Lamarr in *Dishonored Lady*, a film that would eventually go $1.2

million over budget and become the last made by Hedy Lamarr's independent production company.

With thousands of returning servicemen pouring into Los Angeles, the Hollywood Guild Canteen opened an annex in the last week of October. That week, tempers at the film studios cooled when a 33-week-old strike ended. With a three-day pass in his hand, Ira positioned himself on Highway 101 heading south from Santa Barbara and hitched a ride in order to keep the appointment with Billy Gordon in Hollywood.

That free ride ended in a head-on collision 90 miles shy of Hollywood, and Ira ended up in the Army hospital in Santa Barbara. During his two weeks there, doctors treated him for a concussion as well as deep facial and scalp lacerations. Half his head was shaved in order to treat a particularly nasty gash that crossed his left eyebrow and extended to the top of his head. The hospital released Ira in mid–November; in December, in civvies once again, he headed for Hollywood.

In February 1946, Ira received his honorable discharge. After spinning his wheels with the film studios in his postwar plans to become a film actor, he turned to radio; his resume included "radio actor" and "disc jockey" after serving his country in the Aleutians. He made the rounds in Hollywood to advertising agencies, radio shows and their producers, receiving the usual "we'll call you when we need you," and by spring, he was nearly broke. Marjorie suggested that he collect unemployment, but he persevered; in May, Ira read for a part in *The Killers* (1946).

After working with 20th Century–Fox and Warner Bros., Mark Hellinger became an independent producer for Universal-International. *The Killers* proved to be his running start. After purchasing the Ernest Hemingway property, he prepared a budget and began casting. Wherever possible, Hellinger wanted unknowns, has-beens, or almost-wases, and he began scouting around.[25]

"I was reading for a part in Mark Hellinger's *The Killers*," Ira recalled, "and I knew the character I was playing was supposed to be tough, so I gave it the works. I overplayed it and didn't get the part. I guess I looked like a heavy. I had a big scar across my forehead from the automobile accident. I was a mug, for sure!"[26]

Ira didn't get the part, but his screen test card found its way into the files of U-I's casting department: "Name: Ira Grossel. Age: 27. Height: 6'4". Weight: 210 pounds. Type: Mug. Comment: Combination [Humphrey] Bogart–[James] Cagney–[Clark] Gable. Would be okay for tough bits."[27]

Shortly after his movie audition for *The Killers*, a local radio show called him in for an audition. As a result, Ira began his freelance career when he received $14 for a few lines on the 15-minute weekly radio show *That's a Good Idea*, produced by George W. Allen and written by Madelyn Pugh. Ira played as many as eight parts in one show, receiving excellent training in versatility. "I have an adaptable voice," Ira recalled in an interview, "and always had a knack for mimicry. I can do all kinds of voices. I played around doing Gable, [James] Stewart, and Cagney on amateur radio shows. I auditioned for *Major Bowes' Original Amateur Hour* once. I was scared. Poor preparation killed me."[28]

Ira flourished on radio with work on air shows such as *The Casebook of Gregory Hood*, *Tennessee Jed*, *Gene Autry's Melody Ranch* and *The Man Called X*. Radio producer-director Dee Engelbach gave newcomer Ira the opportunity to appear in the top scale *Academy Award* and Dick Powell's *Rogue's Gallery*. As *Rogue's Gallery* began its summer broadcast, Powell introduced Ira to the casting director at Columbia Pictures, who cast the actor in Powell's *Johnny O'Clock* (1947).

Production began for *Johnny O'Clock* in late July, a few days before Ira performed with Henry Fonda in a radio broadcast of *Academy Award*. When film production ended two months later, Ira appeared on the radio show again, this time with Joseph Cotten in the broadcast of the Alfred Hitchcock thriller *Shadow of a Doubt*.

In September, Ira landed a regular job on a radio soap opera, and proposed marriage to Marjorie at Brittingham's, the restaurant at CBS studios. On October 13, 1946, Marjorie became his wife in a small, private ceremony attended by a small group of friends and family. After their honeymoon, they moved into a Hollywood efficiency and Ira reported to NBC for the radio serial *Dr. Paul*, where he earned $40 as a sheriff.

Marjorie appeared in seven films released in 1946. Reviews favored her performance in *Behind the Mask* as well as her singing voice in *The Red Dragon*. A third film, *Cloak and Dagger*, ended that year among the top-grossing films, just one position above *The Killers*.

Before the radio show moved from Hollywood to New York, Ira portrayed the character of Tex Thorne on *The Zane Grey Show*. Ira considered changing his name to Conway (Tex) Thorne, but couldn't give up the radio identity he'd established under his own name. He finally chose a new last name: "Chandler" from the Van Johnson and Esther Williams film *Easy to Wed* (1946). Actor Gerald Mohr suggested a new first name, "Jeff." In the October 1946 issue of the *Academy Players Directory*, the Salkow Agency listed Marjorie Hoshelle in the section "Leading Women," while the Murray Weintraub Agency posted their first listing for "Jeff Chandler" under "Characters and Comedians."

As Jeff's work on radio increased, he benefited from the close proximity of the theaters and studios that made up Hollywood's "Radio City." Located on the corner of Sunset Boulevard and Vine Street, NBC Radio was a 15-minute run west on Sunset from CBS Radio; ABC Studios sat across from NBC and a block south from the Vine Street Theatre, where, in March 1947, Jeff made his first appearance on *The Lux Radio Theatre*.

Lux adapted movies of the day into a radio show format, using the stars of the original motion picture whenever possible. Jeff started out as part of their stable of supporting actors. On April 21, 1947, Barbara Stanwyck and George Brent starred in the *Lux* radio adaptation of the 1946 Warner Bros. drama *My Reputation*, with Jeff in its supporting cast. Brent — well-known for playing opposite screen idols such as Greta Garbo, Ginger Rogers, Bette Davis and Barbara Stanwyck — repeated his screen role as did Miss Stanwyck.

Jeff appeared twice on *Lux* during the month of May. On May 5, with Jeff in the cast, Claudette Colbert and Fred MacMurray reprised the roles they made famous in U-I's 1947 comedy *The Egg and I*. On May 12, Jeff did more than reprise a role *he* created on the screen: he played the more important role of Charlie, the part originally played by John Kellogg in Columbia's 1947 crime drama "Johnny O'Clock," a broadcast that benefited from the appearance of two other members of the original cast: Dick Powell and Lee J. Cobb. Four days after the broadcast, Jeff and Marjorie celebrated the birth of their first daughter, Jamie.

A week later, at CBS Radio, writers Tommy Tomlinson and E. Jack Neuman had fewer than four days, including Memorial Day, to come up with a new dramatic radio show. After auditions the next evening, Neuman and director Sterling Tracy selected Jeff for the starring role as "Dr. Steve Dana" in *The Private Practice of Dr. Dana*.[29]

In early 1947, Neuman and Tracy worked together on another CBS Radio series *The City*. First aired in February, *The City* ended its run on August 3, 1947; the next week, *The Private Practice of Dr. Dana* took over its Sunday evening spot.

By its fifth episode, however, *The Private Practice of Dr. Dana* was receiving unfavorable reviews and headed for trouble. In episode two, "The Joseph Coursey Case," a two-time loser robs a bank, frames an old love, and forces Dr. Dana to treat the wound that's killing him. By the end of the show, the robber, lying in pools of his own perspiration and blood, expires in long, painful gurgles. In episode three, "The Leonard Hazelton Case," fear consumes a musical genius who refuses treatment by any doctor. These storylines apparently were not going over with audiences.

After a number of changes to its format, *The Private Practice of Dr. Dana* became much less a horror story and much more a medical drama with a doctor who truly cared for and helped his patients in warm, touching stories. In episode 46, "The Linda Andrews Case," a foreign object stuck in a baby's lung not only brings two different families together, it also helps save two lives. In episode 49, "The Glenda Barton Case," a seven-year-old adopted girl, surrounded by material wealth that a child can only dream of, slowly starves to death; she's extremely hungry, Dr. Dana determines, but not for food.

On October 6, Katharine Hepburn made a rare appearance on radio when she reprised her film role in the *Lux* broadcast of MGM's 1946 drama *Undercurrent*, with Jeff in the role played in the picture by Robert Mitchum. A week later, Jeff and his wife celebrated their first wedding anniversary.

On November 17, 1947, the *Lux* broadcast of the 1946 Warner Bros. romantic melodrama *Nobody Lives Forever* won the highest rating of the season. Jeff portrayed the character of Al Doyle, the part originally played by actor George Tobias; Ronald Reagan and Jane Wyman, married in real life, portrayed the screen roles originally played by John Garfield and Geraldine Fitzgerald. Reagan had made news earlier that year when he became the president of the Screen Actors Guild, and a few months later when he was hospitalized for pneumonia; Jane Wyman had been in the papers when she signed a new multi-million dollar contract with Warner Bros., shortly before hospitalization because of the loss of a baby born prematurely.[30]

On December 15, Jeff celebrated his twenty-ninth birthday as *Lux* brought to the air the 1947 drama *Magic Town*, featuring James Stewart and Jane Wyman from the original screen cast and Jeff in the role played in the motion picture by Kent Smith. On December 24, *Duffy's Tavern* presented the second of three annual, live radio broadcasts of "Miracle in Manhattan: A Christmas Story," with Jeff as the stranger.

Jeff appeared on the same radio stage with other film stars such as Loretta Young, Victor Mature, Richard Widmark and Gregory Peck. In April 1948, Dana Andrews resumed his picture role in the *Lux* version of the 1947 20th Century–Fox drama *Daisy Kenyon*, with Ida Lupino and Jeff in the roles played in the movie by Joan Crawford and Henry Fonda.

May 1948 marked a number of firsts for Jeff. The Chandlers appeared together in a *Lux* adaptation (of the 1946 adventure film *Cloak and Dagger*); he appeared on the cover of *Radio Life* and in their feature story, "Jeff Chandler — Oh! Doctor!"; and he starred in two radio series. For a 15-week period, listeners heard Jeff in the afternoon on one radio station in *The Private Practice of Dr. Dana*, and that night on another radio station in *The New Adventures of Michael Shayne*. Jeff wrote the next to last episode in the *Dr. Dana* series, "The Steve Dana Case," and at the end of the show, the announcer said that the show had been written by Ira Grossel *and* Jeff Chandler.

On May 24, 1948, *Lux* presented their 617th broadcast with the 1947 Paramount crime drama *I Walk Alone*. Burt Lancaster and Lizabeth Scott repeated their screen roles with Jeff in the supporting cast. At 6:00 P.M., announcer John Milton Kennedy opened the live broadcast, followed by an introduction of the story by host William Keighley. Based on the play *Beggars Are Coming to Town* by Theodore Reeves, the story features Noll Turner and Frankie Madison, fellow gangsters during the Prohibition Era. When a murder occurs during a hijacking job, Turner escapes while Madison takes the rap. At about three minutes into the radio broadcast, the script called for Burt Lancaster to begin the dramatization by reading the part of Madison opposite Jeff's characterization of Dave, a part played by E.G. Marshall in the 1945 play.³¹

Confused about the actual show time, however, Lancaster missed the start of the show. With just seconds to spare, the show's director, Frederic MacKaye, stepped in to read Jeff's part, while Jeff handled Burt Lancaster's role. Dave (played by MacKaye) asks Frankie Madison (played by Jeff) about the fleabag he's in. Frankie says that any room in midtown New York is a good one without bars on it. Fourteen years in prison, and not a visit or a letter from Noll, who had since become a big-

Jeff Chandler as Philip Boynton and Eve Arden as Connie Brooks in *Our Miss Brooks*, 1948.

shot night club proprietor; 1933, Frankie adds, the year he went "up the river" to Sing Sing. With Jeff's "knack for mimicry" and his ability to handle himself well in a theatrical performance no matter the circumstance, the show went on with the listening audience believing that Jeff was Burt Lancaster, who arrived eight minutes late and smoothly eased into his role, with Jeff once again as Dave, as rehearsed.[32]

The E. T. Somlyo Agency now represented Jeff theatrically, while Don W. Sharpe continued to represent him as a radio artist. Sharpe "packaged" radio shows for the networks; he brought together a show's cast and crew and successfully presented the new radio show when the networks needed it the most. In just one year, Sharpe had a proven track record on radio, developing *Richard Diamond, Private Detective* for Dick Powell. For his client Lucille Ball, Sharpe developed *My Favorite Husband*, a package that included producer-director Jess Oppenheimer and writers Bob Carroll Jr. and Madelyn Pugh.

One of the replacements for *Lux* in the summer of 1948 included a new radio series, *Our Miss Brooks*. Jeff had appeared 23 times on *Lux* by the time it ended its thirteenth season. Early on in Jeff's career, the director of *Lux* had come through with a part whenever he could. Now, selected from a large group of aspirants, Jeff won the role of Eve Arden's bashful boyfriend and biology teacher, Philip Boynton, in *Our Miss Brooks*.

CBS had a new high in audience programs originating from Hollywood in the network's fall schedule for 1948, including *Our Miss Brooks* and *My Favorite Husband*. With over 60 performances broadcast each week from four different locations, CBS needed new facilities. So, after October 3, 1948, Studio 3 — one of four audience studios in the new $3 million Mutual-Don Lee Building at 1313 North Vine Street — became the new home of *Our Miss Brooks*.

Morton Fine and David Friedkin wrote for many radio shows, including *Bold Venture, Broadway Is My Beat, Escape, Suspense* and *Yours Truly, Johnny Dollar*. They were also under contract to CBS Radio to write for *Our Miss Brooks*. Fine and Friedkin never received proper air credit for their contribution, while the listening audience heard almost every week as the show closed: "*Our Miss Brooks*, starring Eve Arden, is produced by Larry Berns, written and directed by Al Lewis, with music by Wilbur Hatch." Fine and Friedkin, along with the radio show's director, Al Lewis, and other writers as needed, wrote 33 scripts for the show, beginning with the November 21, 1948, episode, the same week that the show underwent a format revision.[33]

In 1939, Meyer Mishkin, at that time a talent scout in New York City, first saw Jeff from afar at the Feagin School of Dramatic Art, and later at the Millpond Playhouse. Mishkin silently noted an increase in the actor's stage presence and talent, but still couldn't recommend a ticket to Hollywood.

Mishkin moved to Hollywood and worked as the general manager of Huntington Hartford's talent agency. "My first and only agent was a man named Meyer Mishkin," recalled actor William Reynolds, "who discovered me in a little chili bowl of a theater at Pico and Robertson. Meyer was running the Huntington Hartford Agency at the time. Having recently come from New York, he didn't want to sign me up as a client of the Huntington Hartford and then have to redo the contract, because he was going to open his own agency, which he soon did."[34]

Mishkin formally and finally introduced himself to Jeff after seeing him in a fine performance on *Lux*. The next day, they met to discuss theatrical representation; Don W. Sharpe continued to represent Jeff as a radio artist. In the January 1949 edition of the *Academy Players Directory*, Jeff appeared in the section, "Leading Men," representation by Meyer Mishkin of the Hartford Agency; Marjorie in the section, "Leading Women," representation by the Salkow Agency.

On January 10, 1949, the Hollywood Chamber of Commerce agreed to a resolution that changed the landscape of filmland forever: they voted to drop the last four letters from the "Hollywoodland" sign. They also elected to replace the "H," which had fallen off, and overruled a decision made the previous week by the Recreation and Park Commission to *completely* remove the sign. The next day, Angelenos experienced their first recorded snowfall, with passage through the canyons into the San Fernando Valley, just north of "'ollywoodland," impossible. The Chandlers lived in Burbank, northeast of Los Angeles, where the thermometer hit as low as 30 that night.

As the result of work that Mishkin did with U-I, Jeff attended sound casting tests for *Sword in the Desert* on January 10; on February 19, the studio signed him to play "Kurta" in the film. While U-I saw Jeff as a newcomer to film, they acknowledged his radio work, especially his work with virtually all of Hollywood's biggest stars—and in January, Jeff had added Joan Fontaine, Eddie Cantor, and Glenn Ford to that roster. But before U-I and an excited Mishkin could even look at a contract for the actor, the studio first needed to see how Jeff would do in his film role.

Shortly after the release of Marjorie's only film for 1949, *Ladies of the Chorus*, principal photography for *Sword in the Desert* began on March 1, 1949. As outside talent, Jeff had a U-I contract covering a four-week period. Jeff didn't have to attend location filming in Monterey, California, and while he awaited the cast and crew's return to the studio, he added John Wayne to his roster of coworkers with a *Lux* broadcast of the 1948 western *Red River*.

On March 11, shooting continued in the studio for *Sword in the Desert*; Jeff received first feature position in the movie as well as in its advertising. The promotional campaign for *Sword in the Desert* also included coast-to-coast publicity on *The New Adventures of Michael Shayne* and *Our Miss Brooks*.

Meyer Mishkin's hard work paid off: in April 1949, U-I signed Jeff to a long-term contract and assigned him a part in *Abandoned*; by June, a big part came his way in *Broken Arrow*. "Meyer was terrific; a little guy, but tough as could be," Peter Graves recalled. "He'd jut his chin out, talk to the producers, directors, the casting directors, and get what he wanted."[35]

As production ended for *Broken Arrow*, U-I made plans for advance publicity for *Sword in the Desert*. On August 8, Marta Toren and Jeff arrived in New York City where the press kept them busy. U-I received positive response as the result of Jeff's fine performance, both on film and in person, leaving the studio with certainty that they had a new star in Jeff Chandler.[36]

Attendees and honored guests for the August 23, 1949, world premiere of *Sword in the Desert* at the Criterion Theatre on Broadway included John Garfield and Irving Berlin. Jeff returned to Hollywood earlier than Miss Toren because of his weekly commitment on *Our Miss Brooks*.

As the studio made plans for location filming abroad for *Deported*, Jeff went on a local publicity tour for *Sword in the Desert* to San Diego, California, with U-I's Bob Rains (head of the studio's television and radio publicity department), and Jeff's father, Phillip, who by this time had completed parole and relocated to Southern California. Following the real-life deportation of gangster Charles "Lucky" Luciano to Italy, *Deported* starred Jeff as a gangster deported to his native land after a five-year prison sentence in Sing Sing for stealing close to a quarter of a million dollars.

In early October, Gale Storm and Meg Randall made personal appearances as Detroit hosted the world premiere of *Abandoned*. With the arrival later that month of their second daughter, Dana — born nine months after Los Angeles' first recorded snowfall — the Chandlers sold their home in Burbank and rented a larger one in North Hollywood.

With Universal-International, Jeff had the full support of a well-established studio. "Jeff Chandler," recalled Bob Rains, "had a lot of faith in Don W. Sharpe, an aggressive and sharp businessman."[37] Sharpe and U-I came to an agreement on *Screen Directors' Playhouse,* a radio series adaptation of motion pictures introduced each week by the film's director. Sharpe acquired a number of U-I's motion pictures for adaptation, aware of the studio's policy in selling properties to radio that U-I players would appear in. On December 2, 1949, with a plug for *Sword in the Desert*, the *Screen Directors' Playhouse* presented the radio version of U-I's 1948 drama *All My Sons*, featuring Edward G. Robinson from the original screen cast with Jeff in the role played in the film by Burt Lancaster; its guest, the film's director, Irving Reis.

As the year came to a close, the studio saw a substantial increase in requests for pictures of Jeff. After running out of their initial portrait run, the studio arranged new portrait sittings with the star; newspapers and magazines alike promoted his growing celebrity. With celebrity came photos and articles for all the important fan magazines. Stars of the day valued their exposure in magazines such as *Movie Life*, *Motion Picture*, *Screenland* and *Photoplay*.

On January 13, 1950, Jeff made his second appearance in the *Screen Directors' Playhouse* with their presentation of the RKO-International 1945 drama *Tomorrow Is Forever*. Claudette Colbert reprised her film role with Jeff in the role played in the film by Orson Welles.

While radio agent Sharpe looked out for Jeff's ventures on the air, Mishkin opened his own theatrical agency. In April 1950, Mishkin's roster of clients included supporting actor John Alvin as well as character actors John Qualen, Sandra Gould, Adelaide Klein, and Peter Leeds. That month, the agency took on at least one new client: in the April 1950 edition of the *Academy Players Directory*, Jeff *and* Marjorie appeared with representation by the Mishkin Agency.

In mid–1950, Harry S. Ackerman, director of programming for CBS Radio West, offered radio agent Sharpe an opportunity for Jeff to star in *Romance*, a summer replacement radio show for *Life with Luigi*. The timing was perfect for the summer break of *Our Miss Brooks*, scheduled to begin June 4, 1950 — the show's first break since it began in mid–1948. Sharpe also worked at getting Jeff out of his contract to CBS Radio for *Our Miss Brooks* so Jeff could star in a Sharpe radio package similar to those put together for Lucille Ball and others. *Romance* became an early collaboration between producer-director Norman Macdonnell and writer-editor John Meston, later responsible for radio's *Gunsmoke*. Jeff's contract with CBS Radio went unbroken; he spent the latter part of the summer of 1950 in Hawaii for location filming of *Bird of Paradise*. When *Romance* went to air, it starred William Conrad (who would later star as Matt Dillon in *Gunsmoke* for nine seasons) and Georgia Ellis (who would play Kitty in that show).[38]

As *Broken Arrow* went to new heights at the box office, U-I's fan mail receipts reached new heights for Piper Laurie, Marta Toren, Shelley Winters, Rock Hudson, Audie Murphy and Jeff. Three of those players—Miss Laurie, Hudson and Jeff—were voted filmland's favorites of the future by the readers of *Photoplay*. Columnist Hedda Hopper's choice for the film stars of 1951 included newcomers Debbie Reynolds, Charlton Heston and Jeff. In their 1950 issue, *Who's Who in Hollywood* listed Jeff in their biographies of Hollywood's best.

On Lincoln's birthday, February 12, 1951, Academy Award nominations for 1950 were announced and included a nomination for Jeff as Best Supporting Actor in *Broken Arrow*. The next day—the day before Valentine's Day—Jeff announced that he and Marjorie had separated. Unable to locate an apartment, Jeff moved into his studio suite at U-I.

They weren't able to come to an agreement, however, and a week later, Marjorie hired a lawyer to handle their divorce. With the marriage dissolved, she hoped to resume her film career under the name of "Marjorie Hoshelle."

Jeff Chandler and his wife, Marjorie, look on as their eldest daughter, Jamie, offers a taste of her candy bar to her younger sister, Dana, in 1951.

Variety reviewed the Chandlers in two 20th Century–Fox releases: on March 12, Jeff in *Bird of Paradise*; on March 13, Marjorie in *I Can Get It for You Wholesale*. Jeff began to date red-haired beauty Ann Sheridan. Paramount awarded Miss Sheridan her first screen role the result of winning a beauty contest in 1933. She signed in 1936 with Warner Bros., who promoted her as the "Oomph Girl," and appeared along with Marjorie in *Thank Your Lucky Stars* (1943).

After 20th Century–Fox made arrangements with U-I to share Jeff's contract, they cast him in *Broken Arrow*, *Two Flags West* and *Bird of Paradise*. The deal between U-I and Fox called for Jeff to do a total of six pictures; U-I stipulated that when Fox used him, they would give him equal billing with any star in the picture. Fox used him as fast as they could, but dropped the option because of time limitations. They wanted Jeff in *The Day the Earth Stood Still* (1951), *The Secret of Convict Lake* (1951), *Les Miserables* (1952) and *Lydia Bailey* (1952), but U-I couldn't let him go because of Jeff's obligations to his studio.

Despite their separation, Marjorie accompanied Jeff to the 23rd annual Academy Awards presentation at the RKO Pantages Theatre on March 29, 1951. *All About Eve* (1950), nominated for 14 Academy awards, won six that night, including Best Supporting Actor (George Sanders).

Marta Toren came to the U.S. in 1947 and made 11 films within four years, including *Sword in the Desert* and *Deported*. In 1951, Jeff dated Marta a couple of times, and when the Swedish movie actress returned to Europe, Jeff resumed seeing Ann Sheridan. On May 5, 1951, they attended the opening of *I Was a Communist for the FBI* (1951). The couple also hit various night spots including the Sportsmen's Lodge on Ventura Boulevard as well as a private party held for them, the Van Johnsons and Desi Arnaz and Lucille Ball.

In May 1951, actor William "Hopalong Cassidy" Boyd opened "Hoppyland," an 80-acre park near the beach community of Venice, California. Jeff and Marjorie took four-year-old Jamie and 18-month-old Dana to the kiddyland section of the park for pony rides and good eats.

Jeff volunteered his time to help charities such as Bonds of Israel, and that summer he helped Father Patrick Peyton, creator of radio's *Family Theater*. Five thousand people turned out for the star-studded charity event held at the McCarthy estate in Beverly Hills. Roddy McDowall, Charles Boyer, Loretta Young and Jeff were among the many celebrities who autographed Father Peyton's book *The Ear of God*.

In late 1952, the Chandlers reconciled and signed a two-year lease on a home west of Sunset and Vine, within walking distance of Schwab's Drugstore and the headquarters for *Family Theater*. Their reconciliation marked Marjorie's last appearance, as a leading woman or otherwise, in the *Academy Players Directory*.

In 1947, with fewer than 15,000 television sets in the U.S., crowds gathered around store windows to watch television. By 1950, television replaced radio as the dominant mass entertainment medium in industrialized countries, with almost five million television sets in the U.S. alone; by 1951, that number almost tripled.

Of all the radio programs that Jeff appeared in, ten of them were new to the air in 1947, while two were broadcast for the last time; in 1951, however, those numbers reversed. Only one of those programs were new to the air, while nine were heard for the last time, including Lucille Ball's *My Favorite Husband*.

Don W. Sharpe helped establish Desilu Productions, and as their exclusive representative, helped bring Lucille Ball's *I Love Lucy* (as well as the producer-director and writers of radio's *My Favorite Husband*) to television in the fall of 1951. As part of their ongoing struggle to keep the ever-growing television-viewing public in movie theaters, the Council of Motion Picture Organizations (COMPO) formed "Movietime, USA," a public relations project to bring Hollywood to the heartland of America.

In October 1951, Jeff and Marjorie celebrated their fifth wedding anniversary while on tour in Cleveland for COMPO. Twenty-nine tours went on the road that year, and each one represented Hollywood's best in actors, directors and industry personnel. Jeff and Marjorie, along with actress Geraldine Brooks, director Fletcher Markle and screenwriter Jesse Lasky Jr., appeared at official functions, women's clubs, school and church events. "I had a chance to meet people in both big cities and small towns and I found out how important motions pictures are to all of them," Jeff said after the tour. "We in Hollywood have a responsibility. I hope we will always meet it."[39]

On January 8, 1952, Frank Sinatra arranged a party at the Ambassador Hotel on Wilshire Boulevard after a preview of *Meet Danny Wilson*. Guests included the Chandlers as well as music industry professionals Sammy Cahn, Jack Pleis, David Rose, Paul Weston and Victor Young. Inspired, Jeff and Marjorie later vacationed in Lake Arrowhead, California, where they cowrote a song.

On May 29, Jeff made his singing debut on the radio program *Club 88 Starring Peggy Lee*. Miss Lee began singing professionally in the mid–1930s, and by 1952 had established herself as one of the top singers, recording for Capitol and Decca Records. Jeff sang "You Made Me Love You" and joined Miss Lee on "Walking My Baby Back Home." "I heard the show at a party and reaction to Jeff's voice, particularly among the women, was great," said Bob Rains. "All of them thought he could really 'sell' them a song." Rains proposed that Jeff record the song "Because of You." He didn't record the cut, but the proposal evolved into a deal with Decca.[40]

Bob Rains is responsible, to a large degree, for the path that Jeff Chandler took that led to his recording contract with Decca Records. "It's true," said Bob Rains, "and when I suggested it to Jeff, he thought I was kidding." Jeff later told Bob, "I never thought singing in the shower would earn me money later on."[41]

Beginning in the summer of 1952, Jeff, Mishkin and U-I worked out a new contract that doubled Jeff's old salary, making him one of the studio's highest paid stars. Jeff's contract, however, prevented him from doing a television version of *Our Miss Brooks*—or any television show, for that matter. In November 1952, the television show *Our Miss Brooks*, filmed on the Desilu Productions set, aired with

Robert Rockwell as Eve Arden's bashful boyfriend, while Jeff continued with the radio role each Sunday night.[42]

On January 19, 1953, Jeff agreed to proceed with recording for Decca, with profits to be divided equally between himself and U-I. That evening, 68 percent of all television sets in the U.S. tuned in to *I Love Lucy* in order to see Lucy give birth to fictional Little Ricky (Desi Arnaz, Jr. in real life). A month later, Lucille Ball and Desi Arnaz signed an $8 million contract to continue *I Love Lucy* through 1955.

On March 30, 1953, the giveaway television show *The Big Payoff* moved to the West Coast for two weeks. With former Miss America Bess Myerson and Randy Meriman as emcees, the broadcast from Hollywood lent an aura of glamour to a show normally broadcast from New York City. Earlier that month, CBS-TV launched a beauty contest open to all girls over 15 and residing in Southern California. Its judges: Jeff, Tony Curtis and Rock Hudson, who, on March 30, appeared on the show and announced the four winners from the 100 auditioned. Each winner received a two-week television modeling contract on the show.

In mid–1953, Jeff's contract with *Our Miss Brooks* ended, and as his last performance of that show aired, requests from studios arrived at U-I for Jeff's services: Warner Bros. wanted him for the lead in an outdoor adventure with director David Lean; MGM wanted him for a Greer Garson movie; and RKO was also vying for his services. U-I declined all outside requests because of their star's busy schedule: three movies (one a cameo role), personal appearances in Chicago and New York City, his recording contract and a position as a judge of the Miss America and Miss Universe pageants in Long Beach, California.

Jeff's schedule also included finding a new place to live when Marjorie told him to move out of their two-story colonial; she called the separation a case of incompatibility. Seen around town with Marilyn Maxwell, Gloria de Haven, Bella Darvi, Julie Adams, Mamie Van Doren and Susan Hayward, Jeff lived in his bungalow on the studio lot before finding an apartment in Studio City.

A bungalow served as a combination office and dressing room and many stars at U-I considered their bungalow a second home. With Jeff working and living in his, he filled it with family pictures and curios from his career, including the plaque he received for his Academy Award nomination in *Broken Arrow*, the service helmet he wore in *Red Ball Express*, a dart blowpipe from *East of Sumatra*, and an old long rifle from *Yankee Pasha*.

A contract dispute between U-I and CBS Radio kept Jeff from a scheduled appearance on a February broadcast of the radio show *Suspense*. Jeff starred, instead, in "My True Love's Hair," the October 19 broadcast. The story, based on a popular 1875 folk ballad, aired one week before *Suspense*'s presentation of "Dutch Schultz," the true account of the events leading up to the murder of the gangster, which starred Broderick Crawford.

Jeff Chandler

On November 12, Jeff's boss, William Goetz, ended his association with the studio after he and Milton R. Rackmil, president of U-I, were unable to reach an agreement on a new contract. As one of the top three moviemaking executives in Hollywood, Goetz won the *Look Magazine* Industry Achievement Award for 1952. Upon Goetz's departure, Edward Muhl became the studio's new Vice President in Charge of Production.

More than 700 of the top names in Hollywood honored Darryl F. Zanuck at a banquet for the third annual "Milestone" Award; Jesse L. Lasky and Louis B. Mayer were its previous recipients. Zanuck received the "Silver Wreath of Honor," with this legend: "The Screen Producers Guild presents to Darryl F. Zanuck this wreath of honor for his historic contribution to the American motion picture. November 22, 1953." Special guests included Jack L. Warner and Shirley Temple. Other notables attending the black-tie affair: Edward Arnold, Clifton Webb, Van Johnson, and Jeff Chandler accompanied by actress Terry Moore.[43]

On March 8, 1954, Marjorie sued for divorce in Superior Court on charges of cruelty. One month later, she won by default. The court approved a property settlement of almost $50,000 a year; it included custody of and financial support for the children and made Marjorie, Jamie and Dana permanent beneficiaries in insurance policies totaling $65,000. "As a result of his complete and continuous absorption in his career, he was not a companion in any way," the actress said, adding that the actor suffered from chronic fatigue and always fell asleep no matter where they were.[44]

In mid–April 1954, U-I cast Jeff as Detective Gallagher, the lead role in *Six Bridges to Cross*. By the middle of May, wardrobe, sound and makeup casting had been done. On May 20, however, Ed Muhl suspended Jeff in response to a letter he received from the actor who asked, in part, to be relieved of his current production assignment. Within just a few days and after a meeting with the actor and his agent, the studio lifted the suspension. U-I then cast Jeff in a new production and assigned George Nader, instead, to play the lead in *Six Bridges to Cross*.

In the fall of 1954, Jeff opened the fourth World Series game between the New York Giants and the Cleveland Indians by singing the "Star Spangled Banner," and appeared a few days later as a mystery guest on television's *What's My Line?*

In 1954, fan magazines such as *Modern Screen*, *Motion Picture*, *Movie Life*, *Movie Spotlight*, *Movieland*, *Photoplay* and *Screen Album* covered Jeff well over a hundred times in articles and photographs. In popularity polls conducted by the major fan magazines, Jeff consistently placed among the Top Ten, along with Tony Curtis, Rock Hudson, and Audie Murphy. Each month, an average of 8,000 fan letters arrived for the four stars.

Jeff and Marjorie reconciled by March 15, 1955, beating the deadline of their final divorce decree by only a few weeks. To celebrate their reunion, they accepted an invitation as guests of Leo Durocher in Phoenix, Arizona, where the Chandlers shared a grandstand box at a New York Giants exhibition baseball game. On March 19, they returned to Los Angeles, where Jeff prepared for location filming in the Virgin Islands followed by the debut of his nightclub act at the Grand Opening of the Hotel Riviera in Las Vegas. The timing of their reconciliation and trip to Phoenix, however, conflicted with an invitation for the actor to appear on *I Love Lucy*.

Ten days before the Chandlers reconciled, Sam Marx of *I Love Lucy* approached U-I with the interest in obtaining Jeff Chandler, Rock Hudson, or Tony Curtis— with the names shown in the order of the show's preference — and the studio decided on Rock Hudson.[45] This event marked the first time U-I allowed one of their contract players to appear on a *filmed* television show; previous appearances were only allowed on *live* television.[46]

On the day that the Chandlers attended the exhibition game in Phoenix, Desilu filmed episode number 123, "In Palm Springs." During that season of *I Love Lucy*, the Ricardos and Mertzes headed to Hollywood from New York. Starstruck, Lucy had hilarious encounters with various celebrities in their own backyards. Those who signed to play themselves on other episodes included Richard Widmark, Harpo Marx, Van Johnson and Cornel Wilde. "In Palm Springs" involved a quarrel between Lucy and Ethel and their husbands that resulted in a weekend for the wives, without Ricky or Fred, in Palm Springs, where they realize that they've taken rooms next to Rock Hudson. Broadcast on April 25, "In Palm Springs" received a rating/share of 44.0/62.[47]

On Saturday, April 2, 1955, the Chandlers left on a publicity tour for *Foxfire*. They went by train on Union Pacific's *City of Los Angeles* to Chicago, then on to New York City for Jeff's point of departure for location filming in the Virgin Islands for *Away All Boats*.

The Hotel Riviera, the ninth hotel to open on the Las Vegas Strip, opened its doors on April 21, 1955, with Liberace as its opening show. With the song "Foxfire" three weeks away from release, Jeff opened in the Riviera's Clover Room on May 11, backed by Ray Sinatra and His Orchestra. Liberace received $50,000 a week, the most ever paid to a Las Vegas entertainer; Jeff, $90,000 for his three-week stand.

Dressed in a dark suit, white shirt, black four-in-hand tie and black shoes, Jeff entertained an opening-night audience of 600 that included Tony Curtis, Janet Leigh, Rosemary Clooney and Lucille Ball. Part of his act covered the song "Six Bridges to Cross" and a special number: "I'm Not Cochise Any More," a takeoff on his role as the Apache chief.

In October 1955, U-I passed on a request from NBC's *Colgate Variety Hour* for Jeff as guest conductor of the Hollywood Bowl Symphony Orchestra. On October 16, Shirley Jones, Gordon MacRae and Yul Brynner joined Dean Martin and

Jerry Lewis in a salute to Richard Rodgers and Oscar Hammerstein before a crowd of 15,000 at the Hollywood Bowl. A serious Jerry Lewis, instead of Jeff, conducted the orchestra on a Rodgers and Hammerstein overture; to close the show, the entire cast led the audience in a stirring songfest from *Oklahoma!*.

That month, the Chandlers celebrated their ninth wedding anniversary at the Beverly Hills Bali Room, where Marjorie received a present from Jeff every hour on the hour.

In November, U-I signed Esther Williams for the lead in *The Unguarded Moment* (1956), her first for the studio. An early synopsis of *Raw Wind in Eden* (1958), to be her second film for the studio, revealed that "the people involved in making a picture of this type automatically invite the close scrutiny of the confidential-type magazines into their personal lives."[48]

"Jeff's an enigma," remembered Arline Gray, Jeff's receptionist and Meyer Mishkin's secretary for three years beginning in late 1956. After responding to an ad for a secretary and an address—and nothing else—the Mishkin Agency hired Ms. Gray when she proved not to be the starstruck type. "He brooded a lot," she added. "That's the first impression I got the first day I met Jeff."[49]

As Jeff and Mishkin formed Earlmar Productions for independent film productions, plans began to fill the lead role for *Ben-Hur* (1959). Before signing Charlton Heston, MGM sought the likes of Rock Hudson and Burt Lancaster, and, at one point, their chief of production, Dore Schary, wanted Jeff Chandler for the role. At first, the film's producer Sam Zimbalist disagreed, but later decided that if the studio acquired William Wyler to direct, then Zimbalist would take Jeff Chandler. In 1956, however, MGM let Dore Schary go, then signed Heston for the lead with Wyler as its director. Zimbalist died during the film's preparation.[50]

In May 1957, Jeff met Esther Williams for the first time at a party when production ended for *The Lady Takes a Flyer*. With Jeff planning to have his family in Italy during location filming of *Raw Wind in Eden*, U-I made plans for them to travel by boat as they wouldn't fly. On June 19, the Chandlers sailed on the *Queen Mary* out of New York.

Jeff earned $200,000 for his work at Columbia Pictures in *Jeanne Eagels* (1957). When he returned to U-I to costar in *Raw Wind in Eden*, Jeff also returned to a lower salary, while Esther Williams earned $200,000. U-I not only made all of the arrangements for the Chandlers during the 45-day shooting schedule in Italy, the studio also paid for all of their expenses, including transportation, lodging, a nursemaid for the children and a car and chauffeur when needed.

As rumors about Jeff and Esther becoming closer than just friends reached stateside, Mishkin arrived on location just five days before production ended on *Raw Wind in Eden*. After location filming ended in Italy, Marjorie went from Europe to New York, then to Los Angeles, while Jeff went to Los Angeles and then New York, but each alone in their travels. The columns soon reported trouble for the Chandlers as well as domestic trouble for Esther Williams and her husband, Ben Gage.

On October 17, four days after their eleventh wedding anniversary, Jeff and Marjorie separated for the last time. Jeff and Esther (who had asked for a separation from her husband) had their first date on December 2; four days later, Marjorie sued for divorce, charging extreme mental cruelty. Jeff in turn gave her a monthly allowance, paid many of her bills, and gave her full use of their house on Loring Avenue in West Los Angeles.

Jeff and Esther soon owned matching Lincoln Continental convertibles. In July 1958, they attended the premiere of *The Vikings* (1958), while *Photoplay*'s gossip columnist Rona Barrett made an early prediction that wedding bells would not ring for the couple. The next month, location filming for *Thunder in the Sun* (1959) kept Jeff on the West Coast, while Esther attended the opening of *Raw Wind in Eden* in Atlantic City. When she went to Seattle, he helped close the gap. "Jeff was the happiest when he and Esther were together," remembered Arline Gray. "Jeff loved Esther so much that he arranged for flowers to be sent to her, every hour on the hour, for days on end."[51]

Jeff purchased the two-story Beverly Hills home on San Ysidro Drive previously owned by Tony Curtis and Janet Leigh; Rita Hayworth, Danny Kaye, William Wyler and Mary Pickford became his new neighbors. When fire threatened the hillside homes above Beverly Hills on New Year's Eve, 1958, Jeff spent the evening entertaining only a small handful of invited party guests as he watered down his property with garden hoses. The Tony Curtises and others evacuated their homes; three hours later, roadblocks came down after the fire department got a handle on the blaze.

Gossip columns in the *National Police Gazette* and *Hollywood Secrets* followed Jeff and Esther's every step through 1959. For the promotion of *A Stranger in My Arms* (1959), Jeff agreed to a conference call with an East Coast newspaper, but only under the condition that he wouldn't talk about his private life; if he were asked any such questions, the call would be terminated.

Marjorie won her divorce from Jeff in June; Esther from Ben in November. The court awarded Marjorie the family home along with a car, cash, furs, jewelry, monthly alimony and child support. Marjorie told the court that she suffered from an ulcer and needed psychiatric treatment, the result of Jeff's complete absorption in his career. Jeff appeared during the court proceedings, but neither contested or testified; three weeks before, he quietly filed a new will that left his fortune to Jamie and Dana with no provision for Marjorie.

The day after his divorce, Jeff bought Esther a diamond ring; in August, earrings for her birthday. The divorce allowed him to keep, among other things, his business. In addition to his activities at his office on South La Cienega that included Chandler Music, Jeff added August Productions, a new independent film production company. With location filming in various states as well as recording sessions for a new album, Jeff didn't spend a lot of time on South La Cienega. "Jeff's father, Phillip, spent a lot of time in the office, sitting in Jeff's chair, not really doing anything," remembered Arline Gray. "He somehow knew when Jeff wouldn't be there; Phillip would just show up, in a beautiful suit and tie."[52]

By the end of the decade, Mishkin's representation had expanded considerably; the roster that began the decade with supporting and character actors, ended it with costars and stars. "In 1959, I changed agents, going with Meyer Mishkin, who had such a happy group and a friendly place," recalled Peter Graves. "He represented a couple of notable gals and a lot of tall guys. Meyer liked having them tower over him: Chuck Connors, Peter Graves, Jeff Chandler, Lee Marvin — and there was Charles Buchinski [Bronson], too."[53]

The size of the *Academy Players Directory* best represents the flood of actors into the motion picture capital of the world. In 1955, the volume numbered over 600 pages; in 1960, over 1000. Membership in the Screen Actors Guild from 1950 to 1960 nearly doubled. Of the 14,000 S.A.G. members in February 1960, 75 percent earned $10,000 or less a year. A list of the world's wealthiest and most famous personalities included the name of Jeff Chandler, one of a hundred members who made over $100,000 a year. In 1960, Jeff would earn close to five times that amount.

On March 7, 1960, a S.A.G. strike against seven of the eight major motion picture studios occurred when new contract talks broke off over the issue of movie residual payments. The strike, the first of its kind in the history of Hollywood, forced the layoff of thousands at Allied Artists, Columbia, Walt Disney Productions, MGM, Paramount, Fox and Warner Bros. U-I avoided the strike and its effects when they became the first major studio to sign a pact giving actors a portion of profits from any post–1948 film sold to television.[54]

Union negotiators, including James Cagney, Glenn Ford, Gregory Peck, Jeff Chandler and S.A.G. President Ronald Reagan, met as early as December 1959 in the hopes of reaching an agreement. Negotiations continued through January, and on February 18, 1960, a meeting of a hundred actors, among them John Wayne, David Niven, Glenn Ford, Debbie Reynolds and Jeff, at the home of Tony Curtis and Janet Leigh resulted in unanimous support of S.A.G. On March 2, Glenn Ford held a meeting with many young and working actors, stating that a S.A.G. strike would not be morally justified if it meant the unemployment of thousands. Jeff, present at the meeting at the Curtises' home, found himself reluctant, when asked by *Variety*, "to speak disparagingly of Ford, but if he intended to say those things, why didn't he say them then?"[55]

From Flatbush to Filmland

After signing in January with one of the biggest agencies in Hollywood, Jeff appeared in the March 1960 edition of the *Academy Players Directory*: the William Morris Agency, management; Meyer Mishkin, personal management. As the strike halted the production of two dozen feature films at the studios, Hollywood's unemployed leading men represented by the William Morris Agency included James Arness, Lloyd Bridges, Robert Mitchum and Robert Taylor.

On March 9, a full-page ad purchased and placed not by S.A.G. members, but by motion pictures actors as a service to actors, appeared in *Variety*. Headed "We Voted to Back Our Guild Board," its 25 signatories included Lauren Bacall, Bing Crosby, Bette Davis, Joan Fontaine, Bob Hope, Spencer Tracy and Jeff Chandler.[56]

Jeff and Esther attended a meeting of nearly 4000 actors when S.A.G. held a union rally at the Hollywood Palladium on March 13. Autograph seekers mobbed Myrna Loy, Van Heflin and Ernest Borgnine as well as Ronald Reagan, who ran the two-hour meeting. On April 8, the 33-day-old strike ended when S.A.G. reached an agreement with the studios over residuals.

With Jeff and Esther's divorces final in June 1960, *Movieland and TV Time* reported that Esther wore a "friendship" ring from Jeff on her engagement finger. *Photoplay* reported, however, that the couple weren't talking about wedding plans set for July.

In December 1959, the Arab League's Israel Boycott Office blacklisted Elizabeth Taylor and banned the showing in Arab countries of any of her movies. Miss Taylor's offense: the purchase of $100,000 of Israeli bonds. In January 1960, the minister of national guidance of the United Arab league issued a similar order that banned the movies of Eartha Kitt and Edward G. Robinson because of their pro–Israel activities.[57]

In early July 1960, Jeff arrived in Israel for location filming of *A Story of David*. The Arab League's Israel Boycott Office soon blacklisted both him and Danny Kaye for their pro–Israel activities. Actor Danny Kaye, who made *Assignment Children*, a picture for the United Nations filmed in several countries, found himself, like Jeff, banned from entering any Arab country because he started production in Israel.[58]

After returning stateside, Jeff traveled to Michigan, Illinois, Nebraska, Utah, Idaho, Colorado and Kentucky—not for a movie promotional tour, but for Citizens for Kennedy. Former All-American football player Byron "Whizzer" White headed the group of luminaries from the movie, sport and intellectual worlds. Those appearing at a rooftop Kennedy rally in Indianapolis, Indiana, on November 4: baseball star Stan Musial and White; authors James Michener and Arthur Schlesinger, Jr.; and movie stars Shelley Winters and Jeff Chandler, who introduced Kennedy.

Their schedule involved numerous speeches and plane rides; an average day consisted of meetings, interviews with the press and talks with community groups. After the first session, White saw past Jeff's Hollywood persona and made him the chairman of their group. Michener saw in Jeff their best political speaker. "He had a brilliant grasp of American history," the author wrote. "Most of the effective speeches were suggested by him, and most of the telling sallies of wit were his."[59]

As the end of 1960 neared, Esther left Jeff and chose Fernando Lamas as the new love in her life. *Photoplay* romantically linked Esther to Lamas after he appeared as a guest star in her television special *Esther Williams at Cypress Gardens*. After 70 million tuned in to watch a closely fought presidential debate, America began their love affair with "Camelot" when they chose Senator John F. Kennedy as president over Vice-President Richard M. Nixon.

Jeff's ex-wife observed her forty-third birthday on January 7, 1961, as the actor, cast and crew drove seven hours north of Los Angeles for location filming of *Return to Peyton Place* in the town of Mammoth Lakes. The mountain resort, located on the eastern edge of the Sierra Nevada mountain range, is home to some of the best snowfall in the state, lending authenticity to the winter scenes in the movie overlooking the town of "Peyton Place."

Heavy snow fell in Washington, D.C., the night before the presidential inauguration, but thoughts of canceling the activities were overruled. The former Democratic senator's tour the previous fall through Republican strongholds in eight states had been a success. On January 20, Chief Justice Earl Warren swore in John F. Kennedy as the thirty-fifth President. Five days later came the first live televised presidential press conference.

As the end of the month approached, with his contractual obligations complete for *Return to Peyton Place*, Jeff began making plans for *Merrill's Marauders*. This film would be shot entirely on location in the Philippines, allowing for a 36-day shooting schedule, with a target to finish in 30 days, weather permitting. Milton Sperling, its producer, also oversaw *Cloak and Dagger* (1946). Gary Cooper starred in the latter with Marjorie Hoshelle portraying Ann Dawson, a femme spy; *Merrill's Marauders* was originally written for Gary Cooper.

Before leaving for the Philippines, Jeff bought dinner for British actress Judy Campbell at the Islander on La Cienega's Restaurant Row in Beverly Hills. *Photoplay* reported that Jeff still carried a torch for Esther Williams; "The Islander" was the working title for his movie with Esther, *Raw Wind in Eden*. Miss Campbell, a leading lady onscreen since the 1940s, accompanied Jeff when they went to Dean Martin's Dino's Lodge on the Sunset Strip to catch some late-night entertainment.

Saturday evening, March 4, Pan American Flight 811 left International Airport in Los Angeles for a Monday morning arrival in Manila via Honolulu. Passengers included the lead and supporting actors of *Merrill's Marauders*: Ty Hardin,

From Flatbush to Filmland

Peter Brown, Will Hutchins, Claude Akins, and Jeff Chandler. The connecting flight from Hawaii arrived on time. Filming began 24 hours later.

On April 14, Jeff worked nearly 12 hours in the Pasimil Compound for native village scenes in *Merrill's Marauders*. The next day, a telegram sent from Manila to Warner Bros. described the actor in severe pain as the result of twisting his back violently during filming the day before.[60] Jeff insisted that filming continue and treatment began under the care of doctors at Clark Air Force Base in the Philippines with pain-killing medication, followed by a series of injections. Each injection failed to give the movie star relief; he slept in traction, and between scenes, he was treated with heat and ice applications.

From *Sword in the Desert* to *Raw Wind in Eden*, Dr. N. Edward Gourson, known as "Dr. Hollywood," had examined Jeff for cast insurance before production began on each of his movies at U-I. Gourson, staff physician to movie studios since the early 1940s, had treated many actors including Barbara Stanwyck, Ava Gardner, Cary Grant, John Wayne, and helped get Charlie Chaplin back on his feet after the comedian accidentally severed an Achilles tendon.[61]

An old leg injury caused Jeff to conceal a limp during the production of *War Arrow* and *Yankee Pasha*. For that condition, he later received considerable medical treatment. From 1951 to 1956, Gourson's physical exams accepted Jeff under U-I's insurance, "except for disability due to back condition," or "except for disability due to sciatica." Weeks of location filming for *Merrill's Marauders* in the jungles, mountains and swamps of the Philippines had not been kind to Jeff's preexisting back condition.

On May 5, Jeff flew home, conferred with his doctor and underwent diagnostic procedures. His doctor said that only surgery would relieve his physical condition, so arrangements were made for Jeff to undergo corrective surgery of a ruptured disk, a common operation.

Esther Williams' last motion picture, *The Big Show* (1961), went into nationwide release on May 10, while the *Los Angeles Examiner* became the first newspaper to report Jeff's planned surgery. Three days later, Jeff entered the Culver City Hospital on Hughes Avenue, one of the medical facilities closest to his home in Beverly Hills. Dr. Marvin A. Korbin, a skilled and experienced neurosurgeon, would perform the surgery.

A relatively minor operation, the procedure involved the removal of a small, non-elastic protrusion in a torsion of the ligament that ran down his vertebral column. The extrusion, impinging on his spinal nerves, was the cause of his great pain.

On Saturday, May 13, Jeff underwent his first surgery. On the same day, actor Gary Cooper died of cancer, and the Hollywood Hills were on fire. Starting the night before, the fire eventually destroyed eight homes and over 800 acres in a ten-mile perimeter. The prolonged Southern California drought and low humidity were perfect conditions for a fire driven by winds that sometimes reached 67 m.p.h. Full containment was achieved early Sunday, Mother's Day, with the help of over 100 firefighting units and hundreds of police to handle the huge traffic jams that resulted in and around Hollywood and Vine. Sixty-year-old Gary Cooper's last moments were spent with family members at his Holmby Hills home, just two miles from Jeff's Beverly Hills home.

On May 16, Jeff's eldest daughter, Jamie, turned fourteen. The next day, Jeff went into shock because of hemorrhaging in the abdomen. The exact origin of the bleeding was unknown. On May 18, doctors performed a second surgery, a seven-hour emergency operation that required a transfusion of 55 pints of blood in an attempt to save his life.

Jeff's mother, ex-wife and father visited the hospital during the marathon surgery; the latter two were strong enough to hold vigil. Whereas the first operation had entered through his back, the second entered through the abdomen as the doctors explored, looking for the site of hemorrhage.

Unknown to the doctors, an accidental nick during the first surgery had opened a hole in the abdominal aorta. Such situations have been documented; an accident does not necessarily mean carelessness. Yet in Jeff's case, because he suffered from hardening of the arteries, proper blood clotting couldn't occur. The wound remained open after the first operation, and blood began to seep into his abdomen.[62]

Hours into the second surgery, the surgeon discovered the hole in the abdominal aorta, but attempts to close the wound were futile. Medical specialists from UCLA arrived and replaced part of the abdominal aorta.

The first time he hemorrhaged, Jeff lost all of the antibodies necessary to fight off bacteria. Treatment included antibiotics, but he couldn't produce antibodies fast enough and bacteria began to multiply. Special nurses, assigned to watch Jeff 24 hours a day, cared for a man barely clinging to life; condition, grave.

As Jeff battled for survival, his secretary spent much of Friday at his bedside handling a great deal of mail, telephone calls and telegrams from well-wishers, including letters from friends in the world of baseball. Bill Rigney, manager of the Los Angeles Angels and former manager of Jeff's favorite team, the San Francisco Giants, checked on his condition daily. As the weekend approached, the hospital expected Jeff to pass the crisis by Monday, but Dr. Korbin refused to discuss the case with reporters.

Midweek, the hospital took Jeff off the critical list. When Thursday arrived, Jeff said that he wanted to get up and go home; the hospital allowed him to sit up in bed. On May 26, however, Jeff underwent a third surgery because of further hemorrhaging; condition, critical.

On Saturday, Jeff experienced complications from the third surgery. By the next morning, Jeff had somewhat improved, yet by early afternoon, his condition worsened and he fell unconscious. The Associated Press issued a biographical sketch of the film star to be used only in the event of his death.

As Memorial Day arrived, the toxins in Jeff's system reached an alarming height as he fought for his life. On June 1, Jeff came off the critical list, making slow, steady improvement. Jeff asked to see his business manager; Ed Traubner visited him on June 6.

Two days later, Jeff experienced an inflammation of the gallbladder and underwent a fourth operation without a public announcement. When further inflammation set in, the lungs were the next organs to become completely overwhelmed. When his condition worsened on the morning of June 16, the hospital summoned his ex-wife and father to his bedside. Jeff Chandler died at 4:35 P.M. Saturday, June 17, 1961. The cause of death was tentatively attributed to blood poisoning and pneumonia.

On June 19, Malinow and Silverman Mortuary oversaw the funeral at Temple Isaiah in West Los Angeles. Rabbi Albert Lewis, a friend of Jeff's from the war, performed the ceremony. Mourners nearly filled the 1000-seat red-brick temple. Along with Jeff's family were Steve Broidy, president of Allied Artists; Spyros Skouros, president of 20th Century–Fox; and David A. Lipton and Edward Muhl, vice-presidents of U-I.

Actors in attendance included Edward G. Robinson, Kim Novak, Mickey Rooney, Sammy Davis, Jr., Janet Leigh, Shelley Winters and Peter Graves. "In June 1961, Meyer was still my agent; Jeff was a friend," recalled Peter Graves. "My wife and I went to his funeral; a terrible and tragic thing. I remember how sad and broken up his children were; Meyer was simply shattered by it. It was a privilege to have known and worked with Jeff Chandler; he was quite a man."[63]

"Everybody was just sick when Jeff died," remembered William Reynolds. "The whole town was shocked and grief stricken. The futility of this great career, everything great going for him, and then this, something so pointless. Everyone was just beside themselves. Meyer never really recovered, he was just never the same after that."[64]

"Who's to say just why this happened," entertainer George Jessel wrote of his friend. "Some say his constitution was weakened by the break up of his marriage. Others say he was hurt even more by the breaking up of his love affair with Esther."[65]

Jeff's passing affected not only those in Hollywood, but a Hollywood-hopeful from Great Britain. Angela von Mizener, a pen pal of Jeff's throughout the 1950s who met the star about a year before his death, recalled, "I'd done theatre in London and dreamed of becoming an actress, with a trip planned for California. Jeff said he'd help me in any way he could, and he certainly could have, but it was not to be. I was heartbroken when he died, long, long before his time. The world lost a sensitive, gentle man, and a fine actor."[66]

After a 200-car procession, private internment occurred a few miles southwest of Culver City Hospital in Hillside Memorial Park. Rabbi Lewis performed the eulogy; cantor Robert Nadel sang the liturgical music. Pallbearers for the bronze-colored solid steel casket were Hoby Landrith, Bill Rigney, Tony Curtis, Gerald Mohr, Meyer Mishkin, Ed Traubner, Byron Kane and Jess Rand. Entombment occurred in a crypt in the mausoleum's Hall of Graciousness.

Jeff's will named attorney Edward M. Rose as executor of the late actor's estate. In the third week of June, Los Angeles Superior Court assigned Rose as special administrator. Jeff's original will was missing, but a copy of it did exist, and the court gave Rose permission to search Jeff's Beverly Hills home, sealed since his death to protect the estate's assets, for the will. Valued at $600,000, the estate left everything to Jeff's daughters and included cash, securities, properties and interest in a number of motion pictures.

Jeff's executor, Edward Rose, was graduate of Fordham University and a close personal friend of the late actor. His legal career included service to the State of New York in the 1930s as a deputy district attorney in the office of district attorney Thomas E. Dewey.[67] Rose received his acceptance to the New York State Bar in 1928 and to the California State Bar in May 1948, the same month that Jeff filled in for a late Burt Lancaster on the *Lux* broadcast of *I Walk Alone*.

Rumors swept Hollywood when Jeff's autopsy revealed the fourth operation on June 8; later, a fifth, although unverified operation, also came to light. His death certificate listed the immediate cause of death as "shock — peripheral vascular collapse" due to "staphylococci septicemia" and "pneumonitis" with "bone marrow depression" as a significant condition that contributed to death.[68]

The film community wanted to know if the actor died under unfortunate and unavoidable circumstances or because of medical negligence. A petition initiated by actors Clint Walker (TV's *Cheyenne*), Trevor Bardette (*The Mating Game*) and Chuck Hicks (*Merrill's Marauders*) circulated the movie lots of Warner Bros., Revue and others. The petition requested "that an investigation be conducted by the Guild to evaluate the facts" of Jeff's death. "No one we contacted refused to sign it," said Walker.[69] On the evening of June 27, Walker presented the petition, signed by more than 150 members of the Screen Actors Guild, to the guild's president.

On June 28, the director of the State Bureau of Hospitals in Berkley, California, announced the formation of a committee to investigate Jeff's death. Later that day, Dr. David M. Brotman, medical director of the Culver City Hospital, stated that the hospital "is not trying to hide anything."[70]

The Los Angeles Supervisor of the State Bureau of Hospitals headed the investigating committee, assisted by the San Diego Supervisor of the Bureau. The chief of the housing and institutions section of the Los Angeles County Health Department also assisted; the rest of the investigative team included members of the State Department of Public Health. Launched on July 1, the investigation focused on the nursing, record-keeping and cleanliness of Culver City Hospital, reviewing Jeff's hospital records and those of patients, past and present. The purpose was to determine if Culver City Hospital was in compliance with the Hospital Licensing Act.

As Independence Day approached, the bureau's investigation continued; *Boxoffice* reported that action by the Screen Actors Guild into Jeff's death would be unlikely.[71] After consulting with attorney Edward M. Rose and the State Bureau of Hospitals, the Board of Directors of the Screen Actors Guild held a regularly scheduled meeting on July 10. (Their headquarters, located on Sunset Blvd. near Courtney Avenue, stood a block away from where the Chandlers lived in the early 1950s). After reviewing the petition and documents submitted to them after Jeff's death, the guild declined to investigate the matter, and gave the documents to the bureau and Rose for their investigation.

The State Bureau of Hospitals completed its investigation of Culver City Hospital on July 12, with their report forwarded to the chief of the Hospital Licensing Section of the State Department of Public Health in Berkeley. Nine days later, Dr. David M. Brotman received the findings and recommendations from the chief of the State Bureau of Hospitals. Dr. Brotman, accompanied by an attorney representing Culver City Hospital, held a press conference at the Biltmore on Saturday, July 22, making public the bureau's report. The report recommended 23 improvements (to record-keeping, repair and maintenance procedures) and acknowledged five corrections done during the bureau's investigation. Public opinion prompted Dr. Brotman to release the report's findings, originally scheduled to be made public September 15, when a new law was to go into effect. The report, in the form of a letter from the chief of the bureau, did not mention Jeff.

On July 27, attorney Irving H. Green, a medical malpractice lawyer acting for Marjorie, launched an investigation into Jeff's death. Green, a specialist in negligence and malpractice law, requested full reports from the doctors involved as well as the Culver City Hospital. The hospital risked a court order for documents not turned in voluntarily. As the month drew to a close, Dr. Brotman prepared to turn over all of Jeff's medical records—a 500-page document—to attorneys Rose and Green.

On September 8, attorney Green attended a Friday meeting of the Junior Bar Association in Beverly Hills, where he hinted at a $1 million lawsuit as his office had not received the pathologist's report from the Culver City Hospital. Three days later, the lawyers joined the same team: attorney Edward M. Rose received permission from Superior Court to employ attorney Irving H. Green in order to determine if they should pursue a malpractice lawsuit. Four days later, a new California law went into effect, making private hospital records public if permission is granted by the patient himself or his representatives and heirs.

On September 25, attorney Irving H. Green filed a $1.5 million suit in Superior Court. The suit sought $1 million for Jeff's children and $500,000 for additional expenses, including medical, hospital and funeral expenses as well as the loss of Jeff's earnings, estimated at $10,000 a week at the time of his death. The suit named over two dozen doctors, including Dr. Marvin A. Korbin, and Culver City Hospital as defendants.

On October 31, 1961, actor Sheldon Allman reported to work at Warner Bros. as a voice stand-in for Jeff Chandler in order to complete production of *Merrill's Marauders*.

Thousands attended a five-hour exhibition at the Ames Art Gallery in Beverly Hills on Sunday, November 5, followed by four days of auctions, the result of a court-ordered liquidation of over 1,500 items from Jeff's Beverly Hills and Palm Springs homes. Replaceable items sold to the highest bidder — treasure hunters and collectors alike — included books, cameras, appliances and luggage. Irreplaceable items included a lifetime of awards, citations and recognition for Jeff's contribution to the world of entertainment and to charity.[72] Two months later, a real estate investor purchased the late actor's Beverly Hills home.

On February 20, superior court judge Mervyn Aggeler approved a $233,358.42 settlement in the $1.5 million wrongful death and malpractice suit. Included in its terms: each of Jeff's daughters received $70,000, held in trust until they reached 21, and Jeff's medical and hospital bills were canceled.

Who's Who in Hollywood, an annual publication, featured photographs and biographies of hundreds of actors and actresses in filmland. Over the years, the magazine's coverage of Jeff Chandler included him in various categories: "Super Stars: the Older Set" (1954), "The Brightest Stars" (1956), "The Golden Circle" (1957), "Top of the Crop: Super Stars" (1958) and "Royalty Hollywood-Style: Super Stars" (1959). After 12 consecutive years of covering his career in filmland, *Who's Who in Hollywood* ended 1962 with their tribute to Jeff "... and now, good-bye."

The Films

*Films are listed according to year of copyright
and are alphabetically arranged within that year.*

The Invisible Wall

A 20th Century–Fox Picture. © 1947. Released October 1947. Ad line: "Booze–Blondes–Bullets, the Direct Trail to Skid Row!" Aka "Flamingo." Running time, 73 minutes; black & white; Crime.

Rating: *The Motion Picture Guide,* ☆½

Credits: Produced by Sol M. Wurtzel; associate producer, Howard J. Sheehan Sr.; directed by Eugene Forde; assistant director, Paul Wurtzel; screenplay by Arnold Belgard; original story by Howard J. Green and Paul Frank; original music by Dale Butts; musical direction by Morton Scott; art direction by Walter Koessler; set decoration by Al Greenwood; hair styles by Irene Beshon; make-up by Don Cash; sound technician, Max M. Hutchinson; cinematography by Benjamin Kline; film editing by Frank Baldridge and William F. Claxton.

Cast: Don Castle (Harry Lane), Virginia Christine (Mildred Elsworth), Richard Gaines (Richard Elsworth), Arthur Space (Hanford), Edward Keane (Marty Floyd), Jeff Chandler (Al Conway), Harry Cheshire (Hamilton), Mary Gordon (Mrs. Bledsoe), Harry Shannon (Det. Capt.), Rita Duncan (Alice Jamison).

Synopsis: A World War II veteran's involvement in the numbers racket leads him to Las Vegas, blackmail and murder.

Behind the Scenes: Sol M. Wurtzel joined the Fox Film Corp. in 1914, and opened their West Coast studio in 1917. When the company merged with 20th Century Pictures, he became executive producer at 20th Century–Fox, heading the B-picture unit. The year 1947 marked writer Paul Frank's last feature and director Eugene Francis Forde's last film after 19 years in Hollywood. *The Hollywood Reporter* said that *The Invisible Wall* "has a smattering of suspense and enough of the homey touch to find rather general appeal."[1]

Jeff Chandler

Reviews: "Compact, attention-holding dramatic entertainment. Well-produced, performed."—*Film Daily*, October 17, 1947. Additional Reviews: *Boxoffice*, 10/18/47; *Motion Picture Herald*, 10/18/47; *The New York Times*, 11/01/47; *Variety*, 10/10/47.

Johnny O'Clock

A Columbia Picture. © 1947. Released March 1947. Ad line: "Johnny's Dangerous ... But That's How His Women Like Him!" Columbia production number 850. Running time, 95 minutes; black & white; Crime Drama.

Ratings: *The Motion Picture Guide*, ★★★½; *Leonard Maltin's Movie and Video Guide*, ★★½; *New York Daily News*, ★★★½; *Halliwell's Film Guide*, 0

Credits: Producers, Jerry Giesler and Edward G. Nealis; assistant producer, Milton Holmes; directed by Robert Rossen; assistant director, Carl Hiecke; screenplay by Robert Rossen; original story by Milton Holmes; musical score by George L. Duning; musical direction by M. W. Stoloff; production associate, Lehman Katz; production design by Stephen Goosson and Cary Odell; set decoration by James Crowe; gowns by Jean Louis; sound by Jack Haynes; cinematography by Burnett Guffey; film editing by Al Clark and Warren Low.

Cast: Dick Powell (Johnny O'Clock), Evelyn Keyes (Nancy Hobbs), Lee J. Cobb (Inspector Koch), Ellen Drew (Nelle Marchettis), Nina Foch (Harriet Hobbs), Thomas Gomez (Pete Marchettis), John Kellogg (Charlie), Jim Bannon (Chuck Blayden), Mabel Paige (slatternly woman), Phil Brown (hotel clerk), Jeff Chandler (Turk), Kit Guard (Punchy).

Synopsis: The junior partner in a gambling house is a suspect in the homicide of a crooked cop and his girl, but the dead girl's sister helps clear him.

Behind the Scenes: Robert Rossen boxed professionally in his native New York before starting his career in Hollywood as a writer for Warner Bros. in the 1930s and, later, for director Lewis Milestone. Rossen's directorial debut occurred in 1947 with the prize fighting flick *Body and Soul* and *Johnny O'Clock*, his first for Columbia.

Sport fans may spot boxing and baseball greats in front of and behind the camera in *Johnny O'Clock*. After coaching fight scenes for the legendary cowboy star Tom Mix, retired boxing great Dave Montrose joined the props department at Columbia. Bob Perry, Gene Delmont, Charlie St. George, Cy Schindell, Sammy Shack and Ralph Volkie, all members of the boxing community, appeared as casino dealers; Charles Mueller, formerly of the St. Louis Cardinals and the Phillies, as bodyguard.[2]

Film exhibitors in the U.S. chose among the newer screen talent of the season the players most likely to achieve major stardom, and Quigley Publications called them "Stars of Tomorrow."³ Evelyn Keyes, a Star of Tomorrow, 1947, began her career as a nightclub dancer and later played Scarlett O'Hara's younger sister in *Gone with the Wind* (1939). Film exhibitors in the U.S. voted Dick Powell as one of the Top Box-Office Stars for 1935–36.

For Powell's first under the Columbia banner, the studio turned Stage One into a gambling casino. Filled with gambling equipment valued at over $50,000, the lavish set included roulette wheels, dice tables as well as professional croupiers imported from Las Vegas.⁴ *Liberty* reviewed the film as "a slick offering of hot spots and cold corpses."⁵

Reviews: "This is exceptional picture-making judged by any standards."—*The Hollywood Reporter*, January 16, 1947. "*Johnny O'Clock* is an exciting, expertly-acted thriller."—*Motion Picture Herald*, January 4, 1947. Additional Reviews: *Boxoffice*, 01/18/47; *Los Angeles Times*, 04/10/47; *Motion Picture Exhibitor*, 01/08/47; *The New York Times*, 03/27/47; *Variety*, 01/14/47.

Comments by Jeff Chandler: "One day when Dick Powell and I were standing around after rehearsal for [the radio detective drama] *Rogue's Gallery*, he asked me 'Ever thought of doing any picture work, kid?' I'd thought about it since my school days at Feagin [School of Dramatic Art]. I don't know whether that showed up when I answered 'Yeah' to Powell that day or not! At any rate, he said to meet him the next morning at Columbia Picture studios, and that's just about the way I got into my first flicker. I think the director put me into Powell's own *Johnny O'Clock* just to get even with Dick for foisting me off on him!"⁶

Roses Are Red

A 20th Century–Fox Picture. © 1947. Released December 1947. Ad line: "Roses are Red — With the Heart-Blood of Murder." Running time, 67 minutes; black & white; Crime.

Rating: *The Motion Picture Guide,* ☆

Credits: Produced by Sol M. Wurtzel; assistant producer, Howard J. Sheehan Sr.; directed by James Tinling; assistant director, Maurice Vaccarino; story and screenplay by Irving Elman; original music by Rudy Schrager; musical supervision by David Chudnow; art direction by Walter Koessler; production assistant, Clifford R. Gans; set decoration by Al Greenwood; hair styles by Irene Beshon; make-up by Don Cash; sound by John Carter; cinematography by Benjamin Kline; film editing by Frank Baldridge.

Cast: Don Castle (Robert A. Thorne and Don Carney), Peggy Knudsen (Martha McCormack), Patricia Knight (Jill Carney), Joe Sawyer (Wall), Jeff Chandler (Knuckle), Paul Guilfoyle (Cooley), Charles McGraw (Duke), Charles Lane (Lipton), Douglas Fowley (Ace Oliver), James Arness (Ray), Edward Keane (Jim Locke).

Synopsis: In an effort to gain full control of the city, a newly-elected district attorney is kidnapped by a crooked political boss and replaced by an ex-convict.

Behind the Scenes: Howard J. Sheehan Sr. joined the Fox Film Corporation in 1914, and later became executive Vice President of Fox West Coast Theaters, where he built the showcase Wilshire Theatre in Beverly Hills. As associate producer, he worked on five motion pictures in 1947; James Tinling directed two of those films, including *Roses are Red*. Tinling arrived in Hollywood in 1925 and served as an apprentice assistant director under Howard Hawks. "The story," wrote the *Motion Picture Exhibitor*, "is unfolded in a tense, suspenseful style."[7]

Reviews: "*Roses are Red* is standard supporting feature material." — *Variety*, October 30, 1947. "Has smart script, action, good cast." — *The Hollywood Reporter*, October 30, 1947. Additional Reviews: *Monthly Film Bulletin*, 09/49; *Motion Picture Herald*, 11/08/47; *The New York Times*, 11/15/47.

Abandoned

A Universal-International Picture. © 1949. Released October 1949. Ad line: "No Name for Her Baby ... Only a Price!" Universal-International production number 1608. Aka "Abandoned Woman," "Illegitimate," "One Way Out." Running time, 79 minutes; black & white; Crime.

Ratings: *The Motion Picture Guide*, ☆☆☆; *Leonard Maltin's Movie and Video Guide*, ☆½; *New York Daily News*, ☆☆½; *Halliwell's Film Guide*, 0

Credits: Produced by Jerry Bresler; assistant producer, William Holland; directed by Joseph M. Newman; story and screenplay by Irwin Gielgud, with additional dialogue by William Bowers; music by Walter Scharf; art direction by Robert Boyle and Bernard Herzbrun; production manager, Howard J. Christie; set decorations by Russell A. Gausman and Ruby R. Levitt; hair styles by Emmy Eckhardt and Joan St. Oegger; make-up by Emile LaVigne and Bud Westmore; costume design by Yvonne Wood; sound by Leslie I. Carey and Joe Lapis; cinematography by William H. Daniels; film editing by Edward Curtiss.

Cast: Dennis O'Keefe (Mark Sitko), Gale Storm (Paula Considine), Jeff Chandler (Chief McRae), Meg Randall (Dottie Jensen), Raymond Burr (Kerric), Marjorie Rambeau (Mrs. Donner), Jeanette Nolan (Maj. Ross), Mike Mazurki (Hoppe), Will Kuluva ("Little Guy" DeCola), David Clarke (Harry), William Page (Scoop), Sid Tomack (Mr. Humes), Perc Launders (Dowd), Steve Darrell (Brenn), Clifton Young (Eddie), Ruth Sanderson (Mrs. Spence).

Synopsis: A newspaperman helps a distraught woman track down the murderer of her sister and the whereabouts of the dead girl's baby — somewhere in the dark, mob-infested underworld of Los Angeles.

Behind the Scenes: In early May 1949, location filming occurred in the Maternity Hospital of the Salvation Army in the Montecito Heights section of Los Angeles. A semi-documentary on the black market of illegitimate babies, *Abandoned* supported the Salvation Army's fight against baby adoption racketeering, and marked the second movie for Jeff Chandler and Gale Storm under contract to U-I. Jeff first worked with the film's star, Dennis O'Keefe, in 1948 on *Lux*; O'Keefe came to U-I on loan-out as part of the studio's policy of casting its new players with established stars. For the promotion of *Abandoned*, U-I made available to theater owners various tools, including posters, lobby cards and a free record album featuring Jeff. The studio provided an announcer's script with the disc, allowing radio commentators to have a "personal" interview with the star.[8] Because of his good performance in *Sword in the Desert*, U-I strengthened Jeff's name by giving him the catch line "sensation of *Sword in the Desert*" in their promotion of *Abandoned*. The *Motion Picture Herald* called the movie "an interesting melodrama of crime and scientific investigation."[9]

Reviews: "Jeff Chandler scores decisively in the spot of a district attorney."—*The Hollywood Reporter*, October 5, 1949; "Jeff Chandler, as the District Attorney, is a business-like official, who really talks and acts like a D.A."—*Los Angeles Examiner*, October 29, 1949. Additional Reviews: *Boxoffice*, 10/15/49; *Monthly Film Bulletin*, 10/49; *Motion Picture Exhibitor*, 10/12/49; *Motion Picture Herald*, 10/08/49; *The New York Times*, 10/27/49; *Variety*, 10/05/49.

Comments by the Director: "We had a very good cast. Dennis O'Keefe, Gale Storm, Jeff Chandler, and this was Jeff's first big part."—*Joseph M. Newman*[10]

Comments by a Fan: "Jeff Chandler's performance rates applause. Even though his part was a less important one, he stole almost every scene he was in. He has a memorable and fascinating voice, and is very personable in appearance. In my opinion, he's made of 'star stuff.' I'd sure like to see him 'starring' and soon!"[11]

Mr. Belvedere Goes to College

A 20th Century–Fox Picture. © 1949. Released May 1949. Ad line: "The Amazing Mr. Belvedere is Back Again and Funnier Than Ever." Running time, 88 minutes; black & white; Comedy.

Ratings: *The Motion Picture Guide*, ☆☆☆; *Leonard Maltin's Movie and Video Guide*, ☆☆; *New York Daily News*, ☆☆☆½; *Halliwell's Film Guide*, ☆

Credits: Produced by Samuel G. Engel; directed by Elliott Nugent; assistant director, Arthur Jacobson; written by Mary Loos, Mary McCall Jr., and Richard Sale, based on a character created by Gwen Davenport; original music and musical direction by Alfred Newman; orchestrator, Edward Powell; art direction by Richard Irvine and Lyle Wheeler; production manager, Charles R. Hall; set decorations by Thomas Little; hair styles by Irene Brooks, Annabell Levy, and Marie

Walters; make-up by Ben Nye; wardrobe by Charles Le Maire; costume design by Bonnie Cashin; sound by Roger Heman and E. Clayton Ward; cinematography by Lloyd Ahern; film editing by Harmon Jones.

Cast: Clifton Webb (Lynn Belvedere), Shirley Temple (Ellen Baker), Tom Drake (Bill Chase), Alan Young (Avery Brubaker), Jessie Royce Landis (Mrs. Chase), Kathleen Hughes (Kay Nelson), Taylor Holmes (Dr. Gibbs), Alvin Greenman (Corny Whittaker), Paul Harvey (Dr. Keating), Barry Kelly (Griggs), Bob Patten (Joe Fisher), Jeff Chandler (Pratt), Clancy Cooper (McCarthy), Lotte Stein (Marta).

Synopsis: Unable to collect a literary award unless he has a college degree, a genius goes to college, where a journalism student threatens to expose his secret.

Behind the Scenes: Elliott Nugent brought to this film his experience in directing comedies with stars such as Bob Hope and Danny Kaye. Samuel G. Engel, who began his career at the studio in the 1930s, produced *Sitting Pretty* (1948), the first of the Mr. Belvedere movies. Clifton Webb's role in the latter earned him an Academy award-nomination for Best Actor.

During a four-year period in the mid–1930s, America chose child star Shirley Temple as the number one box-office attraction. After a sixteen-year absence, Miss Temple returned to the same stage at 20th Century–Fox where she made her film debut. *Motion Picture Herald* proclaimed *Mr. Belvedere Goes to College* a "load of laughs."[12]

Reviews: "Sequel scores hit for witty genius."—*The Hollywood Reporter*, April 1, 1949. "The film is funny. It had the house in an uproar."—*Los Angeles Times*, May 7, 1949. Additional Reviews: *Boxoffice*, 04/09/49; *Motion Picture Exhibitor*, 04/13/49; *The New York Times*, 04/16/49; *Variety*, 04/01/49.

Among the Top-Grossing Films of 1949: $3,650,000[13]

The Rugged O'Riordans

A Universal-International Picture. © 1949. Released January 1950. Ad line: "Rough as its Name! Reckless as its People! Epic Drama Filmed in Australia's Most Savage Wilderness!" Aka "The Sons of Matthew," "Conqueror of the Green Kingdom." Running time, 87 minutes; black & white; Drama.

Rating: *The Motion Picture Guide,* ☆☆

Credits: Produced and directed by Charles Chauvel; associate producer, Elsa Chauvel; screenplay by Charles and Elsa Chauvel; adapted in part by Maxwell Dunn; narration and wild lines by Jeff Chandler; music directed and composed by Henry Cripps; sound by Clive Cross; cinematography by Carl Kayser and Bert Nicholas; film editing by Terry Banks.

Cast: Michael Pate (Shane), Wendy Gibb (Cathy), John O'Malley (Matthew), Thelma Scott (Jane), Ken Wayne (Barney), John Unicombe (Terry), John Ewart (Mickey), Tommy Burns (Luke), Jimmy White (Mickey as a boy).

Synopsis: The story of a clan of hardy pioneers as they carve an existence out of the Australian bush country and jungles.

Behind the Scenes: Hollywood released 382 feature films in 1948, while Australia seldom released three in one year. Without known movie actors available, Charles Chauvel, who discovered Errol Flynn, turned to the Australian stage and radio. Accomplished radio performers head the cast of the film, with Thelma Scott the only actor with former movie experience. Filmed in its entirety in the jungles of Lamington National Park, *The Rugged O'Riordans* marked Chauvel's third production in a 24-year period to receive American bookings.[14]

Over a year of location filming in the jungle occurred because of torrential rainstorms that pummeled the cast and crew. Jeff attended two sessions at U-I for the film: one for narration, and the other for wild lines, or "wild tracks," where the actor said lines that didn't record properly the first time. *Boxoffice* proclaimed that the movie "is one of few from Australia and is worth seeing because it is different."[15]

Reviews: "There are no names to exploit nor anything unusual about the story and its treatment except some fine acting and excellent photography."—*Motion Picture Herald*, December 17, 1949. "Interesting story, well-acted roles, good direction and production."—*The Exhibitor*, December 21, 1949. Additional Reviews: *Harrison's Reports*, 12/24/49; *Monthly Film Bulletin*, 01/02/50; *Variety*, 12/14/49.

Sword in the Desert

A Universal Picture. © 1949. Released October 1949. Ad line: "Their Names Were Known Only in Whispers ... But Their Deeds Wrote the Headlines of the World!" Universal Picture production number 1601. Aka "Desert Legion," "The Night Watch," "Sword in the Sand." Running time, 100 minutes; black & white; War Drama.

Ratings: *The Motion Picture Guide*, ☆☆☆½; *Leonard Maltin's Movie and Video Guide*, ☆☆½; *New York Daily News*, ☆☆☆½; *Halliwell's Film Guide*, 0

Credits: Produced by Robert Buckner; directed by George Sherman; assistant director, Frank Shaw; original story by Robert Buckner; music by Frank Skinner; art direction by Alexander Golitzen; set decorations by A. Roland Fields and Russell A. Gausman; hair styles by Ruby Felker and Joan St. Oegger; make-up by Emile LaVigne and Bud Westmore; sound by Glenn E. Anderson and Leslie I. Carey; cinematography by Irving Glassburg; film editing by Otto Ludwig.

Cast: Dana Andrews (Mike Dillon), Marta Toren (Sabra), Stephen McNally (David Vogel), Jeff Chandler (Kurta), Phillip Friend (Lt. Ellerton), Hugh French (Maj. Sorrell), Liam Redmond (McCarthy), Lowell Gilmore (Maj. Stephens), Stanley Logan (Col. Bruce Evans), Hayden Rorke (Capt. Beaumont), George Tyne (Dov), Peter Coe (Tarn), Paul Marion (Jeno), Martin Lamont (Capt. Fletcher), David

Jeff Chandler

Wolfe (Gershon), Campbell Copelin (Sgt. Chapel), Art Foster (Sgt. Rummins), Gilchrist Stuart (radio operator), Emil Rameau (old man).

Synopsis: In 1947, an American blockade-runner smuggles Jewish refugees from Europe into the Holy Land, but finds himself trapped by the British and is forced to escape with the refugees.

Behind the Scenes: Robert Montgomery, Paulette Goddard and Burgess Meredith found interest in *Sword in the Desert* early on; Van Heflin and Ann Blyth

Stephen McNally, Dana Andrews, and Marta Toren with Jeff Chandler (kneeling) in a publicity photo for *Sword in the Desert* (1949, Universal-International).

were originally cast as the leads.[16] With the final cast in place, U-I canceled a Technicolor commitment followed by extensive wardrobe tests made with infrared film. Heavy use of infrared occurred — shooting day scenes for night — because 80% of the story occurred at night.[17] During the summer of 1949, the studio wrote, produced and recorded a free record album with Jeff to be used in the promotion of *Sword in the Desert*. Further promotion included a plane trip to San Diego where Jeff attended a press luncheon followed by newspaper interviews and radio broadcasts. The *Motion Picture Herald* said the film "will keep them on the edges of the seats."[18]

Reviews: "*Sword in the Desert* marks the screen introduction of Chandler. He makes a rousing film debut."—*Film Daily*, August 24, 1949. "Jeff Chandler, as the lead, is an exciting new personality — an actor with a wide range of talent."—*The Hollywood Reporter*, August 24, 1949. Additional Reviews: *Boxoffice*, 09/03/49; *Monthly Film Bulletin*, 04/05/50; *Motion Picture Exhibitor*, 08/31/49; *The New York Times*, 08/25/49; *Variety*, 08/24/49.

Comments by the Head of Television-Radio Promotion, Universal-International: "Jeff Chandler was reachable, touchable and had no phony Hollywood airs. That's what made him so popular and liked by everyone. He always mingled with the crew and extras."—*Bob Rains*[19]

Abbott and Costello in the Foreign Legion

A Universal-International Picture. © 1950. Released August 1950. Ad line: "The Newest and Funniest by Far! And Their First in a Year!" Universal-International production number 1628. Aka "Foreign Legion." Running time, 80 minutes; black & white; Comedy.

Ratings: *The Motion Picture Guide*, ☆☆; *Leonard Maltin's Movie and Video Guide*, ☆☆; *New York Daily News*, ☆☆; *Halliwell's Film Guide*, 0

Credits: Produced by Robert Arthur; directed by Charles Lamont; assistant director, Milton Carter; screenplay by John Grant, Martin Ragaway and Leonard Stern, based on a story by D. D. (Bud) Beauchamp; narration by Jeff Chandler; musical direction by Joseph Gershenson; art direction by Bernard Herzbrun and Eric Orbom; production manager, Edward Dodds; set decorations by Russell A. Gausman and Ray Jeffers; hair styles by Joan St. Oegger; make-up by Bud Westmore; sound by Leslie I. Carey and Robert Pritchard; cinematography by George Robinson; film editing by Frank Gross.

Cast: Bud Abbott (Jonesy), Lou Costello (Max Hotchkiss), Patricia Medina (Nicole), Walter Slezak (Axmann), Douglass Dumbrille (Hamud El Khalid), Leon Belasco (Hassam), Marc Lawrence (Frankie), Wee Willie Davis (Abdullah), Tor Johnson (Abou Ben), Sam Menacker (Bertram), Fred Nurney (Commandant), Paul

Fierro (Ibn), Henry Corden (Ibrim), Jack Raymond (Ali Ami), Jack Shutta (thug), Harry Wilson (thug), Ernesto Morelli (thug), Jack Davidson (thug), Chuck Hamilton (thug).

Synopsis: Pressed for cash by a racketeer and after their wrestler runs away from Brooklyn to Algiers, a couple of wrestling promoters follow in pursuit to North Africa only to be tricked into joining the Foreign Legion.

Behind the Scenes: The rise to fame as movie comedians for Bud Abbott and Lou Costello began in radio. *The Abbott and Costello Show* started as the summer replacement for *The Fred Allen Show* in 1940, returning to the air as a regular program in 1942 until 1949. In the late 1930s, Universal adopted a policy of developing star values, finding this successful after signing under contract Donald O'Connor, Deanna Durbin, and, in 1939, Abbott and Costello. John Grant, Abbott and Costello's chief writer, began with the comedy team in 1938. D. D. (Bud) Beauchamp's writing credits include *The Wistful Widow of Wagon Gap* (1947), produced by Robert Arthur. The successful Abbott and Costello feature *Buck Privates Come Home* (1946) marked Arthur's debut production at Universal, while Charles Lamont's directorial career began with shorts for Mack Sennett, the "King of Comedy." The *Motion Picture Herald* told its readers that *Abbott and Costello in the Foreign Legion* has its "rib ticklers" and "belly-laugh moments."[20]

Reviews: "Amusing comedy."—*Motion Picture Exhibitor*, July 19, 1950. "Abbott and Costello are at it again, this time in 'The Foreign Legion,' and there's plenty of fun offered for the fans and family trade situations."—*Variety*, July 12, 1950. Additional Reviews: *Boxoffice*, 07/22/50; *Film Daily*, 07/19/50; *The Hollywood Reporter*, 07/12/50; *Los Angeles Times*, 07/29/50; *Monthly Film Bulletin*, 08/50; *The New York Times*, 08/14/50.

Among the Top-Grossing Films of 1950: $1,275,000[21]

Broken Arrow

A 20th Century–Fox Picture. © 1950. Released July 1950. Ad line: "When Tomahawk and Carbine Split the West Asunder ... These Three Stood Alone — In Glory!" Aka "Warpaint," "Arrow," "Blood Brothers." Running time, 92 minutes; Technicolor; Western.

Ratings: *The Motion Picture Guide*, ☆☆☆½; *Leonard Maltin's Movie and Video Guide*, ☆☆☆; *New York Daily News*, ☆☆☆; *Halliwell's Film Guide*, ☆

Credits: Produced by Julian Blaustein; directed by Delmer Daves; assistant director, Jasper Blystone; screenplay by Michael Blankfort, based on the book *Blood Brother* by Elliott Arnold (New York: Duell, Sloane and Pearce, 1947); original music by Hugo Friedhofer; musical direction by Alfred Newman; orchestra by Edward Powell; art direction by Albert Hogsett and Lyle Wheeler; production man-

The Films

Apache chief Cochise (Jeff Chandler) and scout Tom Jeffords (James Stewart) in *Broken Arrow* (1950, 20th Century–Fox).

ager, Stanley Goldsmith; set decorations by Thomas Little and Fred J. Rode; hair styles by Stephanie Garland; make-up by Ben Nye; costume design by Rene Hubert; wardrobe director, Charles Le Maire; sound by Bernard Freericks and Harry M. Leonard; cinematography by Ernest Palmer; film editing by J. Watson Webb Jr.

Cast: James Stewart (Tom Jeffords), Jeff Chandler (Cochise), Debra Paget (Sonseeahray), Basil Ruysdael (Gen. Howard), Will Geer (Ben Slade), Joyce MacKenzie (Terry), Arthur Hunnicutt (Duffield), Raymond Bramley (Col. Bernall), Jay Silverheels (Goklia), Argentina Brunetti (Nalikadeya), Jack Lee (Boucher), Robert Adler (Lonergan), Robert Griffin (Lowrie), Billy Wilkerson (Juan), Mickey Kuhn (Chip Slade), John War Eagle (Nahilzay), Robert Foster Dover (Machogee).

Synopsis: In 1870's Arizona, an ex-Army scout, disgusted with the constant battles between the Apaches and frontiersmen, boldly plans a visit to the feared Apache leader to propose peace.

Jeff Chandler

Behind the Scenes: Onscreen for more than a decade as *Broken Arrow* went into production in June 1949, James Stewart received an Academy award for *The Philadelphia Story* (1940) as well as Academy award-nominations for *Mr. Smith Goes to Washington* (1939) and *It's a Wonderful Life* (1946). Jeff first worked with Stewart in December 1947 on *The Lux Radio Theatre*. Six months later, Jeff appeared in the *Lux* broadcast of "You Were Meant for Me," starring Dan Dailey and Donna Reed and featuring that week's intermission guest, 20th Century–Fox starlet, Debra Paget. Under U-I's employment agreement with the star, Jeff had the right to do one radio performance a week, and with filming outside the Los Angeles city limits, he would receive twenty-four hours off in order to do the broadcast. While in Flagstaff, Arizona, for location filming for *Broken Arrow*, 20th Century–Fox paid for his travel expenses. In order to meet his contractual agreements for the radio broadcast of *Our Miss Brooks*, Jeff flew from Flagstaff to Hollywood three out of the five weekends. Cooler weather in New York City, along with the release of a number of new movies, accounted for an upward swing in film business on Broadway in the summer of 1950: *Broken Arrow* premiered at the Roxy Theatre with the Andrews Sisters on stage. In order to break even, the film had to gross over $3.25 million, a challenge that the solemn western more than met. As U-I delayed the release of *Deported* in order to take advantage of Jeff's performance in *Broken Arrow*, the *Motion Picture Herald* said of the latter, "Chandler brings a great deal of dignity to the part of 'Cochise.' Much of the credit must go to him."[22]

Reviews: "Brilliant job on every hand. Lacks nothing. Audiences have never seen anything like this one."—*Film Daily*, June 14, 1950. "The acting is in the superior class, with all turning in a fine job, with perhaps special mention due Chandler."—*Motion Picture Exhibitor*, June 21, 1950. Additional Reviews: *Boxoffice*, 06/07/50; *The Hollywood Reporter*, 06/12/50; *Los Angeles Times*, 08/19/50; *Monthly Film Bulletin*, 08/50; *The New York Times*, 07/21/50; *Variety*, 06/12/50.

Among the Top-Grossing Films of 1950: $3,550,000[23]

Academy Award Nominations (1950): Best Supporting Actor, Jeff Chandler; Writing (Screenplay), Michael Blankfort; Cinematography (Color), Ernest Palmer.

Golden Globe Award (1950): Best Film Promoting International Understanding.

Writers Guild of America Award (1950): Best-Written American Western: Michael Blankfort.

Comments by the Vice President in Charge of Production, 20th Century–Fox: "The best scenes in the picture were Jimmy's [James Stewart's] death scene and the scenes in the tent between [Jeff] Chandler and Jimmy."—*Darryl F. Zanuck*[24]

Comments by Jeff Chandler: "'Cochise' made my career."[25]

The Films

Deported

A Universal-International Picture. © 1950. Released November 1950. Ad line: "He Had a Talent for Trouble ... A Greedy Gun ... And a Taste for Gaudy Women." Universal-International production number 1607. Aka "Fox in Chains," "Native's Return," "Paradise Lost." Running time, 88 minutes; black & white; Crime.

Ratings: *The Motion Picture Guide*, ☆☆½; *Leonard Maltin's Movie and Video Guide*, ☆☆½; *New York Daily News*, ☆☆☆; *Halliwell's Film Guide*, 0

Credits: Produced by Robert Buckner; directed by Robert Siodmak; assistant directors, Ronnie Rondell, Tom Shaw; screenplay by Robert Buckner, based on a short story by Lionel S. B. Shapiro; music by Frank Skinner; musical direction by Walter Scharf; art direction by Bernard Herzbrun and Nathan Juran; production manager, Charles Stallings; set decorations by John Austin and Russell A. Gausman; hair styles by Joan St. Oegger; make-up by Bud Westmore; gowns by Orry Kelly; sound by Leslie I. Carey and Joe Lapis; cinematography by William H. Daniels; film editing by Ralph Dawson.

Cast: Marta Toren (Contessa Di Lorenzi), Jeff Chandler (Vic Smith), Claude Dauphin (Bucelli), Marina Berti (Gina), Silvio Minciotti (Armando Sparducci), Mimi Aguglia (Teresa), Richard Rober (Bernardo Gervase), Phillip Dakin (Wickruff), Adriano Ambrogi (Father Genaro), Ermino Spalla (Beniamino Bardi), Guido Celano (Aldo Brescia), Michail Tor (Ernesto Pampiglione), Rosanna Lucarelli (Maria), Maria Carli (Serefina), Carlo Rizzo (Guido Caruso).

Synopsis: After serving time in a U.S. prison, a hoodlum is deported to his native Italy where he proceeds to defraud a beautiful countess while courting the black market.

Behind the Scenes: In 1929, Robert Siodmak's directorial debut occurred in Germany, four years before the Nazi takeover. After calling Hollywood home for six years, Siodmak earned an Academy award-nomination for *The Killers* (1946). In August 1949, U-I assigned him to direct *Deported* under a deal whereby he would deliver to the studio one picture a year. Cities for location filming of *Deported* included Rome and Naples as well as Siena, where half the town turned out to see Marta and Jeff present Italy's first Grauman's Chinese Theater-type courtyard at the 1200-seat Odeon Theatre.[26] After U-I cast Jeff in the lead, CBS Radio agreed to release Jeff from three consecutive radio broadcasts of *Our Miss Brooks*. U-I understood the importance of Jeff's presence in Hollywood for the October 23, 1949 radio broadcast of *Our Miss Brooks*: the actor had exactly 19 days in Italy; in order to complete filming, the cast and crew had several days without him. The studio then kept track of Jeff's trip from Italy to Hollywood in great detail. For his return flight, three different reservations were made on two different airlines. U-I knew of Jeff's exact location at each leg of his journey with reports such as Jeff is "at this moment over the Atlantic," "in New York," and "delayed in Indiana." He arrived in Hollywood on time and the broadcast of *Our Miss Brooks* with Jeff went on as scheduled. Marta Toren returned from Italy a couple of days later and accompanied Jeff to the studio, where they continued filming. Although location filming in Italy delayed the celebration of Jeff and Marjorie's third wedding anniversary, international travel arrangements coincided nicely with the birth of their second daughter, Dana, on the 29th of October. "Marta Toren was one of the loveliest ladies I ever worked with," recalled Bob Rains. "Jeff and Marta were very close and her death [in 1957] upset him greatly."[27] Miss Toren helped promote *Deported* by touring Canada with Canadian-born writer, Lionel S. B. Shapiro. In their review of the movie, the *Motion Picture Exhibitor* wrote that "Toren is as attractive as ever, while Chandler turns in another able performance."[28]

Reviews: "*Deported* has several things in its favor. Foremost among these is the portrayal of the gangster by Jeff Chandler, an actor of exceptional ability and authority."—*Los Angeles Daily News*, November 8, 1950.

"Chandler Unmasked: It is pleasant to discover that Jeff Chandler is a young man and a competent performer, even divested of the title and accessories of 'chief' which he wore in such films as *Sword in the Desert* and *Broken Arrow*."—*Los Angeles Times*, November 8, 1950.

Additional Reviews: *Boxoffice*, 10/28/50; *Film Daily*, 10/10/49; *The Hollywood Reporter*, 10/18/50; *Monthly Film Bulletin*, 06/50; *Motion Picture Herald*, 10/21/50; *The New York Times*, 11/02/50; *Variety*, 10/18/50.

Costar Comments: "Some 10,000 people visited the sets. And before we left, they opened their version of Grauman's Chinese. I put my hand and foot prints and wrote my name in the concrete."—*Marta Toren*[29]

Double Crossbones

A Universal-International Picture. © 1950. Released April 1951. Ad line: "Yo-Ho-Ho-Ho ... It's a Battle of Fun!" Universal-International production number 1621. Aka "Half Pint Buccaneer." Running time, 75 minutes; Technicolor; Musical/Comedy.

Ratings: *The Motion Picture Guide*, ☆☆; *Leonard Maltin's Movie and Video Guide*, ☆☆; *New York Daily News*, ☆☆☆; *Halliwell's Film Guide*, 0

Credits: Produced by Leonard Goldstein; directed by Charles T. Barton; assistant director, Fred Frank; screenplay by Oscar Brodney, with additional dialogue by John Grant, based on a story by Oscar Brodney and John Grant, written by Leonard Goldstein; narration by Jeff Chandler; musical direction by Frank Skinner; art direction by Alexander Golitzen and Bernard Herzbrun; production manager, Howard J. Christie; set decorations by John Austin and Russell A. Gausman; hair styles by Doris Harris and Joan St. Oegger; make-up by Emile LaVigne and

Bud Westmore; costume design by Yvonne Wood; sound by Leslie I. Carey and Richard DeWeese; cinematography by Maury Gertsman; film editing by Russell Schoengarth.

Cast: Donald O'Connor (Dave Crandall), Helena Carter (Lady Sylvia Copeland), Will Geer (Tom Botts), John Emery (Gov. Elden), Hope Emerson (Mistress Ann Bonney), Stanley Logan (Lord Montrose), Kathryn Givney (Lady Montrose), Hayden Rorke (Malcolm Giles), Morgan Farley (Caleb Nicholas), Charles McGraw (Capt. Ben Wickett), Alan Napier (Capt. Kidd), Robert Barrat (Henry Morgan), Louis Bacigalupi (Blackbeard), Glenn Strange (Capt. Ben Avery), Gregg Martell (Issac Wells).

Synopsis: A timid shop apprentice in the colonial Carolinas escapes arrest when a British official mistakes him as a murderous cutthroat, but ends up forced to act the part of a pirate.

Behind the Scenes: Through the 1920s and into the 1930s, Paramount employed Charles T. Barton in various capacities; for his work as Assistant Director, he received an Academy award at the 6th Annual Academy Awards Presentation. In the 1940s, Barton directed Abbott and Costello features for U-I, while Leonard Goldstein successfully produced comedies such as the Ma & Pa Kettle features for the studio.

Donald O'Connor, a Star of Tomorrow, 1943, appeared in the popular comedy *Francis* (1950) shortly before taking the starring role in *Double Crossbones*. The *Motion Picture Herald* called the film a "thoroughly entertaining musical comedy."[30]

Reviews: "It may be that people who like swashbucklers don't like to see them satirized, but if they'll pardon a light approach, they'll enjoy *Double Crossbones*." — *Los Angeles Mirror*, May 12, 1951.

Additional Reviews: *Boxoffice*, 12/02/50; *Film Daily*, 11/21/50; *The Hollywood Reporter*, 11/20/50; *Monthly Film Bulletin*, 06/50; *Motion Picture Exhibitor*, 12/20/50; *The New York Times*, 04/27/51; *Variety*, 11/20/50.

Two Flags West

A 20th Century–Fox Picture. © 1950. Released November 1950. Ad line: "Savages Are Beating the Drums of War ... Whetting the Arrow for the Kill ... And Brave Men Stand at the Gateway to Glory ... In Their Dream of Empire." Aka "Trumpet to the Morn." Running time, 92 minutes; black & white; Western.

Ratings: *The Motion Picture Guide*, ☆☆☆; *Leonard Maltin's Movie and Video Guide*, ☆☆; *New York Daily News*, ☆☆☆; *Halliwell's Film Guide*, ☆

Credits: Produced by Casey Robinson; directed by Robert Wise; assistant director, William Eckhardt; screenplay by Casey Robinson, adapted from an unpublished story by Frank S. Nugent and Curtis Kenyon; original music by Hugo

Jeff Chandler

Friedhofer; musical direction by Alfred Newman; orchestra by Earle Hagen and Maurice de Packh; art direction by Chester Gore and Lyle Wheeler; production manager, Sam Wurtzel; set decorations by Thomas Little and Fred J. Rode; hair styles by Lillian Hokom; make-up by Ben Nye and Allan Snyder; costume design by Edward Stevenson; sound by Alfred Bruzlin and Harry M. Leonard; cinematography by Leon Shamroy; film editing by Louis Loeffler.

Cast: Joseph Cotten (Col. Clay Tucker), Linda Darnell (Mary Kenniston), Jeff Chandler (Kenniston), Cornel Wilde (Capt. Mark Bradford), Dale Robertson (Lem), Jay C. Flippen (Sgt. Terrance Duffy), Noah Beery (Cy Davis), Harry Von Zell (Ephraim Strong), John Sands (Lt. Adams), Arthur Hunnicutt (Sgt. Pickens).

Synopsis: In exchange for their freedom, Confederate prisoners head west to assist the Union Army in their fight against the Indians. After their arrival at the frontier post, however, they become involved with a brutal, anti–Confederate commandant.

Behind the Scenes: Jeff first performed with Joseph Cotten in 1946 on radio's *Academy Award*; two years later, with Cotten and Cornel Wilde in separate broadcasts of *Lux*. Awards for outstanding achievement brought to the set included the Venice Film Festival award to Cotten for *Portrait of Jennie* (1948) and an Academy award-nomination to Wilde for *A Song to Remember* (1944).

The "two flags" in *Two Flags West* are those of the Union and the Confederacy. During the Civil War, Confederate prisoners headed west to help the Union fight Indians, and in *Two Flags West*, they head for Ft. Thorn, New Mexico. The cast and crew locationed for six weeks near Santa Fe, New Mexico, and Jeff commuted to Hollywood for live broadcasts of *Our Miss Brooks*. In its review of the film, the *Los Angeles Times* wrote, "The shooting, when it finally starts, is terrific."[31]

Reviews: "If anyone could be said to be truly outstanding it is Jeff Chandler whose interpretation of an uncompromising Confederate-hater, tortured by his love for his dead brother's wife, is a superb piece of acting."—*The Hollywood Reporter*, October 9, 1950.

"Good outdoor adventure show."—*Motion Picture Exhibitor*, October 11, 1950.

Additional Reviews: *Film Daily*, 10/10/50; *Monthly Film Bulletin*, 12/50; *Motion Picture Herald*, 10/14/50; *The New York Times*, 10/13/50; *Variety*, 10/11/50.

Comments by the Vice President in Charge of Production, 20th Century–Fox: "He [Jeff Chandler] is a very great actor, and when I say great, I mean it. He has the stature, the power, and yet with it all he has a very wonderful personality. I think you will find out with his natural power and strength that you can afford to underwrite him in many scenes, that you could even afford to give him a sense of humor."—*Darryl F. Zanuck*[32]

Costar Comments: "Jeff Chandler is a dreamboat, good actor, and a real down-to-earth guy."—*Linda Darnell*[33]

The Films

Comments by Jeff Chandler: "In the movie role of Major Kenniston, I was a very complex character with more frustrations than any mere corporal could afford to have."[34]

Bird of Paradise

A 20th Century–Fox Picture. © 1951. Released March 1951. Ad line: "Volcanic! The Story of Polynesian Love on the 'Islands!'" Running time, 100 minutes; Technicolor; Romance/Adventure.

Ratings: *The Motion Picture Guide*, ★½; *Leonard Maltin's Movie and Video Guide*, ★★; *New York Daily News*, ★★½; *Halliwell's Film Guide*, 0

Credits: Directed by Delmer Daves; associate producer, Harmon Jones; assistant director, Jasper Blystone; written by Delmer Daves, adapted from the play *Bird of Paradise* by Richard Walton Tully, in: (synopsis) *Best Plays of 1909/1919*; and *The Yearbook of the Drama in America* (New York: Dodd, Mead, 1919); original music by Daniele Amfitheatrof; associate musical director, Ken Darby; orchestra by Edward Powell; art direction by Albert Hogsett and Lyle Wheeler; set decorations by Thomas Little and Fred J. Rode; make-up by Ben Nye; costume design by Travilla; wardrobe supervisor, Charles Le Maire; sound by W. D. Flick and Roger Heman; cinematography by Winton C. Hoch; film editing by James B. Clark.

Cast: Louis Jourdan (Andre Laurence), Debra Paget (Kalua), Jeff Chandler (Tenga), Everett Sloane (The Beachcomber), Maurice Schwartz (The Kahuna), Jack Elam (The Trader), Prince Lei Lani (Chief), Otto Waldis (Skipper), Alfred Zeisler (Van Hook), Mary Ann Ventura (Noanoa), David K. Bray (Chanter), Sam Monsarrat (Tenga's friend), Violet Nathaniel (Chieftess), Solomon Pa (Chief's Man), Maiola Kalili (cook), Jane Robisa (woman).

Synopsis: A South Seas romance between a white man and a native island girl ends when she leaps into an erupting volcano to appease the anger of the gods.

Behind the Scenes: In May 1950, photographers filmed the eruption of Mauna Loa, a 13,680 foot high active volcano in Hawaii; that footage appears as the climax of *Bird of Paradise*. The next month, the cast and crew arrived for eight weeks location filming. During those two months and during his second loanout from U-I to 20th, Jeff traveled round trip from Hawaii to Hollywood in order to appear in the live radio broadcasts of *Our Miss Brooks*.

Cinematography, handled by cameraman Winton C. Hoch, reflects his twenty years with the Technicolor Motion Picture Corporation, where he assisted in the development of the company's three-color system. Hoch won an Academy award for *She Wore a Yellow Ribbon* (1949) and shared the Oscar honors for *Joan of Arc* (1948).

Publicity for the motion picture included the song "Bird of Paradise" (music, Peter de Rose; lyrics, Malia Rosa). "Inspired by the 20th Century–Fox Technicolor

Production," the song's sheet music featured scenes from the movie, along with the film's billing. The *Hollywood Citizen-News* proclaimed that *Bird of Paradise* "is one of the most beautiful motion pictures ever made."[35]

Reviews: "So forceful is this rapidly rising young actor [Jeff Chandler] as the American-educated native, and college friend of the Frenchman, that he practically makes the picture his star property."—*Los Angeles Examiner*, March 24, 1951.

"Chandler demonstrates his increasing mettle as an actor in a colorful role in which he blends modernness of thought with ancient philosophies."—*Variety*, March 12, 1951.

Additional Reviews: *Boxoffice*, 03/17/51; *The Hollywood Reporter*, 03/12/51; *Los Angeles Times*, 03/24/51; *Monthly Film Bulletin*, 07/51; *Motion Picture Exhibitor*, 03/14/51; *Motion Picture Herald*, 03/17/51; *The New York Times*, 03/15/51.

Among the Top-Grossing Films of 1951: $1,650,000[36]

Comments by Jeff Chandler: "Whenever a new film assignment comes along, one of two things happen. I either get overdressed or underdressed."[37]

Flame of Araby

A Universal-International Picture. © 1951. Released January 1952. Ad line: "The Desert Drums Out Their Rhythm of Romance and Passion ... and All Araby Cheers the Daring Deeds of the Swashbuckling Tamerlane ... as He Claims a Princess as His Own." Universal-International production number 1612. Aka "Flame of the Desert," "Wildfire." Running time, 76 minutes; Technicolor; Adventure/Drama.

Ratings: *The Motion Picture Guide*, ☆☆; *Leonard Maltin's Movie and Video Guide*, ☆☆½; *New York Daily News*, ☆☆½; *Halliwell's Film Guide*, 0

Credits: Produced by Leonard Goldstein; associate producer, Ross Hunter; directed by Charles Lamont; story and screenplay by Gerald Drayson Adams; musical direction by Joseph Gershenson; art direction by Hilyard Brown and Bernard Herzbrun; set decorations by Oliver Emert and Russell A. Gausman; hair styles by Joan St. Oegger; make-up by Bud Westmore; costume design by Bill Thomas; sound by Leslie I. Carey and Richard DeWeese; cinematography by Russell Metty; film editing by Ted J. Kent.

Cast: Maureen O'Hara (Princess Tanya), Jeff Chandler (Tamerlane), Lon Chaney Jr. (Borka Barbarossa), Buddy Baer (Hakim Barbarossa), Maxwell Reed (Prince Medina), Richard Egan (Capt. Fezil), Dewey Martin (Yak), Royal Dano (Basra), Susan Cabot (Clio), Judith Braun (Calu), Henry Brandon (Mallik), Neville Brand (Kral), Tony Barr (Malat), Frederic Berest (Ibid).

Synopsis: A sheik and his wild Arabian black stallion are urged into a race that will result in either his marriage to a princess or her forced marriage to one of two evil chieftains.

The Films

Behind the Scenes: Location filming for *Flame of Araby* took place 215 miles north of Los Angeles, and coincided with a water shortage in Southern California; the studio filmed the water sequences by building its own waterfall. The set measured fifty feet high and more than thirty feet wide, big enough to allow the Arabian stallions to mysteriously disappear in this romantic adventure. *The Hollywood Reporter* wrote, "Jeff Chandler swashbuckles sufficiently to set femme pulses palpitating."[38]

Reviews: "Spectacular photography in brilliant Technicolor, lavish-to-the-point-of-fantasy costuming, and a plentitude of swashbuckling action characterize Universal-International's adventure-romance film, *Flame of Araby*."—*Los Angeles Examiner*, December 26, 1951.

Additional Reviews: *Boxoffice*, 11/24/51; *Film Daily*, 11/19/51; *Monthly Film Bulletin*, 03/52; *Motion Picture Exhibitor*, 11/21/51; *Motion Picture Herald*, 11/24/51; *The New York Times*, 12/20/51; *Variety*, 11/16/51.

Among the Top-Grossing Films of 1952: $1,500,000[39]

Iron Man

A Universal-International Picture. © 1951. Released August 1951. Ad line: "She Bought His Deadly Fists with Kisses—and Sold Them for Cash!" Universal-International production number 1662. Running time, 81 minutes; black & white; Drama.

Ratings: *The Motion Picture Guide*, ★★½; *Leonard Maltin's Movie and Video Guide*, ★★½; *New York Daily News*, ★★★; *Halliwell's Film Guide*, 0

Credits: Produced by Aaron Rosenberg; associate producer, John W. Rogers; directed by Joseph Pevney; assistant directors, Phil Bowles and John Sherwood; screenplay by Borden Chase and George Zuckerman, based on the book *Iron Man* by W. R. Burnett (New York: Dial Press, 1930); musical direction by Joseph Gershenson; art direction by Robert Boyle and Bernard Herzbrun; production manager, Edward Dodds; set decorations by John Austin and Russell A. Gausman; hair styles by Joan St. Oegger; make-up by Bud Westmore; costume design by Bill Thomas; sound by Leslie I. Carey and Joe Lapis; cinematography by Carl Guthrie; film editing by Russell Schoengarth.

Cast: Jeff Chandler (Coke Mason), Evelyn Keyes (Rose Warren), Stephen McNally (George Mason), Joyce Holden (Tiny), Rock Hudson (Speed O'Keefe), Jim Backus (Max Watkins), James Arness (Alex), Paul Javor (Pete), Steve Martin (Joe Savella), Eddie Simms (Jackie Bowden), George Baxter (Herb Riley), Raymond Gray (Jo Jo Meyers), Walter "Whitey" Ekwart (Whitey).

Synopsis: A poor coal miner who only wants to be a small businessman is instead urged into the ring by his greedy brother when he shows promise as a boxer because of his brutal killer instinct.

Rock Hudson and Joyce Holden with Jeff Chandler (center) as Coke Mason, a boxer with a killer instinct, in *Iron Man* (1951, Universal-International).

Behind the Scenes: U-I allowed three weeks before the start of *Iron Man* for Jeff, Rock Hudson and James Arness to get in condition for the boxing scenes. U-I's physical instructor Frankie Van, ex-boxing star and noted ring referee, managed the fight sequences, with the trainees taking full advantage of the studio gym. The facility, the finest on the West Coast, included exercise rooms, a solarium, sun deck, steam rooms, massage tables, reducing equipment and a rock steam bath.

Joyce Holden, Miss Southern California, 1949, rehearsed with the cast for five days before production began for the film. The *Motion Picture Exhibitor* said, "Chandler is tops as the killer-fighter, and the rest of the cast is above average."[40]

Reviews: "Jeff Chandler is one of the most dynamic and durable new actors in Hollywood. He turns in a powerful characterization as a savage prizefighter in this picture, and does this without much help from the writers, the director and from the supporting cast."—*Los Angeles Daily News*, August 20, 1951.

"More Than Clod: Chandler is excellent in his performance, and except that as a man he seems naturally to possess intelligence far above that of the dumb ox he portrays, you can hardly criticize the casting."—*Los Angeles Times*, August 21, 1951.

Additional Reviews: *Boxoffice*, 07/07/51; *The Hollywood Reporter*, 07/02/51; *Monthly Film Bulletin*, 09/51; *Motion Picture Herald*, 07/07/51; *The New York Times*, 08/20/51; *Variety*, 07/4/51.

Among the Top-Grossing Films of 1951: $1,000,000[41]

Meet Danny Wilson

A Universal-International Picture. © 1951. Released December 1951. Ad line: "It's Frankie and Shelley ... That Dynamite Pair! ... When They Tangle, the Screen Explodes with Romantic Excitement!" Universal-International production number 1679. Running time, 83 minutes; black & white; Musical/Drama.

Ratings: *The Motion Picture Guide*, ☆☆☆☆; *Leonard Maltin's Movie and Video Guide*, ☆☆½; *New York Daily News*, ☆☆½; *Halliwell's Film Guide*, 0

Credits: Produced by Leonard Goldstein; associate producer, Don McGuire; directed by Joseph Pevney; assistant directors, Frank Shaw and Les Warner; story and screenplay by Don McGuire; musical direction by Joseph Gershenson; art direction by Bernard Herzbrun and Nathan Juran; unit production manager, Edward Dodds; set decorations by Russell A. Gausman and Julia Heron; hair styles by Joan St. Oegger; make-up by Bud Westmore; costume design by Bill Thomas; sound by Leslie I. Carey and Richard DeWeese; cinematography by Maury Gertsman; film editing by Virgil W. Vogel.

Cast: Frank Sinatra (Danny Wilson), Shelley Winters (Joy Carroll), Alex Nicol (Mike Ryan), Raymond Burr (Nick Driscoll), Vaughn Taylor (Hatcher), Tommy Farrell (Tommy Wells), Carl Sklover (cab driver), Jeff Chandler (cameo appearance), Tony Curtis (cameo appearance).

Synopsis: In his rise to the top, a crooner hooks up with a cafe thrush and gives half his income thereafter to the gangster-type running the swank nightclub where she performs.

Behind the Scenes: After acting experience on Broadway and in Hollywood, *Meet Danny Wilson* became Joseph Pevney's seventh as director for U-I. Columbia brought Brooklyn-raised Shelley Winters to Hollywood in 1943, where she became a Star of Tomorrow, 1951.

Frank Sinatra, stage, radio and nightclub performer known by his fans as "The Voice," performed nine all-time favorites including "That Old Black Magic" and "I've Got a Crush on You." In late July 1951, guest artists Tony Curtis and Jeff Chandle attended location filming at Ciro's Nightclub in Hollywood. "Names," wrote the *Motion Picture Exhibitor*, "should prove a factor in the selling."[42]

Reviews: "*Meet Danny Wilson* is a bright drama, with comedy and songs liberally interlarded to make it a good and profitable entry in the regular runs."— *Variety*, January 11, 1952.

Additional Reviews: *Boxoffice*, 01/19/52; *Film Daily*, 01/23/52; *The Hollywood Reporter*, 01/11/52; *Los Angeles Times*, 02/08/52; *Monthly Film Bulletin*, 12/51; *Motion Picture Herald*, 01/19/52; *The New York Times*, 03/27/52.

Comments by Tony Curtis: "Jeff Chandler was the best of men—charming, elusive, somewhat cynical, introspective."[43]

Comments by Jeff Chandler: "Oddly enough, in our six years at U-I, we've only worked together in one picture—a gag guest appearance in *Meet Danny Wilson*. Maybe you remember. In the same scene, [Frank] Sinatra trips and two guests in tuxedos pick him up. Inside the tuxes were Curtis and Chandler. Brief as it was, we had a ball."[44]

Smuggler's Island

A Universal-International Picture. © 1951. Released May 1951. Ad line: "Danger Zones of the China Seas! Where Smuggler and Adventuress Fight for the Orient's Stolen Riches!" Universal-International production number 1642. Aka "Yangtze Pirates." Running time, 75 minutes; Technicolor; Adventure.

Ratings: *The Motion Picture Guide*, ☆☆; *Leonard Maltin's Movie and Video Guide*, ☆☆; *New York Daily News*, ☆☆½

Credits: Produced by Ted Richmond; directed by Edward Ludwig; assistant director, Bill Holland; screenplay by Leonard Lee, story and adaptation by Herb Margolis and Louis Morheim; musical direction by Joseph Gershenson; art direction by Alexander Golitzen and Bernard Herzbrun; set decorations by A. Roland Fields and Russell A. Gausman; hair styles by Joan St. Oegger; make-up by Bud Westmore; costume design by Bill Thomas; sound by Leslie I. Carey and Robert Pritchard; cinematography by Maury Gertsman; film editing by Ted J. Kent.

Cast: Jeff Chandler (Steve Kent), Evelyn Keyes (Vivian Craig), Phillip Friend (Allan Craig), Marvin Miller (Bok-Ying), Ducky Louie (Kai Lun), H. T. Tsiang (Chang), Leon Lontoc (native aide).

Synopsis: An American Navy veteran working in the Far East as a deep-sea diver falls for a sultry woman who persuades him to recover $200,000 in illegal gold.

Behind the Scenes: In 1940, Atlanta-born Evelyn Keyes failed a screen test given by a Universal talent scout. After Universal merged with International Pictures, forming Universal-International, Miss Keyes signed a contract with U-I; *Smuggler's Island* became her first assignment.

During the editing phase of the motion picture, the sound of the Pacific Ocean

Gold smuggler Vivian Craig (Evelyn Keyes) and deep-sea diver Steve Kent (Jeff Chandler) in *Smuggler's Island* (1951, Universal-International).

when Jeff crash-lands an airplane didn't please director Edward Ludwig. He brought in sound-effects editor, Jack Foley, to make the water sound "wetter." Foley's name became identified with doing synchronized sound effects manually—"Foley artist"—when he chose to do the water effects live in the studio with a large tank of water, instead of using sounds from U-I's library of recorded sound effects.[45]

As one of Hollywood's tallest actors, Jeff naturally spoke down when he said his lines. With the camera shooting head-on, however, only the top of the actor's head appeared in some of his close-ups. The cameraman's answer to the situation called for the elimination of many of Jeff's close-ups with another, resulting in getting Jeff's face on film.[46] "Chandler," wrote the *Motion Picture Herald*, "turns in his usual good performance as a diamond-in-the rough he-man."[47]

Reviews: "As an adventure thriller, *Smuggler's Island* is pretty exciting stuff."—*Los Angeles Examiner*, May 19, 1951.

Jeff Chandler

"Increasing marquee strength of Jeff Chandler, costar with Evelyn Keyes, will accelerate its chances at box office."—*Variety*, April 13, 1951.

Additional Reviews: *Boxoffice*, 04/21/51; *The Hollywood Reporter*, 04/13/51; *Los Angeles Times*, 05/19/51; *Monthly Film Bulletin*, 05/51; *Motion Picture Exhibitor*, 04/25/51; *The New York Times*, 05/24/51.

Among the Top-Grossing Films of 1951: $1,050,000[48]

Comments by Jeff Chandler: "Of all my parts, I think I enjoyed playing just plain Jeff Chandler—a nondescript American down on his luck in *Smuggler's Island*."[49]

The Battle at Apache Pass

A Universal-International Picture. © 1952. Released April 1952. Ad line: "Cochise! Geronimo! ... Blood Brothers of Vengeance Against the U.S. Cavalry!" Universal-International production number 1677. Aka "The Battle of Apache Pass." Running time, 85 minutes; Technicolor; Western.

Ratings: *The Motion Picture Guide*, ☆☆; *Leonard Maltin's Movie and Video Guide*, ☆☆½; *New York Daily News*, ☆☆½; *Halliwell's Film Guide*, 0

Credits: Produced by Leonard Goldstein; associate producer, Ross Hunter; directed by George Sherman; assistant director, William Holland; story and screenplay by Gerald Drayson Adams; music by Hans J. Salter; art direction by Bernard Herzbrun and Richard H. Riedel; set decorations by Oliver Emert and Russell A. Gausman; sound by Leslie I. Carey and Corson Jowett; cinematography by Charles Boyle; film editing by Ted J. Kent.

Cast: John Lund (Maj. Colton), Jeff Chandler (Cochise), John Hudson (Lt. Bascom), Susan Cabot (Nona), Jay Silverheels (Geronimo), Beverly Tyler (Mary Kearny), Bruce Cowling (Neil Baylor), Richard Egan (Sgt. Reuben Bernard), Jack Elam (Mescal Jack), Tommy Cook (Little Elk), Regis Toomey (Dr. Carter), James Best (Corp. Hassett), Richard Garland (Culver), William Reynolds (Lem Bent), Hugh O'Brian (Lt. Robert Harley), Palmer Lee (Joe Bent), Paul Smith (Trumpeter Ross), Jack Ingram (Johnny Ward), John Baer (Pvt. Bolin).

Synopsis: A U.S. Cavalry Officer teams with Cochise, the leader of the Apaches, in order to prevent the ensuing bloodshed when a villainous government Indian Affairs representative incites delusions of grandeur in Geronimo.

Behind the Scenes: John Lund's appearance in *The Battle at Apache Pass* marked his first in a Western at U-I and Jeff Chandler's first at the studio as "Cochise." Eighteen-year-old William Reynolds signed with Paramount in 1950, and portrayed the sons of James Mason in *Desert Fox* (1951) and Laurence Olivier in *Carrie* (1952), before going to U-I.

Three weeks for the cast and crew in Utah coincided with the summer break of *Our Miss Brooks*. Location filming occurred in the Moab area; pre-filming activities included the recruitment of Navajo Indians from Monument Valley. With their war paint running in the 112-degree heat, *Desert Magazine* reported that production went smoothly for the Navajos "playing Apache under a Mohawk Indian Geronimo and a white Cochise in the artificial atmosphere of a Hollywood set."[50]

For the promotion of the film, U-I made available to theater owners various tools, including a free recorded interview with Jeff. Further publicity included a nation-wide Apache Indian tour and the release of the movie novelization *The Battle at Apache Pass* written by Harold Conrad; published by Avon Publishing Company. *The Hollywood Reporter* told its readers that the movie is "a colorful, rousing saga of the war against the Apaches."[51]

Reviews: "Chandler is as able as usual."—*Motion Picture Exhibitor*, April 9, 1952.

"Both Lund and Chandler make a nice impression in their roles, the latter doing particularly well."—*Motion Picture Herald*, April 5, 1951.

Additional Reviews: *Boxoffice*, 04/05/52; *Los Angeles Times*, 04/07/52; *Monthly Film Bulletin*, 07/52; *The New York Times*, 05/10/52; *Variety*, 04/02/52.

Among the Top-Grossing Films of 1952: $2,000,000[52]

Costar Comments: "When I went to U-I, I did a western with a crew cut! Us kids under contract there played small parts, bigger parts, whatever was available. Jeff wasn't really a contract player; Rock Hudson was. We didn't socialize with Jeff as he was much older and respected to get involved with. Jeff was kind of a stand-alone person in that environment, perhaps in any environment. From the steam room in the gym at U-I, we'd hear him complain of the hair growing back on his chest after shaving it for his role as 'Cochise.'"—*William Reynolds*[53]

Comments by Jeff Chandler: "We slept in beautifully furnished air-conditioned motel apartments. Never was more comfortable in my life! And the thousand or so inhabitants of Moab are without doubt the friendliest people I have ever met."[54]

Because of You

A Universal-International Picture. © 1952. Released November 1952. Ad line: "Was She a Gun Moll ... Or a Sacrificing Mother?" Universal-International production number 1708. Aka "Magic Lady." Running time, 95 minutes; black & white; Romance.

Ratings: *The Motion Picture Guide*, ☆½; *Leonard Maltin's Movie and Video Guide*, ☆☆; *New York Daily News*, ☆☆½; *Halliwell's Film Guide*, 0

Credits: Produced by Albert J. Cohen; directed by Joseph Pevney; assistant director, Frank Shaw; screenplay by Ketti Frings, based on a story by Thelma Robin-

Jeff Chandler

son; music by Frank Skinner; art direction by Robert Clatworthy and Bernard Herzbrun; set decorations by John Austin and Russell A. Gausman; hair styles by Joan St. Oegger; make-up by Bud Westmore; costume design by Bill Thomas; sound by Leslie I. Carey and Glenn E. Anderson; cinematography by Russell Metty; film editing by Virgil W. Vogel.

Cast: Loretta Young (Christine Carroll), Jeff Chandler (Steve Kimberly), Alex Nicol (Mike Monroe), Frances Dee (Susan Arnold), Alexander Scourby (Dr. Breen), Lynne Roberts (Rosemary Balder), Gayle Reed (Kim), Morris Ankrum (Dr. Travis), Mae Clarke (Peachie), Billy Wayne (George), Frances Karath (Judy), Jeri Weil (Kim, 3 years), Betty Reilly (singer).

Synopsis A nurse falls in love with a wounded World War II pilot, but fails to tell him about her sordid past when they marry.

Behind the Scenes: At fourteen, Loretta Young broke into films in *Naughty But Nice* (1927). During the next two decades, the movie industry topped the country for those who earned $75,000 a year or more; in 1941, Miss Young earned

Steve Kimberly (Jeff Chandler) and Christine Carroll (Loretta Young) share a kiss in *Because of You* (1952, Universal-International).

The Films

$89,000. She won an Academy award for *The Farmer's Daughter* (1947), and recreated that motion picture role during the thirteenth season of *The Lux Radio Theatre*, a broadcast with Jeff in two small roles.

Music for the film included the songs "Here's Your Kiss" (music, Milton Rosen; lyrics, Everett Carter) and "Because of You" (music, Dudley Wilkinson; lyrics, Arthur Hammerstein). The sheet music for the latter, a song previously waxed by Les Baxter for Capitol Records, Louis Armstrong for Decca Records and other recording artists, appeared in stores with a new special edition cover: a close-up of Miss Young and Jeff, along with the film's billing.[55]

Miss Young's first movie under a two-picture agreement with U-I, *Because of You* became Jeff's first in finery. He enjoyed playing the role of an ex–Air Force Major opposite the Academy award-winning actress, his first emotional role. A leading man, the actor reasoned, hasn't arrived until he has starred in a woman's picture.[56] The *Motion Picture Herald* wrote that the film "has a way of blending laughter with tears that will win over the ladies."[57]

Reviews: "Loretta Young Magnificent."—*Hollywood Citizen-News*, November 20, 1952.

"*Because of You* is a gripping and moving drama of turbulent romance and mother love, highlighted by splendid acting and direction."—*The Hollywood Reporter*, October 9, 1951.

Additional Reviews: *Boxoffice*, 10/18/52; *Film Daily*, 10/09/52; *Los Angeles Times*, 11/20/52; *Monthly Film Bulletin*, 11/52; *Motion Picture Exhibitor*, 10/04/52; *The New York Times*, 12/04/52; *Variety*, 10/09/52.

Comments by Jeff Chandler: "Do you think women will recognize me with my clothes on?"[58]

Red Ball Express

A Universal-International Picture. © 1952. Released May 1952. Ad line: "The Never-Before-Told Story of the Army's Devil Drivers!" Universal-International production number 1688. Running time, 83 minutes; black & white; War.

Ratings: *The Motion Picture Guide*, ☆☆½; *Leonard Maltin's Movie and Video Guide*, ☆☆½; *New York Daily News*, ☆☆☆; *Halliwell's Film Guide*, 0

Credits: Produced by Aaron Rosenberg; directed by Budd Boetticher; screenplay by John Michael Hayes, based on a story by Marcel Klauber and Billy J. Grady; music by Milton Rosen and Frank Skinner; musical direction by Joseph Gershenson; art direction by Bernard Herzbrun and Richard H. Riedel; set decorations by Oliver Emert and Russell A. Gausman; hair styles by Joan St. Oegger; make-up by Bud Westmore; sound by Leslie I. Carey and Joe Lapis; cinematography by Maury Gertsman; film editing by Edward Curtiss.

Jeff Chandler

Cast: Jeff Chandler (Lt. Chick Campbell), Alex Nicol (Sgt. Red Kallek), Charles Drake (Pvt. Ronald Partridge), Jacqueline Duval (Antoinette), Sidney Poitier (Corp. Andrew Robertson), Judith Braun (Joyce McClellan), John Hudson (Tank Sgt. Max), Hugh O'Brian (Pvt. Wilson), Jack Kelly (Pvt. John Heyman), Palmer Lee (Tank Lt.), John Pickard (Maj.), Howard Petrie (Gen. Gordon), Bubber Johnson (Pvt. Taffy Smith), Robert Davis (Pvt. Dave McCord), David Friedman (first mechanic), Syl Lamont (Jones), Frank Chase (Pvt. Higgins).

Synopsis: A World War II officer heads a tough crew of unsung heroes in German-occupied territory as they work round-the-clock to supply fuel and ammunition to General George Patton's tank divisions as they move towards Paris.

Behind the Scenes: *Red Ball Express* became Alex Nicol's third film with Jeff, after *Meet Danny Wilson* and *Because of You*. Also trained at the Feagin School of Dramatic Art, Nicol made his stage debut a year before Jeff did.

Oscar "Budd" Boetticher arrived in Hollywood in 1941, made his debut as director in 1944, and later shared an Academy award-nomination for original story in *The Bullfighter and the Lady* (1951). His directorial outfit customarily consisted of a pair of denims, a pullover shirt and a hat that had seen better days; this helped the actors feel more comfortable on the set.

Hundreds of men from the U.S. Army Transportation Corp were used as extras when, in November 1951, the cast and crew arrived in Ft. Eustis, Virginia, for location filming. In railroad jargon, "Red Ball" means top priority freight.[59] The citizens of nearby Newport News formed their own "Red Ball Express," delivering actors to the set ontime and supplied hot lunches.[60] The actors found, however, that they produced more efficiently when caterers replaced the traditional southern food — spoon bread, snap beans, goober soup and the like — with a steak and potato diet.

As part of the film's promotion, U-I made available to theater owners a free recorded interview featuring Alex Nicol. The *Motion Picture Herald*, in their review of the film, called it an "excellent job of film making."[61]

Reviews: "Chandler delivers a strong, straightforward performance, and Nicol, in an unsympathetic role, handles his part effectively."—*Variety*, April 30, 1952.

"Story of transport corps has the angles for selling."—*Motion Picture Exhibitor*, May 7, 1952.

Additional Reviews: *Film Daily*, 04/30/52; *The Hollywood Reporter*, 04/30/52; *Monthly Film Bulletin*, 08/52; *The New York Times*, 05/30/52.

Among the Top-Grossing Films of 1952: $1,500,000[62]

Comments by the Director: "An actor who sees his director in informal clothes is an actor who is put immediately at ease. I think a lot of the over-acting performances of a decade or so ago were caused by the director, looking for all the world as though he had just stepped out of a Brooks Brothers window, scaring the hell out of the actors. I don't scare anyone with my get-up. I do get a lot of laughs, though, and I like to keep my actors happy!"—*Budd Boetticher*[63]

Comments by Jeff Chandler: "In case no one around Hollywood has heard of us for a long time, we're still down here in the deep south making *Red Ball Express*. Your Brooklyn Boy has acquired a 'you-all' accent and a taste for snap beans, spoon bread and goober soup. (What the hell *is* goober soup?)"[64]

Son of Ali Baba

A Universal-International Picture. © 1952. Released September 1952. Ad line: "Storming the Screen with Romantic Adventure!" "Jeff was unique, being both a successful radio and movie actor. Like Alan Ladd, Jeff was a very good radio actor first."—*William Reynolds*.[65] Universal-International production number 1680. Running time, 75 minutes; Technicolor; Adventure.

Ratings: *The Motion Picture Guide*, ☆☆½; *Leonard Maltin's Movie and Video Guide*, ☆☆; *New York Daily News*, ☆☆½; *Halliwell's Film Guide*, 0

Credits: Produced by Leonard Goldstein; associate producer, Ross Hunter; directed by Kurt Neumann; story and screenplay by Gerald Drayson Adams; opening narration by Jeff Chandler; music by Herman Stein; musical direction by Joseph Gershenson; art direction by Bernard Herzbrun and Emrich Nicholson; set decorations by John Austin and Russell A. Gausman; hair styles by Joan St. Oegger; make-up by Bud Westmore; costume design by Rosemary Odell; sound by Glenn E. Anderson and Leslie I. Carey; cinematography by Maury Gertsman; film editing by Virgil W. Vogel.

Cast: Tony Curtis (Kashma Baba), Piper Laurie (Kiki), Susan Cabot (Tala), William Reynolds (Mustafa), Hugh O'Brian (Hussein), Victor Jory (Caliph), Gerald Mohr (Capt. Youssef), Robert Barrat (Commandant), Leon Belasco (Babu), Morris Ankrum (Ali Baba), Alice Kelley (Calu), Barbara Knudson (Theda), Milada Mladova (Zaza), Gregg Palmer (Farouk), Phillip Van Zandt (Kareeb), Katherine Warren (Princess Karma).

Synopsis: Training as a cadet at the Persian Military Academy, the son of Ali Baba gives refuge to an escaped slave who is really a princess kidnapped by an evil Caliph who wants to trap Ali Baba and gain his treasure.

Behind the Scenes: Ross Hunter's Hollywood career began in the mid–1940s in front of the camera as an actor, and expanded his range to that of associate producer. Kurt Neumann directed foreign versions of Universal pictures after being brought to Hollywood from his native Germany in the late 1920s by Carl Laemmle Jr. Neumann became a feature director early in the 1930s, bringing to this film an accent on fantasy. The *Los Angeles Examiner* wrote that the *Son of Ali Baba* was a "lavish fare."[66]

Reviews: "*Son of Ali Baba* is a pleasant fairy tale of exciting deeds of derring-do which should appeal to lovers of high adventure."—*The Hollywood Reporter*, August 13, 1952.

"Ali Baba 'Son' film enjoyable."—*Hollywood Citizen-News*, October 2, 1952.

Additional Reviews: *Boxoffice*, 08/23/52; *Film Daily*, 08/19/52; *Los Angeles Times*, 10/02/52; *Monthly Film Bulletin*, 10/52; *Motion Picture Exhibitor*, 08/27/52; *Motion Picture Herald*, 08/23/52; *The New York Times*, 08/16/52; *Variety*, 08/13/52.

Among the Top-Grossing Films of 1952: $1,250,000[67]

Yankee Buccaneer

A Universal-International Picture. © 1952. Released October 1952. Ad line: "From the Battle-Torn Seas of the Spanish Main Comes a Rousing Tale of Adventure!" Universal-International production number 1700. Aka "The Ship Without a Country." Running time, 86 minutes; Technicolor; Adventure.

Ratings: *The Motion Picture Guide*, ☆☆; *Leonard Maltin's Movie and Video Guide*, ☆☆½; *New York Daily News*, ☆☆½

Credits: Produced by Howard J. Christie; directed by Frederick de Cordova; story and screenplay by Charles K. Peck Jr.; musical direction by Joseph Gershenson; art direction by Robert Boyle and Bernard Herzbrun; set decorations by Oliver Emert and Russell A. Gausman; make-up by Bud Westmore; costume design by Bill Thomas; sound by Leslie I. Carey and Joe Lapis; cinematography by Russell Metty; film editing by Frank Gross.

Cast: Jeff Chandler (Com. David Porter), Scott Brady (Lt. David Farragut), Suzan Ball (Countess Margarita), Joseph Calleia (Count Domingo Del Prado), George Mathews (Link), Rodolfo Acosta (Poulini), David Janssen (Beckett), Joseph Vitale (Scarjack), Michael Ansara (Romero), James Parnell (Redell), Jay Silverheels (lead warrior).

Synopsis: An American man-of-war poses as a pirate ship in order to uncover a pirate fleet in the tropics.

Behind the Scenes: *Yankee Buccaneer* followed the Howard J. Christie-produced, Errol Flynn-swashbuckler *Against All Flags* (1952). Christie, the production manager on *Abandoned*, took advantage of a new marine set on the studio's back lot, where workers transformed one end of a huge lake into a buccaneer's den. Over 600 tons of sand, palm trees and boulders were utilized in the conversion.[68] Set decorator Russell A. Gausman brought to the set the Academy award honors he shared for Interior Decoration in *The Phantom of the Opera* (1943).

Mohawk Indian Jay Silverheels began his career in Hollywood in the 1940s in film and radio, most notably in *The Lone Ranger* television series; this film marked his third with Jeff, following *Broken Arrow* and *The Battle at Apache Pass*. The *Motion Picture Herald* called the film a "good adventure tale."[69]

Reviews: "The big, bad, bold buccaneer is the choice of the movie-makers once again in a rousing adventure melodrama titled *Yankee Buccaneer.*"—*Hollywood Citizen-News*, September 17, 1952.

"*Yankee Buccaneer* is a very creditable job of story-telling, with its fast paced direction and fine production."—*Los Angeles Examiner*, September 17, 1952.

Additional Reviews: *Boxoffice*, 09/27/52; *Film Daily*, 09/18/52; *The Hollywood Reporter*, 09/12/52; *Los Angeles Times*, 09/17/52; *Monthly Film Bulletin*, 01/53; *Motion Picture Exhibitor*, 9/24/52; *Variety*, 09/12/52.

Costar Comments: "That first big role before the camera was enough to take a person's breath away. I speak literally, too. The picture was *Yankee Buccaneer* and I pulled not one, but two, leading men, those tall, dark and handsome fellows, Jeff Chandler and Scott Brady. Not bad for a scared high school graduate (one year removed) who got her start in the movies by making a cake for a baking contest in Santa Maria, huh?"—*Suzan Ball*[70]

East of Sumatra

A Universal-International Picture. © 1953. Released October 1953. Ad line: "For Her Savage Kisses, He Plundered the Last Forgotten Corner of the Earth!" Universal-International production number 1727. Aka "East of Sarawak." Running time, 82 minutes; Technicolor; Adventure.

Ratings: *The Motion Picture Guide*, ☆☆☆; *Leonard Maltin's Movie and Video Guide*, ☆☆½; *Halliwell's Film Guide*, ☆

Credits: Produced by Albert J. Cohen; directed by Budd Boetticher; assistant director, Tom Shaw; screenplay by Frank Gill Jr., based on a story by Louis L'Amour and Jack Natteford, as adapted by Jack Natteford; musical direction by Joseph Gershenson; art direction by Robert Boyle and Bernard Herzbrun; set decorations by Russell A. Gausman and Joseph Kish; hair styles by Joan St. Oegger; make-up by Bud Westmore; costume design by Bill Thomas; sound by Glenn E. Anderson and Leslie I. Carey; cinematography by Clifford Stine; film editing by Virgil W. Vogel.

Cast: Jeff Chandler (Duke Mullane), Marilyn Maxwell (Lory Hale), Anthony Quinn (Kiang), Suzan Ball (Minyera), John Sutton (Daniel Catlin), Jay C. Flippen (Mac), Scatman Crothers (Baltimore), Eugene Iglesias (Paulo), Peter Graves (cowboy), Aram Katcher (Atib), Earl Holliman (Cupid), Anthony Eustrel (Clyde), James Craven (Drake), John Warburton (Keith), Michael Dale (copilot), Mylee Haulani (native girl), Suzanne Ridgway (native girl), Nancy Westbrook (native girl), Mario Lamm (native man), Maiola Kalili (native man).

Synopsis: A chief engineer and his mining crew set up camp on a Pacific island reportedly loaded with mineral wealth, but anger the island's king when mining supplies are delivered instead of food promised to the natives in exchange for their labor.

Jeff Chandler

Duke Mullane (Jeff Chandler) and native king Kiang (Anthony Quinn) in *East of Sumatra* (1953, Universal-International).

Behind the Scenes: In August 1952, U-I reviewed *East of Sumatra* with John Wayne as its star. The studio later considered Humphrey Bogart along with Rhonda Fleming, Arlene Dahl and Rita Gam.[71] As the native island king, the studio chose Anthony Quinn, an Academy award-winner for his role in *Viva Zapata!* (1952).

Production began in November 1952, bringing actor-jazz artist Scatman Crothers to the set, who sang "Strange Land," a tune he penned for the movie.[72] The studio originally cast Jeff with actress-singer Marilyn Maxwell, a Star of Tomorrow, 1945, in *Outside the Wall* (1950), but she starred, instead, with Richard Basehart when the studio sent Jeff to Italy for *Deported*.

Guests at a rough-cut screening of *East of Sumatra* were impressed by a young, clean-cut, positive screen personality by the name of Peter Graves; some moviegoers were heard to ask, "Who is that guy?"[73] Sara Hamilton of the *Los Angeles Examiner* wrote, "The lushness of a South Pacific isle provides the setting for the main feature with Jeff Chandler dominating the story, the action, the women, the natives and the whole bloomin' works. Quite a man, this Universal star."[74]

Reviews: "Chandler turns in an excellent portrayal of a rugged, two-fisted mining engineer with a yen for women and liquor."—*The Hollywood Reporter*, September 11, 1953.

Additional Reviews: *Film Daily*, 09/14/53; *Los Angeles Times*, 09/12/53; *Monthly Film Bulletin*, 10/53; *Motion Picture Exhibitor*, 09/23/53; *Motion Picture Herald*, 09/19/53; *Variety*, 11/05/53.

Costar Comments: "I first met Jeff in 1952, when I was just beginning as an actor. I wasn't under contract with U-I, but they were interested, casting me in *East of Sumatra*. Jeff starred, with Tony Quinn as the mean island chieftain. I walked out on the set that first morning and Jeff and I exchanged greetings as we sat down to read the scene. I was part of Jeff's team as he came down to explore the island."—*Peter Graves*[75]

Costar Comments: "My rival in the story is one of the most dynamic and vital brunettes on the screen today, Suzan Ball. She's really vivid. But who gets Jeff in the fadeout? Poor little Marilyn, the fragile blonde."—*Marilyn Maxwell*[76]

Comments by a Fan: "Any female in her right mind would see any picture with Jeff Chandler. He is the All-American he-man."[77]

The Great Sioux Uprising

A Universal-International Picture. © 1953. Released July 1953. Ad line: "All the Savage Fury of the Great Plains Indian Wars!" Universal-International production number 1722. Aka "Sioux Uprising." Running time, 80 minutes; Technicolor; Western.

Ratings: *The Motion Picture Guide*, ☆☆; *Leonard Maltin's Movie and Video Guide*, ☆☆½; *New York Daily News*, ☆☆½; *Halliwell's Film Guide*, 0

Credits: Produced by Albert J. Cohen and Leonard Goldstein; directed by Lloyd Bacon; assistant director, Jesse Hibbs; screenplay by Melvin Levy, J. Robert Bren, and Gladys Atwater, based on a story by J. Robert Bren and Gladys Atwater, with additional dialogue by Frank Gill Jr.; musical direction by Joseph Gershenson; art direction by Alexander Golitzen and Alfred Sweeney; set decorations by Russell A. Gausman and Joseph Kish; hair styles by Joan St. Oegger; make-up by Bud Westmore; costume design by Bill Thomas; sound by Glenn E. Anderson and Leslie I. Carey; cinematography by Maury Gertsman; film editing by Edward Curtiss.

Cast: Jeff Chandler (Jonathan Westgate), Faith Domergue (Joan Britton), Lyle Bettger (Stephen Cook), Peter Whitney (Ahab Jones), Stacy Harris (Uriah), Stephen Chase (Maj. McKay), Walter Sande (Joe Baird), Charles Arnt (Gist), Glenn Strange (Stand Watie), John War Eagle (Red Cloud), Julia Montoya (Heyoka), Ray Bennett (Sgt. Manners), Dewey Drapeau (Teo-Ka-Ha), Boyd "Red" Morgan (Ray), Lane Bradford (Lee), Jack Ingram (Sam), Clem Fuller (Jake).

Synopsis: A former Union captain turns to horse trading in private life and must stop a horse rustler from provoking a war between U.S. Army troops and the Sioux Indians.

Behind the Scenes: In August 1952, casting for the female lead focused on Alexis Smith, with alternates including Suzan Ball and Faith Domergue, a protégée of and under contract to Howard Hughes from 1941 to 1950. The latter joined the cast two months later when location filming began in Pendleton, Oregon, where demands for pictures and biographies of the stars ran high along with a mob of requests for personal appearances.[78]

According to the studio's sound technician, Jeff's voice allowed for a strong, virile output. After U-I and CBS Radio came to an agreement on a schedule, Jeff commuted from Oregon to Hollywood for live radio broadcasts of *Our Miss Brooks*. In their review of the film, *Motion Picture Herald* said that "the principals behave with proper gusto."[79]

Reviews: "A colorful, well-made action picture of horse thievery and chicanery against the Indians."—*The Hollywood Reporter*, June 24, 1953.

Additional Reviews: *Boxoffice*, 07/07/53; *Los Angeles Times*, 08/01/53; *Monthly Film Bulletin*, 11/53; *Motion Picture Exhibitor*, 07/01/53; *The New York Times*, 07/18/53; *Variety*, 06/24/53.

Among the Top-Grossing Films of 1953: $1,350,000[80]

Comments by a Studio Publicist: "Chandler on his own has given an okay to many people for outside activities which is wonderful. I've never seen an actor so conscientious about appointments, interviews and personal appearances."—*Fred Banker*[81]

Comments by the Sound Technician: "Jeff brings his voice up from the middle of his stomach. That's real muscle and brawn level. I don't register a male voice with as much sex in it as Jeff's for years at a stretch."—*Glenn E. Anderson*[82]

Comments by Jeff Chandler: "For a while I thought I had been typed as a movie Indian. I used to wake up in the middle of the night, worrying about it. In fact, when I made *The Battle at Apache Pass* I told the studio I wanted it to be my last Indian part. After all, how many good starring Indian roles come along in Hollywood?"[83]

Taza, Son of Cochise

A Universal-International Picture. © 1953. Released February 1954. Ad line: "He Led the Apache Nation Against Geronimo's Pillaging Hordes!" Universal-International production number 1743. Aka "Son of Cochise." Running time, 79 minutes; Technicolor; (2-D, 3-D); Western.

The Films

Ratings: *The Motion Picture Guide*, ★★½; *Leonard Maltin's Movie and Video Guide*, ★★½; *New York Daily News*, ★★★; *Halliwell's Film Guide*, 0

Credits: Produced by Ross Hunter; directed by Douglas Sirk; assistant director, Tom Shaw; screenplay by George Zuckerman, story and adaptation by Gerald Drayson Adams; music by Frank Skinner; art direction by Bernard Herzbrun and Emrich Nicholson; set decorations by Oliver Emert and Russell A. Gausman; hair styles by Joan St. Oegger; make-up by Bud Westmore; costume design by Jay A. Morley Jr.; sound by Glenn E. Anderson and Leslie I. Carey; cinematography by Russell Metty; film editing by Milton Carruth.

Cast: Rock Hudson (Taza), Barbara Rush (Oona), Gregg Palmer (Capt. Burnett), Bart Roberts (Naiche), Morris Ankrum (Grey Eagle), Ian MacDonald (Geronimo), Richard H. Cutting (Cy Hegan), Joe Sawyer (Sgt. Hamma), Robert Burton (Gen. Crook), Eugene Iglesias (Chato), Lance Fuller (Lt. Willis), Brad Jackson (Lt. Richards), James Van Horn (Skinya), Charles Horvath (Kocha), Robert Hoy (Lobo), Jeff Chandler (Cochise).

Synopsis: On his deathbed, Apache Chief Cochise asks his son Taza to try and keep the peace, but Taza's brother plans to unite their tribe with that of Geronmio against the white man.

Behind the Scenes: On June 11, 1953 and in Moab, Utah, Jeff made a final appearance as Cochise, in the prologue to *Taza, Son of Cochise*. The death of Cochise did not receive billing during the picture's advertising, a decision U-I made in early July. For the advertising of the film, U-I relied on the strength of the name of Cochise. In their review of the film, *Variety* said that Douglas Sirk's direction "is forceful, aimed at making every scene an eye-filling experience."[84]

Reviews: "*Taza, Son of Cochise*, it is nice to report, is a soundly-made Western, loaded with action, replete with color, and just the right length."—*Hollywood Citizen-News*, February 11, 1954.

"'Taza' is another fine credit in the long list of entertaining pictures which the brilliant young producer, Ross Hunter, has made for Universal-International."—*Los Angeles Examiner*, February 11, 1954.

Additional Reviews: *Film Daily*, 02/10/54; *The Hollywood Reporter*, 01/20/54; *Los Angeles Times*, 02/14/54; *Monthly Film Bulletin*, 06/54; *Motion Picture Exhibitor*, 01/27/54; *Motion Picture Herald*, 01/30/54.

Among the Top-Grossing Films of 1954: $1,100,000[85]

Comments by Jeff Chandler: "The character of Cochise made me a star and I have become very attached to him. I hate to see him die off, but, after playing him twice, I felt that it would be bad for me to portray him again and again and become too identified with him. However, Cochise has brought me wonderful luck and I felt this was the least I could do for him: to play his death with dignity and drama and pass on the tradition of Cochise to another actor."[86]

Jeff Chandler

Comments by a Fan: "Since Jeff Chandler is my favorite — it seems as though he should receive screen recognition at either the beginning or the end of the picture. You have to give him credit for not being too big a star to take that small part."[87]

Sign of the Pagan

A Universal-International Picture. © 1954. Released December 1954. Ad line: "Against His Ruthless Pagan Lusts ... The Power of a Woman's Love!" Universal-International production number 1758. Aka "Attila the Conqueror." Running time, 92 minutes; Technicolor (CinemaScope); Adventure/Historical Drama.

Ratings: *The Motion Picture Guide,* ☆½; *Leonard Maltin's Movie and Video Guide,* ☆☆½; *New York Daily News,* ☆☆☆½; *Halliwell's Film Guide,* 0

Credits: Produced by Albert J. Cohen; directed by Douglas Sirk; assistant

Roman centurion Marcian (Jeff Chandler) and Princess Pulcheria (Ludmilla Tcherina) in *Sign of the Pagan* (1954, Universal-International).

The Films

director, John Sherwood; screenplay by Oscar Brodney and Barre Lyndon, story by Oscar Brodney; music by Hans J. Salter and Frank Skinner; musical direction by Joseph Gershenson; art direction by Alexander Golitzen and Emrich Nicholson; set decorations by Oliver Emert and Russell A. Gausman; hair styles by Joan St. Oegger; make-up by Bud Westmore; costume design by Bill Thomas; sound by Leslie I. Carey and Corson Jowett; cinematography by Russell Metty; film editing by Al Clark.

Cast: Jeff Chandler (Marcian), Jack Palance (Attila), Ludmilla Tcherina (Princess Pulcheria), Rita Gam (Kubra), Jeff Morrow (Gen. Paulinus), Allison Hayes (Ildico), Eduard Franz (Astrologer), George Dolenz (Emperor Theodosius), Sara Shane (Myra), Alexander Scourby (Chrysaphius), Howard Petrie (Gundahar), Michael Ansara (Edecon), Leo Gordon (Bleda), Pat Hogan (Sangiban), Robo Bechi (Chilothe), Moroni Olsen (Pope Leo I), Fred Nurney (Chamberlain), Sim Iness (Herculanus), Charles Horvath (Olt), Glenn Thompson (Seyte), Chuck Roberson (Mirrai), Rusty Wescoatt (Tula).

Synopsis: A dramatization of the life of Attila, King of the Huns, a just ruler feared for his savagery, covering his rise as a humble Christian Roman to general and emperor.

Behind the Scenes: The Fifth Century spectacle *Sign of the Pagan* became U-I's second in CinemaScope and Jeff's fourth with producer Albert J. Cohen. Jack Palance, a Star of Tomorrow, 1953, portrayed Attila the Hun—"the Scourge of the Gods"—with two Academy award-nominations under his belt from *Sudden Fear* (1952) and *Shane* (1953). With experience on the New York stage, Rita Gam—who portayed the daughter to Palance's Attila—made her Hollywood debut in *The Thief* (1952).

The art director incorporated into this film props from Hollywood's past: *Ben-Hur* (1926), the biggest epic of the silent screen, provided armored breastplates; *All Quiet on the Western Front* (1930), a milestone in filmmaking, furnished bayonets refashioned into Roman short swords; and *The Hunchback of Notre Dame* (1923), a masterpiece of Hollywood's silent era, lent shoulder pads originally worn by Lon Chaney Sr.

Promotion of the movie included the release of *Sign of the Pagan*, a book based on the screenplay written by Roger Fuller and published by Dial Press. Other publicity tools included an extensive national magazine advertising campaign and a recorded interview with Jeff made available, free of charge, to theater owners.[88] *Motion Picture Herald* called the film a "handsome, effective spectacle."[89]

Reviews: "Most of the ingredients for rousing, eye-filling spectacle are here. The historical background alone would seem a natural for Technicolor and wide screen."—*The New York Times*, February 14, 1955.

"Top flight costumed actioner on Atilla, the Hun, with entertainment values for hearty box-office possibilities."—*Variety*, November 10, 1954.

Jeff Chandler

Additional Reviews: *Film Daily*, 11/09/54; *The Hollywood Reporter*, 11/08/54; *Los Angeles Times*, 12/24/54; *Monthly Film Bulletin*, 01/55.

Among the Top-Grossing Films of 1954: $2,500,000[90]

Costar Comments: "Jeff Chandler was fun! I had the pleasure of playing Attila the Hun's daughter in *Sign of the Pagan* to his Roman soldier. Between scenes of intense athletic feats—we had a broadsword fight in one scene, he threw me in a Roman swimming pool in another and we rode horses together in yet another— we exchanged current jokes and giggled a lot. Not only was he intelligent and a fine actor, he had a hell of a good sense of humor. I'll never forget the huge bowl of penny bubble gum he kept handy in his personal trailer. Whereas Jack Palance offered drinks, director Douglas Sirk offered coffee, Jeff was ever ready with his bubble gum."—*Rita Gam*[91]

Comments by Jeff Chandler: "We have a great performance by Jack Palance in the role of Attila and if I don't miss my guess, Jack is going to get considerable consideration for an Academy award nomination when this picture is shown. We also have a very lovely French importation, Ludmilla Tcherina, who plays one of the leading ladies. Rita Gam, who has certainly made her mark in the last couple of years in motion pictures, is the other leading lady. There's a guy named Chandler in there somewhere, too."[92]

War Arrow

A Universal-International Picture. © 1954. Released January 1954. Ad line: "The Reckless Beat of their Hearts Matched the Thundering Throb of the War Drums!" Universal-International production number 1736. Aka "Brady's Bunch." Running time, 78 minutes; Technicolor; Western.

Ratings: *The Motion Picture Guide*, ★★½; *Leonard Maltin's Movie and Video Guide*, ★★

Credits: Produced by John W. Rogers; directed by George Sherman; assistant director, Frank Shaw; story and screenplay by John Michael Hayes; musical direction by Joseph Gershenson; art direction by Alexander Golitzen and Bernard Herzbrun; set decorations by Russell A. Gausman and Joseph Kish; make-up by Bud Westmore; costume design by Edward Stevenson; sound by Leslie I. Carey and Richard DeWeese; cinematography by William H. Daniels; film editing by Frank Gross.

Cast: Maureen O'Hara (Elaine Corwin), Jeff Chandler (Maj. Howell Brady), Suzan Ball (Avis), Charles Drake (Sgt. Luke Schermerhorn), John McIntire (Col. Jackson Meade), Noah Beery (Sgt. Agustus Wilks), Henry Brandon (Maygro), Dennis Weaver (Pino), Brad Jackson (Lt.), James Bannon (Capt. Roger Corwin), Jay Silverheels (Satanta), Steve Wyman (Capt. Neil).

The Films

U.S. Army major Howell Brady (Jeff Chandler) and widow Elaine Corwin (Maureen O'Hara) in *War Arrow* (1954, Universal-International).

Synopsis: Disregarding the protests of his commanding officer, a U.S. Army major trains a group of friendly Seminole Indians from the East to fight the hostile Kiowa Indians in the West.

Behind the Scenes: For *War Arrow*, the studio gave Jeff first position in equal billing with Maureen O'Hara. Miss O'Hara, a performer on radio as a child in her native Ireland, first worked with Jeff in 1948 on *The Lux Radio Theatre*.

As of April 1953, Miss O'Hara had appeared in fourteen broadcasts of *Lux*, compared to John McIntire's twenty. McIntire, a commanding character actor who came to Hollywood in the 1940s, saw considerable experience in radio, most notably in the news documentary and dramatization *The March of Time*. Suzan Ball, a Star of Tomorrow, 1954, also made an appearance on *Lux* in 1951 as starlet for U-I.

Location filming in Nogales, AZ, included the transportation of one of the largest movie-trained horses, a creature 17½ hands high. Jeff, one of Hollywood's tallest actors, wore low-heeled cowboy boots to keep him from towering above his fellow players.

As part of its $1.5 million campaign for twelve pictures released during the first four months of 1954, U-I stressed the box-office strength of its two stars. "Jeff Chandler and Maureen O'Hara head the cast of this big, well-paced Western, beautifully photographed," wrote the *Motion Picture Herald*.[93]

Reviews: "Chandler turns in a strong, believable performance as an Army major sent to a Texas outpost to put down a troublesome Kiowa uprising."—*The Hollywood Reporter*, December 8, 1953.

"Jeff Chandler comes off best."—*Los Angeles Examiner*, January 14, 1954.

Additional Reviews: *Film Daily*, 12/17/53; *Los Angeles Times*, 01/14/54; *Monthly Film Bulletin*, 04/54; *Motion Picture Exhibitor*, 12/16/53; *The New York Times*, 01/15/54; *Variety*, 12/08/53.

Among the Top-Grossing Films of 1954: $1,400,000[94]

Costar Comments: "Jeff kisses me oftener than he does his horse."—*Maureen O'Hara*[95]

Costar Comments: "At the fadeout, I lose Maureen to Jeff, of course, but I'm not complaining. The scenes I have with her before that happens still make me feel twenty years younger."—*John McIntire*[96]

Comments by Jeff Chandler: "It's great riding a big horse, but I need two steps in midair to reach the stirrup."[97]

Yankee Pasha

A Universal-International Picture. © 1954. Released April 1954. Ad line: "A Passionate Love That Became the Strangest Adventure Ever Told!" Universal-International production number 1747. Running time, 84 minutes; Technicolor; Adventure Romance.

Ratings: *The Motion Picture Guide*, ☆☆½; *Leonard Maltin's Movie and Video Guide*, ☆☆½; *New York Daily News*, ☆☆☆; *Halliwell's Film Guide*, 0

Credits: Produced by Howard J. Christie; directed by Joseph Pevney; assistant director, Joseph E. Kenny; screenplay by Joseph Hoffman, based on the book *Yankee Pasha, The Adventures of Jason Starbuck* by Edison Marshall (New York: Farrar, Straus and Company, 1947); musical direction by Joseph Gershenson; art direction by Bernard Herzbrun and Eric Orbom; costume design by Rosemary Odell; cinematography by Carl Guthrie; film editing by Virgil W. Vogel.

Cast: Jeff Chandler (Jason Starbuck), Rhonda Fleming (Roxana Reil), Mamie Van Doren (Lilith), Lee J. Cobb (sultan), Bart Roberts (Omar-Id-Din), Hal March (Hassan Serdar), Tudor Owen (Elias Derby), Arthur Space (Richard O'Brien), Benny Rubin (Zimil), Harry Lauter (Dick Bailey), John Day (First Mate Miller),

The Films

Rosalind Hayes (Eliza), Forbes Murray (Mr. Reil), Christiane Martel (French girl), Myrna Hansen (third girl), Kinuko Ito (harem girl), Ingrid Mills (harem girl), Maxine Morgan (harem girl), Alicia Ibanez (harem girl), Synove Gulbrandsen (harem girl), Emita Arosemena (harem girl).

Synopsis: After a beautiful American woman is captured by pirates and sold into the harem of Barbary raiders, an American swashbuckler travels to Morocco to free her.

Behind the Scenes: In the summer of 1953, U-I offered contracts to eight participants of the Miss Universe Pageant. The first four signed term contracts; the remaining four signed on a weekly basis. Appearing in *Yankee Pasha* as the "Miss Universe Beauties": Miss France, Christiane Martel (Miss Universe, 1953); Miss USA, Myrna Hansen, (1st runner-up); Miss Japan, Kinuko Ito (2nd runner-up); Miss South Africa, Ingrid Mills (semi-finalist); Miss Australia, Maxine Morgan (contestant); Miss Uruguay, Alicia Ibanez (semi-finalist); Miss Norway, Synove Gulbrandsen (semi-finalist); and Miss Panama, Emita Arosemena.[98]

In their promotion of the film, U-I stressed their casting Jeff with another of Hollywood's most exciting actresses: Rhonda Fleming. Miss Fleming, a native of Los Angeles, grew up in Hollywood and made her film debut in *Spellbound* (1945). Along with Milo Anderson, Hollywood couturier of personal wardrobes for Jane Wyman, Bette Davis, Ann Sheridan and others, Miss Fleming and Jeff participated as judges in the July 1953 Miss USA and Miss Universe contests.

Edison Marshall's book played an active part in advertising the movie: a Book League selection, *Yankee Pasha, The Adventures of Jason Starbuck* sold over 2.5 million copies. In its review of the romantic adventure, *Motion Picture Herald* wrote, "Rarely has a man fought so valiantly for a woman or over such a wide sweep of geography as Jeff Chandler in *Yankee Pasha*."[99]

Reviews: "Lively action in fast swashbuckler."—*The Hollywood Reporter*, December 5, 1954.

"It has the combination of a romantic-melodramatic tale, the lure of harems, etc., plenty of attractive damsels, action and other ingredients which make the ticket register hum."—*Motion Picture Exhibitor*, March 24, 1954.

Additional Reviews: *Film Daily*, 04/07/54; *Los Angeles Times*, 03/18/54; *Monthly Film Bulletin*, 05/54; *The New York Times*, 04/19/54; *Variety*, 03/12/54.

Among the Top-Grossing Films of 1954: $1,250,000[100]

Costar Comments: "The character of Lilith is a silly, pretty little chatterbox of a slave girl who is given to Jeff as a gift by the sultan, played by Lee J. Cobb. And what slave girl wouldn't have loved to be a gift to Jeff Chandler? With that big square jaw and broad shoulders, salt-and-pepper hair, what's not to love? Jeff was one of the nicest stars I ever worked with."—*Mamie Van Doren*[101]

Jeff Chandler

Female on the Beach

A Universal-International Picture. © 1955. Released September 1955. Ad line: "Now ... Joan's Got Jeff! Living the Kind of Love That Most Women Want But are Afraid to Dare!" Universal-International production number 1788. Aka "Besieged Heart," "Woman on the Beach." Running time, 97 minutes; black & white; Crime Drama.

Ratings: *The Motion Picture Guide*, ☆☆; *Leonard Maltin's Movie and Video Guide*, ☆☆; *New York Daily News*, ☆☆☆; *Halliwell's Film Guide*, 0

Credits: Produced by Albert Zugsmith; directed by Joseph Pevney; assistant director, John Sherwood; screenplay by Robert Hill and Richard Alan Simmons, based on the play *The Besieged Heart* by Robert Hill; musical direction by Joseph Gershenson; art direction by Robert Clatworthy and Alexander Golitzen; set decorations by Oliver Emert and Russell A. Gausman; hair styles by Joan St. Oegger; make-up by Bud Westmore; costume design by Sheila O'Brien; sound by Leslie I.

Widow Lynn Markham (Joan Crawford) suspects beachcomber Drummond Hall (Jeff Chandler) of murder in *Female on the Beach* (1955, Universal-International).

The Films

Carey and Robert Pritchard; cinematography by Charles B. Lang; film editing by Russell Schoengarth.

Cast: Joan Crawford (Lynn Markham), Jeff Chandler (Drummond Hall), Jan Sterling (Amy Rawlinson), Cecil Kellaway (Osbert Sorenson), Natalie Schafer (Queenie Sorenson), Charles Drake (Lt. Galley), Judith Evelyn (Eloise Crandall), Stuart Randall (Frankovitch), Marjorie Bennett (Mrs. Murchison), Romo Vincent (Pete Gomez).

Synopsis: After moving into a beach house, a gambler's widow marries a mysterious, shiftless beachcomber whom she soon suspects of having been involved in the murder of another woman, the former lessor.

Behind the Scenes: Joan Crawford made her film debut in *Pretty Ladies* (1925), and by the 1930s, stood among the ten best moneymaking stars. Under contract to MGM with such lumanaries as Clark Gable and Greta Garbo, Miss Crawford earned almost $200,000 from the studio in 1941, and nearly the same in 1942. After the studio ended her contract, she won an Academy award for Best Actress in *Mildred Pierce* (1945). Miss Crawford and Jeff first worked together in 1951 on a radio adaptation of MGM's *The Secret Heart* (1946). With Jeff as her leading man—at her request—Miss Crawford appeared in nearly all of the scenes shot for *Female on the Beach*, her first for U-I.[102]

Charles B. Lang, one of Hollywood's finest cinematographers, received his first assignment in 1926. He won an Academy award for *A Farewell to Arms* (1933); in *Sudden Fear* (1952), Joan Crawford received a nomination for Best Actress and Lang a nomination for Black-and-White Cinematography. Jan Sterling received an Academy award-nomination as well as the Golden Globe Award for Best Supporting Actress in *The High and the Mighty* (1954).

As part of the film's promotion, the Victor Young Orchestra recorded the song "Female on the Beach" (music, Sonny Burke), released in July 1955. Miss Crawford and Jeff appeared on the sheet music's cover along with billing for the film. U-I also made available to theater owners a free recorded interview featuring Miss Crawford.[103] For its review of the film, the *Los Angeles Examiner* proclaimed that *Female on the Beach* "is quite a movie. Suspense, suspicion and Jeff Chandler have a real go at it—results in a thoroughly intriguing tale."[104]

Reviews: "Joan Crawford, Jeff Chandler top-lining romantic melodrama of sex and murder at the beach. Good prospects."—*Variety*, July 13, 1955.

"Well-done is this study in suspense, drama, and romance."—*Motion Picture Exhibitor*, July 27, 1955.

Additional Reviews: *The Hollywood Reporter*, 07/12/55; *Los Angeles Times*, 09/22/55; *Monthly Film Bulletin*, 07/55; *Motion Picture Herald*, 07/16/55; *The New York Times*, 08/20/55.

Comments by the Film's Star: "If you think that was tender, you should catch me next week when Jeff makes love to me on the deck of a steamer. I simply shove him overboard."—*Joan Crawford*[105]

Comments by Jeff Chandler: "For a long time, it just never occurred to anyone that I should be doing anything but adventure stories in which I could be an Indian, cowboy or the like. Once in a while I got a chance to kiss the girl, but most of the time I was winding up with my horse, riding off into the Technicolor sunset. In a way, I'm glad I got a chance to play so many swashbuckling roles. Gave me a chance to get in proper athletic trim for this one!"[106]

Comments by a Fan: "Love that Jeff Boy!"[107]

Foxfire

A Universal-International Picture. © 1955. Released July 1955. Ad line: "Jane's Got Jeff! The Story of an Impatient Love!" Universal-International production number 1777. Running time, 92 minutes; Technicolor; Drama.

Ratings: *The Motion Picture Guide*, ☆☆; *Leonard Maltin's Movie and Video Guide*, ☆☆½; *New York Daily News*, ☆☆☆; *Halliwell's Film Guide*, 0

Credits: Produced by Aaron Rosenberg; directed by Joseph Pevney; assistant director, Ronnie Rondell; screenplay by Ketti Frings, based on the book *Foxfire* by Anya Seton (Boston: Houghton Mifflin Company, 1950); music by Frank Skinner; music supervised by Joseph Gershenson; art direction by Robert Clatworthy and Alexander Golitzen; set decoration by Russell A. Gausman and Ruby R. Levitt; hairstyles by Joan St. Oegger; hairstyles for Jane Russell by Stephanie McGrew; make-up by Bud Westmore; make-up for Jane Russell by Layne Britton; costume design by Bill Thomas; sound by Leslie I. Carey and Robert Pritchard; cinematography by William H. Daniels; film editing by Ted J. Kent.

Cast: Jane Russell (Amanda), Jeff Chandler (Jonathan Dartland), Dan Duryea (Hugh Slater), Mara Corday (Maria), Frieda Inescort (Mrs. Lawrence), Barton MacLane (Mr. Mablett), Robert F. Simon (Ernest Tyson), Eddy C. Waller (old Larky), Celia Lovsky (Princess Saba), Charlotte Wynters (Mrs. Mablett), Lillian Bronson (Mrs. Potter), Arthur Space (Foley), Phil Chambers (Mr. Riley), Robert Bice (Walt Whitman), Guy Wilkerson (Mr. Barton), Mary Carroll (Mrs. Riley), Vici Raaf (Cleo), Grace Lenard (Rose), Lisabith Fielding (Mrs. Foley).

Synopsis: A half–Apache mining engineer marries a New York society girl who gives up all the comforts of her former life when the newlyweds settle down in a remote mining town in Arizona.

Behind the Scenes: In late 1953, an agreement between U-I and June Allyson for her starring role in *Foxfire* required her approval, by the end of the year, of screenplay, leading males and director. If the studio cast Jeff in the leading male role, the studio had Miss Allyson's automatic approval.

The Films

East Coast society girl Amanda (Jane Russell) and half–Apache Jonathan Dartland (Jeff Chandler) in *Foxfire* (1955, Universal-International).

A survey, however, determined who the public wanted to see play opposite Jeff in *Foxfire*: Jeanne Crain, Arlene Dahl, Susan Hayward, Jane Russell, Elizabeth Taylor or Lana Turner. Men in the survey chose Miss Russell for the starring role, women in the survey placed Miss Russell near the top of their choices, and teenagers surveyed preferred Susan Hayward, with Jeanne Crain as their second choice.[108]

U-I tentatively cast Jeanne Crain in the lead, until the Russ-Field Corporation asked to borrow Jeff to costar in their own production of a film starring Jane Russell. The studio agreed if Miss Russell would appear in one of their films. U-I screened a print of *Because of You* for the actress who thought highly of Jeff and liked the work director Joe Pevney did in the 1952 film. The Russ-Field film was never produced, and *Foxfire*, director Pevney's seventh with Jeff, became Miss Russell's first for U-I.[109]

Two opportunities arose before *Foxfire* where Jeff almost worked with Dan

Duryea, a Star of Tomorrow, 1946. In early 1949, U-I signed Jeff for a part in *Johnny Stool Pigeon* with Howard Duff, Shelley Winters and Duryea. Another commitment, however, forced Jeff to withdraw from the role eventually played by Wally Maher. Five months later, U-I signed Jeff for the lead in *One Way Street*, a role that later went to James Mason, and costarred Marta Toren and Duryea.

Publicity for the movie included the song "Foxfire" (music, Henry Mancini; lyrics, Jeff Chandler) and its sheet music, issued by Northern Music Company, with Miss Russell and Jeff on its cover. Decca Records also made available a colorful record streamer for use in record stores as a special tie-in to Jeff's other Decca recordings. The *Motion Picture Exhibitor* in their review found the film to be an "interesting drama."[110]

Reviews: "An off-beat love story by novelist Anya Seton plus sexy Jeff Chandler and sexier Jane Russell to play the principals in the imaginative romance — that's *Foxfire*."—*Los Angeles Examiner*, January 30, 1955.

Additional Reviews: *The Hollywood Reporter*, 06/14/55; *Los Angeles Times*, 06/30/55; *Monthly Film Bulletin*, 06/55; *Motion Picture Herald*, 06/18/55; *The New York Times*, 07/14/55; *Variety*, 06/14/55.

Among the Top-Grossing Films of 1955: $1,900,000[111]

Comments by the Film's Star: "At last I'm working with a guy who's tall enough so I can wear my high heels."—*Jane Russell*[112]

Comments by Jeff Chandler: "We had a lot of fun in the wilds of the Arizona desert where the unit was on location."[113]

Comments by a Fan: "Mr. Chandler improves with every picture, and his voice is terrific."[114]

The Littlest Outlaw

A Walt Disney Picture. © 1955. Released January 1956. Ad line: "So Heartwarming! So Entertaining! So Unusual!" Walt Disney production number 4104. Aka, "The General's Horse." Running time, 75 minutes; Technicolor; Children's Drama.

Ratings: *The Motion Picture Guide*, ☆☆☆ ; *Leonard Maltin's Movie and Video Guide*, ☆☆☆

Credits: Produced by Larry Lansburgh; executive producer, Walt Disney; directed by Roberto Gavaldon; assistant director, Jesus Marin; screenplay by Bill Walsh, from an unpublished story by Larry Lansburgh; music by William Lava; orchestration by Charles Maxwell; production manager, Luis Sanchez Tello; set decoration by Rafael Suarez; sound by Manuel Topete; cinematography by Alex Phillips; film editing by Carlos Savage; second unit camera, J. Carlos Carbajal.

Cast: Pedro Armendariz (Gen. Torres), Joseph Calleia (The Padre), Rodolfo Acosta (Chato), Andres Velazquez (Pablito), Pepe Ortiz (Matador, played by himself), Laila Maley (Celita), Gilberto Gonzalez (Tiger), Jose Torvay (Vulture), Jose Angel Espinosa "Ferrusquilla" (Senor Garcia), Enriqueta Zazueta (Senora Garcia), Senor Lee (Gypsy), Carlos Ortigoza (Doctor), Margarito Luna (Silvestre), Ricardo Gonzales (Marcos), Maria Eugenia (The Bride), Pedrito Vargas (The Groom).

Synopsis: A young boy risks everything in order to save the life of a mistreated horse ordered destroyed for throwing the daughter of a general.

Behind the Scenes: Recording sessions for the musical score to *The Littlest Outlaw* occurred in June 1954. Jeff wrote the lyrics to four of its songs, while William Lava composed the music: "The Littlest Outlaw (A Boy)," "El Padre," "This Lovely Night," and "The Moon Won't Let You Tell a Lie." Bob Jackman wrote the words for two other William Lava tunes, but, in the end, the studio used the song "Doroteo (The Automobile Song)," music and lyrics by Edmundo Santos; the other songs were used instrumentally only.[115] The *Motion Picture Herald* said that *The Littlest Outlaw* "will steal your heart."[116]

Reviews: "New Disney film 'a honey.'"—*Los Angeles Examiner*, December 26, 1955.

"Good Disney live action entry."—*Motion Picture Exhibitor*, January 11, 1956.

Additional Reviews: *Boxoffice* 12/24/55; *Film Daily*, 12/28/55; *The Hollywood Reporter*, 12/20/55; *Monthly Film Bulletin*, 08/56; *The New York Times*, 12/27/55; *Variety*, 12/20/55.

Among the Top-Grossing Films of 1956: $1,600,000[117]

The Nat "King" Cole Musical Story

A Universal-International Picture. © 1955. Released December 1955. Ad line: "Swing and Roll with Nat 'King' Cole Singing His Favorite Record Hits!" Universal-International production number 7136. Running time, 18 minutes; Technicolor (CinemaScope); Musical Short.

Credits: Produced and directed by Will Cowan; screenplay by Maxine Dioguardi; narration by Jeff Chandler; music conducted by Nelson Riddle; art direction by Eric Orbom; sound by Leslie I. Carey; cinematography by George Robinson; film editing by Tom Conlon Jr.

Cast: Nat "King" Cole (as himself), John Collins (as himself), Charles Harris (as himself), Lee Young (as himself), Ray Walker (Carlos Gastel), Douglas Evans (Evans), Billy Wayne (drunk), Richard Reeves (manager), Robert Lynn (doctor).

Synopsis: *The Nat "King" Cole Musical Story* traces the musical career of Nat "King" Cole, who performs "That's My Girl," "Pretend," and "Darling, Je Vous Aime Beaucoup." "Sweet Lorraine," "Route 66," and "Straighten Up and Fly Right" are performed by Nat "King" Cole and His Trio.

Jeff Chandler

Behind the Scenes: In the spring of 1955, Nat "King" Cole filmed this two-reel musical short based on his life; Jeff Chandler recorded the narration a short time later. Leslie I. Carey, head of U-I's Sound Department, came to this production fresh from his win of an Academy award for his work in *The Glenn Miller Story* (1953). U-I screened the featurette in November 1955 at the Academy Award Theatre on Melrose Avenue in Los Angeles as a curtain raiser for their pre-showing of *All That Heaven Allows* (1955). *Motion Picture Exhibitor* rated *The Nat "King" Cole Musical Story*, "Excellent."[118]

Reviews: "An excellent biographical-type musical which traces the career of Nat 'King' Cole, currently one of the hottest singing stars on record, TV and in nightclubs. Cole has had so many Hit Parade records in the past few years that he has an army of teenage devotees and the short rates marquee billing, especially in the neighborhood and family spots."—*Boxoffice*, December 10, 1955.

Additional Reviews: *Motion Picture Herald*, 03/17/56.

One Desire

A Universal-International Picture. © 1955. Released August 1955. Ad line: "A Tidal Wave of Raw Human Emotion … Brought to the Screen With All of the Surging Passion of the Best-Selling Novel From Which It was Made … An Unforgettable Movie Experience." Universal-International production number 1787. Aka "Tacey," "Tacy Cromwell." Running time, 94 minutes; Technicolor; Drama.

Ratings: *The Motion Picture Guide*, ☆☆½; *Leonard Maltin's Movie and Video Guide*, ☆☆½; *New York Daily News*, ☆☆½; *Halliwell's Film Guide*, 0

Credits: Produced by Ross Hunter; directed by Jerry Hopper; assistant director, Tom Shaw; screenplay by Robert Blees and Lawrence Roman, based on the book *Tacey Cromwell* by Conrad Richter (New York, A. A. Knopf, 1942); music by Frank Skinner; musical supervision by Joseph Gershenson; art direction by Carroll Clark and Alexander Golitzen; set decorations by John Austin and Russell A. Gausman; hair styles by Joan St. Oegger; make-up by Bud Westmore; costume design by Bill Thomas; sound by Glenn E. Anderson and Leslie I. Carey; cinematography by Maury Gertsman; film editing by Milton Carruth.

Cast: Anne Baxter (Tacey Cromwell), Rock Hudson (Clint Saunders), Julie Adams (Judith Watrous), Carl Benton Reid (Senator Watrous), Natalie Wood (Seely Dowder), Betty Garde (Mrs. O'Dell), William Hopper (MacBain), Barry Curtis (Nugget Saunders), Adrienne Marden (Marjorie Huggins), Fay Morley (Flo), Vici Raaf (Kate), Lynn Millan (Bea), Smoki Whitfield (Sam), Robert Hoy (fireman), John Daheim (fireman).

Synopsis: An ex-saloon hostess' efforts to start a new life with a retired gambler are thwarted by a spoiled banker's daughter.

Behind the Scenes: Decca Records released three singles in three consecutive weeks during the summer of 1955: Jeff's "A Little Love Can Go a Long, Long Way — Only the Very Young," Victor Young's "Female on the Beach — I Love Your Gypsy Heart," and "Happy-Go-Lucky — One Desire."

With orchestra by Sonny Burke, Karel Wagner, the winner of a record contest, sang "Happy-Go-Lucky" from the U-I drama *The Rawhide Years* (1955); the flip side, "One Desire" (music, Henry Mancini; lyrics, Jeff Chandler) covered by Gene Boyd, another contest winner.

In promoting the movie, Northern Music Company issued a special title page for the sheet music, while U-I made available to theater owners a free radio interview record featuring Anne Baxter. "*One Desire* rates as great woman's picture," wrote *The Hollywood Reporter*.[119]

Reviews: "Universal-International has pulled all stops on this romantic tear-jerker."—*Variety*, July 6, 1955.

Additional Reviews: *Los Angeles Times*, 07/21/55; *Monthly Film Bulletin*, 07/55; *Motion Picture Exhibitor*, 07/13/55; *Motion Picture Herald*, 07/09/55; *The New York Times*, 09/03/55.

Six Bridges to Cross

A Universal-International Picture. © 1955. Released February 1955. Ad line: "Does this Smile ... Hide the Secret Behind the Great $2,500,000 Boston Robbery?" Universal-International production number 1770. Aka "Million Dollar Holdup," "Anatomy of a Crime," "Five Bridges to Cross." Running time, 96 minutes; black & white; Crime.

Ratings: *The Motion Picture Guide*, ☆☆½; *Leonard Maltin's Movie and Video Guide*, ☆☆½; *New York Daily News*, ☆☆☆½; *Halliwell's Film Guide*, 0

Credits: Produced by Aaron Rosenberg; directed by Joseph Pevney; assistant director, Ronnie Rondell; screenplay by Sydney Boehm, based on the book *Anatomy of a Crime* by Joseph F. Dinneen (New York: Scribner, 1954); musical supervision by Joseph Gershenson; art direction by Robert Clatworthy and Alexander Golitzen; set decorations by Russell A. Gausman and Ruby R. Levitt; hair styles by Joan St. Oegger; make-up by Bud Westmore; costume design by Jay A. Morley Jr.; sound by Leslie I. Carey and Joe Lapis; cinematography by William H. Daniels; film editing by Russell Schoengarth.

Cast: Tony Curtis (Jerry Florea), Julie Adams (Ellen Gallagher), George Nader (Edward Gallagher), Jay C. Flippen (Vincent Concannon), Kendall Clark (Sanborn), Sal Mineo (Jerry Florea as a boy), Jan Merlin (Andy Norris), Richard Castle (Skids Radzievich), William Murphy (Red Flanagan), Kenny Roberts (Red Flanagan as a boy), Peter Avramo (Hymie Weiner), Hal Conklin (Jerry's attorney), Don Keefer (Sherman).

Jeff Chandler

Synopsis: The story of a petty thief who, although adopted by a kindly policeman, embarks upon a life of crime, becomes a gangster and seeks redemption only after his most notorious crime.

Behind the Scenes: Tony Curtis, Sammy Davis Jr. and Jeff enjoyed a close friendship ever since Davis first played Ciro's in March 1951. In October 1954, Jeff and Davis discussed the song "Six Bridges to Cross" with Charles F. Simonelli, Executive In-Charge of National Promotion for U-I. Simonelli, in turn, presented a publicity angle to Milton R. Rackmil, cofounder of Decca Records and president of Universal Pictures: why not have Sammy record a song written by Jeff in a picture starring Tony?[120]

Earlier that year, Davis signed with Decca, and one of his first singles "Hey There" reached the top of the charts in early October. As U-I made arrangements for Davis to record *Six Bridges to Cross* that would be heard over the film's ending credits, the singer's popularity reached new heights. A survey of disc jockeys, covering the first ten months of 1954, positioned Davis at #7 in their list of new male vocalists who they thought had the greatest chance in becoming a top male vocalist (the list included Harry Belefonte at #15; Jeff at #18).[121] Davis, headlining the Will Mastin Trio, began a month-long engagement at the New Frontier in Las Vegas. On November 14, 1954, Davis performed to a nationwide television audience on NBC's *The Colgate Comedy Hour*.

With Davis scheduled to record the title track on Saturday morning, November 20, Henry Mancini, Jeff and an orchestra were assembled at U-I. When the morning passed without Davis' arrival, Jeff, on a hunch, located the singer through the sheriff's department. Hospitalized in San Bernadino, California, an automobile accident on Route 66 between Las Vegas and Universal City had cost the entertainer his left eye.

Discharged from the hospital by the end of November, the singer had no time to waste because of the scheduled February 1955 release of the film. On December 26, Davis recorded the song "Six Bridges to Cross" (music, Henry Mancini; lyrics, Jeff Chandler), backed by an orchestra conducted by Joseph Gershenson. Decca rushed the record into production for the Boston opening of the film as the music publishing company rushed into print the sheet music that featured Tony Curtis and film credits on the cover.

Davis performed at Ciro's on January 24, 1955 to standing ovation, the same day Decca released the title song on the West Coast. By the end of the month, movie advertisements nationwide proclaimed "Hear the new Decca Record hit *Six Bridges to Cross* sung by the sensational Sammy Davis Jr."[122]

Reviews: "New crime melodrama tense and suspenseful."—*Hollywood Citizen-News*, February 3, 1955.

"Tony Curtis becomes a star in *Six Bridges to Cross*."—*Los Angeles Mirror-News*, February 4, 1955.

Additional Reviews: *The Hollywood Reporter*, 01/14/55; *Monthly Film Bulletin*, 03/55; *Motion Picture Exhibitor*, 01/26/55; *Motion Picture Herald*, 01/22/55; *The New York Times*, 01/22/55; *Variety*, 01/14/55.

Among the Top-Grossing Films of 1955: $1,800,000[123]

Comments by Jeff Chandler: "*Six Bridges to Cross* is the best thing he's done so far, a role closer to the basic Tony, the tough guy with a heart of gold."[124]

The Spoilers

A Universal-International Picture. © 1955. Released January 1956. Ad line: "Rex Beach's Immortal Saga of the Yukon!" Universal-International production number 1790. Running time, 82 minutes; Technicolor; Western.

Ratings: *The Motion Picture Guide*, ☆☆½; *Leonard Maltin's Movie and Video Guide*, ☆☆½; *New York Daily News*, ☆☆☆; *Halliwell's Film Guide*, ☆

Credits: Produced by Ross Hunter; directed by Jesse Hibbs; assistant director, Frank Shaw; screenplay by Oscar Brodney and Charles Hoffman, based on the book *The Spoilers* by Rex Beach (New York: A. L. Burt Company, 1905); musical direction by Joseph Gershenson; art direction by Alexander Golitzen and Alfred Sweeney; set decorations by John Austin and Russell A. Gausman; hair styles by Joan St. Oegger; make-up by Bud Westmore; costume design by Bill Thomas; sound by John A. Bolger Jr. and Leslie I. Carey; cinematography by Maury Gertsman; film editing by Paul Weatherwax.

Cast: Anne Baxter (Cherry Malotte), Jeff Chandler (Roy Glennister), Rory Calhoun (Alex McNamara), Ray Danton (Blackie), Barbara Britton (Helen Chester), John McIntire (Dextry), Wallace Ford (Flapjack Simms), Carl Benton Reid (Judge Stillman), Raymond Walburn (Mr. Skinner), Ruth Donnelly (Duchess), Willis Bouchey (Jonathan Struve), Forrest Lewis (Banty Jones), Roy Barcroft (The Marshal), Dayton Lummis (Wheaton), John Harmon (Kelly), Paul McGuire (Thompson), Frank Sully (miner).

Synopsis: Partners in an Alaskan gold mine succeed in protecting their rich claim from a conniving Gold Commissioner and a corrupt Federal judge.

Behind the Scenes: Anne Baxter, a Star of Tomorrow, 1943, won the Golden Globe and Academy award for Best Supporting Actress in *The Razor's Edge* (1946). Miss Baxter and Jeff first worked together in 1948 on *The Lux Radio Theatre's* broadcast of "Gentleman's Agreement"; Miss Baxter played the Dorothy McGuire movie role with Jeff in the role earlier taken by John Garfield.

As the filming of *The Spoilers* proceeded, the cast were often reminded that although many of the sourdoughs went broke during the days of the 1899 Alaskan Gold Rush, the grocers and hotel-keepers cleaned up: a ham and egg breakfast cost $10; a pound of the poorest cuts of beef, $1.60; a pint of champagne, $15; a hotel

Saloon owner Cherry Malotte (Anne Baxter) and gold mine owner Roy Glennister (Jeff Chandler) in *The Spoilers* (1955, Universal-International).

room, $25 — without bath, window curtains or floor rugs; the cheapest whiskey, $8 — cash or gold dust.[125] "The Baxter, Chandler, Calhoun names will assure a satisfactory payoff," wrote *Motion Picture Exhibitor*.[126]

Reviews: "Chandler is just right as the rugged miner who has two dames crazy over him and Calhoun is the most plausible villain seen in some time." — *The Hollywood Reporter*, December 6, 1955.

"Ross Hunter's production assures this Rex Beach film classic of becoming a five-time winner at the box office."—*Motion Picture Herald*, December 10, 1955.

Additional Reviews: *Boxoffice* 12/10/55; *Film Daily*, 12/27/55; *Los Angeles Times*, 12/29/55; *Monthly Film Bulletin*, 10/55; *The New York Times*, 12/24/55; *Variety*, 12/06/55.

Among the Top-Grossing Films of 1956: $1,400,000[127]

Comments by Jeff Chandler: "I thought I was being had by the supermarkets until I started work in this picture. Now I feel I'm getting everything at bargain rates."[128]

Costar Comments: "Talk about today's high cost of living — they had us all beat."—*Rory Calhoun*[129]

Away All Boats

A Universal-International Picture. © 1956. Released August 1956. Ad line: "Screamed From the Raw Throats of Fighting Men, Torn From the Hearts of Their Love-Lonesome Women, Away All Boats ... Away! The Battle Cry of the South Pacific." Universal-International production number 1793. Running time, 114 minutes; Technicolor (VistaVision); War.

Ratings: *The Motion Picture Guide*, ☆☆; *Leonard Maltin's Movie and Video Guide*, ☆☆½; *New York Daily News*, ☆☆☆½; *Halliwell's Film Guide*, 0

Credits: Produced by Howard J. Christie; directed by Joseph Pevney; assistant directors, Marshall Green, Terry Nelson, Jim Welch; screenplay by Ted Sherdeman, based on the book *Away All Boats* by Kenneth M. Dodson (Boston: Little, Brown, 1954); music by Frank Skinner; musical supervision by Joseph Gershenson; art direction by Alexander Golitzen and Richard H. Riedel; production manager, Tom Shaw; set decorations by Oliver Emert and Russell A. Gausman; hair styles by Joan St. Oegger; make-up, Bud Westmore; sound by Leslie I. Carey and Joe Lapis; cinematography by William H. Daniels; film editing by Ted J. Kent.

Cast: Jeff Chandler (Capt. Jebediah S. Hawks), George Nader (Lt. Dave MacDougall), Julie Adams (Nadine MacDougall), Lex Barker (Com. Quigley), Keith Andes (Dr. Bell), Richard Boone (Lt. Fraser), William Reynolds (Ens. Kruger), Charles McGraw (Lt. Mike O'Bannion), Jock Mahoney (Alvick), John McIntire (old man), Frank Faylen (Chief Phillip E. "Pappy" Moran), Grant Williams (LTJG Sherwood), David Janssen (talker), Floyd Simmons (LTJG Robinson), Kendall Clark (Lt. Jackson), James Westerfield ("Boats" Torgeson), Don Keefer (Ens. Twitchell), Raymond Bailey (RADM Stacy Bander), Hal Baylor (Chaplain Hughes), Sam Gilman (Lt. Jim Randall), Jarl Victor ("Sacktime" Riley), Arthur Space (Dr. Flynn), George Dunn (Gilbert Hubert), Parley Baer (Dr. Gates), Charles Horvath (Boski), John Pickard (Maj. Scott), Rod Williams (Capt. Blanchard), Robert Hoy (sailor #1), Henry Wills (sailor #2), Chuck Courtney (helmsman), Gerard Masterson (sailor), Ralph Scalzo (Willicut).

Synopsis: Hard-boiled Captain Jebediah S. Hawks undertakes the training of a green crew before they experience the harshness of World War II combat aboard the USS *Belinda*, a Navy attack transport in the Pacific.

Behind the Scenes: Sammy Davis Jr. performed at the Copa in New York in April 1955; Jeff and Marjorie were there three out of the five nights; Davis, in turn, saw Jeff off at the airport as he left for location filming for *Away All Boats*. The headquarters for the production of the sea story were in Charlotte Amalie of St. Thomas in the Virgin Islands.

Lex Barker, George Nader, producer Howard J. Christie and Jeff made personal appearances on a local television program for the benefit of the USO, entertaining five thousand navy personnel who lined the decks of the U.S. aircraft carrier *Saipan*. Before his engagement at the Riviera Hotel in Las Vegas, Jeff previewed his night club act before hundreds of sailors and officers, giving them a great performance[130]

The book *Away All Boats* by Kenneth M. Dodson finished eighth among the ten best-selling books of 1954, and promoted the film quite effectively. As part of their promotion, U-I made available to theater owners a free record album featuring a personal interview with Jeff.

On April 3, 1956, Jeff attended the press preview of *Away All Boats* at the Baldwin Theatre on South La Brea Avenue at Rodeo Drive in Los Angeles. In the weeks that followed, movie ads appeared in magazines nationwide, including a full-page review in the *Film Daily*, the first ever granted a Universal picture. *Family Weekly* declared, "Chandler is now U-I's top box-office star!"[131]

Reviews: "U-I planned *Away All Boats* as its Big One for 1956, and those plans have been carried out with resounding success."—*The Hollywood Reporter*, May 11, 1956.

"U-I's *Away All Boats* is a BIG movie done on a BIG scale. It's exciting, action-filled, colorful, and frequently spectacular."—*Los Angeles Examiner*, July 20, 1956.

Additional Reviews: *Boxoffice*, 05/12/56; *Film Daily*, 05/11/56; *Los Angeles Times*, 07/19/56; *Motion Picture Exhibitor*, 05/16/56; *Motion Picture Herald*, 05/12/56; *The New York Times*, 08/17/56; *Variety*, 05/16/56.

Among the Top-Grossing Films of 1956: $3,500,000[132]

Costar Comments: "Jeff had this presence that was appropriate both in person and in the character he played in *Away All Boats*. He was excellent in that movie, and I don't think he had to work very much to carry off the part, it wasn't a huge feat. The character he portrayed projected a part of what Jeff was—a dignified person. He was a helluva guy."—*William Reynolds*[133]

Comments by Jeff Chandler: "We lived in a plush hotel, one of the finest resort spots in the world, but actually I only slept there, for I spent most of my time at sea. I've gone on about twenty film location trips to the four corners of this interesting Earth, and someday I'm going back to see what all those places look like."[134]

Brooklyn Goes to Las Vegas

A Universal-International Picture. © 1956. Released February 1956. Universal-International production number 6582. Running time, 9 minutes; black & white; Variety View Series; Comedy Short.

Credits: Produced by Thomas Mead; directed and written by Arthur Cohen; narration by Harold Huber; music direction by Joseph Gershenson; music conducted by Milton Rosen; film editing by Ed Bartsch.

Cast: Phil Foster (Brooklyn), Jeff Chandler, Joe E. Lewis, Marilyn Maxwell, Al Ritz, Harry Ritz, Jimmy Ritz.

Synopsis: A native of Brooklyn comments on the hotels, the casinos, the nightclub entertainment and the marriage laws in Las Vegas.

Behind the Scenes: Arthur Cohen, U-I's short-subjects director, received an Academy award-nomination at the 20th Annual Academy Awards Presentation for his short subject *Brooklyn, U.S.A.* (1946). A native of Brooklyn, New York, comedian Phil Foster, known also as "Mr. Brooklyn Dodger," performed on many of the big television variety programs of the 1950s, including *The Ed Sullivan Show*.

The famous nightclub star, Joe E. Lewis, called the El Rancho in Las Vegas "home." The Ritz Brothers became the first name act to play Las Vegas, performing at the El Rancho for $7,500 a week in 1945, the year film exhibitors chose Marilyn Maxwell a Star of Tomorrow. Miss Maxwell, nightclub entertainer and actress, performed as a vocalist for Ted Weems and His Orchestra in the 1930s, and in the 1940s, on radio's *The Abbott and Costello Show*. The *Motion Picture Exhibitor* rated *Brooklyn Goes to Las Vegas*, "Good."[135]

Reviews: "The Brooklyn character visits fabulous Las Vegas with its gambling spots and its beautiful hotels. Some of the famous places and people are featured in this one."—*Motion Picture Herald*, June 9, 1956.

Pillars of the Sky

A Universal-International Picture. © 1956. Released October 1956. Ad line: "This Was the Night of the Tomahawk and the Cross!" Universal-International production number 1808. Aka "Frontier Fury;" "The Tomahawk and the Cross." Running time, 95 minutes; Technicolor (CinemaScope); Western.

Ratings: *The Motion Picture Guide*, ☆☆½; *Leonard Maltin's Movie and Video Guide*, ☆☆½; *New York Daily News*, ☆☆☆; *Halliwell's Film Guide*, 0

Jeff Chandler

Credits: Produced by Robert Arthur; directed by George Marshall; assistant director, Marshall Green; screenplay by Sam Rolfe, based on the book *Frontier Fury* by Will Henry; musical supervision by Joseph Gershenson; art direction by Alexander Golitzen and Bill Newberry; set decorations by Oliver Emert and Russell A. Gausman; hair styles by Joan St. Oegger; make-up by Bud Westmore; costume design by Rosemary Odell; sound by Leslie I. Carey and Frank H. Wilkinson; cinematography by Harold Lipstein; film editing by Milton Carruth.

Cast: Jeff Chandler (First Sgt. Emmett Bell), Dorothy Malone (Calla Gaxton), Ward Bond (Dr. Joseph Holden), Keith Andes (Capt. Tom Gaxton), Lee Marvin (Sgt. Lloyd Carracart), Sydney Chaplin (Timothy), Willis Bouchey (Col. Edson Stedlow), Alberto Morin (Sgt. Major Frenchy Desmonde), Richard Hale (Isaiah), Michael Ansara (Kamiakin), Olive Carey (Mrs. Anne Avery), Floyd Simmons (Lt. Hammond), Glen Kramer (Lt. Winston), Pat Hogan (Jacob), Frank de Kova (Zachariah), Felix Noriego (Lucas), Paul Smith (Morgan), Walter Coy (Maj. Donahue), Martin Milner (Waco), Robert Ellis (Albie), Ralph Votrian (Musie), Charles Horvath (Sgt. Dutch Williams), Orlando Rodriguez (Malachi), Terry Wilson (Capt. Fanning), Dan Borzage (soldier), Phillip Kieffer (Maj. Randall), Gilbert Conner (Elijah).

Synopsis: The head of the scouts attached to the U.S. Cavalry tries to warn off the cavalry from building a road and fort on Indian territory in order to avoid a bloody conflict with the Christianized Indians of the area.

Behind the Scenes: During July 1954, producer Robert Arthur and director John Ford discussed *Pillars of the Sky* with John Wayne as its star; Ford, its director. Ford went on to direct Wayne in *The Searchers* (1956) for Warner Bros., and U-I signed Jeff for the lead in *Pillars of the Sky*.

Beginning in mid–August 1955, the cast and crew of 150 locationed for nearly six weeks in the rugged east country near Pondosa, Oregon. Abundant in riches such as its towering evergreens and snowcapped peaks, Oregon drew settlers by the thousands in the early 1800s; *Pillars of the Sky* takes place in 1868.

George Marshall, veteran of 40 years and hundreds of motion pictures, made his film debut as an extra at Universal in 1912, and began directing Westerns in 1916. The supporting cast for *Pillars of the Sky* included Olive Carey, married to late actor Harry Carey for 34 years, until his death in 1947. Miss Carey, a Universal leading lady from 1914 to 1918, met her husband after being cast in a serial by George Marshall.[136] Of the film, *Motion Picture Exhibitor* wrote, "The cast is good, and the director and production efficient."[137]

Reviews: "*Pillars of the Sky* good historical western story."—*The Hollywood Reporter*, August 7, 1956.

"*Pillars of the Sky* heap good movie."—*Los Angeles Examiner*, September 14, 1956.

Additional Reviews: *Film Daily*, 08/08/56; *Los Angeles Times*, 09/13/56; *Monthly Film Bulletin*, 05/56; *Motion Picture Herald*, 08/11/56; *The New York Times*, 10/13/56; *Variety*, 08/07/56.

Among the Top-Grossing Films of 1956: $1,500,000[138]

Comments by Jeff Chandler: "In this picture I find myself playing opposite the noble Indian chiefs—and envying them. I always did like portraying a man who says a lot in a few words and Indian roles have that as their main characteristic. They're a real challenge to an actor."[139]

Comments by a Fan: "Jeff Chandler is a wonderful actor."[140]

Toy Tiger

A Universal-International Picture. © 1956. Released July 1956. Ad line: "Tim's Back! … With a Tiger by the Tail and the World by the Heart!" Universal-International production number 1814. Running time, 88 minutes; Technicolor (CinemaScope); Comedy.

Ratings: *The Motion Picture Guide*, ☆☆; *Leonard Maltin's Movie and Video Guide*, ☆☆½; *New York Daily News*, ☆☆☆; *Halliwell's Film Guide*, 0

Credits: Produced by Howard J. Christie; directed by Jerry Hopper; assistant directors, Terry Nelson and Frank Shaw; story and screenplay by Ted Sherdeman, based on a story by Marcella Burke and Frederick Kohner; musical supervision by Joseph Gershenson; art direction by Alexander Golitzen and Richard H. Riedel; production manager, Edward Dodds; set decorations by John Austin and Russell A. Gausman; hair styles by Joan St. Oegger; make-up by Bud Westmore; costume design by Rosemary Odell; sound by Leslie I. Carey and Corson Jowett; cinematography by George Robinson; film editing by Milton Carruth.

Cast: Jeff Chandler (Rick Todd), Laraine Day (Gwen Taylor), Tim Hovey (Timmie Harkinson), Richard Haydn (John Fusenot), Cecil Kellaway (James Fusenot), David Janssen (Larry Tripps), Judson Pratt (Mike Wyman), Jacqueline de Wit (Edna), Brad Morrow (Freddy Doobin), Butch Bernard ("Owly" Kimmel), Robert Anderson (State Trooper).

Synopsis: In order to impress his classmates, a lonely, fatherless child in a boy's school persuades his mother's art director to portray the father he has only imagined.

Behind the Scenes: After Tim Hovey's debut in *Queen Bee* (1955), Jerry Hopper directed the child actor in *The Private War of Major Benson* (1955). Laraine Day, a Star of Tomorrow, 1941, made her screen debut in 1937, and worked at RKO and MGM before signing on with U-I to play Hovey's mother in *Toy Tiger*. Supporting cast included Cecil Kellaway, and David Janssen in his second film with Jeff after *Away All Boats*.

Playing art director to Miss Day's advertising executive and father to Tim's imaginary parent—the first light comedy role in his film career—proved to be a challenge to Jeff even though he had played more physically-challenging roles before. *Motion Picture Exhibitor* called the film an "amusing comedy for the family trade."[141]

Reviews: "Chandler gives a graceful, warmly human performance, a triumph of aplomb and acting balance."—*Motion Picture Herald*, April 21, 1956.

"Universal-International has a most entertaining family comedy in *Toy Tiger*."—*Variety*, April 17, 1956.

Additional Reviews: *Boxoffice*, 04/21/56; *The Hollywood Reporter*, 04/17/56; *Los Angeles Times*, 07/05/56; *Monthly Film Bulletin*, 07/56; *The New York Times*, 01/30/56.

Among the Top-Grossing Films of 1956: $1,400,000[142]

Costar Comments: "Jeff was such fun. He took me and my stand-in to lunch every single day."—*Laraine Day*[143]

Comments by Jeff Chandler: "I've been beaten, belted, bopped and burned for screen roles in the past, but for sheer physical exertion I don't think anything can equal doing a picture with twenty-five little boys. Believe me, they're a great bunch of kids, but I'll still take being thrown down a flight of stairs by Rory Calhoun any day of the week."[144]

Comments by a Fan: "I enjoyed the picture thoroughly. Jeff Chandler makes a good comedian."[145]

Drango

A United Artists Picture. © 1957. Released February 1957. Ad line: "One Man Against a Town Gone Mad With Lust!" "When Jeff began casting for *Drango*, he said to Meyer [Mishkin], 'Get me Peter Graves!' I read the script, but something else came up. When Jeff heard I wasn't available for the part, he said to Meyer, 'Get me another Peter Graves!'"—*Peter Graves*[146] Running time, 92 minutes; black & white; Drama.

Ratings: *The Motion Picture Guide*, ☆☆☆; *Leonard Maltin's Movie and Video Guide*, ☆☆; *New York Daily News*, ☆☆½; *Halliwell's Film Guide*, 0

Credits: Produced by Hall Bartlett, Jules Bricken, and Jeff Chandler; executive producer, Meyer Mishkin; directed by Hall Bartlett and Jules Bricken; assistant director, Nathan Barragar; screenplay by Hall Bartlett; music by Elmer Bernstein; art direction by George Van Marter; production manager, Lee Lukather; set decoration by George Milo; hair styles by Lillian Shore; make-up by Steve Drumm; wardrobe by Neva Bourne and Richard Chaney; sound by Vick Appel; cinematography by James Wong Howe.

Cast: Jeff Chandler (Maj. Clint Drango), John Lupton (Marc), Joanne Dru

The Films

Jeff Chandler wearing the uniform of Union major Clint Drango — and the hat of producer of *Drango* (1957, United Artists).

(Kate Calder), Morris Ankrum (Henry Calder), Ronald Howard (Clay Allen), Julie London (Shelby Ransom), Donald Crisp (Judge Allen), Helen Wallace (Mrs. Allen), Walter Sande (Dr. Blair), Parley Baer (George Randolph), Amzie Strickland (Mrs. Randolph), Charles Horvath (Ragan), Barney Phillips (Rev. Giles Cameron), David Stollery (Jeb Bryant), Mimi Gibson (Ellen Bryant), Paul Lukather (Burke), Damian O'Flynn (Blackford), Edith Evanson (Mrs. Blackford).

Synopsis: After the Civil War, a former Union officer faces hatred and hostility when he is sent to aid in the reconstruction of a small Georgia town, in the very area his troops pillaged and burned during Sherman's march to the sea.

Behind the Scenes: In early 1956, Jeff became an independent motion picture producer when he formed Earlmar Productions. With his agent, Meyer Mishkin, they signed a contract with United Artists that allowed complete financing for six pictures. Meanwhile, Jeff's new, non-exclusive three-year contract with U-I, signed when his exclusive, seven-year contract ended, called for Jeff to deliver two pictures a year to that studio until 1959.

Location filming for *Drango*, Earlmar's first production, began in June 1956, in and around St. Francisville, Louisiana, because of the availability of several plantation homes. Casting for the film included leading lady Joanne Dru and veteran actor Donald Crisp, both of whom Jeff had worked with on *Lux*. *Drango* introduced to American audiences 39-year-old, British-born actor Ronald Howard, son of the late Leslie Howard. Fresh from an engagement at The Interlude on the Sunset Strip in Los Angeles, singer-actress Julie London portrayed a disillusioned and confused southern belle.

Academy award-winning cinematographer James Wong Howe approved the film's setting, while Elmer Bernstein composed and conducted its soundtrack, his fifth motion picture score. Liberty Records released the film's soundtrack that pictured Jeff on the front cover as Major Clint Drango, and film credits on the back cover. As part of the publicity for the film, Chandler Music, a company formed by Jeff, released the sheet music for the song "Somehow" (music, Elmer Bernstein; lyrics, Alan Alch). "A fine cast, headed by Jeff Chandler, under the expert hand of Hall Bartlett, who had a hand in the producing, directing and writing, give excellent performances," reported *Motion Picture Exhibitor*.[147]

Reviews: "*Drango* is, in sum, a memorable production that should arouse some critical attention and strong audience reaction."—*The Hollywood Reporter*, January 9, 1957.

"There is nothing mild about *Drango*, a first-rate film which tells a raw and violent tale of the post–Civil War period in a small Southern town devastated by the Union soldiers of General Sherman."—*Los Angeles Examiner*, January 31, 1957.

Additional Reviews: *Film Daily*, 01/17/57; *Los Angeles Times*, 02/01/57; *Monthly Film Bulletin*, 05/57; *Motion Picture Herald*, 01/12/57; *Variety*, 01/09/57.

Jeanne Eagels

A Columbia Picture. © 1957. Released August 1957. Ad line: "She is Eager, Young, Sensual, Luminous, Arrogant, Vain, Shimmering, Drifting, Unbridled, Passionate, Impudent ... She is Icy, Bewitched, Defiant, Glistening, Childlike, Brazen, Breathtaking, Exultant, Vulgar, Tender, Cruel ... She is Animal, Impulsive, Piquant, Damned, Loved, Hated, Adored." "Jeff was the least Hollywood and the most unselfish, sensitive man (other than Jimmy Stewart) that I have ever been fortunate enough to know. He had a wonderful sense of humor and a gift for giving of himself. I will always miss him and hold his memory close to my heart."—*Kim Novak*[148] Columbia Pictures production number 8403. Aka, "The Jeanne Eagels Story." Running time, 114 minutes; black & white; Drama.

The Films

Ratings: *The Motion Picture Guide*, ★★½; *Leonard Maltin's Movie and Video Guide*, ★★½; *New York Daily News*, ★★★; *Halliwell's Film Guide*, ★

Credits: Produced and directed by George Sidney; assistant director, Charles S. Gould; screenplay by John Fante, Daniel Fuchs and Sonya Levien, based on a story by Daniel Fuchs; music by George L. Duning; musical direction by M. W. Stoloff; orchestration by Arthur Morton; art direction by Ross Bellah; set decorations by William Kiernan and Alfred E. Spencer; hair styles by Helen Hunt; make-up by Ben Lane; costume design by Jean Louis; sound by Franklin Hansen Jr. and John Livadary; cinematography by Robert Planck; film editing by Viola Lawrence and Jerome Thoms.

Cast: Kim Novak (Jeanne Eagels), Jeff Chandler (Sal Satori), Agnes Moorehead (Mme. Neilson), Charles Drake (John Donahue), Larry Gates (Al Brooks),

Sal Satori (Jeff Chandler) and Jeanne Eagels (Kim Novak) in *Jeanne Eagels* (1957, Columbia).

Jeff Chandler

Virginia Grey (Elsie Desmond), Gene Lockhart (Equity Board President), Joe de Santis (Frank Satori), Murray Hamilton (Chick O'Hara).

Synopsis: A story based on the triumphant, tormented and tragic life of stage and screen actress Jeanne Eagels, whose fame skyrocketed in the 1920s with the Broadway play, "Rain."

Behind the Scenes: After the success of Columbia's *The Eddy Duchin Story* (1956), producer-director George Sidney again chose Kim Novak, a Star of Tomorrow, 1955, for the lead in *Jeanne Eagels*. On loan-out from U-I, Jeff costarred with Miss Novak, voted one of 1956's ten best moneymaking stars. Supporting cast included Agnes Moorehead, who began her acting career playing small parts on Broadway in 1928, the year before Jeanne Eagels died.

Miss Novak's Jeanne Eagels found international praise as Sadie Thompson in "Rain," a play based on a Somerset Maugham story. Harry Cohn, head of Columbia, groomed Miss Novak and Rita Hayworth to stardom; the latter in *Miss Sadie Thompson* (1953) a Columbia remake of "Rain."

For the promotion of the film, Jeff recorded the movie's ballad "Half of My Heart" (music, George L. Duning; lyrics, Ned Washington), released by Liberty Records in July 1957. In August and September, *Jeanne Eagels* became a box-office winner. "Miss Novak," wrote the *Motion Picture Herald*, "is already a strong box-office attraction. This picture should send her star rating up to a new high."[149]

Reviews: "*Jeanne Eagels* has the elements for box-office hit."—*The Hollywood Reporter*, July 19, 1957.

"Performances by the principals are uniformly excellent, and Novak is radiant in the title role."—*Motion Picture Exhibitor*, July 24, 1957.

Additional Reviews: *Boxoffice*, 07/20/57; *Film Daily*, 07/24/57; *Monthly Film Bulletin*, 10/57; *Motion Picture Herald*, 07/20/57; *The New York Times*, 08/31/57; *Variety*, 07/19/57.

Among the Top-Grossing Films of 1957: $3,100,000[150]

Comments by Jeff Chandler: "But even when she's dressed in one of those black cotton tents they called a bathing suit back in 1921, you'll recognize Kim's charms. Trying to hide her assets is like trying to conceal an elephant in a phone booth."[151]

Comments by the Film's Star: "Don't be discouraged. I can't cut much of a figure in this, but Jeanne Eagels was quite a girl. Try to catch me near the end of her story, when I've taken a drink."—*Kim Novak*[152]

Man in the Shadow

A Universal-International Picture. © 1957. Released January 1958. Ad line: "Violence and Fear Gripped This Land of the Lawless!" Universal-International production

The Films

number 1845. Aka "Alone Together," "Pay the Devil," "I Pay the Devil," "Seeds of Wrath." Running time, 80 minutes; black & white (CinemaScope); Western.

Ratings: *The Motion Picture Guide*, ☆☆½; *Leonard Maltin's Movie and Video Guide*, ☆☆½; *New York Daily News*, ☆☆½; *Halliwell's Film Guide*, ☆

Credits: Produced by Albert Zugsmith; directed by Jack Arnold; assistant director, David Silver; story and screenplay by Gene L. Coon; music by Hans J. Salter; musical supervision by Joseph Gershenson; art direction by Alexander Golitzen and Alfred Sweeney; set decorations by John Austin and Russell A. Gausman; make-up by Bud Westmore; costume design by Bill Thomas; sound by Leslie I. Carey and Joe Lapis; cinematography by Arthur E. Arling; film editing by Edward Curtiss.

Cast: Jeff Chandler (Ben Sadler), Orson Welles (Virgil Renchler), Colleen Miller (Skippy Renchler), Ben Alexander (Ab Begley), Barbara Lawrence (Helen Sadler), John Larch (Ed Yates), James Gleason (Hank James), Royal Dano (Aiken Clay), Paul Fix (Herb Parker), Leo Gordon (Chet Huneker), Martin Garralaga (Jesus Cisneros), Mario Siletti (Tony Santoro), Charles Horvath (Len Bookman), William Schallert (Jim Shaney), Joseph J. Greene (Harry Youngquist), Forrest Lewis (Jake Kelley), Harry Harvey (Dr. Creighton), Joe Schneider (Juan Martin), Mort Mills (gateman).

Synopsis: An honest sheriff decides to find out the facts, at any cost, of the murder of a laborer in the employ of a rich and powerful ranch owner.

Behind the Scenes: During a self-imposed exile abroad, Orson Welles returned briefly to the U.S., and in October 1956, U-I signed the director-producer-screenwriter-actor for *Man in the Shadow*. The film, Jeff's last with U-I as an exclusive, contracted artist, gave him second costar billing with Mr. Welles. Arthur E. Arling, camera operator for *Gone With the Wind* (1939), handled the cinematography in this contemporary black-and-white, horseless western.

When the studio paved over their Western Street, originally built in 1915, cars and trucks replaced horses. Troughs and hitching rails, once used regularly by Western stars such as Harry Carey and his steed, disappeared, replaced by modern devices such as traffic lights and parking meters. In *Man in the Shadow*, the open range became the place where the sheriff, instead of cattle, is roped and tied. Gone, too, is the lawman's cowpuncher boots, duds and holstered horse pistol, replaced by a pair of chukkas, a khaki shirt, trousers and a snub-nosed pistol in his waistband.[153] *Motion Picture Exhibitor* found the film to be an "interesting programmer."[154]

Reviews: "Chandler gives a characteristically convincing performance and Welles makes his part felt with unusual strength and interest."—*The Hollywood Reporter*, November 26, 1957.

"'Man in Shadow' Brilliant."—*Los Angeles Examiner*, January 30, 1958.

Herb Parker (Paul Fix, *left*) provides cover as sheriff Ben Sadler (Jeff Chandler) prepares to handcuff ranch owner Virgil Renchier (Orson Welles) in *Man in the Shadow* (1957, Universal-International).

Additional Reviews: *Boxoffice*, 12/07/57; *Film Daily*, 12/05/57; *Los Angeles Times*, 01/30/58; *Monthly Film Bulletin*, 07/57; *Motion Picture Exhibitor*, 12/11/57; *Motion Picture Herald*, 12/07/57; *The New York Times*, 01/23/58; *Variety*, 11/26/57.

Comments by Jeff Chandler: "You should see some of the scenes with our heroine, Colleen Miller. She wears tight-fitting English jodhpurs and low-cut blouses that are real crazy. And in the big climax scene, there she is in a filmy nightgown silhouetted by the headlights of a dozen cars. Oh, I tell you, westerns have changed!"[155]

Costar Comments: "I never expected to get glamorous on a ranch in Texas. The studio certainly took me literally when I said I'd like a chance to reveal myself in a glamour role for a change."—*Colleen Miller*[156]

The Films

The Tattered Dress

A Universal-International Picture. © 1957. Released April 1957. Ad line: "Every Guy in Town Knew the Dame in *The Tattered Dress*!" Universal-International production number 1840. Running time, 93 minutes; black & white (CinemaScope); Crime Drama.

Ratings: *The Motion Picture Guide*, ★★½; *Leonard Maltin's Movie and Video Guide*, ★★½; *New York Daily News*, ★★★; *Halliwell's Film Guide*, 0

Credits: Produced by Albert Zugsmith; directed by Jack Arnold; assistant director, David Silver; story and screenplay by George Zuckerman; musical supervision by Joseph Gershenson; art direction by Alexander Golitzen and Bill Newberry; set decorations by John Austin and Russell A. Gausman; make-up by Bud Westmore; costume design by Jay A. Morley Jr.; sound by Leslie I. Carey and Robert Pritchard; cinematography by Carl Guthrie; film editing by Edward Curtiss.

Cast: Jeff Chandler (James Gordon Blane), Jeanne Crain (Diane Blane), Jack Carson (Nick Hoak), Gail Russell (Carol Morrow), Elaine Stewart (Charleen Reston), George Tobias (Billy Giles), Edward Andrews (Lester Rawlings), Phillip Reed (Michael Reston), Edward C. Platt (Ralph Adams), Paul Birch (Frank Mitchell), Alexander Lockwood (Paul Vernon), Edwin Jerome (Judge Johnson), William Schallert (court clerk), Joseph Granby (second jury foreman), Frank Scannell (Cal Morrison), Marina Orschel (girl by pool), Ingrid Goude (girl by pool).

Synopsis: A criminal lawyer who wins an acquittal for a murderer is framed by a vengeful sheriff for bribing a juror.

Behind the Scenes: In July 1956, Jeff greeted seventy-five participants of the 1956 Miss Universe Pageant at U-I's main gate, along with an equal number of members from the press. The studio treated their guests to a tour of the lot, publicity photo sessions that included stars such as Maureen O'Hara and Jose Ferrer, and finished with a dinner in the commissary. The Pageant resulted in Carol Morris (Miss USA) as Miss Universe, Marina Orschel (Miss Germany) in second place and in third, Ingrid Goude (Miss Sweden); the latter two made their film debut in *The Tattered Dress* as pool side guests at "The Sun Club."

Actress Jeanne Crain, a California-born model crowned Miss Long Beach of 1941, first worked with Jeff on *Lux*. Albert Zugsmith produced his third with Jeff, who received support from not one, but two Stars of Tomorrow: former model Elaine Stewart, 1954, and Gail Russell, 1947.

In August 1956, members of the legal profession visited the courtroom set and observed how Jeff, whose longest courtroom scene ran nearly six minutes, handled himself as a trial lawyer. The actor won applause from cast, crew and the visitors; among the set's guests: famed Los Angeles trial lawyer, Jerry Giesler, who helped Jeff as coach and technical advisor. *Motion Picture Exhibitor* reported, "Jeff

Diane Blane (Jeanne Crain) lends support to her estranged husband, criminal lawyer James Gordon Blane (Jeff Chandler) in *The Tattered Dress* (1957, Universal-International).

Chandler handles himself particularly well in his first black and white CinemaScope film for the company."[157]

Reviews: "U-I's *The Tattered Dress* is a conventional melodrama with a surprisingly high-powered cast." — *The Hollywood Reporter*, February 26, 1957.

"Excellently produced, directed and acted, *The Tattered Dress* takes a place well above the majority of courtroom dramas, and is made especially good by Jeff Chandler's clean-cut delivery of his sometimes lengthy speeches as a criminal attorney." — *Los Angeles Times*, April 4, 1957.

Additional Reviews: *Boxoffice*, 03/02/57; *Film Daily*, 02/26/57; *Monthly Film Bulletin*, 05/57; *Motion Picture Herald*, 03/02/57; *The New York Times*, 03/15/57; *Variety*, 02/26/57.

Among the Top-Grossing Films of 1957: $1,430,000[158]

Comments by Trial Lawyer: "Jeff is very good. He handles himself extremely well and is most believable. I wish I could sound so good and I also wish I was as handsome." — *Jerry Giesler*[159]

The Films

Comments by Jeff Chandler: "The script is modern, intelligent and believable. I wear my own clothes, I don't have a fist fight every ten pages and I'm not required to ride a single horse."[160]

The Lady Takes a Flyer

A Universal-International Picture. © 1958. Released March 1958. Ad line: "They Teased in Tokyo, Kissed in Casablanca, Fought in France, and Forgave in Every Romantic Land on the Map!" Universal-International production number 1856. Aka "A Game Called Love," "Lion in the Sky," "Wonderful," "Wild and Wonderful." Running time, 95 minutes; Eastmancolor (CinemaScope); Drama.

Ratings: *The Motion Picture Guide*, ☆☆; *Leonard Maltin's Movie and Video Guide*, ☆☆½; *New York Daily News*, ☆☆☆; *Halliwell's Film Guide*, 0

Credits: Produced by William Alland; directed by Jack Arnold; assistant director, David Silver; screenplay by Danny Arnold, developed from an unpublished

Maggie (Lana Turner) shares a tender moment with husband Mike Dandridge (Jeff Chandler) in *The Lady Takes a Flyer* (1958, Universal-International).

Jeff Chandler

story by Edmund H. North; music by Herman Stein; musical supervision by Joseph Gershenson; art direction by Alexander Golitzen and Richard H. Riedel; set decorations by Oliver Emert and Russell A. Gausman; make-up by Bud Westmore; costume design by Bill Thomas; sound by Leslie I. Carey and Corson Jowett; cinematography by Irving Glassberg; film editing by Sherman Todd.

Cast: Lana Turner (Maggie Colby), Jeff Chandler (Mike Dandridge), Richard Denning (Al Reynolds), Andra Martin (Nikko Taylor), Chuck Connors (Phil Donahue), Reta Shaw (Nurse Kennedy), Alan Hale Jr. (Frank Henshaw), Jerry Paris (Willie Ridgley), Dee J. Thompson (Collie Minor), Nestor Paiva (Childreth), James Doherty (tower officer).

Synopsis: Partners in marriage and in a plane ferrying business disagree when they have their first child: she seeks domesticity, while he's always absent delivering planes around the world.

Behind the Scenes: After being "discovered" in a cafe across the street from Hollywood High, Lana Turner made her film debut in 1937 and soon became known as the "Sweater Girl" for MGM, the most successful studio of the 1930s. Twenty years later, U-I signed Miss Turner for the leading role in *The Lady Takes a Flyer*, a property purchased in 1956, and originally intended for Clark Gable. The air drama became producer Jack Arnold's third with Jeff, and the actor's first under his new, non-exlusive contract with the studio.

Location filming included scenes at a military base outside Phoenix, Arizona, where the air force maintained hundreds of surplus World War II planes. After Maggie marries Mike, Miss Turner's form-flitting flight gear matches that worn by her costar. *Motion Picture Exhibitor* reported that, "Lana Turner and Jeff Chandler make a good pair in this drama."[161]

Reviews: "A lusty, rollicking comedy drama with the sole aim of entertaining has been turned out in *The Lady Takes a Flyer*."—*Film Daily*, January 27, 1958.

"Lana Turner delightfully romps through this sparkling domestic adventure drama that is as modern as a sack dress and is entertaining from beginning to end."—*The Hollywood Reporter*, January 14, 1958.

Additional Reviews: *Boxoffice*, 01/20/58; *Los Angeles Times*, 02/28/58; *Motion Picture Herald*, 01/18/58; *The New York Times*, 01/30/58; *Variety*, 01/14/58.

Among the Top-Grossing Films of 1958: $1,000,000[162]

Comments by Jeff Chandler: "If every woman pilot wore clothes like Lana's, our airports would be more crowded than the Hollywood Freeway in a Sunday afternoon jam."[163]

Comments by the Film's Star: "All I can say, is that it's the nearest thing I know to wearing a glove all over the body."—*Lana Turner*[164]

Comments by a Fan: "Loved Lana and Jeff."[165]

The Films

Raw Wind in Eden

A Universal-International Picture. © 1958. Released October 1958. Ad line: "Only Here on This Nameless Island Could They Be Male and Female — Nothing Else!" "Jeff was a formidable leading man. He had played 'Cochise,' the head of the Apache Indian Nation, he had played wagon train masters and more. Because of my height, 5'8", I needed a tall, strong leading man. Jeff fit the bill effectively. He made an ordinary script come alive more impressively."— Esther Williams[166] Universal-International production number 1864. Aka "The Islander." Running time, 93 minutes; Eastmancolor (CinemaScope); Drama.

Ratings: *The Motion Picture Guide*, ☆½; *Leonard Maltin's Movie and Video Guide*, ☆☆½; *New York Daily News*, ☆☆½; *Halliwell's Film Guide*, 0

Credits: Produced by William Alland; directed by Richard Wilson; assistant director, Terry Nelson; screenplay by Elizabeth and Richard Wilson, based on an unpublished story by Dan Lundberg and Elizabeth Wilson; music by Hans J. Salter; musical supervision by Joseph Gershenson; art direction by Alexander Golitzen and Alfred Ybarra; set decoration by Russell A. Gausman; make-up by Bud Westmore; sound by Leslie I. Carey and Umberto Picistrelli; cinematography by Enzo Serafin; film editing by Russell Schoengarth.

Cast: Esther Williams (Laura), Jeff Chandler (Mark Moore, Scott Moorehouse), Rossana Podesta (Costanza Varno), Carlos Thompson (Wally Drucker), Rik Battaglia (Gavino), Eduardo de Filippo (Urbano Varno).

Synopsis: When their plane crashes in the Mediterranean, a fashion model and a playboy are stranded on an island with the lone wolf who rescued them.

Behind the Scenes: Esther Williams made her film debut in 1942, and by 1947, was one of America's Top Ten Box-Office Stars. Publicity at MGM billed Miss Williams, a former model and swimming champion, as "Hollywood's Mermaid," for many of her films included precisely-choreographed underwater ballet sequences. In November 1956, William Alland signed Miss Williams for the starring role in *Raw Wind in Eden*.

After joining Orson Welles's *Mercury Theatre* in the late 1930s, William Alland became the assistant director of that company's radio series, while Richard Wilson acted as its production assistant. Until 1951, Alland worked in many of Mr. Welles's films and radio shows; Wilson in all of them. Projects for director Wilson prior to *Raw Wind in Eden* included *Man with the Gun* (1955) with Robert Mitchum and *The Big Boodle* (1957) with Errol Flynn.

The cast and crew locationed in a remote area off the coast of Italy for five weeks, where workmen built dressing rooms, bathrooms, and a two-story stone house. Further work involved carving out beach coves as well as trails cut into cliffs overlooking the Mediterranean. The beaching and re-launching of a 40-foot boat

Mark Moore (Jeff Chandler) and Laura (Esther Williams) under the spell of their passion in *Raw Wind in Eden* (1958, Universal-International).

became the art director's greatest challenge: the heavy vessel finally moved easily with the help of a cradle, cable, winch and two dozen sweaty hands.

Upon his arrival in Rome en route to location filming, hundreds of movie fans and dozens from the press took Jeff by surprise. Always health-conscious, the star often jogged the few miles to the set, where his wardrobe included slacks by Sy DeVore, footwear by Clarks Goodwins, and shirts by Portofino, Beverly Hills.[167]

When plane-crash survivor Laura (Esther Williams) learns she'll be stranded on an island for five weeks—with a gun-toting man who's on the lam—she hoists a nylon slip as a distress signal. When the hosiery disappears, Mark (Jeff Chandler) helps her raise a petticoat as a second signal. When that garment goes missing, the clothes horse hoists a third piece from her fashionable wardrobe, and wonders: Is the lone wolf a crazy crook? *Film Daily* called the film a "drama of fiery emotions."[168]

Reviews: "The cast is a strong one. Jeff Chandler is a fine actor whatever role he plays, and remains in character throughout."—*Hollywood Citizen-News*, October 22, 1958.

"*Raw Wind in Eden* is a mixture of sophistication, peasantry, romance, mystery and memories."—*Los Angeles Examiner*, October 9, 1958.

Additional Reviews: *The Hollywood Reporter*, 07/22/58; *Los Angeles Times*, 10/09/58; *Monthly Film Bulletin*, 07/58; *Motion Picture Exhibitor*, 08/06/58; *Motion Picture Herald*, 07/26/58; *The New York Times*, 09/20/58; *Variety*, 07/23/58.

Among the Top-Grossing Films of 1958: $1,100,000[169]

Comments by Jeff Chandler: "I was literally bowled over by the big crowd [upon arrival in Rome]. This should be enough to convince everyone that Hollywood is still a live force in the world."[170]

The Jayhawkers

A Paramount Picture. © 1959. Released October 1959. Ad line: "Against the Background of a Turbulent Era When Civil War Was a Flaming Cloud on History's Horizon... A Tremendous Motion Picture!" Running time, 110 minutes; Technicolor (VistaVision); Western.

Ratings: *The Motion Picture Guide*, ☆☆; *Leonard Maltin's Movie and Video Guide*, ☆☆½; *New York Daily News*, ☆☆☆; *Halliwell's Film Guide*, 0

Credits: Produced by Melvin Frank and Norman Panama; directed by Melvin Frank; written by Melvin Frank, Joseph Petracca, Frank Fenton and A. I. Bezzerides; music by Jerome Moross; art direction by Roland Anderson and Hal Pereira; set decorations by Sam Comer and Darrell Silvera; costume design by Edith Head; sound by Lyle Figland and Winston Leverett; cinematography by Loyal Griggs; film editing by Everett Douglas.

Cast: Jeff Chandler (Luke Darcy), Fess Parker (Cam Bleeker), Nicole Maurey (Jeanne Dubois), Henry Silva (Lordan), Herbert Rudley (Gov. Col. Wm. Clayton), Frank de Kova (Evans), Don Megowan (China), Leo Gordon (Jake), Shari Lee Bernath (Marthe), Jimmy Carter (Paul).

Synopsis: A lawless, Napoleonic-like raider envisions ruling pre–Civil War Kansas as the territory moves toward statehood.

Behind the Scenes: Melvin Frank and Norman Panama first collaborated on a play while attending college in their native Chicago, and by 1938, were Hollywood-bound. They began writing for radio shows such as *Command Performance* and *The Bob Hope Show*. Their first film collaboration, *My Favorite Blonde* (1942), produced one of Bob Hope's best motion pictures and launched their career. Their joint efforts included comedies for Cary Grant, Dick Powell and Danny Kaye as well as *The Trap* (1959), a thriller for Paramount starring Richard Widmark.

On loan-out from U-I for *The Jayhawkers*, Jeff costarred with French-born Nicole Maurey and Fess Parker, an unknown when signed by Walt Disney in 1954 to star in the television program *Davy Crockett*. Jeff's able support included Henry Silva, a trigger-happy hatchet man zeroed in on Fess Parker. *Motion Picture Exhibitor* wrote that *The Jayhawkers* was a "good action entry."[171]

Reviews: "Large-scale outdoor action drama of ambition and conflict."—*Film Daily*, October 15, 1959.

Additional Reviews: *The Hollywood Reporter*, 10/15/59; *Los Angeles Times*, 10/06/59; *Monthly Film Bulletin*, 02/60; *Motion Picture Herald*, 10/17/59; *Variety*, 10/15/59.

Among the Top-Grossing Films of 1959: $450,000 (as of October)[172]

Comments by the Producer-Director-Writer: "The power-mad character has always threatened human freedom. We had long wanted to use this theme in a story about the American past, and when we found this story, it clicked. Of course, it's fictionalized but the conflicts are not. Jeff Chandler plays Luke Darcy, a frontier Napoleon who is defeated by a French woman, Nicole Maurey. She has fled tyranny in Europe and is not about to turn her Kansas homestead into a doormat for despots."—*Melvin Frank*[173]

Costar Comments: "Jeff was very easy to work with, very approachable—a guy. A movie star by profession. Gregory Peck was the same way. Gregory Peck could have been an architect, a teacher. They were different in personality, but took themselves seriously. Being an actor wasn't such a big deal, it was a job, a job like any other. They liked what they did and they enjoyed it."—*Henry Silva*[174]

The Mating Game

A Metro-Goldwyn-Mayer Picture. © 1959. Released March 1959. Ad line: "Filmed on Location in the Haystack!" Aka "Noah's Ark." Running time, 96 minutes; Metrocolor (CinemaScope); Comedy.

Ratings: *The Motion Picture Guide*, ☆☆☆; *Leonard Maltin's Movie and Video Guide*, ☆☆☆; *New York Daily News*, ☆☆☆; *Halliwell's Film Guide*, 0

The Films

Credits: Produced by Phillip Barry Jr.; directed by George Marshall; assistant director, Al Jennings; screenplay by William Roberts, based on the book *The Darling Buds of May* by H. E. Bates (Boston: Little, Brown, 1958); music by Jeff Alexander; art direction by Malcolm Brown and William A. Horning; set decorations by Henry Grace and Arthur Krams; hair styles by Sydney Guilaroff; make-up by William Tuttle; costume design by Helen Rose; cinematography by Robert Bronner; film editing by John McSweeney Jr.

Cast: Debbie Reynolds (Mariette Larkin), Tony Randall (Lorenzo Charlton), Paul Douglas (Pop Larkin), Fred Clark (Oliver Kelsey), Una Merkel (Ma Larkin), Phillip Ober (Wendell Burnshaw), Phillip Coolidge (Rev. Osgood), Charles Lane (Bigelow), Trevor Bardette (Chief Guthrie), Bill Smith (Barney), Addison Powell (DeGroot), Rickey Murray (Lee Larkin), Donald Losby (Grant Larkin), Cheryl Bailey (Victoria Larkin), Caryl Bailey (Susan Larkin).

Behind the Scenes: Jeff Alexander and Jeff Chandler composed "cues" (the individual musical sequences that make up a film's score) for the romantic comedy *The Mating Game*.[175] In 1948, when the Jeff Alexander Orchestra and Chorus handled the music for radio's *Amos 'n' Andy*, the arranger-composer had already provided background music for half a dozen motion picture studios. In April 1951, Alexander and Chandler worked on a radio broadcast of *Hollywood Star Playhouse*; Alexander in charge of the music, Chandler its star.

Chandler last worked with director George Marshall in *Pillars of the Sky*, where on location, Chandler worked briefly on the title song for that film. Circumstances beyond his control, however, prevented him from completing the song, one that would have followed the songs "Foxfire" and "Six Bridges to Cross."

The soundtrack identified each cast member with a specific instrument such as the piccolo with Debbie Reynolds; the trumpet with Fred Clark. Debbie Reynolds, onscreen from 1950 and a Star of Tomorrow, 1952, recorded the song "The Mating Game" on MGM Records. The *Motion Picture Exhibitor* proclaimed the film to be, "highly amusing."[176]

Reviews: "*The Mating Game* is one of the funniest pictures I've ever seen."—Jack Moffitt, *The Hollywood Reporter*, February 18, 1959.

"*The Mating Game* runs on laughter."—*Los Angeles Times*, March 1, 1959.

Additional Reviews: *Film Daily*, 02/18/59; *Monthly Film Bulletin*, 06/59; *Motion Picture Herald*, 02/21/59; *The New York Times*, 04/30/59; *Variety*, 02/18/59.

Among the Top-Grossing Films of 1959: $2,500,000 (as of March)[177]

A Stranger in My Arms

A Universal-International Picture. © 1959. Released February 1959. Ad line: "From the Passion-Dipped Pen of Robert Wilder, Author of *Written on the Wind*." "Jeff was

Jeff Chandler

a sterling sort of fellow, an honest man, kindness itself. More than Jeff Chandler, he was Ira Grossel, a nice human being."—*Peter Graves*[178] Universal-International production number 1879. Aka "And Ride a Tiger." Running time, 88 minutes; black & white (CinemaScope); Drama.

Ratings: *The Motion Picture Guide*, ☆☆½; *Leonard Maltin's Movie and Video Guide*, ☆☆½; *New York Daily News*, ☆☆☆; *Halliwell's Film Guide*, 0

Credits: Produced by Ross Hunter; directed by Helmut Kautner; assistant directors, Phil Bowles and Wilbur Mosier; screenplay by Peter Berneis, based on the book *And Ride a Tiger* by Robert Wilder (New York: Putnam, 1951); musical supervision by Joseph Gershenson; art direction by Alexander Golitzen and Richard H. Riedel; set decorations by Russell A. Gausman and Julia Heron; hair styles by Larry Germain; make-up by Bud Westmore; costume design by Bill Thomas; sound by Leslie I. Carey and Robert Pritchard; cinematography by William H. Daniels; film editing by Frank Gross.

Widow Christina Beasley (June Allyson) and test pilot Yarnell (Jeff Chandler) in *A Stranger in My Arms* (1959, Universal-International).

Cast: June Allyson (Christina Beasley), Jeff Chandler (Yarnell), Sandra Dee (Pat Beasley), Charles Coburn (Vance), Mary Astor (Mrs. Beasley), Peter Graves (Donald), Conrad Nagel (Harley Beasley), Hayden Rorke (Marcus), Reita Green (Bessie Logan).

Synopsis: An Air Force Major falls in love with the wife of a buddy who took his own life during the Korean War, and helps her face up to a domineering mother-in-law who must have her dead son a hero, at any cost.

Behind the Scenes: In October 1957, U-I signed June Allyson for *A Stranger in My Arms*. Onscreen from 1943, Miss Allyson became one of America's Top Ten Box-Office Stars in 1955, after the success of a number of musicals at MGM in the 1940s and U-I's *The Glenn Miller Story* (1953). Support for *A Stranger in My Arms* included Charles Coburn, rising star Sandra Dee as well as silent and sound film star Mary Astor.

In production through late 1957, *A Stranger in My Arms* became Ross Hunter's seventh with Jeff. Hunter, who became U-I's most reliable moneymaker with the drama *Magnificent Obsession* (1954), received support from William H. Daniels, responsible for the Academy award-nominated cinematography in *Cat on a Hot Tin Roof* (1958).

After becoming the controlling stockholders of Universal in 1952, Decca Records consolidated with Music Corporation of America (MCA) in 1959. U-I released *A Stranger in My Arms* in February that year, and MCA purchased the studio. The transition included the temporary closure of U-I as they reevaluated what the public wanted to see. "As with other recent Universal releases," wrote the Editor of *Variety*, the industry's most important trade journal, "a refusal of customary trade reviewing courtesies forced *Variety* to catch [the film] after actual public exhibition began. To exhibitors, let it be pointed out that the tardy publication is not this paper's fault."[179]

Reviews: "The picture is a tribute to the writer, producer, director and cast. It will entertain all who enjoy fine moving drama."—*Hollywood Citizen-News*, March 10, 1959.

Additional Reviews: *Los Angeles Times*, 03/05/59; *Monthly Film Bulletin*, 03/59; *The New York Times*, 03/04/59; *Variety*, 03/12/59.

Costar Comments: "U-I offered me a cameo roll in *A Stranger in My Arms*. It was a nice scene with Jeff and me in a raft at sea where I tried to fight him and jump overboard."—*Peter Graves*[180]

Ten Seconds to Hell

A United Artists Picture. © 1959. Released July 1959. Ad line: "Danger: Don't Touch! Five Tons of Live Blockbuster—Daring a Man to Touch its Fuse!" Aka "Six-To-

One," "The Phoenix," "The Extra Edge." Running time, 93 minutes; black & white; Drama.

Ratings: *The Motion Picture Guide*, ☆☆½; *Leonard Maltin's Movie and Video Guide*, ☆☆½; *New York Daily News*, ☆☆½ *Halliwell's Film Guide*, 0

Credits: Produced by Michael Carreras; directed by Robert Aldrich; screenplay by Robert Aldrich and Teddi Sherman, based on the book *The Phoenix* by Lawrence P. Bachmann (London: Collins, 1955); music by Kenneth V. Jones; art direction by Ken Adam; sound by Heinz Garbowski; cinematography by Ernest Laszlo; film editing by James Needs and Henry Richardson.

Cast: Jeff Chandler (Karl Wirtz), Jack Palance (Koertner), Martine Carol (Margot), Robert Cornthwaite (Loeffler), Dave Willock (Tillig), Wes Addy (Sulke), Jimmy Goodwin (Globke), Virginia Baker (Frau Bauer), Richard Wattis (Maj. Haven), Nancy Lee (Ruth Sulke).

Synopsis: A post–World War II bomb squad in Berlin make a pact to pool half their pay; after six months, their savings are to be split among whoever is left.

Behind the Scenes: Robert Aldrich started his career in Hollywood during the 1940s as assistant to notable directors such as Charlie Chaplin and Lewis Milestone. He made his directorial debut in 1953, followed by awards in 1955 and 1956 from the Film Festivals in Venice and Berlin.

Berlin, badly damaged by Allied bombing during World War II, served as the backdrop for *Ten Seconds to Hell*. Littered with hundreds of unexploded bombs, the city employed a bomb disposal unit that rendered harmless 8,500 bombs since the end of the war, and diffused a 500-pound blockbuster 200 yards from the Hotel Am Zoo that housed the actors, producer and director, nine days into location filming.[181]

In late March 1958 and with the help of its producer, Jeff made personal appearances in Hanover, Germany, for the opening of *Drango*. Hampered by severe cold and gale winds, however, an old back ailment kept him from returning to the set of *Ten Seconds to Hell* for four days in early April 1958. The average daily temperature for the late winter and early spring in Berlin is about half that of Palm Springs, where Jeff went for a "winter break" once filming ended. *Motion Picture Exhibitor* called the film a "suspenseful drama."[182]

Reviews: "Drama of ticking excitement set in post-war Berlin. Solid performances." —*Film Daily*, July 15, 1959.

"U-A's *Ten Seconds to Hell* is off-beat enough and well enough done to merit a nod." —*Los Angeles Times*, September 18, 1959.

Additional Reviews: *The Hollywood Reporter*, 07/15/59; *Monthly Film Bulletin*, 06/59; *Motion Picture Herald*, 07/18/59; *The New York Times*, 07/18/59; *Variety*, 07/15/59.

Comments by Jeff Chandler: "When I was a boy back in P.S. [Public School]

181, who would have believed my acting ambitions would carry me so far from home. Finally, when Berlin got too lonely, I put in a long-distance call—just to hear familiar sounds emanating from the Brown Derby at Hollywood and Vine!"[183]

Thunder in the Sun

A Paramount Picture. © 1959. Released May 1959. Ad line: "The Brawling, Sprawling Story of a Proud People's Way West!" Aka "Between the Thunder and the Sun," "The Gun and the Arrow." Running time, 81 minutes; Technicolor; Western.

Ratings: *The Motion Picture Guide*, ☆½; *Leonard Maltin's Movie and Video Guide*, ☆☆½; *New York Daily News*, ☆☆☆; *Halliwell's Film Guide*, 0

Credits: Produced by Clarence Greene; directed by Russell Rouse; assistant directors, Bert Chervin and William Reineck; screenplay by Russell Rouse, based on an original story by Guy Trosper and James Hill, as adapted by Stewart Stern; music by Cyril Mockridge; art direction by Boris Leven; costume design by Charles Le Maire; cinematography by Stanley Cortez; film editing by Chester W. Schaeffer; choreography by Pedro de Cordoba.

Cast: Susan Hayward (Gabrielle Dauphin), Jeff Chandler (Lon Bennett), Jacques Bergerac (Pepe Dauphin), Blanche Yurka (Louise Dauphin), Carl Esmond (Andre Dauphin), Fortunio Bonanova (Fernando Christophe), Bertrand Castelli (Edmond Duquette), Felix Locher (Danielle), Veda Ann Borg (Marie).

Synopsis: A group of French Basques, impoverished by the Napoleonic Wars, migrate to California in 1847 with the dream of starting a new life and reestablishing their vineyards.

Behind the Scenes: Clarence Greene and Russell Rouse began working together in the mid–1940s after leaving their native New York, forming a partnership not unlike Melvin Frank and Norman Panama. Actors such as Glenn Ford, Ray Milland, and Edmund O'Brien starred in their sometimes out-of-the-ordinary joint efforts. Their writing collaboration resulted in an Academy award-nomination for *The Well* (1951) and an Academy award for *Pillow Talk* (1959).

Susan Hayward made her screen debut in 1937, became a Top Ten Box-Office Star by 1952, and received an Academy award for Best Actress in *I Want to Live!* (1958). Location filming for *Thunder in the Sun* took the actress, the cast and crew to five states: Arizona, California, Colorado, Nevada and New Mexico. The film also included actors from five countries: Susan Hayward and Jeff Chandler (U.S.), Jacques Bergerac (France), Blanche Yurka (Czechoslovakia), Carl Esmond (Austria) and Fortunio Bonanova (Spain). The *Hollywood Citizen-News* called the film "an offbeat picture, a powerfully exciting, suspense filled drama."[184]

Reviews: "Outdoor adventure drama with unique story appeal and sturdy marquee cast. A solid grosser."—*Film Daily*, March 25, 1959.

Wagon train scout Lon Bennett (Jeff Chandler) and Gabrielle Dauphin (Susan Hayward) in *Thunder in the Sun* (1959, Paramount).

"Off-beat entry has angles."—*Motion Picture Exhibitor*, April 8, 1959.

Additional Reviews: *Boxoffice*, 04/06/59; *The Hollywood Reporter*, 03/23/59; *Los Angeles Times*, 04/30/59; *Monthly Film Bulletin*, 01/12/60; *Motion Picture Herald*, 03/28/59; *The New York Times*, 08/09/58; *Variety*, 03/25/59.

Among the Top-Grossing Films of 1959: $1,500,000 (as of April)[185]

Comments by Jeff Chandler: "Our story is based on fact. Official records were kept in Salt Lake City and Fort Laramie, Wyoming, listing all wagon trains going West. And the Basques from the French-Spanish border actually brought over the vine plants that started the wine industry in California."[186]

The Plunderers

An Allied Artists Picture. © 1960. Released November 1960. Ad line: "There was *Shane*, *High Noon*, *Red Bravo* ... Now the New Giant of Western Suspense!" Allied

The Films

Artists production number 7399. Running time, 94 minutes; black & white; Drama.

Ratings: *The Motion Picture Guide*, ☆☆☆; *Leonard Maltin's Movie and Video Guide*, ☆☆½; *New York Daily News*, ☆☆; *Halliwell's Film Guide*, 0

Credits: Produced and directed by Joseph Pevney; associate producer, Jess Rand; executive producer, Scott R. Dunlap; assistant director, Bob Saunders; adapted from a story and screenplay by Bob Barbash; music by Leonard Rosenman; music editing by Richard C. Harris; art direction by David Milton; production manager, Edward Morey Jr.; set decoration by Joseph Kish; make-up by Emile LaVigne; wardrobe by Norah Sharpe and Roger Weinberg; sound by Ralph Butler and Charles Schelling; cinematography by Eugene Polito; film editing by Tom McAdoo.

Cast: Jeff Chandler (Sam Christy), John Saxon (Rondo), Dolores Hart (Ellie Walters), Marsha Hunt (Kate Miller), Jay C. Flippen (Sheriff McCauley), Ray Stricklyn (Jeb), James Westerfield (Mike Baron), Dee Pollock (Davy), Roger Torrey (Mule), Harvey Stephens (Doc Fuller), Vaughn Taylor (Jess Walters), Joseph Hamilton (Abilene), Ray Ferrell (Billy Miller), William Challee (1st citizen), Ken Patterson (2nd citizen), Ella Ethridge (Mrs. Phelps).

Synopsis: Four teenage hoodlums terrorize a peaceful western town, until a one-armed Civil War hero steps in to put a stop to their brazen antics.

Behind the Scenes: In August 1959, three years after Earlmar Productions' singleton venture *Drango*, Jeff formed August Productions and announced *The Plunderers* as its first project. Originally a Dragon production for Gold Medal studios in the east, the project headed west, where it made the rounds at Columbia and 20th before landing at Allied Artists. In January 1960, Steve Broidy, President of Allied, signed Jeff to a contract, but with a Screen Actors Guild strike called in March against seven of the eight major studios—including Allied—production began in May, a month and a day after the strike ended.

Broidy began his career at Monogram—the original corporate name of Allied—in 1933 as sales manager and became its president in 1945. That year, Jeffrey Bernerd produced for Monogram *Black Market Babies* with Marjorie Hoshelle Chandler followed by three more with the actress in 1946: *Behind the Mask*, *The Red Dragon* and *The Strange Mr. Gregory*. Scott R. Dunlap, executive producer on *The Plunderers*, began his career in 1915, worked in every capacity of movie making and, in 1947, became Executive Assistant to Broidy.

The film, director Joseph Pevney's ninth with Jeff, featured a teenage rat pack: Ray Stricklyn, Dee Pollock, Roger Torrey and John Saxon, a Star of Tomorrow, 1959. Marsha Hunt, a former operatic soprano and John Robert Powers model, widely know for her work in behalf of World Refugee year, celebrated her Silver Anniversary in Hollywood with the picture's release. "Joseph Pevney's direction achieves an atmosphere charged with suspense," wrote *Motion Picture Herald*.[187]

Reviews: "Powerfully played melodrama of the old west in which the anatomy of fear and the impact of violence are searchingly explored and vividly demonstrated."—*Film Daily*, November 4, 1960.

"Performances are good and action sequences well handled."—*Motion Picture Exhibitor*, November 9, 1960.

Additional Reviews: *Boxoffice*, 11/14/60; *The Hollywood Reporter*, 11/04/60; *Los Angeles Times*, 04/06/61; *Monthly Film Bulletin*, 01/61; *Motion Picture Herald*, 11/12/60; *Variety*, 11/09/60.

Costar Comments: "He [Jeff Chandler] was widely liked and admired. A very dear man and a generous, unassuming actor."—*Marsha Hunt*[188]

Comments by Jeff Chandler: "It's post–Civil War. Not a western, though the locale is the West—Texas in 1868. The central figures are four kids, juvenile delinquents on horseback, who ride into a town and proceed to take it over. In fact, they turn it practically into a siege. I play a veteran who has lost the use of his right arm and is resigned to a half-existence, with an it's-none-of-my-business attitude, until I see my mistake and pitch in."[189]

A Story of David

A British Lion Picture. © 1960. Released Theatrically Abroad: April 1961. Released Domestically on Television: November 1962. Ad Line: "The Sword That Challenged the Iron Might of Tyranny!" Aka "David the Outlaw" and "David the Hunted." Running time, 104 minutes; Eastmancolor; Biblical Drama.

Rating: *The Motion Picture Guide*, ☆☆

Credits: Produced by George Pitcher; directed by Herbert (Bob) McNaught; screenplay by Gerry Day and Terence Maple; music by Kenneth V. Jones; sound by Arthur Ridout; art director, Allan Harris; photography by Arthur Ibbetson.

Cast: Jeff Chandler (David), Basil Sydney (Saul), David Knight (Johnathan), Peter Arne (Doeg), Barbara Shelley (Abigail), Donald Pleasence (Nabal), Robert Brown (Jashobeam), Richard O'Sullivan (Abiathar), David Davies (Abner), Martin Wyldeck (Hezro), John Van Eyssen (Joab), Angela Browne (Michal), Zena Marshall (Naomi), Charles Carson (Ahimelech), Alec Mango (Kudruh).

Synopsis: A dramatization of the middle years in the life of David and his opposition to King Saul for the throne of Israel.

Behind the Scenes: On January 25, 1949, David Ben-Gurion became Israel's first Prime Minister. Later that year, U-I released *Sword in the Desert*, the first motion picture about the birth of the modern state of Israel. In 1960, Prime Minister Ben-Gurion received Jeff Chandler during location filming *A Story of David*, the first British-made Biblical spectacle and the first motion picture with a Biblical background to be filmed in the Holy Land.[190]

The Films

Other Biblical dramas started at the time included *King of Kings* (1961) filmed in Spain and starred Jeffrey Hunter. *A Story of David* followed a similar pattern to that of *Macbeth* (1960), filmed in Scotland and London by director George Schaefer for NBC-TV's *Hallmark Hall of Fame*. Director Bob McNaught filmed *A Story of David* so that it could be released domestically on television and abroad on the wide-screen in theaters.

The film's origins began in 1956 when Screen Gems announced that William Goetz would produce a television series *The Book of Books* based on Biblical stories dealing with figures such as David, Peter, and others. The series never aired, and in 1959, ABC-TV announced that Goetz would produce two hour-long biblical dramas based on the life of David for ABC-TV. The dramas were produced, not by Goetz, but by George Pitcher.

Jeff's debut on American television, the result of a deal Goetz made with ABC-TV, was scheduled for the Fall season of 1960–61, along with the television debut of Gary Cooper on NBC's *Project 20*, Danny Kaye's variety show for CBS-TV, and NBC's *Macbeth*. ABC postponed the release of *A Story of David* (originally scheduled as a two-part drama *David the Outlaw* and *David the Hunted*), after Jeff's death.

Reviews: "Chandler's portrayal of David was a typical performance by the late actor: one of quiet, understated strength, masculinity and appeal."—*Variety*, November 28, 1962.

"The religious element, handled with ease and reticence, is manifest mainly in the fact that David (Jeff Chandler, a surprisingly moving performance) is sustained by an entirely personal conviction that his actions are guided by the hand of God."—*Monthly Film Bulletin*, August 1962.

Additional Reviews: *ABC Film Review*, 3/61; *Daily Cinema*, 07/62; *Kine Weekly*, 07/62.

Television Nielsen Rating History: November 18, 1962 — 20.6, ABC-TV Premiere.[191]

Comments by Jeff Chandler: "I don't want to make pictures in other countries; I want to stay home. But suddenly there are not enough pictures being made here. All other countries are giving inducements to companies and to players; even a little country like Israel is trying to formulate a plan for subsidy. Our government still taxes the hell out of its people; somebody ought to wake 'em up!"[192]

Comments by a Fan: "I first wrote to Jeff in 1951, and after seeing *Red Ball Express*, I wrote him every seven months or so, and he always replied. I met him eight years later, when he came to London to do interior scenes for *A Story of David*. It was a privilege to have shared hugs, laughter and friendship with such a fascinating man."[193]

Jeff Chandler

Return to Peyton Place

A 20th Century–Fox Picture. © 1961. Released May 1961. Ad line: "It Begins Where *Peyton Place* Left Off!" Running time, 122 minutes; Color by De Luxe (CinemaScope); Drama.

Ratings: *The Motion Picture Guide*, ☆☆½; *Leonard Maltin's Movie and Video Guide*, ☆☆; *New York Daily News*, ☆☆☆; *Halliwell's Film Guide*, ☆

Credits: Produced by Jerry Wald; associate producer, Curtis Harrington; directed by Jose Ferrer; assistant director, David Hall; screenplay by Ronald Alexander, based on the book *Return to Peyton Place* by Grace Metalious (New York: J. Messner, 1959); music by Franz Waxman; art direction by Hans Peters and Jack Martin Smith; set decorations by Fred Maclean and Walter M. Scott; hair styles by Helen Turpin; make-up by Ben Nye; costume design by Don Feld; sound by Warren B. Delaplain and Bernard Freericks; cinematography by Charles G. Clarke; film editing by David Bretherton.

Cast: Carol Lynley (Allison MacKenzie), Jeff Chandler (Lewis Jackman), Eleanor Parker (Connie), Mary Astor (Roberta Carter), Robert Sterling (Mike

Author Allison MacKenzie (Carol Lynley) and publisher Lewis Jackman (Jeff Chandler) in *Return to Peyton Place* (1961, 20th Century–Fox).

Rossi), Luciana Paluzzi (Raffaella), Brett Halsey (Ted), Gunnar Hellstrom (Lars), Tuesday Weld (Selena Cross), Kenneth MacDonald (Dexter), Bob Crane (Peter White), Bill Bradley (Mark Steele), Tim Durant (John Smith), Max Showalter (Nick Parker), Pitt Herbert (Mr. Wadley), Warren Parker (Lupus Wolf).

Synopsis: The secrets of a small New England town are revealed when an author's book is published.

Behind the Scenes: Strikes against the major studios by the Writers Guild of America and the Screen Actors Guild in early 1960 held up the production of *Return to Peyton Place*. As a result, the script, originally written for summertime in Maine, went from "hot" to "cold," when the story's summer theater actor became a ski instructor. Production began in December 1960 in the Los Angeles studio, except for location filming of the winter scenes in Northern California. The delays also affected the film's casting as Joan Crawford and Bette Davis were unavailable for the role of Roberta Carter, a part later given to Mary Astor.[194]

Brooklyn-born Jerry Wald, in Hollywood from the 1930s, produced many of the most successful Warner Bros. films of the 1940s. Twice Academy award-nominated Jose Ferrer made his directorial debut in the 1950s, and oversaw the film's creative aspects with the help of Carol Lynley, Tuesday Weld and Brett Halsey, all promising newcomers of the 1960s. *Motion Picture Exhibitor* called the film, "well-made and well-portrayed."[195]

Reviews: "*Return to Peyton Place* is lifted above the average of most romantic melodramas by some fine directorial touches on the part of Jose Ferrer."—*Motion Picture Herald*, May 6, 1961.

"Slick, soap-operatic follow-up to Jerry Wald's earlier hit, though not quite equal of its predecessor."—*The New York Times*, May 6, 1961.

Additional Reviews: *Boxoffice*, 05/08/61; *Film Daily*, 05/02/61; *The Hollywood Reporter*, 05/01/61; *Los Angeles Times*, 05/11/61; *Monthly Film Bulletin*, 06/61; *Variety*, 05/01/61.

Among the Top-Grossing Films of 1961: $3,000,000 (as of May)[196]

Merrill's Marauders

A Warner Bros. Picture. © 1962. Released July 1962. Ad line: "The Men Who 'Couldn't' Go On ... the Mission that 'Couldn't' Be Done... the Picture that Can't Be Forgotten!" Warner Bros. production number 457. Aka "The Marauders." Running time, 98 minutes; Technirama (CinemaScope); War.

Ratings: *The Motion Picture Guide*, ☆☆☆½; *Leonard Maltin's Movie and Video Guide*, ☆☆½; *New York Daily News*, ☆☆☆½; *Halliwell's Film Guide*, 0

Credits: Produced by Milton Sperling; directed by Samuel Fuller; assistant director, William Kissel; story by Samuel Fuller and Milton Sperling, based on the book *The Marauders* by Charlton Ogburn Jr. (New York: Harper & Brothers, Publishers, 1956); music by Howard Jackson; production supervisor, William Magginetti; make-up by Gordon Bau; sound by Francis M. Stahl; cinematography by William Clothier; film editing by Folmar Blangsted.

Cast: Jeff Chandler (Brig. Gen. Merrill), Ty Hardin (Stock), Peter Brown (Bullseye), Andrew Duggan (Maj. Nemey, "Doc"), Will Hutchins (Chowhound), Claude Akins (Sgt. Kolowicz), John Hoyt (Gen. Stilwell), Charles Briggs (Muley), Chuck Roberson (officer), Chuck Hayward (officer), Paul Edwards (Chris), Jack C. Williams (medic), Chuck Hicks (Corp. Doskis), Lt. Col. Sam Wilson (Lt. Col. Bannister), Pancho Magalona (Taggy).

Synopsis: With the threat of the Japanese joining the Germans during World War II, a U.S. Army Brigadier General commands a band of GIs through the Burmese jungle, despite disease, fatigue, and death.

Behind the Scenes: Milton Sperling produced a number of movies for Gary Cooper including *Blowing Wild* (1953) and *The Court-Martial of Billy Mitchell* (1955), a military drama based on a historical incident. Samuel Fuller made his directorial debut in the late 1940s and looked forward to working with Cooper, but lost the actor to cancer after production started on the film.

Warner Bros. postponed the release of *Merrill's Marauders* until a year after its star's death; the motion picture became one of Jeff's top-grossing films. "Chandler too infrequently got roles with the kind of masculine plausibility he deserved; he did well with this one," wrote the *New York Herald Tribune*.[197]

Reviews: "Chandler delivers a superb performance, perhaps his best in a career which ended so tragically."—*Motion Picture Herald*, May 23, 1962.

"Jeff Chandler's last role, as Brigadier General Frank Merrill, is one of his best."—*Variety*, May 9, 1962.

Additional Reviews: *Boxoffice*, 05/21/62; *Film Daily*, 05/15/62; *The Hollywood Reporter*, 05/08/62; *Los Angeles Times*, 05/27/62; *Monthly Film Bulletin*, 08/62; *Motion Picture Exhibitor*, 05/16/62; *The New York Times*, 06/14/62.

Among the Top Grossing Films of 1962: $1,500,000 (as of June)[198]

Costar Comments: "Working on *Merrill's Marauders* was tougher than my Army basic training. In '61, Warner Bros. sent a bunch of U.S. actors to Clark Air Force Base in the Philippines to re-fight the Japanese in World War II Burma. We all pretended to be heroes, but the only real hero in that snake-infested jungle was Jeff Chandler. Most Hollywood 'stahs' would have packed it in and returned stateside after suffering injuries similar to his. He stuck it out, sucked it in, and fought to the bloody end. Jeff Chandler gave his life for *Merrill's Marauders*."—*Will Hutchins*[199]

Comments by Jeff Chandler: "The physical stuff is really hard for me. The fighting, the running, the jumping on horses, or climbing a cliff. I have a fear of height, anyway. I get dizzy."[200]

Recordings (Music and Spoken Word)

Entries are in chronological order

Included in the recordings listed immediately below are songs Chandler performed that were written by others, songs he wrote himself, and songs he wrote in collaboration with others. Songwriting credits included in the listings enable the reader to distinguish among these categories. Titles of singles (one song per side) are in quotation marks. Titles of albums are in **bold italics**.

Listed in a separate category (see page 129) are songs Chandler wrote that were recorded by others. This category includes only two songs, "One Desire" and "Six Bridges to Cross." Chandler's spoken word recordings (audio books) are listed in a third category (see page 129).

Musical Recordings by Chandler

"I Should Care" / "More Than Anyone"

Released March 1954. Decca Records 9-29004, format: 45 rpm; 29004, format: 78 rpm.

Ratings: *The Billboard*, Good to Satisfactory; *Down Beat*, Fair.

Credits: Musical direction by Sonny Burke; music conducted by Gordon Jenkins; musical supervision by Joseph Gershenson; orchestra by Victor Young and His Singing Strings; vocal by Jeff Chandler.

Songs: *I Should Care* (Cahn-Stordahl-Weston) • *More Than Anyone* (De Paul-Raye).

Behind the Scenes: Violinist and orchestra leader Victor Young came to Hollywood in the early 1920s and worked with Sid Grauman. He began his career as arranger and composer of movie music a decade later, while audiences heard his orchestral accompaniments on various radio programs such as *The Al Jolson Show*.

Jeff Chandler

After Decca Records' birth in August 1934, the record company's first roster of artists included Bing Crosby and Victor Young. At Decca, Young recorded movie scores and conducted for other Decca artists including Tommy Dorsey and Judy Garland. As a songwriter, Young worked on a number of hits including a collaboration with Sam Lewis that resulted in the song "Street of Dreams," a hit for Bing Crosby (#13, 1933) and Frank Sinatra and the Pied Pipers (#17, 1942).

Like Victor Young, Sonny Burke studied violin as a child. After Burke's orchestra work in New York, he moved to Hollywood where he composed and arranged for film and radio shows such as *Club 88 Starring Peggy Lee*. In order to determine his first record for Decca, U-I arranged for Jeff to sing a number of songs in a public performance, while backed by an orchestra conducted by Sonny Burke. In September 1953, Jeff sang for hundreds of high school and college students at the Balboa Rendezvous Ballroom.

In late November 1953 and with arranger George Jenkins in attendance, Jeff recorded the song "I Should Care." Decca then set-up round-the-clock promotion that included record signings and personal appearances on radio stations throughout Southern California. In the spring of 1954, Jeff became a best-selling artist for the record company and an established crooner when his record sales topped 300,000.

Reviews: *I Should Care*: "Here's a passionate ballad. Chandler belts it out okay." *More Than Anyone*: "Tasteful side, Chandler sings the ballad with nice phrasing."—*The Billboard*[1]

Additional Reviews: *Down Beat*, 04/21/54; *Song Hits*, 07/54.

Comments by Jeff Chandler: "I've been going over hundreds of songs with Sonny [Burke], old and new. We know we have to find something just right for this first record. Unless it's pretty big, I'll just be a movie actor who thinks he can sing."[2]

"That's All She's Waiting to Hear" / "Lamplight"

Released July 1954. Decca Records 9-29175, format: 45 rpm; 29175, format: 78 rpm.

Ratings: *The Billboard*, Good.

Credits: Vocal by Jeff Chandler with orchestra (with The Ralph Brewster Singers on "That's All She's Waiting to Hear").

Songs: *That's All She's Waiting to Hear* (Chandler-Lava) • *Lamplight* (Shelton).

Behind the Scenes: For the song "That's All She's Waiting to Hear," Jeff formed Chandler Music Company and shared writing credits with one of Hollywood's most prolific film composers, William Lava. Lava arrived in Hollywood in the 1930s after working in Chicago where he arranged music for bands and radio. He scored music for hundreds of films at RKO, Republic and Warner Bros. before joining U-I.

Promotion for the recording included Jeff's appearance in June 1954 on the radio show *Juke Box Jury* broadcast nationwide. Played "blind" for a panel that included lyricist and composer Johnny Mercer, the record first received their unanimous vote that it would be a hit before the panel met its recording artist.

Reviews: *That's All She's Waiting to Hear*: "Chandler sells this new ditty with quiet charm." *Lamplight*: "Chandler's name power is enough to get this one some action." — *The Billboard*[3]

Additional Reviews: *Song Hits*, 10/54; *Variety*, 06/23/54.

Comments by Jeff Chandler: "I write a few numbers myself and, as well as singing them on records, I'm able to print the sheet music, too, through a publishing company I've formed."[4]

Jeff Chandler Sings

Released 1954. Decca Records ED 2150, format: extended play 45 rpm.

Credits and Songs: Same as Decca Records 9-29004 and 9-29175.

"Always" / "Everything Happens to Me"

Released November 1954. Decca Records 9-29345, format: 45 rpm; 29345, format: 78 rpm.

Ratings: *The Billboard*, Good.

Credits: Orchestra by Jack Pleis; vocal by Jeff Chandler (with Chorus on "Always").

Songs: *Always* (Berlin) • *Everything Happens to Me* (Dennis-Adair).

Behind the Scenes: Jeff's third song "Always," waxed shortly before production began for *Female on the Beach*, featured the Jack Pleis Orchestra, Decca's house band. Composer, arranger and pianist Jack Pleis recorded albums with his orchestra and worked with other Decca artists such as Theresa Brewer, Kitty Kallen, and The Four Aces.

By only its second week of release, "Always" sold 85,000 copies. Promotion included radio appearances in late November 1954, followed a month later by television appearances and a contest held by *Movieland*. The magazine awarded a number of prizes, including a package to fifty winners of autographed records from six top recording artists: The Ames Brothers, Nat "King" Cole, Vic Damone, Eddie Fisher, Johnnie Ray and Jeff Chandler.

Reviews: *Always*: "Another first-rate job here and on another fine standard piece of material." *Everything Happens to Me*: "Flick star Chandler lends his commercial sound and selling ability to one of the better standard tunes." — *The Billboard*[5]

Additional Reviews: *Variety*, 11/17/54.

Comments by Jeff Chandler: "The receptions from the kids at these teenage affairs have been wonderful. Jeff Chandler the actor or Jeff Chandler the singer is something only my first records will prove."[6]

"When Spring Comes" / "My Prayer"

Released February 1955. Decca Records 9-29405, format: 45 rpm; 29405, format: 78 rpm.
    Ratings: *The Billboard*, Good.
    Credits: Orchestra by Jack Pleis; vocal by Jeff Chandler.
    Songs: *My Prayer* (Kennedy-Boulanger) • *When Spring Comes* (Lippman-Dee).
    Reviews: *When Spring Comes*: "Pretty tune receives a quiet reading from the movie star." *My Prayer*: "The evergreen is sung nicely by Chandler." — *The Billboard*[7]
    Additional Reviews: *Down Beat*, 03/09/55.

"Foxfire" / "Shaner Maidel"

Released June 1955. Decca Records 9-29532, format: 45 rpm; 29532, format: 78 rpm.
    Ratings: *The Billboard*, Good; *Down Beat*, Three-Star Disc.
    Credits: Orchestra by Sonny Burke; vocal by Jeff Chandler with The Rhythmaires.
    Songs: *Foxfire* (Mancini-Chandler) • *Shaner Maidel* (Duna-Shaw).
    Reviews: *Foxfire*: "That very good movie actor, Jeff Chandler, sings pleasantly, albeit with little 'fire,' on the haunting theme from his new picture, *Foxfire*." *Shaner Maidel*: "Chandler warbles sincerely on a warm folk ditty with a soothing minor melody." — *The Billboard*[8]
    Additional Reviews: *Down Beat*, 06/29/55.

"A Little Love Can Go a Long Long Way" / "Only the Very Young"

Released July 1955. Decca Records 9-29600, format: 45 rpm; 29600, format: 78 rpm.
    Ratings: *The Billboard*, Good; *Down Beat*, Four-Star Disc.
    Credits: Orchestra by Sonny Burke; vocal by Jeff Chandler.
    Songs: *A Little Love Can Go a Long Long Way* (Fain-Webster) • *Only the Very Young* (Torme).

Reviews: *A Little Love Can Go a Long Long Way*: "Chandler warbles attractively on a tune from the Piper Laurie movie musical *Ain't Misbehavin*.'" *Only the Very Young*: "The Universal-International picture star contributes an okay vocal on a lovely Mel Torme ballad with effective lyrics."—*The Billboard*[9]

Additional Reviews: *Down Beat*, 08/24/55; *Variety*, 07/13/55.

Comments by Jeff Chandler: "Sonny (Burke) should take all the praise for breaking me into the disc world, and I'm certainly grateful to him for adding another string to my bow."[10]

"Half of My Heart" / "Hold Me"

Released July 1957. Liberty Records F-55092, format: 45 rpm.
Ratings: *The Billboard*, Good to Excellent.
Credits: Vocal by Jeff Chandler with The Spencer-Hagen Orchestra.
Songs: *Half of My Heart* (Duning-Washington) • *Hold Me* (Schuster-Oppenheim-Little).
Reviews: *Half of My Heart*: "Disk is tastefully produced, not overburdened with instrumentation, and Chandler's vocal is sincere." *Hold Me*: "The great oldie, sung with heart and affecting simplicity by Chandler."—*The Billboard*[11]
Additional Reviews: *Variety*, 07/24/57.

Jeff Chandler Sings to You

Released September 1957. Liberty Records LRP-3067, format: 33⅓ rpm.
Ratings: *The Billboard*, Excellent.
Credits: Produced by Simon Jackson; music arranged and orchestration by Earle Hagen and Herbert Spencer; engineers, Allan Emig and Sherwood Hall; vocal by Jeff Chandler.
Songs: Side One: *A Lovely Way to Spend an Evening* (McHugh-Adamson) • *Hold Me* (Schuster-Oppenheim-Little) • *With My Eyes Wide Open I'm Dreaming* (Gordon-Revel) • *The More I See You* (Warren-Gordon) • *To You* (Dorsey-Shapiro-Davis) • *You and I* (Chandler).
Side Two: *I'll String Along with You* (Warren-Dubin) • *Welcome Stranger* (Mercer) • *I Wished on the Moon* (Ranger-Parker) • *Where am I* (Levey) • *Tell Me* (Chandler) • *Let's Get Lost* (McHugh-Loesser).
Behind the Scenes: Earle Hagen began his career in Hollywood in 1947, handled the orchestration with Maurice de Packh for *Two Flags West* and, by the early 1950s, composed for both film and television. Herbert Spencer began his career in the mid–1930s working at 20th Century–Fox where, under the musical direction of Alfred Newman, he arranged orchestration for numerous films. Together, Her-

bert Spencer and Earle Hagen's credits included *Gentlemen Prefer Blondes* (1953), *There's No Business Like Show Business* (1954), *Carousel* (1956) as well as the television program *Make Room for Daddy*.

Higher and Higher (1943) marked Frank Sinatra's starring debut in which he sang "A Lovely Way to Spend an Evening," the first track on *Jeff Chandler Sings to You*. Other selections are two introduced in the movies, including "The More I See You," from *Diamond Horseshoe* (1945), orchestration in the film by Herbert Spencer; two from Bing Crosby, including "I Wished on the Moon," from *The Big Broadcast of 1936* (1935); two from Dick Powell, including "Let's Get Lost," from *Happy Go Lucky* (1942); and two originals written by Jeff.

Reviews: "Chandler's first Liberty LP should sell briskly on the strength of the cover photo alone. Chandler applies his pleasant baritone to a group of leisurely paced romantic ballads. Actor has powerful fan following and this could be a sleeper."—*The Billboard*[12]

Additional Reviews: *Variety*, 09/18/57.

Warm and Easy

Released May 1958. Liberty Records LRP-3074, format: 33⅓ rpm.

Ratings: *The Billboard*, Good Potential—Will Sell.

Credits: Music arranged and orchestration by Earle Hagen and Herbert Spencer; vocal by Jeff Chandler.

Songs: Side One: I've Got My Love to Keep Me Warm (Berlin) • It Could Happen to You (Van Heusen-Burke) • You're a Sweet Little Headache (Robin-Rainger) • Lovely to Look At (Kern-McHugh-Fields) • Please Make a Pass at My Heart (Chandler) • Should I (Brown-Freed).

Side Two: *Somebody Loves Me* (Gershwin-MacDonald-De Sylva) • *One, Two, Button Your Shoe* (Johnston-Burke) • *Stay as Sweet as You Are* (Gordon-Revel) • *Love is Just Around the Corner* (Gensler-Robin) • *Coincidentally* (Chandler) • *It's Been So Long* (Adamson-Donaldson).

Behind the Scenes: *Warm and Easy* featured four movie selections originally sung by Bing Crosby as well as Dick Powell's "I've Got My Love to Keep Me Warm" from *On the Avenue* (1937); orchestration in the film by Herbert Spencer. Jeff penned two of the album's other selections including "Please Make a Pass at My Heart," a tune he hummed during a scene in *Female on the Beach*. The album also included the song "It Could Happen to You" from the Paramount musical *And the Angels Sing* (1943); music directed in the film by Victor Young. Young, who died of a heart attack just months before the release of Jeff's first album, received twenty-two Academy award-nominations during his career, including a posthumous Academy award for the soundtrack to *Around the World in Eighty Days* (1956).

Reviews: "Chandler sounds somewhat like Sinatra, as he delivers 10 standards and two originals in warm and easy style. Strong orchestra backing helps. His movie fans should go for the set. Attractive cover."—*The Billboard*[13]

Additional Reviews: *Variety*, 06/18/58.

SONGS WRITTEN BY CHANDLER AND RECORDED BY OTHERS

"Six Bridges to Cross"

Released January 1955. A-side: "All of You" (Porter). Decca Records 9-29402, format: 45 rpm; 29402, format: 78 rpm.

Ratings: *The Billboard*, Good.

Credits: Vocal by Sammy Davis Jr. with orchestra. Music and lyrics by Mancini-Chandler.

Reviews: "A pleasant interpretation of a nice ballad, which should benefit from the movie tie-up."—*The Billboard*[14]

Additional Reviews: *Down Beat*, 02/23/55; *Variety*, 01/19/55.

"One Desire"

Released August 1955. A-side: "Happy-Go-Lucky (Hughes-Herbert). Decca Records 9-29584, format: 45 rpm; 29584, format: 78 rpm.

Ratings: *The Billboard*, Satisfactory; *Down Beat*, Three-Star Disc.

Credits: Orchestra by Sonny Burke; vocal by Gene Boyd. Music and lyrics by Mancini-Chandler.

Reviews: *Happy-Go-Lucky*: "Tune is sung sweetly by the thrush, winner of a diskery contest." *One Desire*: "Another contest winner sings another flicker tune capably."—*The Billboard*[15]

Additional Reviews: *Down Beat*, 09/07/55.

SPOKEN WORD RECORDINGS BY CHANDLER

The Adventures of Tom Sawyer

Released 1960. Audio Book Company C-311, format: 7"—16⅔ rpm, nine records.

Credits: Narration by Jeff Chandler.

Behind the Scenes: Founded in 1952, Audio Books, Inc. introduced the 16⅔ rpm, the record industry's fourth speed (after 78 rpm, 33⅓ rpm and 45 rpm). The twenty-six record volume of the King James version of the New Testament became their first "book." Other releases included tales and poems of Edgar Allen Poe and "The Best of Mark Twain." In early 1956, Audio Book records were changed to resemble that of the 45 rpm; previous records had a three-inch center hole and bore no label copy.[16]

Program Notes: "For the first time, recorded in its entirety and presented with great feeling."[17]

Classic Tales of Adventure & Mystery

Released 1960. Audio Book Company LRC 6025, format: 12" 33⅓ rpm, one record; T-6025, format: reel-to-reel tape; TC-6025, format: cassette tape.
　Credits: Narration by Marvin Miller and Jeff Chandler.
　Program Notes: "Favorite highlights from Jack London's *Call of the Wild* and mysteries from Edgar Allen Poe."[18]

The Best of Mark Twain

Released 1961. Audio Book Company LRC 6013, format: 12" 33⅓ rpm, one record; T-6013, format: reel-to-reel tape; TC-6013, format: cassette tape.
　Credits: Narration by Marvin Miller and Jeff Chandler.
　Program Notes: "The rhythm, the humor, the drama and the pulse of life in the last half of 19th century America, as it is preserved by the pen of Mark Twain."[19]

Call of the Wild

Released 1961. Audio Book Company C-312, format: 7"—16⅔ rpm, four records; LP-C 312, format: 12"—16⅔ rpm, two records.
　Credits: Narration by Jeff Chandler.
　Program Notes: "Here is one of the greatest adventure novels ever written. Here, recorded in its entirety for the first time, is Jack London's story of desperate men and the lure of newfound gold in the Klondike. And the story of Buck, a superb dog who had to learn the ancient laws of the wilderness—or die!"[20]

Radio

Entries are in chronological order

1946

Academy Award (CBS); 07/10/46; episode 16, "Young Mr. Lincoln" adapted by Frank Wilson; directed and produced by Dee Engelbach; musical direction by Leith Stevens; cast: Henry Fonda, Ward Bond, Jeff Chandler (as "Ira Grossel").

Suspense (CBS); 07/18/46; episode 202, "Photo Finish"; directed by William Spier; host, Robert Montgomery; cast: Michael O'Shea, Cathy Lewis, Jerry Hausner, Wally Maher, Jay Novello, Jeff Chandler (as "Ira Grossel").

The Cavalcade of America (NBC); 09/02/46; episode 487, "With Cradle and Clock"; produced and directed by Jack Zoller; cast: Herbert Marshall, Mary Jane Croft, Byron Kane, Martha Wentworth, Ramsey Hill, Lurene Tuttle, Ken Peters, Jeff Chandler (as "Ira Grossel"), Eric Snowden, Dorothy Scott, Gloria Gordon, Francis X. Bushman.

Academy Award (CBS); 09/11/46; episode 25, "Shadow of a Doubt" adapted by Frank Wilson; directed and produced by Dee Engelbach; musical direction by Leith Stevens; cast: Joseph Cotten, June Vincent, Jeff Chandler (as "Ira Grossel").

Academy Award (CBS); 10/16/46; episode 30, "Blood On The Sun" adapted by Frank Wilson; directed and produced by Dee Engelbach; musical direction by Leith Stevens; cast: John Garfield, Jeff Chandler (as "Ira Grossel").

Academy Award (CBS); 11/06/46; episode 33, "Cheers for Miss Bishop" adapted by Frank Wilson; directed and produced by Dee Engelbach; musical direction by Leith Stevens; cast: Olivia de Havilland, Jeff Chandler (as "Ira Grossel").

Academy Award (CBS); 12/18/46; episode 39, "Lost Angel" adapted by Frank Wilson; directed and produced by Dee Engelbach; musical direction by

Jeff Chandler

Leith Stevens; cast: Margaret O'Brien, Marissa O'Brien, Jeff Chandler (as "Ira Grossel").

Duffy's Tavern (NBC); 12/25/46; episode 13, "Miracle in Manhattan: A Christmas Story"; directed by Antony Stanford; written by Vincent (Vin) Bogert, Sid Dorfman, H. Finn, the Freedman Bros., Larry Gelbart, Al Johansen and Lou Lasco; music by Matty Malneck; engineer, Charles Norman; announcer, James Wallington; cast: Ed Gardner, Charlie Cantor, Eddie Green, Sandra Gould, Jeff Chandler (as "Ira Grossel"), James Ogg, Ken Peters, Herb Vigran, Tyler McVey, Helen Andrews, Robert Bruce, Jack Kruschen, Franklin Parker, Bud Widom.

1947

The Lux Radio Theatre (CBS); 03/24/47; episode 564, "Smoky"; directed by Frederic MacKaye; host, William Keighley; cast: Joel McCrea, Constance Moore, Bill Johnstone, Noreen Gammill, Jeff Chandler (as "Ira Grossel"), Ken Carson, Eddie Marr, Cliff Clark, Norman Field, Tim Graham, Jack Carrington, Earl Lee, Charles Seel, June Whitley.

The Lux Radio Theatre (CBS); 03/31/47; episode 565, "How Green Was My Valley"; directed by Frederic MacKaye; host, William Keighley; cast: David Niven, Donald Crisp, Sara Allgood, Maureen O'Sullivan, Gale Gordon, Johnny McGovern, Tony Barrett, Clarke Gordon, Jeff Chandler (as "Ira Grossel"), Bill Johnstone, Frederic Worlock, Norman Field, Ramsey Hill, Charles Seel, Gloria Gordon, Claire Verdera, Howard Jeffrey, June Whitley.

The Lux Radio Theatre (CBS); 04/21/47; episode 568, "My Reputation"; directed by Frederic MacKaye; host, William Keighley; cast: Barbara Stanwyck, George Brent, Janet Scott, Frances Robinson, Tommy Cook, Bobby Ellis, Charles Seel, Jeff Chandler (as "Ira Grossel"), Bill Johnstone, Noreen Gammill, Gloria McMillan, Lois Corbett, Louise Lorimer, Leo Sherin.

The Lux Radio Theatre (CBS); 05/05/47; episode 570, "The Egg and I"; directed by Frederic MacKaye; host, William Keighley; cast: Claudette Colbert, Fred MacMurray, Elvia Allman, Frances Robinson, Bill Johnstone, Janet Scott, Billy Roy, Tim Graham, Charles Seel, Noreen Gammill, Jeff Chandler (as "Ira Grossel"), Norman Field, Cliff Clark, Earl Lee, Lois Kennison, Howard Jeffrey, Bobby Ellis, Vance Colvig.

The Lux Radio Theatre (CBS); 05/12/47; episode 571, "Johnny O'Clock"; directed by Frederic MacKaye; host, William Keighley; cast: Dick Powell, Marguerite Chapman, Lee J. Cobb, Janis Carter, Jay Novello, Jeff Chandler (as "Ira Grossel"), Bill Johnstone, Alvina Temple, Edwin Max, Charles Seel, Noreen Gammill, Eddie Marr, Robert Bruce.

Radio

The Hedda Hopper Show: This Is Hollywood (CBS); 05/24/47; episode 34, "Magnificent Obsession"; hostess, Hedda Hopper; cast: Susan Hayward, Lew Ayres, Jeff Chandler (as "Ira Grossel").

The Private Practice of Dr. Dana (Synd.); 06/01/47; episode 1, "The Samuel Jessup Case"; directed by Robert Hafter; written by E. Jack Neuman; music by Eddie Dunstedter; cast: Jeff Chandler (as "Ira Grossel"), Mary Lansing.

The Private Practice of Dr. Dana (Synd.); 06/08/47; episode 2, "The Joseph Coursey Case"; directed by Robert Hafter; written by E. Jack Neuman; music by Eddie Dunstedter; announcer, Alan Botzer; cast: Jeff Chandler (as "Ira Grossel"), Mary Lansing.

The Lux Radio Theatre (CBS); 06/09/47; episode 575, "One More Tomorrow"; directed by Frederic MacKaye; host, William Keighley; cast: Dennis Morgan, Jane Wyman, Alexis Smith, Gale Gordon, Jeff Chandler (as "Ira Grossel"), Frances Robinson, Bill Johnstone, Stanley Waxman, Charles Seel.

Johnny Modero: Pier 23 (Mut.); 06/12/47; "Two-Way Doublecross"; directed by Nat Wolff; written by Herb Margolis and Lou Markheim; music by Harry Zimmerman; announcer, Tony La Frano; cast: Jack Webb, Gale Gordon, William Conrad, Frank Lovejoy, Joan Banks, Jeff Chandler (as "Ira Grossel"), Peter Leeds.

The Private Practice of Dr. Dana (Synd.); 06/15/47; episode 3, "The Leonard Hazelton Case"; directed by Robert Hafter; written by Robert Ryf; music by Eddie Dunstedter; announcer, Alan Botzer; cast: Jeff Chandler (as "Ira Grossel"), Mary Lansing.

Johnny Modero: Pier 23 (Mut.); 06/19/47; "Find Pete Sutro"; directed by Nat Wolff; music by Harry Zimmerman; announcer, Tony La Frano; cast: Jack Webb, Gale Gordon, Jeff Chandler (as "Ira Grossel"), William Conrad, John Garfield, Joan Banks, Jeanne Rogers.

The Private Practice of Dr. Dana (Synd.); 06/22/47; episode 4, "The Janice Manning Case"; directed by Sterling Tracy; written by E. Jack Neuman; music by Eddie Dunstedter; announcer, Alan Botzer; cast: Jeff Chandler (as "Ira Grossel"), Mary Lansing.

The Private Practice of Dr. Dana (Synd.); 06/29/47; episode 5, "The Frederick Jerome Leech Case"; directed by Sterling Tracy; written by E. Jack Neuman; music by Eddie Dunstedter; announcer, Murray Wagner; cast: Jeff Chandler (as "Ira Grossel"), Mary Lansing.

The Private Practice of Dr. Dana (Synd.); 07/06/47; episode 6, "The George Mansfield Bowman III Case"; directed by Sterling Tracy; written by Robert

Jeff Chandler

Ryf; music by Eddie Dunstedter; cast: Jeff Chandler (as "Ira Grossel"), Mary Lansing, Harry Lang, Bernice Barrett, Joe Forte, Byron Kane, Tyler McVey, Berne Surrey.

Mr. President (ABC); 07/10/47; episode 3, "John Quincy Adams"; directed by Dwight Hauser; cast: Edward Arnold, Betty Lou Gerson, Jeff Chandler (as "Ira Grossel").

The Private Practice of Dr. Dana (Synd.); 07/13/47; episode 7, "The Jessica McKee Case"; directed by Sterling Tracy; written by Robert Ryf; music by Eddie Dunstedter; cast: Jeff Chandler.

The Private Practice of Dr. Dana (Synd.); 07/20/47; episode 8, "The Johnnie McCall Case"; directed by Sterling Tracy; written by E. Jack Neuman; music by Eddie Dunstedter; announcer, Murray Wagner; cast: Jeff Chandler.

The Private Practice of Dr. Dana (Synd.); 07/27/47; episode 9, "The Shelby Withers Jr. Case"; directed by Sterling Tracy; written by Robert Ryf; music by Eddie Dunstedter; cast: Jeff Chandler, Mary Lansing.

The Private Practice of Dr. Dana (Synd.); 08/03/47; episode 10, "The John Ellbridge Cleaver Case"; directed by Sterling Tracy; written by Robert Hall and E. Jack Neuman; music by Eddie Dunstedter; cast: Jeff Chandler, Mary Lansing.

Mr. President (ABC); 08/07/47; episode 7, "Theodore Roosevelt"; directed by Dwight Hauser; cast: Edward Arnold, Betty Lou Gerson, Jeff Chandler (as "Ira Grossel").

The Private Practice of Dr. Dana (Synd.); 08/10/47; episode 11, "The Carol Davison Case"; directed by Sterling Tracy; written by Robert Ryf; music by Eddie Dunstedter; cast: Jeff Chandler.

The Private Practice of Dr. Dana (Synd.); 08/17/47; episode 12, "The Johnny Rizzo Case"; directed by Sterling Tracy; written by Larry Roman; music by Eddie Dunstedter; cast: Jeff Chandler, Byron Kane.

The Private Practice of Dr. Dana (Synd.); 08/24/47; episode 13, "The Peter Scarbo Case"; directed by Sterling Tracy; written by Larry Roman; music by Eddie Dunstedter; cast: Jeff Chandler, Mary Lansing, Jack Carroll.

The Private Practice of Dr. Dana (Synd.); 08/31/47; episode 14, "The Adele Van Heusan Case"; directed by Sterling Tracy; written by E. Jack Neuman; music by Eddie Dunstedter; cast: Jeff Chandler, Mary Lansing.

The Lux Radio Theatre (CBS); 09/01/47; episode 579, "Three Wise Fools"; directed by Frederic MacKaye; host, William Keighley; cast: Margaret O'Brien, Lionel Barrymore, Lewis Stone, Edward Arnold, Bill Johnstone, Janet Scott, Earle

Ross, Jeff Chandler (as "Ira Grossel"), Earl Lee, Charles Seel, Anthony Boris, Norman Field, Eddie Marr, Clarke Gordon, George Neise.

The Private Practice of Dr. Dana (Synd.); 09/07/47; episode 15, "The David Ford Case"; directed by Sterling Tracy; written by Robert Ryf; music by Eddie Dunstedter; cast: Jeff Chandler, Mary Lansing.

Family Theater (Mut.); 09/18/47; episode 32, "Strictly Amateurs"; directed by David Young; host, Jimmy Durante; cast: Dennis Day, Barbara Eiler, Jack Kruschen, Jeff Chandler (as "Ira Grossel").

The Private Practice of Dr. Dana (Synd.); 09/21/47; episode 17, "The Irving Richards Case"; directed by Sterling Tracy; written by Robert Ryf; music by Eddie Dunstedter; cast: Jeff Chandler.

The Lux Radio Theatre (CBS); 09/22/47; episode 582, "Two Years Before the Mast"; directed by Frederic MacKaye; host, William Keighley; cast: Alan Ladd, Howard da Silva, Macdonald Carey, Wanda Hendrix, Bill Johnstone, Luis Van Rooten, Billy Roy, Pat Aherne, Jeff Chandler (as "Ira Grossel"), Norman Field, Leo Cleary, Tyler McVey, Robert Griffin, Clarke Gordon, George Sorel, George Neise, Eddie Marr, Donald Morrison, June Whitley.

The Private Practice of Dr. Dana (Synd.); 09/28/47; episode 18, "The Jen Cather Case"; directed by Sterling Tracy; written by Kathleen Hite; music by Eddie Dunstedter; cast: Jeff Chandler, Mary Lansing.

The Private Practice of Dr. Dana (Synd.); 10/05/47; episode 19, "The Bill Carroll Case"; directed by Sterling Tracy; written by Robert Ryf; music by Eddie Dunstedter; cast: Jeff Chandler, Mary Lansing.

The Lux Radio Theatre (CBS); 10/06/47; episode 584, "Undercurrent"; directed by Frederic MacKaye; host, William Keighley; cast: Katharine Hepburn, Robert Taylor, Jeff Chandler (as "Ira Grossel"), Frances Robinson, Janet Scott, Bill Johnstone, Earl Smith, Norman Field, Lois Corbett, Herb Butterfield, Anne Stone, June Whitley.

The Private Practice of Dr. Dana (Synd.); 10/12/47; episode 20, "The Frances Case"; directed by Sterling Tracy; written by Les Farber; music by Eddie Dunstedter; cast: Jeff Chandler, Mary Lansing, Jerry Farber, Jeff Corey, Dawn Bender, Anne Morrison.

The Private Practice of Dr. Dana (Synd.); 10/19/47; episode 21, "The C. L. Tracy, M. D. Case"; directed by Sterling Tracy; written by Robert Ryf; music by Eddie Dunstedter; cast: Jeff Chandler, Mary Lansing.

The Private Practice of Dr. Dana (Synd.); 10/26/47; episode 22, "The Sam

Jeff Chandler

Farnsworth Case"; directed by Sterling Tracy; written by Robert Hall; music by Eddie Dunstedter; cast: Jeff Chandler, Mary Lansing.

The Private Practice of Dr. Dana (Synd.); 11/02/47; episode 23, "The Matilda Fogarty Case"; directed by Sterling Tracy; written by Les Farber; music by Eddie Dunstedter; cast: Jeff Chandler, Mary Lansing, Peggy Webber, Betty Lou Gerson, Cynthia Corley, Tyler McVey.

The Private Practice of Dr. Dana (Synd.); 11/09/47; episode 24, "The Joan Carter Case"; directed by Sterling Tracy; written by Robert Ryf; music by Eddie Dunstedter; cast: Jeff Chandler, Mary Lansing.

The Private Practice of Dr. Dana (Synd.); 11/16/47; episode 25, "The Sandy Bartlett Case"; directed by Sterling Tracy; written by Les Farber; music by Eddie Dunstedter; cast: Jeff Chandler, Mary Lansing, Anne Morrison, Betty Lou Gerson, Tony Barrett, Tom Collins, Joseph Granby, Bill Gould, Joe Schweiger.

The Lux Radio Theatre (CBS); 11/17/47; episode 590, "Nobody Lives Forever"; directed by Frederic MacKaye; host, William Keighley; cast: Jane Wyman, Ronald Reagan, William Conrad, Bill Johnstone, Jeff Chandler (as "Ira Grossel"), Herb Butterfield, Frances Robinson, Edwin Max, Tyler McVey, Eddie Marr, Herbert Rawlinson, Edwin Cooper.

The Private Practice of Dr. Dana (Synd.); 11/23/47; episode 26, "The Ilse Case"; directed by Sterling Tracy; written by Robert Ryf; music by Eddie Dunstedter; cast: Jeff Chandler, Mary Lansing.

The Private Practice of Dr. Dana (Synd.); 11/30/47; episode 27, "The Rita Rowan Case"; directed by Sterling Tracy; written by Les Farber; music by Eddie Dunstedter; cast: Jeff Chandler, Mary Lansing, Bill Gould, Joe Schweiger.

The Private Practice of Dr. Dana (Synd.); 12/07/47; episode 28, "The Eddie Foster Case"; directed by Sterling Tracy; written by Robert Ryf; music by Eddie Dunstedter; cast: Jeff Chandler, Mary Lansing.

Escape (CBS); 12/10/47; episode 18, "An Occurrence At Owl Creek Bridge" adapted by William N. Robson; cast: Harry Bartell, Luis Van Rooten, William Conrad, Bill Johnstone, Jeff Chandler.

The Private Practice of Dr. Dana (Synd.); 12/14/47; episode 29, "The Bill Worthington Case"; directed by Sterling Tracy; written by Les Farber; music by Eddie Dunstedter; cast: Jeff Chandler, Mary Lansing, Bill Gould, Joe Schweiger.

The Lux Radio Theatre (CBS); 12/15/47; episode 594, "Magic Town"; directed by Frederic MacKaye; host, William Keighley; cast: James Stewart, Jane Wyman,

Wally Maher, Jeff Chandler (as "Ira Grossel"), Edwin Cooper, Herb Butterfield, Robert Griffin, Earl Lee, Janet Scott, George Chandler, Bill Johnstone, Horace Murphy, Alex Gerry, Jack Edwards, Norman Field, Billy Roy, Tommy Cook, Gil Stratton Jr., Lois Corbett, Eddie Marr, Marie Windsor, Charles Woolf.

The Private Practice of Dr. Dana (Synd.); 12/21/47; episode 30, "The Sophia Howard Case"; produced and directed by Sterling Tracy; written by Robert Ryf; music by Eddie Dunstedter; cast: Jeff Chandler, Mary Lansing, Betty Lou Gerson, Marlene Ames, Bob Young.

Duffy's Tavern (NBC); 12/24/47; episode 13, "Miracle in Manhattan: A Christmas Story"; directed by Antony Stanford; written by Vincent (Vin) Bogert, Bill Freedman, Morris Freedman, Lou Grant, Al Johansen, Larry Rhine, Phil Sharp and Bob Schiller; music by Matty Malneck; sound by Bob Grapperhaus; engineer, Charles Norman; announcer, Rod O'Connor; cast: Ed Gardner, Charlie Cantor, Eddie Green, Florence Halop, Jeff Chandler (as "Ira Grossel"), Bobby Ellis, Ken Peters, Alan Reed, Tyler McVey, Helen Andrews, Jerry Hausner, Robert Bruce, Eric Rolfe, Franklin Parker, Bud Widom.

The Private Practice of Dr. Dana (Synd.); 12/28/47; episode 31, "The Geraldine Fairfield Case"; produced and directed by Sterling Tracy; written by Tom and Jerry; music by Eddie Dunstedter; cast: Jeff Chandler.

1948

Suspense (CBS); 01/03/48; episode 278, "The Black Curtain"; directed by William Spier; host, Robert Montgomery; cast: Robert Montgomery, Sidney Miller, Conrad Binyon, Jack Kruschen, William Conrad, Jerry Hausner, Paul Frees, Joseph Kearns, Jeff Chandler (as "Ira Grossel").

The Private Practice of Dr. Dana (Synd.); 01/04/48; episode 32, "The Dan Betterly Case"; directed by Sterling Tracy; written by Robert Ryf; music by Eddie Dunstedter; cast: Jeff Chandler, Mary Lansing.

The Lux Radio Theatre (CBS); 01/05/48; episode 597, "The Farmer's Daughter"; directed by Frederic MacKaye; host, William Keighley; cast: Loretta Young, Joseph Cotten, Janet Scott, Cliff Clark, Bill Johnstone, Frances Robinson, Robert Griffin, Leo Cleary, Herbert Rawlinson, Norman Field, Lois Corbett, Herb Butterfield, Jeff Chandler (as "Ira Grossel"), Clarke Gordon, George Neise, June Whitley, Stanley Farrar, Eddie Marr.

The Voyage of the Scarlet Queen (Mut.); 01/07/48; episode 27, "The Derelict and the Wandering Boy" written by Gil Doud; produced by James Burton; music

Jeff Chandler

by Richard Aurandt; announcer, Charles Arlington; cast: Elliott Lewis, Clarke Gordon, Edwin Max, Jeff Chandler, John Dehner, Maya Gregory.

The Private Practice of Dr. Dana (Synd.); 01/11/48; episode 33, "The Lyle Madden, M. D. Case"; directed by Sterling Tracy; written by Robert Ryf; music by Eddie Dunstedter; cast: Jeff Chandler, Mary Lansing, Bob Bruce, Tyler McVey, Lillian Buyeff, Daws Butler.

The Lux Radio Theatre (CBS); 01/12/48; episode 598, "Kiss of Death"; directed by Frederic MacKaye; host, William Keighley; cast: Victor Mature, Coleen Gray, Richard Widmark, Alan Reed, Robert Griffin, Carole Sue Leeds, Norma Jean Nilsson, Jeff Chandler (as "Ira Grossel"), Jack Petruzzi, Marie Windsor, Joseph Bell, Gwen Delano, Edwin Cooper, Eddie Marr, Ed Emerson, Tyler McVey, Larry Dobkin.

The Private Practice of Dr. Dana (Synd.); 01/18/48; episode 34, "The David Turner Case"; directed by Sterling Tracy; written by Adrian Gendot; music by Eddie Dunstedter; cast: Jeff Chandler, Mary Lansing.

The Lux Radio Theatre (CBS); 01/19/48; episode 599, "The Yearling"; directed by Frederic MacKaye; host, William Keighley; cast: Gregory Peck, Jane Wyman, Claude Jarman Jr., James Ogg, Gwen Delano, Jeff Chandler (as "Ira Grossel"), Larry Dobkin, Norman Field, Bill Johnstone, Barney Phillips, George Neise, Eddie Marr, Ann Carter, Noreen Gammill, June Whitley.

The Private Practice of Dr. Dana (Synd.); 01/25/48; episode 35, "The Barbara Dunbar Case"; directed by Sterling Tracy; music by Eddie Dunstedter; cast: Jeff Chandler, Mary Lansing, Betty Lou Gerson, Laurette Fillbrandt, Gerald Mohr.

The Private Practice of Dr. Dana (Synd.); 02/01/48; episode 36, "The Jason King Case"; directed by Sterling Tracy; written by Adrian Gendot; music by Eddie Dunstedter; cast: Jeff Chandler, Mary Lansing.

Escape (CBS); 02/08/48; episode 87, "Snake Doctor" adapted by Fred Howard; directed and produced by Norman Macdonnell; assistant, Ted Rogers; engineer, Stan Carr; music by Wilbur Hatch; sound by Gus Base; announcer, John Jacobs; cast: Jeff Chandler (as "Ira Grossel"), Paul Frees, William Conrad, William Lally, Ruth Perrott, Wilms Herbert, Edgar Barrier.

The Private Practice of Dr. Dana (Synd.); 02/08/48; episode 37, "The Winifred Whitehead Case"; directed by Sterling Tracy; written by Robert Hall; music by Eddie Dunstedter; cast: Jeff Chandler, Mary Lansing.

The Private Practice of Dr. Dana (Synd.); 02/15/48; episode 38, "The Edward L. Russell Case"; directed by Sterling Tracy; written by Robert Ryf; music by Eddie

Dunstedter; cast: Jeff Chandler, Mary Lansing, Hans Conried, Betty Lou Gerson, David Ellis.

The Private Practice of Dr. Dana (Synd.); 02/22/48; episode 39, "The Roy St. John Case"; directed by Sterling Tracy; written by Adrian Gendot; music by Eddie Dunstedter; cast: Jeff Chandler.

The Lux Radio Theatre (CBS); 02/23/48; episode 604, "T-Men"; directed by Frederic MacKaye; host, William Keighley; cast: Dennis O'Keefe, Gail Patrick, Gerald Mohr, Tony Barrett, Lou Merrill, Alan Reed, Bill Johnstone, Carlton KaDell, Jay Novello, Jeff Chandler (as "Ira Grossel"), Frances Robinson, Jack Carrington, Ed Emerson, Robert Griffin, Howard McNear, Eddie Marr, Jack Petruzzi, Truda Marson, Charlie Lung.

The Private Practice of Dr. Dana (Synd.); 02/29/48; episode 40, "The Paul Melville Case"; directed by Sterling Tracy; written by Robert Hall; music by Eddie Dunstedter; cast: Jeff Chandler, Laurette Fillbrandt.

The Private Practice of Dr. Dana (Synd.); 03/07/48; episode 41, "The John Christopher Case"; directed by Sterling Tracy; written by Robert Ryf; music by Eddie Dunstedter; cast: Jeff Chandler, Mary Lansing.

The Private Practice of Dr. Dana (Synd.); 03/14/48; episode 42, "The Valerie Carter Case"; directed by Sterling Tracy; written by Adrian Gendot; music by Eddie Dunstedter; cast: Jeff Chandler, Mary Lansing, Laurette Fillbrandt, Paul Frees, Lillian Buyeff, Tyler McVey.

The Lux Radio Theatre (CBS); 03/15/48; episode 607, "Irish Eyes Are Smiling"; directed by Frederic MacKaye; host, William Keighley; cast: Dick Haymes, Jeanne Crain, Alan Reed, Gerald Mohr, Frances Robinson, Herb Butterfield, Jeff Chandler (as "Ira Grossel"), Bill Johnstone, Joe Forte, Irene Winston, Gwen Delano, Truda Marson, Ed Emerson, Robert Griffin, Eddie Marr, Cliff Clark.

The Private Practice of Dr. Dana (Synd.); 03/21/48; episode 43, "The Bill Meredith Case"; directed by Sterling Tracy; written by Robert Ryf; music by Eddie Dunstedter; cast: Jeff Chandler, Mary Lansing, Gil Stratton Jr., Bill Bouchey, Charlie Lung.

The New Adventures of Michael Shayne (Synd.); 03/28/48; episode 1, "The Man Who Lived Forever"; directed by William P. Rousseau; cast: Jeff Chandler, Charles McGraw.

The Private Practice of Dr. Dana (Synd.); 03/28/48; episode 44, "The Ray Wardell Case"; directed by Sterling Tracy; written by Robert Hall; music by Eddie Dunstedter; cast: Jeff Chandler.

Jeff Chandler

The New Adventures of Michael Shayne (Synd.); 04/04/48; episode 2, "The Case of The Hunted Bride" written by Larry Marcus; directed by William P. Rousseau; cast: Jeff Chandler, Frank Lovejoy.

The Private Practice of Dr. Dana (Synd.); 04/04/48; episode 45, "The Carol Tracy, M. D. Case"; directed by Sterling Tracy; written by Robert Ryf; music by Eddie Dunstedter; cast: Jeff Chandler, Mary Lansing, Betty Lou Gerson, Bill Johnstone.

The Lux Radio Theatre (CBS); 04/05/48; episode 610, "Daisy Kenyon"; directed by Frederic MacKaye; host, William Keighley; cast: Dana Andrews, Ida Lupino, Jeff Chandler (as "Ira Grossel"), Frances Robinson, Bill Johnstone, Gerald Mohr, Ann Carter, Herb Butterfield, Robert Griffin, Irene Winston, Eddie Marr, Truda Marson.

The New Adventures of Michael Shayne (Synd.); 04/11/48; episode 3, "The Case of The Blood-Stained Pearls" written by Larry Marcus; directed by William P. Rousseau; cast: Jeff Chandler, Paul Frees.

The Private Practice of Dr. Dana (Synd.); 04/11/48; episode 46, "The Linda Andrews Case"; directed by Sterling Tracy; written by Gomer Cool; music by Eddie Dunstedter; cast: Jeff Chandler, Mary Lansing, Henry Blair, Laurette Fillbrandt, Bill Bouchey.

The New Adventures of Michael Shayne (Synd.); 04/18/48; episode 4, "The Case of the Phantom Gun"; directed by William P. Rousseau; cast: Jeff Chandler, Jack Webb, William Conrad.

The Private Practice of Dr. Dana (Synd.); 04/18/48; episode 47, "The Melody Windsor Case"; directed by Sterling Tracy; written by Robert Hall; music by Eddie Dunstedter; cast: Jeff Chandler.

The Adventures of Red Ryder (Synd.); 04/20/48; "Roar of the River"; directed by Paul Franklin; written by Albert Van Antwerp and Paul Franklin; cast: Brooke Temple, Johnny McGovern, Horace Murphy, Jeff Chandler.

The New Adventures of Michael Shayne (Synd.); 04/25/48; episode 5, "The Hate that Killed"; directed by William P. Rousseau; written by Robert Ryf; cast: Jeff Chandler, Peter Leeds, Dave Sisenby, William Conrad, Alan Reed, Joan Banks, Eleanor Audley.

The Private Practice of Dr. Dana (Synd.); 04/25/48; episode 48, "The Danny McNear Case"; produced and directed by Sterling Tracy; written by Larry Roman; music by Eddie Dunstedter; cast: Jeff Chandler, Mary Lansing.

The New Adventures of Michael Shayne (Synd.); 05/02/48; episode 6, "The

Case of the Gray-Eyed Blonde"; directed by William P. Rousseau; cast: Jeff Chandler, Jack Webb, Betty Lou Gerson, Paul Frees.

The Private Practice of Dr. Dana (Synd.); 05/02/48; episode 49, "The Glenda Barton Case"; produced and directed by Sterling Tracy; written by Frank C. Burt and Robert Libbott; music by Eddie Dunstedter; cast: Jeff Chandler.

The Lux Radio Theatre (CBS); 05/03/48; episode 614, "Cloak and Dagger"; directed by Frederic MacKaye; host, William Keighley; cast: Ronald Reagan, Lilli Palmer, Jeff Chandler, Herb Butterfield, Bill Johnstone, Norman Field, Regina Wallace, Robert Griffin, Marjorie Hoshelle, Ben Wright, June Whitley, Jay Novello, Jack Petruzzi, Eddie Marr, Charles LaTorre, Janet Scott, Robert Conte.

The New Adventures of Michael Shayne (Synd.); 05/09/48; episode 7, "The Case of the Model Murder"; directed by William P. Rousseau; cast: Jeff Chandler, Jack Webb, Hans Conried.

The Private Practice of Dr. Dana (Synd.); 05/09/48; episode 50, "The Francine Cooper Case"; produced and directed by Sterling Tracy; written by Robert Hall; music by Eddie Dunstedter; cast: Jeff Chandler.

The Lux Radio Theatre (CBS); 05/10/48; episode 615, "Intrigue"; directed by Frederic MacKaye; host, William Keighley; cast: George Raft, June Havoc, Bill Johnstone, Joan Banks, Gerald Mohr, Edmund MacDonald, Tony Barrett, Herb Butterfield, Jeff Chandler, Nora Martin, Marie Windsor, Howard McNear, Eddie Marr, Norma Jean Nilsson, James Ogg, Phillip Bernard, Jerry Farber, Henry Blair.

The New Adventures of Michael Shayne (Synd.); 05/16/48; episode 8, "The Case of the Generous Killer"; directed by William P. Rousseau; cast: Jeff Chandler, Jack Webb.

The Private Practice of Dr. Dana (Synd.); 05/16/48; episode 51, "The Luscious Louie Case"; produced and directed by Sterling Tracy; written by Larry Roman; music by Eddie Dunstedter; cast: Jeff Chandler, Mary Lansing, Charlie Lung.

The Lux Radio Theatre (CBS); 05/17/48; episode 616, "The Homestretch"; directed by Frederic MacKaye; host, William Keighley; cast: Cornel Wilde, Maureen O'Hara, Tim Graham, Frances Robinson, Janet Scott, Tommy Cook, Carlton KaDell, Gerald Mohr, Jeff Chandler, Bill Johnstone, Ben Wright, Rye Billsbury, Jean Vander Pyl, Eddie Marr, Robert Earle, Tyler McVey.

The New Adventures of Michael Shayne (Synd.); 05/23/48; episode 9, "The Pursuit of Death"; directed by William P. Rousseau; cast: Jeff Chandler, Paul Frees.

Jeff Chandler

The Private Practice of Dr. Dana (Synd.); 05/23/48; episode 52, "The Paul Dennison Case"; produced and directed by Sterling Tracy; written by Larry Roman; music by Eddie Dunstedter; cast: Jeff Chandler, Mary Lansing, Paul Frees, Charlie Lung.

The Lux Radio Theatre (CBS); 05/24/48; episode 617, "I Walk Alone"; directed by Frederic MacKaye; host, William Keighley; cast: Burt Lancaster, Lizabeth Scott, Whitfield Connor, Jeff Chandler, Bill Johnstone, Jay Novello, Betty Bryant, Paul Dubov, Kirk Ragan, Norman Field, Howard McNear, Ed Emerson, Eddie Marr.

The New Adventures of Michael Shayne (Synd.); 05/30/48; episode 10, "The Case of the Crooked Wheel"; directed by William P. Rousseau; cast: Jeff Chandler, Frank Lovejoy, William Conrad.

The Private Practice of Dr. Dana (Synd.); 05/30/48; episode 53, "The Clark Adams Case"; produced and directed by Sterling Tracy; written by Frank C. Burt and Robert Libbott; music by Eddie Dunstedter; cast: Jeff Chandler, Mary Lansing, Berry Kroeger, Laurette Fillbrandt.

The Lux Radio Theatre (CBS); 05/31/48; episode 618, "The Miracle of the Bells"; directed by Frederic MacKaye; host, William Keighley; cast: Fred MacMurray, Alida Valli, Frank Sinatra, Bill Johnstone, Herb Butterfield, Veronica Pataky, Carlton KaDell, Gerald Mohr, Jeff Chandler, Howard McNear, Eddie Marr, Norman Field, George Chandler, Herbert Rawlinson, Larry Dobkin, George Neise, Rolfe Sedan, Jack Carrington, Virginia Agnello.

The New Adventures of Michael Shayne (Synd.); 06/06/48; episode 11, "The Case of the Wandering Fingerprints"; directed by William P. Rousseau; cast: Jeff Chandler, Jack Webb.

The Private Practice of Dr. Dana (Synd.); 06/06/48; episode 54, "The Joe Carney Case"; produced and directed by Sterling Tracy; written by Larry Roman; music by Eddie Dunstedter; cast: Jeff Chandler, Mary Lansing, Davis Butler, Bill Bouchey, Laurette Fillbrandt, Bill Gould.

The Lux Radio Theatre (CBS); 06/07/48; episode 619, "Relentless"; directed by Frederic MacKaye; host, William Keighley; cast: Robert Young, Claire Trevor, Jeff Chandler, Frank Richards, Jay Novello, Leo Cleary, Edwin Max, Bill Johnstone, Cliff Clark, Horace Murphy, Tim Graham, Earl Lee, Eddie Marr, Howard McNear.

The New Adventures of Michael Shayne (Synd.); 06/13/48; episode 12, "The Case of the Purloined Corpse"; directed by William P. Rousseau; cast: Jeff Chandler, Jack Webb.

The Private Practice of Dr. Dana (Synd.); 06/13/48; episode 55, "The Nameless Patient Case"; produced and directed by Sterling Tracy; written by Roy Grandey; music by Eddie Dunstedter; cast: Jeff Chandler, Mary Lansing, Anne Morrison.

The New Adventures of Michael Shayne (Synd.); 06/20/48; episode 13, "The Case of the Left-Handed Fan"; directed by William P. Rousseau; cast: Jeff Chandler, Betty Lou Gerson.

The Private Practice of Dr. Dana (Synd.); 06/20/48; episode 56, "The Randolph Grey Case"; produced and directed by Sterling Tracy; written by Larry Roman; music by Eddie Dunstedter; cast: Jeff Chandler, Mary Lansing.

Tell It Again (CBS); 06/20/48; episode 22, "Dr. Jekyll and Mr. Hyde"; directed by Ralph Rose; cast: Jeff Chandler, Herbert Rawlinson, Virginia McDowell, Ramsey Hill, Gordon Gray, Donald Morrison.

Our Miss Brooks (CBS); 06/23/48; episode 0, "Audition Show"; produced and directed by Larry Berns; written by Al Lewis; music by Wilbur Hatch; announcer, Bob Stevenson; cast: Eve Arden, Jeff Chandler, Joe Forte, Richard Crenna, Noreen Gammill.

The New Adventures of Michael Shayne (Synd.); 06/27/48; episode 14, "The Case of the Deadly Dough"; directed by William P. Rousseau; cast: Jeff Chandler, Jack Webb, Charles McGraw.

The Private Practice of Dr. Dana (Synd.); 06/27/48; episode 57, "The Mrs. Margaret Barnstack Case"; produced and directed by Sterling Tracy; written by Roy Grandey; music by Eddie Dunstedter; cast: Jeff Chandler, Mary Lansing.

The Lux Radio Theatre (CBS); 06/28/48; episode 621, "You Were Meant for Me"; directed by Frederic MacKaye; host, William Keighley; cast: Dan Dailey, Donna Reed, Jeff Chandler, Bill Johnstone, Eleanor Audley, Alvina Temple, Herb Butterfield, Howard McNear, Gil Stratton Jr., Eddie Marr, George Neise, Clarke Gordon, Robert Cole.

The New Adventures of Michael Shayne (Synd.); 07/04/48; episode 15, "The Case of the Popular Corpse"; directed by William P. Rousseau; written by Robert Ryf; cast: Jeff Chandler, William Conrad.

The Private Practice of Dr. Dana (Synd.); 07/04/48; episode 58, "The Harold Landry Case"; produced and directed by Sterling Tracy; written by Larry Roman; music by Eddie Dunstedter; cast: Jeff Chandler, Mary Lansing, Herb Butterfield.

Tell It Again (CBS); 07/04/48; episode 24, "The Man Without a Country"; directed by Ralph Rose; cast: Jeff Chandler (as "Ira Grossel"), David Ellis, Stanley Waxman, Jack Kelly, Peter Leeds, Paul Dubov, Joy Hartung, Byron Kane.

Jeff Chandler

Let George Do It (Mut.); 07/05/48; episode 89, "The Man Who Was Murdered Twice"; directed by Don Clark; cast: Bob Bailey, Frances Robinson, Wally Maher, Ramsey Hill, Virginia Gregg, Betty Moran, Peter Leeds, Jeff Chandler.

The Private Practice of Dr. Dana (Synd.); 07/11/48; episode 59, "The Barney Layton Case"; produced and directed by Sterling Tracy; written by Roy Grandey; music by Eddie Dunstedter; cast: Jeff Chandler, Mary Lansing.

Tell It Again (CBS); 07/11/48; episode 25, "Adventures of Baron Munchausen"; directed by Ralph Rose; narration by Jeff Chandler; cast: Harry Lang, Beth Layman, Anne Whitfield, Jerry Farber, Daws Butler, Ken Harvey, Frank Cady, Dorothy Roberts.

The Private Practice of Dr. Dana (Synd.); 07/18/48; episode 60, "The Liza Zernig Case"; produced and directed by Sterling Tracy; written by Larry Roman; music by Eddie Dunstedter; cast: Jeff Chandler, Mary Lansing.

Our Miss Brooks (CBS); 07/19/48; episode 1, "First Show"; produced and directed by Larry Berns; written by Al Lewis and Lee Loeb; music by Wilbur Hatch; sound by Stan Carr; announcer, Bob Stevenson; cast: Eve Arden, Jeff Chandler, Joe Forte, Jane Morgan, Richard Crenna, Noreen Gammill.

The Private Practice of Dr. Dana (Synd.); 07/25/48; episode 61, "The Phillip Martell Case"; produced and directed by Sterling Tracy; written by Larry Roman; music by Eddie Dunstedter; cast: Jeff Chandler.

Our Miss Brooks (CBS); 07/26/48; episode 2, "Weenie-Roast Chaperone"; produced by Larry Berns; directed by Al Lewis; written by Al Lewis and Lee Loeb; music by Wilbur Hatch; announcer, Bob Lemond; cast: Eve Arden, Jeff Chandler, Jane Morgan, Richard Crenna, Gloria McMillan, Dink Trout, Hans Conried, Ezelle Poule.

The Private Practice of Dr. Dana (Synd.); 08/1/48; episode 62, "The Jennifer Carr Case"; produced and directed by Sterling Tracy; written by Larry Roman; music by Eddie Dunstedter; cast: Jeff Chandler.

Our Miss Brooks (CBS); 08/02/48; episode 3, "Camp Okeechobi"; produced by Larry Berns; directed and written by Al Lewis; music by Wilbur Hatch; announcer, Bob Lemond; cast: Eve Arden, Jeff Chandler, Gale Gordon, Jane Morgan, Richard Crenna, Gloria McMillan, Bea Benaderet, Norma Jean Nilsson, Eleanor Audley, Hy Averback.

My Favorite Husband (CBS); 08/06/48; episode 3, "The Portrait"; directed by Harry S. Ackerman; cast: Lucille Ball, Richard Denning, John (Bud) Hiestand, Ruth Perrott, Jeff Chandler (as "Ira Grossel").

Radio

Jeff Regan, Investigator (CBS); 08/07/48; episode 5, "The Story of the Man Who Liked the Mountains"; produced and directed by Sterling Tracy; cast: Jack Webb, Wilms Herbert, Jeff Chandler.

The Private Practice of Dr. Dana (Synd.); 08/08/48; episode 63, "The Tony Garabaldi Case"; produced and directed by Sterling Tracy; written by Roy Grandey; music by Eddie Dunstedter; cast: Jeff Chandler, Mary Lansing.

Our Miss Brooks (CBS); 08/09/48; episode 4, "The $50,000 Endowment"; produced by Larry Berns; directed by Al Lewis; written by Al Lewis and Joseph Quillan; music by Wilbur Hatch; announcer, Bob Lemond; cast: Eve Arden, Jeff Chandler, Gale Gordon, Jane Morgan, Richard Crenna, Gloria McMillan, Eleanor Audley, Veda Vonn, Jay Novello, Paul Frees.

The Private Practice of Dr. Dana (Synd.); 08/15/48; episode 64, "The Lucy Brown Case"; produced and directed by Sterling Tracy; written by Harrison Negley and Larry Roman; music by Eddie Dunstedter; cast: Jeff Chandler, Mary Lansing, Eleanor Audley, Ken Christy, Daws Butler, Marjorie Hoshelle.

Our Miss Brooks (CBS); 08/16/48; episode 5, "Juvenile Delinquency at Madison High"; produced by Larry Berns; directed by Al Lewis; written by Al Lewis and Alan Rader; music by Wilbur Hatch; announcer, Bob Lemond; cast: Eve Arden, Jeff Chandler, Gale Gordon, Jane Morgan, Richard Crenna, Gloria McMillan, Hy Averback, Lester Jay.

Hallmark Playhouse (CBS); 08/19/48; episode 10, "Drums Along the Mohawk"; directed by Dee Engelbach; host, James Hilton; cast: Jeff Chandler.

The Private Practice of Dr. Dana (Synd.); episode 65, 08/22/48; "The State Highway Patrolman Case"; produced and directed by Sterling Tracy; written by Larry Roman; music by Eddie Dunstedter; cast: Jeff Chandler.

Our Miss Brooks (CBS); 08/23/48; episode 6, "The Swiss Chrono-Mono-Thing"; produced by Larry Berns; directed and written by Al Lewis; music by Wilbur Hatch; announcer, Bob Lemond; cast: Eve Arden, Jeff Chandler, Gale Gordon, Jane Morgan, Richard Crenna, Gloria McMillan, Noreen Gammill, Hy Averback, Jack Kruschen.

The Amazing Mr. Malone (ABC); 08/24/48; "Cleanliness is Next to Godliness"; directed by William P. Rousseau; cast: Frank Lovejoy, Jeff Chandler.

The Private Practice of Dr. Dana (Synd.); 08/29/48; episode 66, "The Jessica Lehr Case"; produced and directed by Sterling Tracy; written by Larry Roman; music by Eddie Dunstedter; cast: Jeff Chandler, Mary Lansing, Laurette Fillbrandt, Paul Frees, Berry Kroeger.

Jeff Chandler

The Private Practice of Dr. Dana (Synd.); 09/05/48; episode 67, "The Steve Dana Case"; produced and directed by Sterling Tracy; written by Jeff Chandler and Ira Grossel; music by Eddie Dunstedter; cast: Jeff Chandler, Mary Lansing, Betty Lou Gerson.

The Private Practice of Dr. Dana (Synd.); 09/12/48; episode 68, "The Joe Haydn Case"; produced and directed by Sterling Tracy; written by Roy Grandey; music by Eddie Dunstedter; cast: Jeff Chandler, Joe Forte.

The Whistler (Synd.); 09/15/48; episode 331, "Uncle Ben's Widow"; directed by George W. Allen; cast: Betty Lou Gerson, Theodore von Eltz, Jeff Chandler.

Jeff Regan, Investigator (CBS); 09/18/48; episode 11, "The Story of the Gambler and the Lady"; produced and directed by Sterling Tracy; cast: Jack Webb, Wilms Herbert, Betty Lou Gerson, Marvin Miller, Paul Frees, Charles McGraw, David Ellis, Jeff Chandler (as "Ira Grossel").

Our Miss Brooks (CBS); 09/19/48; episode 7, "The Surprise Wedding Anniversary"; produced by Larry Berns; directed by Al Lewis; written by Al Lewis and Alan Rader; music by Wilbur Hatch; announcer, Bob Lemond; cast: Eve Arden, Jeff Chandler, Gale Gordon, Jane Morgan, Richard Crenna, Gloria McMillan, Noreen Gammill, Dink Trout.

The Lux Radio Theatre (CBS); 09/20/48; episode 625, "Gentleman's Agreement"; directed by Frederic MacKaye; host, William Keighley; cast: Gregory Peck, Anne Baxter, Janet Scott, Jeff Chandler, Frances Robinson, Jacqueline de Wit, Bill Johnstone, Johnny McGovern, Herb Butterfield, Joan Banks, Herbert Rawlinson, Howard McNear, Eddie Marr, Ed Emerson.

Sealtest Variety Theater (NBC); 09/23/48; episode 3, "The Love Pact"; directed by Glenhall Taylor; hostess, Dorothy Lamour; cast: Alan Young, William Powell, Hans Conried, Jeff Chandler.

Our Miss Brooks (CBS); 09/26/48; episode 8, "The Maharaja of Shish Kebab"; produced by Larry Berns; directed by Al Lewis; written by Al Lewis and Alan Rader; music by Wilbur Hatch; announcer, Bob Lemond; cast: Eve Arden, Jeff Chandler, Gale Gordon, Jane Morgan, Richard Crenna, Gloria McMillan, Noreen Gammill, Frank Nelson, Bob Lemond, Lester Jay, Peter Leeds.

Our Miss Brooks (CBS); 10/03/48; episode 1, "Money Management"; produced by Larry Berns; directed by Al Lewis; written by Al Lewis and Alan Rader; music by Wilbur Hatch; announcers, Bob Lemond and Verne Smith; cast: Eve Arden, Jeff Chandler, Gale Gordon, Jane Morgan, Richard Crenna, Gloria McMillan, Noreen Gammill, Ken Harvey, Jack Kruschen, Joe Forte.

Radio

Tell It Again (CBS); 10/03/48; episode 37, "Les Miserables"; directed by Ralph Rose; cast: Marvin Miller, Jeff Chandler.

Hallmark Playhouse (CBS); 10/07/48; episode 16, "Elmer, the Great"; directed by Dee Engelbach; host, James Hilton; cast: Bob Hope, Jeff Chandler, Gerald Mohr.

Our Miss Brooks (CBS); 10/10/48; episode 2, "Crowded School Conditions"; produced by Larry Berns; directed by Al Lewis; written by Al Lewis, Howard Miners and Alan Rader; music by Wilbur Hatch; announcer, Bob Lemond; cast: Eve Arden, Jeff Chandler, Gale Gordon, Jane Morgan, Richard Crenna, Gloria McMillan, Ken Harvey, Ed Quillan, Herb Vigran, Tommy Cook.

The Lux Radio Theatre (CBS); 10/11/48; episode 628, "Larceny"; directed by Frederic MacKaye; host, William Keighley; cast: John Payne, Joan Caulfield, Shelley Winters, Paul Dubov, Dan O'Herlihy, Jeff Chandler, Bill Johnstone, Charlotte Lawrence, Herb Butterfield, Robert Griffin, June Whitley, Ed Emerson, Eddie Marr.

Our Miss Brooks (CBS); 10/17/48; episode 3, "Social Butterfly"; produced by Larry Berns; directed by Al Lewis; assistant director, Carl Harwood; written by Harold Goldman and Al Lewis; music by Wilbur Hatch; sound by Bill Gould; engineer, Pat Walsh; announcers, Bob Lemond, Hal Sawyer and Verne Smith; cast: Eve Arden, Jeff Chandler, Gale Gordon, Jane Morgan, Richard Crenna, Gloria McMillan, Noreen Gammill, Jay Novello, Frank Albertson, Ed Quillan, Gloria Blondell.

The Lux Radio Theatre (CBS); 10/18/48; episode 629, "The Razor's Edge"; directed by Frederic MacKaye; host, William Keighley; cast: Ida Lupino, Mark Stevens, Edgar Barrier, Joseph Kearns, Frances Robinson, Jeff Chandler, Herb Butterfield, Bill Johnstone, Eleanor Audley, Alex Gerry, Rolfe Sedan, Eddie Marr.

Our Miss Brooks (CBS); 10/24/48; episode 4, "The Surprise Party"; produced by Larry Berns; directed by Al Lewis; assistant director, Carl Harwood; written by Mark Kearney, Al Lewis and Jack Price; music by Wilbur Hatch; sound by Bill Gould; engineer, Pat Walsh; announcers, Bob Lemond and Verne Smith; cast: Eve Arden, Jeff Chandler, Gale Gordon, Jane Morgan, Richard Crenna, Gloria McMillan, Noreen Gammill, Frank Nelson, Bea Benaderet.

The Lux Radio Theatre (CBS); 10/25/48; episode 630, "The Secret Heart"; directed by Frederic MacKaye; host, William Keighley; cast: Walter Pidgeon, Deborah Kerr, Rhoda Williams, Scott Elliott, Jeff Chandler, Sam Edwards, Alex Gerry, Marlene Ames, Bill Johnstone, Regina Wallace, June Whitley, Eddie Marr, Harry Blair.

Our Miss Brooks (CBS); 10/31/48; episode 5, "Clay City Football Game"; produced by Larry Berns; directed and written by Al Lewis; assistant director, Carl Harwood; music by Wilbur Hatch; sound by Bill Gould; engineer, Pat Walsh;

Jeff Chandler

announcers, Bob Lemond and Verne Smith; cast: Eve Arden, Jeff Chandler, Gale Gordon, Jane Morgan, Richard Crenna, Gloria McMillan, Noreen Gammill, Wally Maher, Frank Nelson.

Let George Do It (Mut.); 11/01/48; episode 106, "The Flowers That Smelled of Murder"; directed by Don Clark; cast: Bob Bailey, Frances Robinson, Wally Maher, Lurene Tuttle, Jeff Chandler.

Hallmark Playhouse (CBS); 11/04/48; episode 20, "My Friend Flicka"; directed by Dee Engelbach; host, James Hilton; cast: Jeff Chandler, Claude Jarman Jr.

Our Miss Brooks (CBS); 11/07/48; episode 6, "Connie Brooks, the Work Horse"; produced by Larry Berns; directed by Al Lewis; assistant director, Carl Harwood; written by Harold Goldman, Al Lewis and Alan Rader; music by Wilbur Hatch; sound by Bill Gould; engineer, Pat Walsh; announcers, Bob Lemond and Verne Smith; cast: Eve Arden, Jeff Chandler, Gale Gordon, Jane Morgan, Richard Crenna, Gloria McMillan, Noreen Gammill.

Our Miss Brooks (CBS); 11/14/48; episode 7, "Babysitting for Three"; produced by Larry Berns; directed by Al Lewis; assistant director, Carl Harwood; written by Al Lewis and Lester White; music by Wilbur Hatch; sound by Bill Gould; engineer, Pat Walsh; announcers, Bob Lemond and Verne Smith; cast: Eve Arden, Jeff Chandler, Gale Gordon, Jane Morgan, Richard Crenna, Gloria McMillan, Tommy Cook, Jeffrey Silver, Bobby Ellis, Sandra Gould.

The Lux Radio Theatre (CBS); 11/15/48; episode 632, "Body and Soul"; directed by Frederic MacKaye; host, William Keighley; cast: John Garfield, Jane Wyman, Marie Windsor, William Conrad, Wilms Herbert, Janet Scott, Douglas Evans, James Edwards, Carlton KaDell, Jeff Chandler, Bill Johnstone, Herb Butterfield, Leo Cleary, Nora Martin, Eddie Marr, Howard McNear.

Our Miss Brooks (CBS); 11/21/48; episode 8, "June Bride"; produced by Larry Berns; directed by Al Lewis; assistant director, Carl Harwood; written by Morton Fine, David Friedkin and Al Lewis; music by Wilbur Hatch; sound by Bill Gould; engineer, Pat Walsh; announcers, Bob Lemond and Verne Smith; cast: Eve Arden, Jeff Chandler, Gale Gordon, Jane Morgan, Richard Crenna, Gloria McMillan, Mary Jane Croft, Jack Kruschen.

The Lux Radio Theatre (CBS); 11/22/48; episode 633, "The Big Clock"; directed by Frederic MacKaye; host, William Keighley; cast: Ray Milland, Maureen O'Sullivan, William Conrad, Bill Johnstone, Eleanor Audley, Elsie Holmes, Robert Griffin, Paul Dubov, Charlotte Lawrence, Leo Cleary, Stephen Chase, Jeff Chandler, Howard McNear, Jack Kruschen, Eddie Marr, Truda Marson.

Favorite Story (Synd.); 11/23/48; episode 98, "The Dynamiter"; produced by

Jerome Lawrence; host, Ronald Colman; cast: Janet Waldo, William Conrad, Jeff Chandler.

Our Miss Brooks (CBS); 11/28/48; episode 9, "Sunnydale Finishing School"; produced by Larry Berns; directed by Al Lewis; assistant director, Carl Harwood; written by Morton Fine, David Friedkin, Lester White and Al Lewis; music by Wilbur Hatch; sound by Bill Gould; engineer, Pat Walsh; announcers, Bob Lemond and Verne Smith; cast: Eve Arden, Jeff Chandler, Gale Gordon, Jane Morgan, Richard Crenna, Gloria McMillan, Noreen Gammill, Bill Gould.

The New Adventures of Michael Shayne (Synd.); 12/02/48; episode 16, "The Case of the Bayou Monster"; directed by William P. Rousseau; cast: Jeff Chandler, Jack Webb, Betty Lou Gerson.

Our Miss Brooks (CBS); 12/05/48; episode 10, "Tall, Dark and French"; produced by Larry Berns; directed by Al Lewis; assistant director, Carl Harwood; written by Morton Fine, David Friedkin and Al Lewis; music by Wilbur Hatch; sound by Bill Gould; engineer, Pat Walsh; announcers, Bob Lemond and Verne Smith; cast: Eve Arden, Jeff Chandler, Gale Gordon, Jane Morgan, Richard Crenna, Gloria McMillan, Eleanor Audley, Gerald Mohr.

The New Adventures of Michael Shayne (Synd.); 12/09/48; episode 17, "A Problem In Murder"; directed by William P. Rousseau; cast: Jeff Chandler, Jack Webb.

Our Miss Brooks (CBS); 12/12/48; episode 11, "Malcolm the Rabbit"; produced by Larry Berns; directed by Al Lewis; assistant director, Carl Harwood; written by Al Lewis, Alan Rader, Howard Snyder and Hugh Wedlock; music by Wilbur Hatch; sound by Bill Gould; engineer, Pat Walsh; announcers, Bob Lemond and Verne Smith; cast: Eve Arden, Jeff Chandler, Gale Gordon, Jane Morgan, Richard Crenna, Gloria McMillan.

The New Adventures of Michael Shayne (Synd.); 12/16/48; episode 18, "The Case of the High Priced Twins"; directed by William P. Rousseau; cast: Jeff Chandler, Paul Frees.

Our Miss Brooks (CBS); 12/19/48; episode 12, "The Christmas Present"; produced by Larry Berns; directed by Al Lewis; assistant director, Carl Harwood; written by Morton Fine, David Friedkin and Al Lewis; music by Wilbur Hatch; sound by Bill Gould; engineer, Pat Walsh; announcers, Bob Lemond and Verne Smith; cast: Eve Arden, Jeff Chandler, Gale Gordon, Jane Morgan, Richard Crenna, Gloria McMillan, Hal March, Sheldon Leonard, Ken Christy, William Conrad.

Duffy's Tavern (NBC); 12/23/48; episode 12, "Miracle in Manhattan: A Christmas Story"; directed by Antony Stanford; NBC director, John Morris; written by Vincent (Vin) Bogert, Bill Freedman, Morris Freedman, Lou Grant, Seymour Kapetansky, Larry Rhine, Bob Schiller and Phil Sharp; commercial writer, Sylvia Dowling; commercial supervisor, Ruby Irwin; music by Matty Malneck; organist, Merle Clark; sound by Bob Grapperhaus; engineer, Charles Norman; announcer, Ken Peters; cast: Ed Gardner, Charlie Cantor, Eddie Green, Florence Halop, Jeff Chandler, Bobby Ellis, Robert Bruce, Florence Baker, Donald Woods, Betty Lou Gerson, Marvin Miller, Frank Gerstle, Franklin Parker, Scott Elliott.

The New Adventures of Michael Shayne (Synd.); 12/23/48; episode 19, "The Case of the Carnival Killer"; directed by William P. Rousseau; cast: Jeff Chandler, Jack Webb, Hans Conried.

Our Miss Brooks (CBS); 12/26/48; episode 13, "Magic Christmas Tree"; produced by Larry Berns; directed by Al Lewis; assistant director, Carl Harwood; written by Morton Fine, David Friedkin and Al Lewis; music by Wilbur Hatch; sound by Bill Gould; engineer, Pat Walsh; announcers, Bob Lemond and Verne Smith; cast: Eve Arden, Jeff Chandler, Gale Gordon, Jane Morgan, Richard Crenna, Gloria McMillan, Helen Spring, Johnny McGovern.

The New Adventures of Michael Shayne (Synd.); 12/30/48; episode 20, "The Case of the Constant Companion"; directed by William P. Rousseau; cast: Jeff Chandler, Jack Webb, William Conrad, Charles McGraw.

1949

Our Miss Brooks (CBS); 01/02/49; episode 14, "Happy New Year"; produced by Larry Berns; directed by Al Lewis; assistant director, Carl Harwood; written by Morton Fine, David Friedkin and Al Lewis; music by Wilbur Hatch; sound by Bill Gould; engineer, Pat Walsh; announcers, Bob Lemond and Verne Smith; cast: Eve Arden, Jeff Chandler, Gale Gordon, Jane Morgan, Richard Crenna, Gloria McMillan, Gerald Mohr, Eleanor Audley, Hal March, Jack Kruschen.

The Lux Radio Theatre (CBS); 01/03/49; episode 639, "The Mating of Millie"; directed by Frederic MacKaye; host, William Keighley; cast: Glenn Ford, Evelyn Keyes, Jimmy Hunt, Gerald Mohr, Jeff Chandler, Lois Corbett, Charlotte Lawrence, Gwen Delano, Bill Johnstone, Louise Fitch, Eddie Marr.

The Railroad Hour (ABC); 01/03/49; episode 14, "Whoopee" adapted by Bill Demling; chorus by Norman Luboff; orchestra by Carmen Dragon; announcer, Marvin Miller; host, Gordon MacRae; cast: Eddie Cantor, Eileen Wilson, Lou Merrill, Elvia Allman, Joseph Kearns, Jeff Chandler, Jess Kirkpatrick.

Radio

Our Miss Brooks (CBS); 01/09/49; episode 15, "Economy Wave"; produced by Larry Berns; directed by Al Lewis; assistant director, Carl Harwood; written by Morton Fine, David Friedkin, Al Lewis and Alan Rader; music by Wilbur Hatch; sound by Bill Gould; engineer, Pat Walsh; announcers, Bob Lemond and Verne Smith; cast: Eve Arden, Jeff Chandler, Gale Gordon, Jane Morgan, Richard Crenna, Gloria McMillan.

Our Miss Brooks (CBS); 01/16/49; episode 16, "Student Government Day"; produced by Larry Berns; directed by Al Lewis; assistant director, Carl Harwood; written by Morton Fine, David Friedkin, Al Lewis and Lester White; music by Wilbur Hatch; sound by Bill Gould; engineer, Pat Walsh; announcers, Bob Lemond and Verne Smith; cast: Eve Arden, Jeff Chandler, Gale Gordon, Jane Morgan, Richard Crenna, Gloria McMillan, Helen Spring, Hans Conried, Herb Vigran, Hal March.

The Lux Radio Theatre (CBS); 01/17/49; episode 641, "You Gotta Stay Happy"; directed by Frederic MacKaye; host, William Keighley; cast: Joan Fontaine, James Stewart, Frank Albertson, Joseph Kearns, Bill Johnstone, Willard Waterman, Jane Webb, Gil Stratton Jr., Herb Butterfield, Jeff Chandler, George Neise, Cy Kendall, Regina Wallace, Eddie Marr, Gail Bonney, Edwin Max.

Our Miss Brooks (CBS); 01/23/49; episode 17, "Head English Department"; produced by Larry Berns; directed by Al Lewis; assistant director, Carl Harwood; written by Morton Fine, David Friedkin, Al Lewis and Lester White; music by Wilbur Hatch; sound by Bill Gould; engineer, Pat Walsh; announcers, Bob Lemond and Verne Smith; cast: Eve Arden, Jeff Chandler, Gale Gordon, Jane Morgan, Richard Crenna, Gloria McMillan, Mary Jane Croft.

Hallmark Playhouse (CBS); 01/27/49; episode 32, "The Failure"; directed by Dee Engelbach; host, James Hilton; cast: Ward Bond, Jeff Chandler, Gerald Mohr.

Our Miss Brooks (CBS); 01/30/49; episode 18, "Custodian of Student Funds"; produced by Larry Berns; directed by Al Lewis; assistant director, Carl Harwood; written by Morton Fine, David Friedkin, Al Lewis and Lester White; music by Wilbur Hatch; sound by Bill Gould; engineer, Pat Walsh; announcers, Bob Lemond and Verne Smith; cast: Eve Arden, Jeff Chandler, Gale Gordon, Jane Morgan, Richard Crenna, Gloria McMillan, Helen Spring, Frank Nelson.

The Lux Radio Theatre (CBS); 01/31/49; episode 643, "The Street with No Name"; directed by Frederic MacKaye; host, William Keighley; cast: Mark Stevens, Richard Widmark, Lloyd Nolan, John McIntire, Ed Begley, Bill Johnstone, Jeff Chandler, Cliff Clark, Sam Edwards, Eddie Marr, Charlotte Lawrence, Ross Tay-

Jeff Chandler

lor, Paul Dubov, Ed Emerson, Robert Griffin, Harry Lewis, Eleanor Audley, Jay Novello, Edwin Max, Tyler McVey.

Our Miss Brooks (CBS); 02/06/49; episode 19, "Working in the Stockroom"; produced by Larry Berns; directed by Al Lewis; assistant director, Carl Harwood; written by Morton Fine, David Friedkin, Al Lewis and Lester White; music by Wilbur Hatch; sound by Bill Gould; engineer, Pat Walsh; announcers, Bob Lemond and Verne Smith; cast: Eve Arden, Jeff Chandler, Gale Gordon, Jane Morgan, Richard Crenna, Gloria McMillan, Arthur Q. Bryan, Frank Nelson.

The Adventures of Phillip Marlowe (CBS); 02/12/49; episode 20, "The Lonesome Reunion"; produced and directed by Norman Macdonnell; cast: Gerald Mohr, Joan Banks, Edgar Barrier, Virginia Gregg, Jeff Chandler.

Our Miss Brooks (CBS); 02/13/49; episode 20, "Stretch is Ineligible for Basketball Team"; produced by Larry Berns; directed by Al Lewis; assistant director, Carl Harwood; written by Morton Fine, David Friedkin, Al Lewis and Lester White; music by Wilbur Hatch; sound by Bill Gould; engineer, Pat Walsh; announcers, Bob Lemond and Verne Smith; cast: Eve Arden, Jeff Chandler, Gale Gordon, Jane Morgan, Richard Crenna, Gloria McMillan, Leonard Smith, Frank Nelson.

Our Miss Brooks (CBS); 02/20/49; episode 21, "The Frog"; produced by Larry Berns; directed by Al Lewis; assistant director, Carl Harwood; written by Morton Fine, David Friedkin, Al Lewis and Lester White; music by Wilbur Hatch; sound by Bill Gould; engineer, Pat Walsh; announcers, Bob Lemond and Verne Smith; cast: Eve Arden, Jeff Chandler, Gale Gordon, Jane Morgan, Richard Crenna, Gloria McMillan, Gerald Mohr.

Hallmark Playhouse (CBS); 02/24/49; episode 36, "So Big"; directed by Dee Engelbach; host, James Hilton; cast: Virginia Bruce, Jeff Chandler, Howard McNear.

Escape (CBS); 02/26/49; episode 57, "Red Wine"; directed by Norman Macdonnell; cast: Jeff Chandler, Berry Kroeger, Laurette Fillbrandt, Jack Kruschen, Lou Krugman, David Ellis.

The Adventures of Phillip Marlowe (CBS); 02/26/49; episode 22, "The Big Mistake"; directed by Norman Macdonnell; cast: Gerald Mohr, Jeff Chandler.

Our Miss Brooks (CBS); 02/27/49; episode 22, "Stretch has a Problem"; produced by Larry Berns; directed by Al Lewis; assistant director, Carl Harwood; written by Morton Fine, David Friedkin, Al Lewis and Lester White; music by Wilbur Hatch; sound by Bill Gould; engineer, Pat Walsh; announcers, Bob Lemond and Verne Smith; cast: Eve Arden, Jeff Chandler, Gale Gordon, Jane Morgan, Richard Crenna, Gloria McMillan, Leonard Smith, Frank Nelson.

Radio

Our Miss Brooks (CBS); 03/06/49; episode 23, "Faculty Dance"; produced by Larry Berns; directed by Al Lewis; assistant director, Carl Harwood; written by Morton Fine, David Friedkin, Al Lewis and Lester White; music by Wilbur Hatch; sound by Bill Gould; engineer, Pat Walsh; announcers, Bob Lemond and Verne Smith; cast: Eve Arden, Jeff Chandler, Richard Crenna, Frank Nelson, Mary Jane Croft, Jane Morgan, Gale Gordon, Gloria McMillan, Margaret MacDonald.

The Lux Radio Theatre (CBS); 03/07/49; episode 648, "Red River"; directed by Frederic MacKaye; host, William Keighley; cast: John Wayne, Joanne Dru, Walter Brennan, Jeff Chandler, Bernard Phillips, Jeff Corey, Bill Johnstone, Alan Reed, Herb Butterfield, James Ogg, Willard Waterman, Lillian Buyeff, Lou Krugman, Jay Novello, Edwin Max, Eddie Marr.

Hallmark Playhouse (CBS); 03/10/49; episode 38, "And There I Stood with My Piccolo"; directed by Dee Engelbach; host, James Hilton; cast: Meredith Wilson, Jeff Chandler.

Our Miss Brooks (CBS); 03/13/49; episode 24, "Cafeteria Boycott"; produced by Larry Berns; directed by Al Lewis; assistant director, Carl Harwood; written by Morton Fine, David Friedkin, Al Lewis and Lester White; music by Wilbur Hatch; sound by Bill Gould; engineer, Pat Walsh; announcers, Bob Lemond and Verne Smith; cast: Eve Arden, Jeff Chandler, Gale Gordon, Jane Morgan, Richard Crenna, Gloria McMillan, Leonard Smith, William Conrad, Gerald Mohr.

Our Miss Brooks (CBS); 03/20/49; episode 25, "Poetry Mix-up"; produced by Larry Berns; directed by Al Lewis; assistant director, Carl Harwood; written by Morton Fine, David Friedkin, Al Lewis and Joseph Quillan; sound by Bill Gould; engineer, Pat Walsh; announcers, Bob Lemond and Verne Smith; cast: Eve Arden, Jeff Chandler, Gale Gordon, Jane Morgan, Richard Crenna, Gloria McMillan, Leonard Smith.

Our Miss Brooks (CBS); 03/27/49; episode 26, "Does Clay High Want Miss Brooks?"; produced by Larry Berns; directed by Al Lewis; assistant director, Carl Harwood; written by Morton Fine, David Friedkin, Al Lewis, Joseph Quillan and Lester White; sound by Bill Gould; engineer, Pat Walsh; announcers, Bob Lemond and Verne Smith; cast: Eve Arden, Jeff Chandler, Gale Gordon, Jane Morgan, Richard Crenna, Gloria McMillan, Gerald Mohr, Frank Nelson.

Our Miss Brooks (CBS); 04/03/49; episode 27, "Mr. Conklin's Talent Party"; produced by Larry Berns; directed by Al Lewis; assistant director, Carl Harwood; written by Morton Fine, David Friedkin, Al Lewis and Lester White; sound by Bill Gould; engineer, Pat Walsh; announcers, Bob Lemond and Verne Smith; cast: Eve

Jeff Chandler

Arden, Jeff Chandler, Gale Gordon, Jane Morgan, Richard Crenna, Gloria McMillan, Ken Harvey, Mary Jane Croft.

Our Miss Brooks (CBS); 04/10/49; episode 28, "Mr. Conklin's Wake-up Plan"; produced by Larry Berns; directed by Al Lewis; assistant director, Carl Harwood; written by Morton Fine, David Friedkin, Al Lewis, Joseph Quillan and Lester White; sound by Bill Gould; engineer, Pat Walsh; announcers, Bob Lemond and Verne Smith; cast: Eve Arden, Jeff Chandler, Gale Gordon, Jane Morgan, Richard Crenna, Gloria McMillan, Ed Begley, Earle Ross.

Our Miss Brooks (CBS); 04/17/49; episode 29, "Easter Outfit"; produced by Larry Berns; directed by Al Lewis; assistant director, Carl Harwood; written by Morton Fine, David Friedkin, Al Lewis and Lester White; sound by Bill Gould; engineer, Pat Walsh; announcers, Bob Lemond and Verne Smith; cast: Eve Arden, Jeff Chandler, Gale Gordon, Jane Morgan, Richard Crenna, Gloria McMillan, Ed Begley, Mary Jane Croft.

The Damon Runyon Theater (Synd.); 04/24/49; episode 17, "Blonde Mink"; directed by Richard Sanville; cast: John Brown, Jeff Chandler.

The Whistler (Synd.); 04/24/49; episode 360, "Mask for Kinsella"; directed by George W. Allen; cast: Jeff Chandler (as "Ira Grossel"), Frances Robinson, Paul McVey.

Our Miss Brooks (CBS); 04/24/49; episode 30, "Problem Over Clothes"; produced by Larry Berns; directed by Al Lewis; assistant director, Ralph Jones; written by Morton Fine, David Friedkin, Al Lewis, Joseph Quillan and Lester White; music by Wilbur Hatch; sound by Bill Gould; engineer, Pat Walsh; announcers, Bob Lemond and Verne Smith; cast: Eve Arden, Jeff Chandler, Gale Gordon, Jane Morgan, Richard Crenna, Gloria McMillan, Leonard Smith, Earle Ross.

The Damon Runyon Theater (Synd.); 05/01/49; episode 18, "Leopard's Spots"; directed by Richard Sanville; cast: John Brown, Jeff Chandler.

Our Miss Brooks (CBS); 05/01/49; episode 31, "The Grudge Match"; produced by Larry Berns; directed by Al Lewis; assistant director, Ralph Jones; written by Morton Fine, David Friedkin, Al Lewis and Lester White; music by Wilbur Hatch; sound by Bill Gould; engineer, Pat Walsh; announcers, Bob Lemond and Verne Smith; cast: Eve Arden, Jeff Chandler, Gale Gordon, Jane Morgan, Richard Crenna, Gloria McMillan, Leonard Smith.

Our Miss Brooks (CBS); 05/08/49; episode 32, "Mother's Day"; produced by Larry Berns; directed by Al Lewis; assistant director, Ralph Jones; written by Morton Fine, David Friedkin, Al Lewis, Joseph Quillan and Lester White; music by

Wilbur Hatch; sound by Bill Gould; engineer, Pat Walsh; announcers, Bob Lemond and Verne Smith; cast: Eve Arden, Jeff Chandler, Gale Gordon, Jane Morgan, Richard Crenna, Gloria McMillan, Myra Marsh, Frank Nelson.

Our Miss Brooks (CBS); 05/15/49; episode 33, "Friday the 13th"; produced by Larry Berns; directed by Al Lewis; assistant director, Ralph Jones; written by Morton Fine, David Friedkin, Al Lewis and Lester White; music by Wilbur Hatch; engineer, Pat Walsh; announcers, Bob Lemond and Verne Smith; cast: Eve Arden, Jeff Chandler, Gale Gordon, Jane Morgan, Richard Crenna, Gloria McMillan, Leonard Smith.

Our Miss Brooks (CBS); 05/22/49; episode 34, "Peanuts, the Great Dane"; produced by Larry Berns; directed by Al Lewis; assistant director, Ted Rogers; written by Morton Fine, David Friedkin, Al Lewis, Joseph Quillan and Lester White; music by Wilbur Hatch; sound by Bill Gould; engineer, Pat Walsh; announcers, Bob Lemond and Verne Smith; cast: Eve Arden, Jeff Chandler, Gale Gordon, Jane Morgan, Richard Crenna, Gloria McMillan, Leonard Smith, Mary Jane Croft, Pinto Colvig.

Our Miss Brooks (CBS); 05/29/49; episode 35, "Why is Everybody Arguing?"; produced by Larry Berns; directed by Al Lewis; assistant director, Ralph Jones; written by Morton Fine, David Friedkin, Al Lewis and Lester White; music by Wilbur Hatch; engineer, Pat Walsh; announcers, Bob Lemond and Verne Smith; cast: Eve Arden, Jeff Chandler, Gale Gordon, Jane Morgan, Richard Crenna, Gloria McMillan, Vivi Janiss.

Our Miss Brooks (CBS); 06/05/49; episode 36, "Key to the School"; produced by Larry Berns; directed by Al Lewis; assistant director, Ralph Jones; written by Morton Fine, David Friedkin, Al Lewis, Joseph Quillan and Lester White; music by Wilbur Hatch; sound by Bill Gould; engineer, Pat Walsh; announcers, Bob Lemond and Verne Smith; cast: Eve Arden, Jeff Chandler, Gale Gordon, Jane Morgan, Richard Crenna, Gloria McMillan, Bob Jellison, Frank Nelson, Hal March.

Our Miss Brooks (CBS); 06/12/49; episode 37, "The Wishing Well School Dance"; produced by Larry Berns; directed by Al Lewis; assistant director, Ralph Jones; written by Morton Fine, David Friedkin, Al Lewis and Lester White; music by Wilbur Hatch; sound by Bill Gould; engineer, Pat Walsh; announcers, Bob Lemond and Verne Smith; cast: Eve Arden, Jeff Chandler, Gale Gordon, Jane Morgan, Richard Crenna, Gloria McMillan, Leonard Smith, Bob Jellison.

Our Miss Brooks (CBS); 06/19/49; episode 38, "Taxidermy"; produced by Larry Berns; directed by Al Lewis; assistant director, Ralph Jones; written by Morton Fine, David Friedkin, Al Lewis and Joseph Quillan; music by Wilbur Hatch;

Jeff Chandler

sound by Bill Gould; engineer, Pat Walsh; announcers, Bob Lemond and Verne Smith; cast: Eve Arden, Gale Gordon, Jane Morgan, Richard Crenna, Gloria McMillan, Leonard Smith.

Our Miss Brooks (CBS); 06/26/49; episode 39, "June Bride"; produced by Larry Berns; directed by Al Lewis; assistant director, Ralph Jones; written by Morton Fine, David Friedkin, Al Lewis and Lester White; music by Wilbur Hatch; sound by Bill Gould; engineer, Pat Walsh; announcers, Bob Lemond and Verne Smith; cast: Eve Arden, Jeff Chandler, Gale Gordon, Jane Morgan, Richard Crenna, Gloria McMillan, Gerald Mohr, Frank Nelson.

Our Miss Brooks (CBS); 07/03/49; episode 40, "July 4th Weekend"; produced by Larry Berns; directed by Al Lewis; assistant director, Robert Hafter; written by Morton Fine, David Friedkin, Al Lewis and Lester White; music by Wilbur Hatch; engineer, Pat Walsh; announcers, Bob Lemond and Verne Smith; cast: Eve Arden, Jeff Chandler, Gale Gordon, Jane Morgan, Richard Crenna, Gloria McMillan, Howard McNear.

Our Miss Brooks (CBS); 07/10/49; episode 41, "Telegram for Mrs. Davis"; produced by Larry Berns; directed by Al Lewis; assistant director, Robert Hafter; written by Morton Fine, David Friedkin, Al Lewis, Joseph Quillan and Lester White; music by Wilbur Hatch; sound by David Light; engineer, Pat Walsh; announcers, Bob Lemond and Verne Smith; cast: Eve Arden, Gale Gordon, Jane Morgan, Richard Crenna, Gloria McMillan, Jerry Hausner, Joseph Kearns, Peter Leeds.

Our Miss Brooks (CBS); 07/17/49; episode 42, "The Conklin Carelessness Code"; produced by Larry Berns; directed by Al Lewis; written by Morton Fine, David Friedkin, Al Lewis and Lester White; music by Wilbur Hatch; engineer, Pat Walsh; announcers, Bob Lemond and Verne Smith; cast: Eve Arden, Jeff Chandler, Gale Gordon, Jane Morgan, Richard Crenna, Gloria McMillan.

Our Miss Brooks (CBS); 07/24/49; episode 43, "Pensacola Popovers"; produced by Larry Berns; directed by Al Lewis; written by Morton Fine, David Friedkin, Al Lewis, Joseph Quillan and Lester White; music by Wilbur Hatch; engineer, Pat Walsh; announcers, Bob Lemond and Verne Smith; cast: Eve Arden, Jeff Chandler, Gale Gordon, Jane Morgan, Richard Crenna, Gloria McMillan.

Our Miss Brooks (CBS); 07/31/49; episode 44, "Will Connie Resign?"; produced by Larry Berns; directed by Al Lewis; assistant director, Carl Harwood; written by Al Lewis, Joseph Quillan and Lester White; music by Wilbur Hatch; engineer, Pat Walsh; announcers, Bob Lemond and Verne Smith; cast: Eve Arden, Jeff Chandler, Gale Gordon, Jane Morgan, Richard Crenna, Gloria McMillan, Gloria Blondell.

Radio

Our Miss Brooks (CBS); 08/07/49; episode 45, "Hot Weather at Summer School"; produced by Larry Berns; directed by Al Lewis; assistant director, Carl Harwood; written by Al Lewis, Joseph Quillan and Lester White; music by Wilbur Hatch; sound by Bill Gould; engineer, Pat Walsh; announcers, Bob Lemond and Verne Smith; cast: Eve Arden, Jeff Chandler, Gale Gordon, Jane Morgan, Richard Crenna, Gloria McMillan, Leonard Smith.

Our Miss Brooks (CBS); 08/14/49; episode 46, "Snodgrass Barbecue"; produced by Larry Berns; directed by Al Lewis; assistant director, Carl Harwood; written by Al Lewis, Joseph Quillan and Lester White; music by Wilbur Hatch; sound by Bill Gould; engineer, Pat Walsh; announcers, Bob Lemond and Verne Smith; cast: Eve Arden, Jeff Chandler, Gale Gordon, Jane Morgan, Richard Crenna, Gloria McMillan, Leonard Smith, Bob Jellison.

Our Miss Brooks (CBS); 08/21/49; episode 47, "Conklin's Anniversary"; produced by Larry Berns; directed by Al Lewis; assistant director, Carl Harwood; written by Al Lewis, Joseph Quillan and Lester White; music by Wilbur Hatch; sound by Bill Gould; engineer, Pat Walsh; announcers, Bob Lemond and Verne Smith; cast: Eve Arden, Jeff Chandler, Gale Gordon, Jane Morgan, Richard Crenna, Gloria McMillan, Vivi Janiss.

The Whistler (Synd.); 08/21/49; episode 377, "Confession"; directed by Sterling Tracy; cast: Bill Forman, Jeff Chandler, Larry Dobkin, Wilms Herbert, Doris Singleton, Herb Butterfield, Tyler McVey, Mary Lansing.

Dragnet (NBC); 08/25/49; episode 12, "Police Academy"; directed by William P. Rousseau; cast: Jack Webb, Barton Yarborough, Jeff Chandler, Mario Koski.

The Damon Runyon Theater (Synd.); 08/28/49; episode 35, "Social Error"; directed by Richard Sanville; cast: John Brown, Jeff Chandler.

Our Miss Brooks (CBS); 08/28/49; episode 48, "Madison Summer Athletic Festival"; produced by Larry Berns; directed by Al Lewis; assistant director, Ralph Jones; written by Al Lewis, Joseph Quillan and Lester White; music by Wilbur Hatch; sound by Bill Gould; engineer, Pat Walsh; announcers, Bob Lemond and Verne Smith; cast: Eve Arden, Jeff Chandler, Gale Gordon, Jane Morgan, Richard Crenna, Gloria McMillan, Mary Jane Croft.

The Whistler (Synd.); 09/04/49; episode 379, "Smart Girl"; directed by Sterling Tracy; cast: Bill Forman, Mary Lansing, Charles Seel, William Conrad, Byron Kane, Bill Bouchey, Jeff Chandler (as "Ira Grossel").

Family Theater (Mut.); 09/07/49; episode 134, "The Song of Roland"; directed

Jeff Chandler

by Jaime del Valle; hostess, Terry Moore; cast: Jeff Chandler, John Dehner, Charles Lund, Robert Griffin, Dennis Hoey, Lou Krugman, Ted Osborne.

Hollywood Star Theater (NBC); 09/10/49; "Promise of Murder"; directed by Jack Van Nostrand and Nat Wolff; hostess, Margaret O'Brien; cast: Rita Lynn, Norma Jean Nilsson, Alan Reed, Jeff Chandler (as "Ira Grossel"), David Ellis.

Four-Star Playhouse (NBC); 09/11/49; "Paradise, U.S.A."; directed by Warren Lewis; cast: Rosalind Russell, Jeff Chandler (as "Ira Grossel"), Dan O'Herlihy, Ken Christy, Shepard Menken.

Our Miss Brooks (CBS); 09/11/49; episode 49, "Board of Education Visit"; produced by Larry Berns; directed by Al Lewis; assistant director, Ralph Jones; written by Al Lewis, Joseph Quillan and Lester White; music by Wilbur Hatch; sound by Bill Gould; engineer, Pat Walsh; announcers, Bob Lemond and Verne Smith; cast: Eve Arden, Jeff Chandler, Gale Gordon, Jane Morgan, Richard Crenna, Gloria McMillan, Leonard Smith.

Our Miss Brooks (CBS); 09/18/49; episode 50, "Faculty Cheerleader"; produced by Larry Berns; directed by Al Lewis; assistant director, Ralph Jones; written by Al Lewis, Joseph Quillan and Lester White; music by Wilbur Hatch; sound by Bill Gould; engineer, Pat Walsh; announcers, Bob Lemond and Verne Smith; cast: Eve Arden, Jeff Chandler, Gale Gordon, Jane Morgan, Richard Crenna, Gloria McMillan, Mary Jane Croft.

Our Miss Brooks (CBS); 09/25/49; episode 51, "Framing Mr. Boynton"; produced by Larry Berns; directed by Al Lewis; assistant director, Ralph Jones; written by Al Lewis, Joseph Quillan and Lester White; music by Wilbur Hatch; sound by Bill Gould; engineer, Pat Walsh; announcers, Bob Lemond and Verne Smith; cast: Eve Arden, Jeff Chandler, Gale Gordon, Jane Morgan, Richard Crenna, Gloria McMillan, Hal March.

The Damon Runyon Theater (Synd.); 10/23/49; episode 43, "Palm Beach Santa Claus"; directed by Richard Sanville; cast: John Brown, Jeff Chandler.

Our Miss Brooks (CBS); 10/02/49; episode 52, "Rival Football"; produced by Larry Berns; directed by Al Lewis; assistant director, Ralph Jones; written by Al Lewis, Joseph Quillan and Lester White; music by Wilbur Hatch; sound by Bill Gould; engineer, Pat Walsh; announcers, Bob Lemond and Verne Smith; cast: Eve Arden, Gale Gordon, Jane Morgan, Richard Crenna, Gloria McMillan, Leonard Smith, Frank Nelson, Leif Erickson.

Our Miss Brooks (CBS); 10/09/49; episode 53, "A Note from Mr. LeBlanc"; produced by Larry Berns; directed by Al Lewis; assistant director, Ralph Jones;

written by Al Lewis, Joseph Quillan and Lester White; music by Wilbur Hatch; sound by Bill Gould; engineer, Pat Walsh; announcers, Bob Lemond and Verne Smith; cast: Eve Arden, Gale Gordon, Jane Morgan, Richard Crenna, Gloria McMillan, Gerald Mohr.

Our Miss Brooks (CBS); 10/16/49; episode 54, "Safety School Advisor"; produced by Larry Berns; directed by Al Lewis; assistant director, Ralph Jones; written by Al Lewis, Joseph Quillan and Lester White; music by Wilbur Hatch; sound by Bill Gould; engineer, Pat Walsh; announcers, Bob Lemond and Verne Smith; cast: Eve Arden, Gale Gordon, Jane Morgan, Richard Crenna, Gloria McMillan, Leonard Smith, Bob Jellison, Ed Begley.

Our Miss Brooks (CBS); 10/23/49; episode 55, "Gifts for Mr. Boynton"; produced by Larry Berns; directed and written by Al Lewis; assistant director, Ralph Jones; music by Wilbur Hatch; sound by Bill Gould; engineer, Pat Walsh; announcers, Bob Lemond and Verne Smith; cast: Eve Arden, Jeff Chandler, Gale Gordon, Jane Morgan, Richard Crenna, Gloria McMillan, Mary Jane Croft.

Our Miss Brooks (CBS); 10/30/49; episode 56, "Halloween"; produced by Larry Berns; directed and written by Al Lewis; assistant director, Ralph Jones; music by Wilbur Hatch; sound by Bill Gould; engineer, Pat Walsh; announcers, Bob Lemond and Verne Smith; cast: Eve Arden, Jeff Chandler, Gale Gordon, Jane Morgan, Richard Crenna, Gloria McMillan, Leonard Smith, Vivi Janiss.

Our Miss Brooks (CBS); 11/06/49; episode 57, "Ma Chere, Miss Brooks"; produced by Larry Berns; directed by Al Lewis; assistant director, Ralph Jones; written by Al Lewis and Joseph Quillan; music by Wilbur Hatch; sound by Bill Gould; engineer, Pat Walsh; announcers, Bob Lemond and Verne Smith; cast: Eve Arden, Jeff Chandler, Gale Gordon, Jane Morgan, Richard Crenna, Gloria McMillan, Gerald Mohr.

Our Miss Brooks (CBS); 11/13/49; episode 58, "Mix-up Over an Elephant"; produced by Larry Berns; directed by Al Lewis; assistant director, Ralph Jones; written by Al Lewis and Joseph Quillan; music by Wilbur Hatch; sound by Bill Gould; engineer, Pat Walsh; announcers, Bob Lemond and Verne Smith; cast: Eve Arden, Jeff Chandler, Gale Gordon, Jane Morgan, Richard Crenna, Gloria McMillan, Leonard Smith, Vivi Janiss, Hal March, Jerry Hausner.

Our Miss Brooks (CBS); 11/20/49; episode 59, "Party Line"; produced by Larry Berns; directed by Al Lewis; assistant director, Ralph Jones; written by Al Lewis and Joseph Quillan; music by Wilbur Hatch; sound by Bill Gould; engineer, Pat Walsh; announcers, Bob Lemond and Verne Smith; cast: Eve Arden, Jeff Chandler, Gale Gordon, Jane Morgan, Richard Crenna, Gloria McMillan, Joseph Kearns, Sandra Gould, Lucille Meredith.

Jeff Chandler

Our Miss Brooks (CBS); 11/27/49; episode 60, "Thanksgiving Mix-up"; produced by Larry Berns; directed by Al Lewis; assistant director, Ralph Jones; written by Al Lewis and Joseph Quillan; music by Wilbur Hatch; sound by Bill Gould; engineer, Pat Walsh; announcers, Bob Lemond and Verne Smith; cast: Eve Arden, Jeff Chandler, Gale Gordon, Jane Morgan, Richard Crenna, Gloria McMillan, Virginia Gordon.

The Screen Directors' Playhouse (NBC); 12/02/49; episode 45, "All My Sons"; directed by Bill Karn; guest director, Irving Reis; cast: Edward G. Robinson, Jeff Chandler, Irene Tedrow, Jack Edwards, Helen Andrews.

Our Miss Brooks (CBS); 12/04/49; episode 61, "Handsome New French Teacher"; produced by Larry Berns; directed and written by Al Lewis; assistant director, Ralph Jones; music by Wilbur Hatch; sound by Bill Gould; engineer, Pat Walsh; announcers, Bob Lemond and Verne Smith; cast: Eve Arden, Jeff Chandler, Gale Gordon, Jane Morgan, Richard Crenna, Gloria McMillan, Wally Maher.

Our Miss Brooks (CBS); 12/11/49; episode 62, "Connie is Chaperon"; produced by Larry Berns; directed by Al Lewis; assistant director, Ralph Jones; written by Al Lewis, Joseph Quillan and Lester White; music by Wilbur Hatch; sound by Bill Gould; engineer, Pat Walsh; announcers, Bob Lemond and Verne Smith; cast: Eve Arden, Jeff Chandler, Gale Gordon, Jane Morgan, Richard Crenna, Gloria McMillan, Mary Jane Croft.

Family Theater (Mut.); 12/14/49; episode 148, "The Other Wise Man"; directed by Jaime del Valle; host and narrator, Otto Kruger; cast: Jeff Chandler, Norman Field, Gloria Hunter, Virginia Eiler, John Dehner, Robert Griffin, Harold Dryanforth, Mary Lansing.

Our Miss Brooks (CBS); 12/18/49; episode 63, "Christmas Letter Contest"; produced by Larry Berns; directed and written by Al Lewis; assistant director, Ralph Jones; music by Wilbur Hatch; sound by Bill Gould; engineer, Pat Walsh; announcers, Bob Lemond and Verne Smith; cast: Eve Arden, Jeff Chandler, Gale Gordon, Jane Morgan, Richard Crenna, Gloria McMillan, Mary Jane Croft, Hal March.

Our Miss Brooks (CBS); 12/25/49; episode 64, "Magic Christmas Tree"; produced by Larry Berns; directed by Al Lewis; assistant director, Ralph Jones; written by Morton Fine, David Friedkin and Al Lewis; music by Wilbur Hatch; sound by Bill Gould; engineer, Pat Walsh; announcers, Bob Lemond and Verne Smith; cast: Eve Arden, Jeff Chandler, Gale Gordon, Jane Morgan, Richard Crenna, Gloria McMillan, Virginia Gordon, Jeffrey Silver.

1950

Our Miss Brooks (CBS); 01/01/50; episode 65, "New Year's Eve"; produced by Larry Berns; directed and written by Al Lewis; assistant director, Ralph Jones; music by Wilbur Hatch; sound by Bill Gould; engineer, Pat Walsh; announcers, Bob Lemond and Verne Smith; cast: Eve Arden, Jeff Chandler, Gale Gordon, Jane Morgan, Richard Crenna, Gloria McMillan, Jeffrey Silver, Bill Gould.

The Prudential Family Hour of Stars (CBS); 01/08/50; produced by Ken Burton; directed by Jack Johnstone; orchestra by Carmen Dragon; announcer, Truman Bradley; cast: Irene Dunne, Jeff Chandler.

Our Miss Brooks (CBS); 01/08/50; episode 66, "Walter Denton's Editorial"; produced by Larry Berns; directed by Al Lewis; assistant director, Ralph Jones; written by Al Lewis and Joseph Quillan; music by Wilbur Hatch; sound by Bill Gould; engineer, Pat Walsh; announcers, Bob Lemond and Verne Smith; cast: Eve Arden, Jeff Chandler, Gale Gordon, Jane Morgan, Richard Crenna, Gloria McMillan, Leonard Smith, Ed Begley.

The Screen Directors' Playhouse (NBC); 01/13/50; episode 51, "Tomorrow Is Forever"; directed by Bill Karn; guest director, Irving Pichel; cast: Claudette Colbert, Jeff Chandler, Sam Edwards, John McIntire.

Our Miss Brooks (CBS); 01/15/50; episode 67, "Cure that Habit!"; produced by Larry Berns; directed by Al Lewis; assistant director, Ralph Jones; written by Al Lewis, Joseph Quillan and Lester White; music by Wilbur Hatch; sound by Bill Gould; engineer, Pat Walsh; announcers, Bob Lemond and Verne Smith; cast: Eve Arden, Jeff Chandler, Gale Gordon, Jane Morgan, Richard Crenna, Gloria McMillan, Leonard Smith, Francis X. Bushman, William Lally.

The Prudential Family Hour of Stars (CBS); 01/22/50, "Ballerina"; produced by Ken Burton; directed by Jack Johnstone; orchestra by Carmen Dragon; announcer, Truman Bradley; cast: Loretta Young, Jeff Chandler.

Our Miss Brooks (CBS); 01/22/50; episode 68, "Mr. Boynton Interviews for State University"; produced by Larry Berns; directed and written by Al Lewis; assistant director, Ralph Jones; music by Wilbur Hatch; sound by Bill Gould; engineer, Pat Walsh; announcers, Bob Lemond and Verne Smith; cast: Eve Arden, Jeff Chandler, Gale Gordon, Jane Morgan, Richard Crenna, Gloria McMillan, Frank Nelson.

Our Miss Brooks (CBS); 01/29/50; episode 69, "School on Saturday"; produced by Larry Berns; directed by Al Lewis; assistant director, Ralph Jones; written by Al Lewis and Joseph Quillan; music by Wilbur Hatch; sound by Bill Gould; engineer, Pat Walsh; announcers, Bob Lemond and Verne Smith; cast: Eve Arden,

Jeff Chandler

Jeff Chandler, Gale Gordon, Jane Morgan, Richard Crenna, Gloria McMillan, Leonard Smith, Bill Johnstone.

Our Miss Brooks (CBS); 02/05/50; episode 70, "Mr. Boynton and Miss Enright"; produced by Larry Berns; directed and written by Al Lewis; assistant director, Ralph Jones; music by Wilbur Hatch; sound by Bill Gould; engineer, Pat Walsh; announcers, Bob Lemond and Verne Smith; cast: Eve Arden, Jeff Chandler, Gale Gordon, Jane Morgan, Richard Crenna, Gloria McMillan, Mary Jane Croft.

Our Miss Brooks (CBS); 02/12/50; episode 71, "Winter Carnival at Crystal Lake"; produced by Larry Berns; directed and written by Al Lewis; assistant director, Ralph Jones; music by Wilbur Hatch; sound by Bill Gould; engineer, Pat Walsh; announcers, Bob Lemond and Verne Smith; cast: Eve Arden, Jeff Chandler, Gale Gordon, Jane Morgan, Richard Crenna, Gloria McMillan.

Our Miss Brooks (CBS); 02/19/50; episode 72, "Valentine's Day Show"; produced by Larry Berns; directed by Al Lewis; assistant director, Ralph Jones; written by Al Lewis and Joseph Quillan; music by Wilbur Hatch; sound by Bill Gould; engineer, Pat Walsh; announcers, Bob Lemond and Verne Smith; cast: Eve Arden, Jeff Chandler, Gale Gordon, Jane Morgan, Richard Crenna, Gloria McMillan, Leonard Smith.

Our Miss Brooks (CBS); 02/26/50; episode 73, "Formal Banquet"; produced by Larry Berns; directed by Al Lewis; assistant director, Ralph Jones; written by Al Lewis and Joseph Quillan; music by Wilbur Hatch; sound by Bill Gould; engineer, Pat Walsh; announcers, Bob Lemond and Verne Smith; cast: Eve Arden, Jeff Chandler, Gale Gordon, Jane Morgan, Richard Crenna, Gloria McMillan, Leonard Smith, Pattee Chapman.

Our Miss Brooks (CBS); 03/05/50; episode 74, "National Clean-Up"; produced by Larry Berns; directed by Al Lewis; assistant director, Ralph Jones; written by Al Lewis and Joseph Quillan; music by Wilbur Hatch; sound by Bill Gould; engineer, Pat Walsh; announcers, Bob Lemond and Verne Smith; cast: Eve Arden, Jeff Chandler, Gale Gordon, Jane Morgan, Richard Crenna, Gloria McMillan, Leonard Smith.

Our Miss Brooks (CBS); 03/12/50; episode 75, "The 5:00 a.m. Burglar"; produced by Larry Berns; directed by Al Lewis; assistant director, Ralph Jones; written by Al Lewis, Joseph Quillan and Lester White; musical direction by Maurice Carlton; music by Wilbur Hatch; sound by Bill Gould; engineer, Pat Walsh; announcers, Bob Lemond and Verne Smith; cast: Eve Arden, Jeff Chandler, Gale Gordon, Jane Morgan, Richard Crenna, Gloria McMillan, Bob Sweeney.

Our Miss Brooks (CBS); 03/19/50; episode 76, "Madison High Auction"; produced by Larry Berns; directed by Al Lewis; assistant director, Ralph Jones; written by Al Lewis and Joseph Quillan; musical direction by Maurice Carlton; music by Wilbur Hatch; sound by Bill Gould; engineer, Pat Walsh; announcers, Bob Lemond and Verne Smith; cast: Eve Arden, Jeff Chandler, Gale Gordon, Jane Morgan, Richard Crenna, Gloria McMillan, Leonard Smith.

Our Miss Brooks (CBS); 03/26/50; episode 77, "Opening Baseball Game with Clay City"; produced by Larry Berns; directed by Al Lewis; assistant director, Ralph Jones; written by Al Lewis and Joseph Quillan; musical direction by Maurice Carlton; music by Wilbur Hatch; sound by Bill Gould; engineer, Pat Walsh; announcers, Bob Lemond and Verne Smith; cast: Eve Arden, Jeff Chandler, Gale Gordon, Jane Morgan, Richard Crenna, Gloria McMillan, Frank Nelson.

Our Miss Brooks (CBS); 04/02/50; episode 78, "April Fool's Day"; produced by Larry Berns; directed by Al Lewis; assistant director, Ralph Jones; written by Al Lewis, Joseph Quillan and Lester White; musical direction by Maurice Carlton; music by Wilbur Hatch; sound by Bill Gould; engineer, Pat Walsh; announcers, Bob Lemond and Verne Smith; cast: Eve Arden, Jeff Chandler, Gale Gordon, Jane Morgan, Richard Crenna, Gloria McMillan, Leonard Smith, Willard Waterman, Bill Gould.

Our Miss Brooks (CBS); 04/09/50; episode 79, "Easter Egg Dye"; produced by Larry Berns; directed by Al Lewis; assistant director, Ralph Jones; written by Al Lewis, Joseph Quillan and Lester White; musical direction by Maurice Carlton; music by Wilbur Hatch; sound by Bill Gould; engineer, Pat Walsh; announcers, Bob Lemond and Verne Smith; cast: Eve Arden, Jeff Chandler, Gale Gordon, Jane Morgan, Richard Crenna, Gloria McMillan, Leonard Smith.

Our Miss Brooks (CBS); 04/16/50; episode 80, "Tea Leaves"; produced by Larry Berns; directed by Al Lewis; assistant director, Ralph Jones; written by Al Lewis and Joseph Quillan; musical direction by Maurice Carlton; music by Wilbur Hatch; sound by Cliff Thorsness; engineer, Pat Walsh; announcers, Bob Lemond and Verne Smith; cast: Eve Arden, Jeff Chandler, Gale Gordon, Jane Morgan, Richard Crenna, Gloria McMillan.

Our Miss Brooks (CBS); 04/23/50; episode 81, "Economy Drive — Tape Recorder"; produced by Larry Berns; directed by Al Lewis; assistant director, Ralph Jones; written by Al Lewis, Joseph Quillan and Lester White; musical direction by Maurice Carlton; sound by Cliff Thorsness; engineer, Pat Walsh; announcers, Bob Lemond and Verne Smith; cast: Eve Arden, Jeff Chandler, Gale Gordon, Jane Morgan, Richard Crenna, Gloria McMillan, Frank Nelson, Hal March.

Our Miss Brooks (CBS); 04/30/50; episode 82, "Mayor Rides by Madison

Jeff Chandler

High"; produced by Larry Berns; directed by Al Lewis; assistant director, Ralph Jones; written by Al Lewis, Joseph Quillan and Lester White; musical direction by Maurice Carlton; engineer, Pat Walsh; announcers, Bob Lemond and Verne Smith; cast: Eve Arden, Jeff Chandler, Gale Gordon, Jane Morgan, Richard Crenna, Gloria McMillan, Leonard Smith, Pattee Chapman.

Our Miss Brooks (CBS); 05/07/50; episode 83, "Miss Brooks Plans for a Barbecue"; produced by Larry Berns; directed by Al Lewis; assistant director, Ralph Jones; written by Al Lewis, Joseph Quillan and Lester White; musical direction by Maurice Carlton; sound by Cliff Thorsness; engineer, Pat Walsh; announcers, Bob Lemond and Verne Smith; cast: Eve Arden, Jeff Chandler, Gale Gordon, Jane Morgan, Richard Crenna, Gloria McMillan, Mary Jane Croft.

Our Miss Brooks (CBS); 05/14/50; episode 84, "Mother's Day Presents"; produced by Larry Berns; directed by Al Lewis; assistant director, Ralph Jones; written by Al Lewis, Joseph Quillan and Lester White; musical direction by Maurice Carlton; sound by Cliff Thorsness; engineer, Pat Walsh; announcers, Bob Lemond and Verne Smith; cast: Eve Arden, Jeff Chandler, Gale Gordon, Jane Morgan, Richard Crenna, Gloria McMillan, Helen Brown, Willard Waterman.

Our Miss Brooks (CBS); 05/21/50; episode 85, "Rare Black Orchid"; produced by Larry Berns; directed by Al Lewis; assistant director, Ralph Jones; written by Al Lewis, Joseph Quillan and Lester White; musical direction by Maurice Carlton; sound by Bill Gould; engineer, Pat Walsh; announcers, Bob Lemond and Verne Smith; cast: Eve Arden, Jeff Chandler, Gale Gordon, Jane Morgan, Richard Crenna, Gloria McMillan.

Our Miss Brooks (CBS); 05/28/50; episode 86, "Traffic Ticket"; produced by Larry Berns; directed by Al Lewis; assistant director, Ralph Jones; written by Al Lewis, Joseph Quillan and Lester White; musical direction by Maurice Carlton; sound by Bill Gould; engineer, Pat Walsh; announcers, Bob Lemond and Verne Smith; cast: Eve Arden, Jeff Chandler, Gale Gordon, Jane Morgan, Richard Crenna, Gloria McMillan, Leonard Smith.

Proudly We Hail (Synd.); 08/01/50; episode 62; produced by C. P. MacGregor; cast: Jeff Chandler.

Our Miss Brooks (CBS); 09/03/50; episode 87, "Beaver Lodge, Room 124"; produced by Larry Berns; directed and written by Al Lewis; assistant director, Ralph Jones; music by Wilbur Hatch; sound by Bill Gould; engineer, Pat Walsh; announcers, Bob Lemond and Verne Smith; cast: Eve Arden, Jeff Chandler, Gale Gordon, Jane Morgan, Richard Crenna, Gloria McMillan, Leonard Smith, William Waterman.

Radio

Our Miss Brooks (CBS); 09/10/50; episode 88, "Conklin Rumors"; produced by Larry Berns; directed by Al Lewis; assistant director, Ralph Jones; written by Arthur Alsberg and Al Lewis; music by Wilbur Hatch; sound by Bill Gould; engineer, Pat Walsh; announcers, Bob Lemond and Verne Smith; cast: Eve Arden, Jeff Chandler, Gale Gordon, Jane Morgan, Richard Crenna, Gloria McMillan, Leonard Smith, Virginia Gordon, Bill Johnstone.

Our Miss Brooks (CBS); 09/17/50; episode 89, "Mr. Boynton's Fire Rescue Practice"; produced by Larry Berns; directed by Al Lewis; assistant director, Ralph Jones; written by Al Lewis and Joseph Quillan; music by Wilbur Hatch; sound by Bill Gould; engineer, Pat Walsh; announcers, Bob Lemond and Verne Smith; cast: Eve Arden, Jeff Chandler, Gale Gordon, Jane Morgan, Richard Crenna, Gloria McMillan, Virginia Gordon, Frank Nelson.

Our Miss Brooks (CBS); 09/24/50; episode 90, "Mr. Conklin Fires the Football Coach"; produced by Larry Berns; directed by Al Lewis; assistant director, Ralph Jones; written by Arthur Alsberg and Al Lewis; music by Wilbur Hatch; sound by Bill Gould; engineer, Pat Walsh; announcers, Bob Lemond and Verne Smith; cast: Eve Arden, Jeff Chandler, Gale Gordon, Jane Morgan, Richard Crenna, Gloria McMillan, Leonard Smith.

Our Miss Brooks (CBS); 10/01/50; episode 91, "Measles"; produced by Larry Berns; directed and written by Al Lewis; assistant director, Ralph Jones; music by Wilbur Hatch; sound by Bill Gould; engineer, Pat Walsh; announcers, Bob Lemond and Verne Smith; cast: Eve Arden, Jeff Chandler, Gale Gordon, Jane Morgan, Richard Crenna, Gloria McMillan, Leonard Smith, Evelyn Barrows.

Our Miss Brooks (CBS); 10/08/50; episode 92, "Walter's Wonderful Radio"; produced by Larry Berns; directed by Al Lewis; assistant director, Ralph Jones; written by Arthur Alsberg and Al Lewis; music by Wilbur Hatch; sound by Bill Gould; engineer, Pat Walsh; announcers, Bob Lemond and Verne Smith; cast: Eve Arden, Jeff Chandler, Gale Gordon, Jane Morgan, Richard Crenna, Gloria McMillan, Dan Tobin.

Our Miss Brooks (CBS); 10/15/50; episode 93, "The School Telephone Bill"; produced by Larry Berns; directed by Al Lewis; assistant director, Ralph Jones; written by Arthur Alsberg and Al Lewis; music by Wilbur Hatch; sound by Bill Gould; engineer, Pat Walsh; announcers, Bob Lemond and Verne Smith; cast: Eve Arden, Jeff Chandler, Gale Gordon, Jane Morgan, Richard Crenna, Gloria McMillan, Leonard Smith, William Conrad, Dan Tobin, Fred Clark.

Adventure Is Your Heritage (Synd.); 10/22/50; episode 2A, "The Skipper's Pants"; directed by Frank Danzig; cast: Jeff Chandler.

Jeff Chandler

Our Miss Brooks (CBS); 10/22/50; episode 94, "Stretch Snodgrass is in Love"; produced by Larry Berns; directed by Al Lewis; assistant director, Ralph Jones; written by Arthur Alsberg and Al Lewis; music by Wilbur Hatch; sound by Bill Gould; engineer, Pat Walsh; announcers, Bob Lemond and Verne Smith; cast: Eve Arden, Jeff Chandler, Gale Gordon, Jane Morgan, Richard Crenna, Gloria McMillan, Leonard Smith, Sandra Gould.

Screen Guild Players (ABC); 10/26/50; episode 479, "Mother Didn't Tell Me"; directed by William (Bill) Lawrence; cast: Dorothy McGuire, Jeff Chandler.

Our Miss Brooks (CBS); 10/29/50; episode 95, "The Stag Party"; produced by Larry Berns; directed by Al Lewis; assistant director, Ralph Jones; written by Arthur Alsberg and Al Lewis; music by Wilbur Hatch; sound by Bill Gould; engineer, Pat Walsh; announcers, Bob Lemond and Verne Smith; cast: Eve Arden, Jeff Chandler, Gale Gordon, Jane Morgan, Richard Crenna, Gloria McMillan, Doris Singleton, Fred Clark.

Family Theater (Mut.); 11/01/50; episode 194, "Stolen Symphony"; directed by Jaime del Valle; cast: Ann Blyth, Jeff Chandler, Sarah Selby, Herb Vigran, Michael Chapin, Cynthia Corley, Gloria McMillan, Ralph Moody, Bill Barron.

Our Miss Brooks (CBS); 11/05/50; episode 96, "Indian Burial Ground"; produced by Larry Berns; directed by Al Lewis; assistant director, Ralph Jones; written by Arthur Alsberg and Al Lewis; music by Wilbur Hatch; sound by Bill Gould; engineer, Pat Walsh; announcers, Bob Lemond and Verne Smith; cast: Eve Arden, Jeff Chandler, Gale Gordon, Jane Morgan, Richard Crenna, Gloria McMillan, Jim Backus.

Our Miss Brooks (CBS); 11/12/50 episode 97, "Trouble with Miss Enright"; produced by Larry Berns; directed by Al Lewis; assistant director, Ralph Jones; written by Arthur Alsberg and Al Lewis; music by Wilbur Hatch; sound by Bill Gould; engineer, Pat Walsh; announcers, Bob Lemond and Verne Smith; cast: Eve Arden, Jeff Chandler, Gale Gordon, Jane Morgan, Richard Crenna, Gloria McMillan, Mary Jane Croft.

The Screen Directors' Playhouse (NBC); 11/16/50; episode 77, "Lifeboat"; directed by Bill Karn; guest director, Alfred Hitchcock; cast: Tallulah Bankhead, Jeff Chandler, Sheldon Leonard, Anne Diamond, Barbara Eiler, Henry Roland, Roy Glenn, Wilms Herbert.

Our Miss Brooks (CBS); 11/19/50; episode 98, "Turkey Dinner"; produced by Larry Berns; directed and written by Al Lewis; assistant director, Ralph Jones; music by Wilbur Hatch; sound by Bill Gould; engineer, Pat Walsh; announcers, Bob Lemond and Verne Smith; cast: Eve Arden, Jeff Chandler, Gale Gordon, Jane Morgan, Richard Crenna, Gloria McMillan, Bill Gould, David Light.

Radio

Our Miss Brooks (CBS); 11/26/50; episode 99, "Driving School"; produced by Larry Berns; directed by Al Lewis; assistant director, Ralph Jones; written by Arthur Alsberg and Al Lewis; music by Wilbur Hatch; sound by Bill Gould; engineer, Pat Walsh; announcers, Bob Lemond and Verne Smith; cast: Eve Arden, Jeff Chandler, Gale Gordon, Jane Morgan, Richard Crenna, Gloria McMillan, Leonard Smith.

Our Miss Brooks (CBS); 12/03/50; episode 100, "Connie and the Measles"; produced by Larry Berns; directed by Al Lewis; assistant director, Ralph Jones; written by Arthur Alsberg and Al Lewis; music by Wilbur Hatch; sound by Bill Gould; engineer, Pat Walsh; announcers, Bob Lemond and Verne Smith; cast: Eve Arden, Jeff Chandler, Gale Gordon, Jane Morgan, Richard Crenna, Gloria McMillan, Leonard Smith.

Our Miss Brooks (CBS); 12/10/50; episode 101, "Madison's Post-Season Game"; produced by Larry Berns; directed by Al Lewis; assistant director, Ralph Jones; written by Al Lewis and Joseph Quillan; music by Wilbur Hatch; sound by Bill Gould; engineer, Pat Walsh; announcers, Bob Lemond and Verne Smith; cast: Eve Arden, Jeff Chandler, Gale Gordon, Jane Morgan, Richard Crenna, Gloria McMillan, Leonard Smith, Fred Clark.

Our Miss Brooks (CBS); 12/17/50; episode 102, "Christmas Clothing Drive"; produced by Larry Berns; directed by Al Lewis; assistant director, Ralph Jones; written by Arthur Alsberg and Al Lewis; music by Wilbur Hatch; sound by Bill Gould; engineer, Pat Walsh; announcers, Bob Lemond and Verne Smith; cast: Eve Arden, Jeff Chandler, Gale Gordon, Jane Morgan, Richard Crenna, Gloria McMillan, Parley Baer.

Our Miss Brooks (CBS); 12/24/50; episode 103, "Magic Christmas Tree"; produced by Larry Berns; directed by Al Lewis; assistant director, Ralph Jones; written by Arthur Alsberg, Morton Fine, David Friedkin and Al Lewis; music by Wilbur Hatch; sound by Bill Gould; engineer, Pat Walsh; announcers, Bob Lemond and Verne Smith; cast: Eve Arden, Jeff Chandler, Gale Gordon, Jane Morgan, Richard Crenna, Gloria McMillan, Virginia Gordon, Mary Jane Croft.

The Hedda Hopper Show (NBC); 12/31/50; episode 12, "A Star is Born"; hostess, Hedda Hopper; produced by the FMB Company; directed by Gil Faust; written by Jackson Gillis and David Victor; music by Frank Worth; sound by Robert Conlon and Wayne Kenworthy; announcer, Art Baker; cast: Jean Hersholt, Lloyd Bridges, Jeff Chandler, Dick Contino, Tony Curtis (as "Anthony Curtis"), Faith Domergue, Howard Keel, Frank Lovejoy, Mala Powers, Jan Sterling, Barry Sullivan, David Wayne.

Our Miss Brooks (CBS); 12/31/50; episode 104, "Exchanging Christmas Presents"; produced by Larry Berns; directed by Al Lewis; assistant director, Ralph Jones; written by Arthur Alsberg and Al Lewis; music by Wilbur Hatch; sound by Bill Gould; engineer, Pat Walsh; announcers, Bob Lemond and Verne Smith; cast: Eve Arden, Jeff Chandler, Gale Gordon, Jane Morgan, Richard Crenna, Gloria McMillan, Virginia Gordon, Joseph Kearns.

1951

Our Miss Brooks (CBS); 01/07/51; episode 105, "New Bus Line"; produced by Larry Berns; directed by Al Lewis; assistant director, Ralph Jones; written by Arthur Alsberg and Al Lewis; music by Wilbur Hatch; sound by Bill Gould; engineer, Pat Walsh; announcers, Bob Lemond and Verne Smith; cast: Eve Arden, Jeff Chandler, Gale Gordon, Jane Morgan, Richard Crenna, Gloria McMillan, Joseph Kearns, Johnny McGovern.

Our Miss Brooks (CBS); 01/14/51; episode 106, "Connie's Old Boyfriend"; produced by Larry Berns; directed by Al Lewis; assistant director, Ralph Jones; written by Arthur Alsberg, Al Lewis and Joseph Quillan; music by Wilbur Hatch; sound by Bill Gould; engineer, Pat Walsh; announcers, Bob Lemond and Verne Smith; cast: Eve Arden, Jeff Chandler, Gale Gordon, Jane Morgan, Richard Crenna, Gloria McMillan, D. J. Thompson.

Our Miss Brooks (CBS); 01/21/51; episode 107, "Mr. Boynton to Leave Madison?"; produced by Larry Berns; directed by Al Lewis; assistant director, Ralph Jones; written by Arthur Alsberg and Al Lewis; music by Wilbur Hatch; sound by Bill Gould; engineer, Pat Walsh; announcers, Bob Lemond and Verne Smith; cast: Eve Arden, Jeff Chandler, Gale Gordon, Jane Morgan, Richard Crenna, Gloria McMillan, Joseph Kearns.

The Lux Radio Theatre (CBS); 01/22/51; episode 730, 01/22/51; "Broken Arrow"; directed by Earl Ebi; host, William Keighley; cast: Burt Lancaster, Jeff Chandler, Debra Paget, Bill Johnstone, William Conrad, Tom Tully, Herb Butterfield, Robert Griffin, Paul Dubov, Jack Negley, Joan Marshall, Dan Riss, Jerry Farber, James Ogg, Joseph Granby, Tyler McVey, Eddie Marr.

Our Miss Brooks (CBS); 01/28/51; episode 108, "Is Martha Conklin Going to Have a Baby?"; produced by Larry Berns; directed by Al Lewis; assistant director, Ralph Jones; written by Arthur Alsberg and Al Lewis; music by Wilbur Hatch; sound by Bill Gould; engineer, Pat Walsh; announcers, Bob Lemond and Verne Smith; cast: Eve Arden, Jeff Chandler, Gale Gordon, Jane Morgan, Richard Crenna, Gloria McMillan, Joseph Kearns, Jerry Hausner, Bill Gould.

Our Miss Brooks (CBS); 02/04/51; episode 109, "Puppy Love, Mr. Barlow, and

Miss Davis"; produced by Larry Berns; directed by Al Lewis; assistant director, Joe Allabough; written by Arthur Alsberg and Al Lewis; music by Wilbur Hatch; sound by Bill Gould; engineer, Pat Walsh; announcers, Bob Lemond and Verne Smith; cast: Eve Arden, Jeff Chandler, Gale Gordon, Jane Morgan, Richard Crenna, Gloria McMillan, Joseph Kearns.

Our Miss Brooks (CBS); 02/11/51; episode 110, "Miss Brooks' Oil Buy for Martha Conklin"; produced by Larry Berns; directed by Al Lewis; assistant director, Joe Allabough; written by Arthur Alsberg, James Fritzell, Al Lewis and Dave Swift; music by Wilbur Hatch; sound by Bill Gould; engineer, Pat Walsh; announcers, Bob Lemond and Verne Smith; cast: Eve Arden, Jeff Chandler, Gale Gordon, Jane Morgan, Richard Crenna, Gloria McMillan, Mary Jane Croft.

Our Miss Brooks (CBS); 02/18/51; episode 111, "Mrs. Davis May Lose Her House"; produced by Larry Berns; directed by Al Lewis; assistant director, Ralph Jones; written by Arthur Alsberg, Al Lewis and Joseph Quillan; music by Wilbur Hatch; sound by Bill Gould; engineer, Pat Walsh; announcers, Bob Lemond and Verne Smith; cast: Eve Arden, Jeff Chandler, Gale Gordon, Jane Morgan, Richard Crenna, Gloria McMillan, Joseph Kearns.

Our Miss Brooks (CBS); 02/25/51; episode 112, "Going Skiing"; produced by Larry Berns; directed by Al Lewis; assistant director, Ralph Jones; written by Arthur Alsberg, James Fritzell, Al Lewis and Joseph Quillan; music by Wilbur Hatch; sound by Bill Gould; engineer, Pat Walsh; announcers, Bob Lemond and Verne Smith; cast: Eve Arden, Jeff Chandler, Gale Gordon, Jane Morgan, Richard Crenna, Gloria McMillan.

Our Miss Brooks (CBS); 03/04/51; episode 113, "Paris, Anyone?"; produced by Larry Berns; directed by Al Lewis; assistant director, Ralph Jones; written by Arthur Alsberg, Al Lewis and Joseph Quillan; music by Wilbur Hatch; sound by Bill Gould; engineer, Pat Walsh; announcers, Bob Lemond and Verne Smith; cast: Eve Arden, Jeff Chandler, Gale Gordon, Jane Morgan, Richard Crenna, Gloria McMillan, Ramsey Hill.

Our Miss Brooks (CBS); 03/11/51; episode 114, "Tex Barton, Basketball Star"; produced by Larry Berns; directed by Al Lewis; assistant director, Ralph Jones; written by Al Lewis and Joseph Quillan; music by Wilbur Hatch; sound by Bill Gould; engineer, Pat Walsh; announcers, Bob Lemond and Verne Smith; cast: Eve Arden, Jeff Chandler, Gale Gordon, Jane Morgan, Richard Crenna, Gloria McMillan, Robert Easton, Bill Gould.

Our Miss Brooks (CBS); 03/18/51; episode 115, "Miss Enright's Birthday Party"; produced by Larry Berns; directed by Al Lewis; assistant director, Ralph Jones;

written by Arthur Alsberg, Al Lewis and Joseph Quillan; music by Wilbur Hatch; sound by Bill Gould; engineer, Pat Walsh; announcers, Bob Lemond and Verne Smith; cast: Eve Arden, Jeff Chandler, Gale Gordon, Jane Morgan, Richard Crenna, Gloria McMillan, Mary Jane Croft, Helen Brown.

Our Miss Brooks (CBS); 03/25/51; episode 116, "How High the Moon"; produced by Larry Berns; directed by Al Lewis; assistant director, Ralph Jones; written by Arthur Alsberg, William Larkin, Al Lewis and Joseph Quillan; music by Wilbur Hatch; sound by Bill Gould; engineer, Pat Walsh; announcers, Bob Lemond and Verne Smith; cast: Eve Arden, Jeff Chandler, Gale Gordon, Jane Morgan, Richard Crenna, Gloria McMillan, Paul McVey.

Our Miss Brooks (CBS); 04/01/51; episode 117, "Economy Drive, Dress Shop Deal"; produced by Larry Berns; directed by Al Lewis; assistant director, Ralph Jones; written by Arthur Alsberg, Al Lewis and Joseph Quillan; music by Wilbur Hatch; sound by Bill Gould; engineer, Pat Walsh; announcers, Bob Lemond and Verne Smith; cast: Eve Arden, Jeff Chandler, Gale Gordon, Jane Morgan, Richard Crenna, Gloria McMillan, Virginia Gordon, Fred Clark.

Our Miss Brooks (CBS); 04/08/51; episode 118, "Medford Reform School at Madison"; produced by Larry Berns; directed by Al Lewis; assistant director, Ralph Jones; written by Arthur Alsberg and Al Lewis; music by Wilbur Hatch; sound by Bill Gould; engineer, Pat Walsh; announcers, Bob Lemond and Verne Smith; cast: Eve Arden, Jeff Chandler, Gale Gordon, Jane Morgan, Richard Crenna, Gloria McMillan, Leonard Smith, Joseph Kearns.

The Screen Directors' Playhouse (NBC); 04/12/51; episode 98, "Hired Wife"; directed by Bill Karn; guest director, William A. Seiter; cast: Rosalind Russell, Jeff Chandler, Robert North, Ken Christy, Jim Backus.

Our Miss Brooks (CBS); 04/15/51; episode 119, "Mr. Conklin's Induction Notice"; produced by Larry Berns; directed by Al Lewis; assistant director, Ralph Jones; written by Al Lewis and Joseph Quillan; music by Wilbur Hatch; sound by Bill Gould; engineer, Pat Walsh; announcers, Bob Lemond and Verne Smith; cast: Eve Arden, Jeff Chandler, Gale Gordon, Jane Morgan, Richard Crenna, Gloria McMillan, Robert Easton.

Hollywood Star Playhouse (CBS); 04/16/51; episode 52, "The God Called Gold"; directed by Jack Johnstone; cast: Jeff Chandler, Will Wright, Parley Baer, Glen Vernon, Howard McNear.

Family Theater (Mut.); 04/18/51; episode 216, "The Promise"; directed by Joseph F. Mansfield; cast: Regis Toomey, Audrey Totter, Jeff Chandler.

Our Miss Brooks (CBS); 04/22/51; episode 120, "The New School Television

Set"; produced by Larry Berns; directed by Al Lewis; assistant director, Ralph Jones; written by Arthur Alsberg, Al Lewis and Joseph Quillan; music by Wilbur Hatch; sound by Bill Gould; engineer, Pat Walsh; announcers, Bob Lemond and Verne Smith; cast: Eve Arden, Jeff Chandler, Gale Gordon, Jane Morgan, Richard Crenna, Gloria McMillan, Robert Easton, Fred Clark, Jim Backus.

Our Miss Brooks (CBS); 04/29/51; episode 121, "Pin-up Pictures"; produced by Larry Berns; directed by Al Lewis; assistant director, Ralph Jones; written by Al Lewis and Joseph Quillan; music by Wilbur Hatch; sound by Bill Gould; engineer, Pat Walsh; announcers, Bob Lemond and Verne Smith; cast: Eve Arden, Jeff Chandler, Gale Gordon, Jane Morgan, Richard Crenna, Gloria McMillan, Fred Clark.

Our Miss Brooks (CBS); 05/06/51; episode 122, "Apartment of the Future"; produced by Larry Berns; directed by Al Lewis; assistant director, Ralph Jones; written by Arthur Alsberg and Al Lewis; music by Wilbur Hatch; sound by Bill Gould; engineer, Pat Walsh; announcers, Bob Lemond and Verne Smith; cast: Eve Arden, Jeff Chandler, Gale Gordon, Jane Morgan, Richard Crenna, Gloria McMillan.

Screen Guild Players (ABC); 05/10/51; episode 507, "The Secret Heart"; directed by William (Bill) Lawrence; cast: Joan Crawford, Jeff Chandler, Sally Forrest, Keefe Brasselle.

Our Miss Brooks (CBS); 05/13/51; episode 123, "Bargain Hats for Mother's Day"; produced by Larry Berns; directed by Al Lewis; assistant director, Ralph Jones; written by Arthur Alsberg and Al Lewis; music by Wilbur Hatch; sound by Bill Gould; engineer, Pat Walsh; announcers, Bob Lemond and Verne Smith; cast: Eve Arden, Jeff Chandler, Gale Gordon, Jane Morgan, Richard Crenna, Gloria McMillan, June Whitley, Robert Easton.

Our Miss Brooks (CBS); 05/20/51; episode 124, "The Bird Rescue and the Sunken Garden"; produced by Larry Berns; directed by Al Lewis; assistant director, Ralph Jones; written by Arthur Alsberg, Al Lewis and Joseph Quillan; music by Wilbur Hatch; sound by Ray Kemper; engineer, Pat Walsh; announcers, Bob Lemond and Verne Smith; cast: Eve Arden, Jeff Chandler, Gale Gordon, Jane Morgan, Richard Crenna, Gloria McMillan.

Suspense (CBS); 05/24/51; episode 430, "Fresh Air, Sunshine, and Murder"; directed by Elliott Lewis; cast: Jeff Chandler, Jack Kruschen, Cathy Lewis, Lou Merrill, Clayton Post, Herb Vigran.

Our Miss Brooks (CBS); 05/27/51; episode 125, "Stretch Wins Yodar Kritch Award for English"; produced by Larry Berns; directed by Al Lewis; assistant director, Ralph Jones; written by Arthur Alsberg, Al Lewis and Joseph Quillan; music

Jeff Chandler

by Wilbur Hatch; sound by Ray Kemper; engineer, Pat Walsh; announcers, Bob Lemond and Verne Smith; cast: Eve Arden, Jeff Chandler, Gale Gordon, Jane Morgan, Richard Crenna, Gloria McMillan, Leonard Smith, Bob Jellison.

Our Miss Brooks (CBS); 06/03/51; episode 126, "Miss Brooks Takes Over Miss Enright's First Aid Class"; produced by Larry Berns; directed by Al Lewis; assistant director, Ralph Jones; written by Arthur Alsberg, Al Lewis and Joseph Quillan; music by Wilbur Hatch; sound by Ray Kemper; engineer, Pat Walsh; announcers, Bob Lemond and Verne Smith; cast: Eve Arden, Jeff Chandler, Gale Gordon, Jane Morgan, Richard Crenna, Gloria McMillan, Mary Jane Croft.

Our Miss Brooks (CBS); 06/10/51; episode 127, "Ladies Good Deed Club Drive"; produced by Larry Berns; directed by Al Lewis; assistant director, Ralph Jones; written by Al Lewis and Joseph Quillan; music by Wilbur Hatch; sound by Ray Kemper; engineer, Pat Walsh; announcers, Bob Lemond and Verne Smith; cast: Eve Arden, Jeff Chandler, Gale Gordon, Jane Morgan, Richard Crenna, Gloria McMillan, Fred Clark.

Guest Star (Synd.); 06/17/51; episode 221, "Jailbreak"; directed by Louis Graf; cast: Jeff Chandler, Peter Leeds, Gerald Mohr.

Our Miss Brooks (CBS); 06/17/51; episode 128, "Romantic Warfare"; produced by Larry Berns; directed by Al Lewis; assistant director, Ralph Jones; written by Al Lewis and Joseph Quillan; music by Wilbur Hatch; sound by Ray Kemper; engineer, Pat Walsh; announcers, Bob Lemond and Verne Smith; cast: Eve Arden, Jeff Chandler, Gale Gordon, Jane Morgan, Richard Crenna, Gloria McMillan, Mary Jane Croft.

Our Miss Brooks (CBS); 06/24/51; episode 129, "Let Hawkins Guide You Through Yonkers"; produced by Larry Berns; directed by Al Lewis; assistant director, Lucien Davis; written by Arthur Alsberg and Al Lewis; music by Wilbur Hatch; sound by Ray Kemper; engineer, Pat Walsh; announcers, Bob Lemond and Verne Smith; cast: Eve Arden, Jeff Chandler, Gale Gordon, Jane Morgan, Richard Crenna, Gloria McMillan, Fred Clark.

Our Miss Brooks (CBS); 07/01/51; episode 130, "Bon Voyage"; produced by Larry Berns; directed by Al Lewis; assistant director, Lucien Davis; written by Arthur Alsberg and Al Lewis; music by Wilbur Hatch; sound by Clark Casey; engineer, Pat Walsh; announcers, Bob Lemond and Verne Smith; cast: Eve Arden, Jeff Chandler, Gale Gordon, Jane Morgan, Richard Crenna, Gloria McMillan, Jim Backus.

The Screen Directors' Playhouse (NBC): 07/05/51; episode 109, "Only Yesterday"; directed by Bill Karn; cast: Mercedes McCambridge, Jeff Chandler.

Radio

O'Hara (CBS); 07/22/51; episode 16, "The Judas Face"; produced and directed by Everett Tomlinson and Sterling Tracy; written by Gilbert Thomas; cast: Jack Moyles, Byron Kane, Sidney Miller, Anne Stone, Jeff Chandler, Edgar Barrier, Fritz Feld.

Suspense (CBS); 09/03/51; episode 437, "Steel River Prison Break"; directed by Elliott Lewis; cast: Jeff Chandler; Barton Yarborough.

The Screen Directors' Playhouse (NBC); 09/07/51; episode 116, "Broken Arrow"; cast: James Stewart, Jeff Chandler, Debra Paget.

Family Theater (Mut.); 09/19/51; episode 237, "The Kiddy Story"; directed by Joseph F. Mansfield; cast: Jeff Chandler, Jane Wyatt, Ken Christy, Verna Felton, James Nusser, George Taylor.

Our Miss Brooks (CBS); 10/07/51; episode 131, "Connie Teaches French"; produced by Larry Berns; directed by Al Lewis; assistant director, Ralph Jones; written by Arthur Alsberg, Al Lewis and Joseph Quillan; music by Wilbur Hatch; sound by Bill Gould; engineer, Pat Walsh; announcers, Bob Lemond and Verne Smith; cast: Eve Arden, Jeff Chandler, Gale Gordon, Jane Morgan, Richard Crenna, Gloria McMillan, Fred Clark.

Our Miss Brooks (CBS); 10/14/51; episode 132, "Is Football Canceled at Madison High?"; produced by Larry Berns; directed and written by Al Lewis; assistant director, Ralph Jones; music by Wilbur Hatch; sound by Bill Gould; engineer, Pat Walsh; announcer, Bob Lemond; cast: Eve Arden, Jeff Chandler, Gale Gordon, Jane Morgan, Richard Crenna, Gloria McMillan, Leonard Smith.

Our Miss Brooks (CBS); 10/21/51; episode 133, "Mr. Boynton's Uncle Visits"; produced by Larry Berns; directed and written by Al Lewis; assistant director, Ralph Jones; music by Wilbur Hatch; sound by Bill Gould; engineer, Pat Walsh; announcer, Bob Lemond; cast: Eve Arden, Jeff Chandler, Gale Gordon, Jane Morgan, Richard Crenna, Gloria McMillan, Nestor Paiva.

Our Miss Brooks (CBS); 10/28/51; episode 134, "Is Miss Brooks Engaged?"; produced by Larry Berns; directed and written by Al Lewis; assistant director, Ralph Jones; music by Wilbur Hatch; sound by Bill Gould; engineer, Pat Walsh; announcer, Bob Lemond; cast: Eve Arden, Jeff Chandler, Gale Gordon, Jane Morgan, Richard Crenna, Gloria McMillan, Mary Jane Croft, Jerry Paris, Ed Begley.

Our Miss Brooks (CBS); 11/04/51; episode 135, "Oui"; produced by Larry Berns; directed and written by Al Lewis; assistant director, Ralph Jones; music by Wilbur Hatch; sound by Bill Gould; engineer, Pat Walsh; announcer, Bob Lemond; cast: Eve Arden, Gale Gordon, Jane Morgan, Richard Crenna, Gloria McMillan, Gerald Mohr.

Jeff Chandler

Our Miss Brooks (CBS); 11/11/51; episode 136, "A Letter from Mr. Boynton"; produced by Larry Berns; directed and written by Al Lewis; assistant director, Ralph Jones; music by Wilbur Hatch; sound by Bill Gould; engineers, Ted Rhodes and Pat Walsh; announcer, Bob Lemond; cast: Eve Arden, Gale Gordon, Jane Morgan, Richard Crenna, Gloria McMillan, Leonard Smith, Sandra Gould.

Our Miss Brooks (CBS); 11/18/51; episode 137, "Mr. Boynton Returns"; produced by Larry Berns; directed and written by Al Lewis; assistant director, Ralph Jones; music by Wilbur Hatch; sound by Bill Gould; engineers, Ted Rhodes and Pat Walsh; announcer, Bob Lemond; cast: Eve Arden, Jeff Chandler, Gale Gordon, Jane Morgan, Richard Crenna, Gloria McMillan, Gloria Gordon, Nestor Paiva.

Our Miss Brooks (CBS); 11/25/51; episode 138, "Miss Brooks Needs a Winter Coat"; produced by Larry Berns; directed and written by Al Lewis; assistant director, Ralph Jones; music by Wilbur Hatch; sound by Bill Gould; engineers, Ted Rhodes and Pat Walsh; announcer, Bob Lemond; cast: Eve Arden, Jeff Chandler, Gale Gordon, Jane Morgan, Richard Crenna, Gloria McMillan, Edwin Max.

Our Miss Brooks (CBS); 12/02/51; episode 139, "Miss Brooks, Head of the English Department?"; produced by Larry Berns; directed and written by Al Lewis; assistant director, Ralph Jones; music by Wilbur Hatch; sound by Bill Gould; engineers, Ted Rhodes and Pat Walsh; announcer, Bob Lemond; cast: Eve Arden, Jeff Chandler, Gale Gordon, Jane Morgan, Richard Crenna, Gloria McMillan, Nestor Paiva.

Our Miss Brooks (CBS); 12/09/51; episode 140, "Annual December Dance"; produced by Larry Berns; directed and written by Al Lewis; assistant director, Ralph Jones; music by Wilbur Hatch; sound by Bill Gould; engineers, Ted Rhodes and Pat Walsh; announcer, Bob Lemond; cast: Eve Arden, Jeff Chandler, Gale Gordon, Jane Morgan, Richard Crenna, Gloria McMillan.

Our Miss Brooks (CBS); 12/16/51; episode 141, "Miss Brooks Makes a Costume for Mr. Boynton"; produced by Larry Berns; directed and written by Al Lewis; assistant director, Ralph Jones; music by Wilbur Hatch; sound by Bill Gould; engineers, Ted Rhodes and Pat Walsh; announcer, Bob Lemond; cast: Eve Arden, Jeff Chandler, Gale Gordon, Jane Morgan, Richard Crenna, Gloria McMillan, Fred Clark, Parley Baer.

Our Miss Brooks (CBS); 12/23/51; episode 142, "Christmas Show"; produced by Larry Berns; directed and written by Al Lewis; assistant director, Ralph Jones; music by Wilbur Hatch; sound by Bill Gould; engineers, Ted Rhodes and Pat Walsh; announcer, Bob Lemond; cast: Eve Arden, Jeff Chandler, Gale Gordon, Jane Morgan, Richard Crenna, Gloria McMillan, Virginia Gordon, Harry Shearer.

Our Miss Brooks (CBS); 12/30/51; episode 143, "Annual Winter Outing"; produced by Larry Berns; directed by Al Lewis; assistant director, Ralph Jones; written by Al Lewis and Joseph Quillan; music by Wilbur Hatch; sound by Bill Gould; engineers, Ted Rhodes and Pat Walsh; announcer, Bob Lemond; cast: Eve Arden, Jeff Chandler, Gale Gordon, Jane Morgan, Richard Crenna, Gloria McMillan, Mary Jane Croft.

The Lux Radio Theatre (CBS); 12/31/51; episode 771, "Bird of Paradise"; directed by Earl Ebi; host, William Keighley; cast: Louis Jourdan, Debra Paget, Jeff Chandler, William Green, Herb Butterfield, Bill Johnstone, Otto Waldis, Lillian Buyeff, Lynn Allen.

1952

Our Miss Brooks (CBS); 01/06/52; episode 144, "Pensacola Popovers"; produced by Larry Berns; directed by Al Lewis; assistant director, Ralph Jones; written by Arthur Alsberg, Al Lewis and Joseph Quillan; music by Wilbur Hatch; sound by Bill Gould; engineers, Ted Rhodes and Pat Walsh; announcer, Bob Lemond; cast: Eve Arden, Jeff Chandler, Gale Gordon, Jane Morgan, Richard Crenna, Gloria McMillan.

Suspense (CBS); 01/07/52; episode 455, "The Case Against Loo Doc"; directed by Elliott Lewis; cast: Jeff Chandler, Herb Butterfield, Lillian Buyeff, William Conrad, Sam Edwards, Byron Kane, Joseph Kearns, Jack Kruschen.

Family Theater (Mut.); 01/08/52; episode 252, "Flight from Home"; directed by Joseph F. Mansfield; cast: Ann Blyth, Jeff Chandler, Martha Shaw, Norma Jean Nilsson, Norman Field, Michael Hayes.

Hollywood Sound Stage (CBS); 01/10/52; episode 5, "Shadow of a Doubt"; directed by Harry Kronman; cast: Ann Blyth, Jeff Chandler.

Our Miss Brooks (CBS); 01/13/52; episode 145, "Psycho-Drama"; produced by Larry Berns; directed by Al Lewis; assistant director, Ralph Jones; written by Arthur Alsberg and Al Lewis; music by Wilbur Hatch; sound by Bill Gould; engineers, Ted Rhodes and Pat Walsh; announcer, Bob Lemond; cast: Eve Arden, Jeff Chandler, Gale Gordon, Jane Morgan, Richard Crenna, Gloria McMillan, Virginia Gordon.

Our Miss Brooks (CBS); 01/20/52; episode 146, "Great Love Letters of History"; produced by Larry Berns; directed by Al Lewis; assistant director, Ralph Jones; written by Arthur Alsberg and Al Lewis; music by Wilbur Hatch; sound by Bill Gould; engineers, Ted Rhodes and Pat Walsh; announcer, Bob Lemond; cast:

Jeff Chandler

Eve Arden, Jeff Chandler, Gale Gordon, Jane Morgan, Richard Crenna, Gloria McMillan, Virginia Gordon, Fred Clark.

Our Miss Brooks (CBS); 01/27/52; episode 147, "Mr Conklin, The Greatest Show on Earth"; produced by Larry Berns; directed by Al Lewis; assistant director, Ralph Jones; written by Arthur Alsberg and Al Lewis; music by Wilbur Hatch; sound by Bill Gould; engineers, Ted Rhodes and Pat Walsh; announcer, Bob Lemond; cast: Eve Arden, Jeff Chandler, Gale Gordon, Jane Morgan, Richard Crenna, Gloria McMillan, Fred Clark.

Our Miss Brooks (CBS); 02/03/52; episode 148, "The Snowball Dance"; produced by Larry Berns; directed by Al Lewis; assistant director, Ralph Jones; written by Al Lewis and Joseph Quillan; music by Wilbur Hatch; sound by Bill Gould; engineers, Ted Rhodes and Pat Walsh; announcer, Bob Lemond; cast: Eve Arden, Jeff Chandler, Gale Gordon, Jane Morgan, Richard Crenna, Gloria McMillan.

Our Miss Brooks (CBS); 02/10/52; episode 149, "Mr. Boynton, Head of the Biology Department?"; produced by Larry Berns; directed by Al Lewis; assistant director, Ralph Jones; written by Al Lewis and Joseph Quillan; music by Wilbur Hatch; sound by Bill Gould; engineers, Robert Chadwick and Pat Walsh; announcer, Bob Lemond; cast: Eve Arden, Jeff Chandler, Gale Gordon, Jane Morgan, Richard Crenna, Gloria McMillan, Ed Begley.

Our Miss Brooks (CBS); 02/17/52; episode 150, "Miss Brooks Follows Mr. Boynton to Eagle Springs"; produced by Larry Berns; directed by Al Lewis; assistant director, Ralph Jones; written by Arthur Alsberg and Al Lewis; music by Wilbur Hatch; sound by Bill Gould; engineers, Pat Walsh and Ralph Wilson; announcer, Bob Lemond; cast: Eve Arden, Jeff Chandler, Gale Gordon, Jane Morgan, Richard Crenna, Gloria McMillan, Mary Jane Croft.

Our Miss Brooks (CBS); 02/24/52; episode 151, "Madison's Birthday Ceremonies for Washington"; produced by Larry Berns; directed by Al Lewis; assistant director, Ralph Jones; written by Al Lewis and Joseph Quillan; music by Wilbur Hatch; sound by Bill Gould; engineers, Pat Walsh and Ralph Wilson; announcer, Bob Lemond; cast: Eve Arden, Jeff Chandler, Gale Gordon, Jane Morgan, Richard Crenna, Gloria McMillan, Lou Merrill.

Our Miss Brooks (CBS); 03/02/52; episode 152, "Miss Brooks Might Lose All Her Furniture"; produced by Larry Berns; directed by Al Lewis; assistant director, Frank Paris; written by Arthur Alsberg and Al Lewis; music by Wilbur Hatch; sound by Bill Gould; engineers, Pat Walsh and Ralph Wilson; announcer, Bob Lemond; cast: Eve Arden, Jeff Chandler, Gale Gordon, Jane Morgan, Richard Crenna, Gloria McMillan.

Radio

Our Miss Brooks (CBS); 03/09/52; episode 153, "Minerva's Husband"; produced by Larry Berns; directed by Al Lewis; assistant director, Frank Paris; written by Arthur Alsberg, Al Lewis and Joseph Quillan; music by Wilbur Hatch; sound by Bill Gould; engineers, Pat Walsh and Ralph Wilson; announcer, Bob Lemond; cast: Eve Arden, Jeff Chandler, Gale Gordon, Jane Morgan, Richard Crenna, Gloria McMillan, Virginia Gordon.

Our Miss Brooks (CBS); 03/16/52; episode 154, "Sh-h-h!"; produced by Larry Berns; directed by Al Lewis; assistant director, Frank Paris; written by Al Lewis and Joseph Quillan; music by Wilbur Hatch; sound by Bill Gould; engineers, Pat Walsh and Ralph Wilson; announcer, Bob Lemond; cast: Eve Arden, Jeff Chandler, Gale Gordon, Jane Morgan, Richard Crenna, Gloria McMillan, Virginia Gordon.

Our Miss Brooks (CBS); 03/23/52; episode 155, "Accident Prevention Week"; produced by Larry Berns; directed by Al Lewis; assistant director, Frank Paris; written by Al Lewis and Joseph Quillan; music by Wilbur Hatch; sound by Bill Gould and Ross Murray; engineers, Lee Crager and Pat Walsh; announcer, Bob Lemond; cast: Eve Arden, Jeff Chandler, Gale Gordon, Jane Morgan, Richard Crenna, Gloria McMillan.

Our Miss Brooks (CBS); 03/30/52; episode 156, "Miss Brooks, Second Delegate?"; produced by Larry Berns; directed by Al Lewis; assistant director, Frank Paris; written by Arthur Alsberg and Al Lewis; music by Wilbur Hatch; sound by Bill Gould; engineers, Lee Crager and Pat Walsh; announcer, Bob Lemond; cast: Eve Arden, Gale Gordon, Jane Morgan, Richard Crenna, Gloria McMillan, Fred Clark.

Lady Esther Screen Guild Players (CBS); 04/03/52; episode 121, "Flesh and Fantasy"; cast: Jeff Chandler, Audrey Totter, Howard McNear, Lou Merrill, Margaret Brayton, Jeffrey Silver, Parley Baer, Paul Dubov, Joseph Granby, Joe Forte.

Our Miss Brooks (CBS); 04/06/52; episode 157, "Miss Brooks Gives Up on Mr. Boynton"; produced by Larry Berns; directed by Al Lewis; assistant director, Bob Hendricks; written by Arthur Alsberg, Al Lewis and Joseph Quillan; music by Wilbur Hatch; sound by Bill Gould; engineers, Ray Erlenborn and Pat Walsh; announcer, Bob Lemond; cast: Eve Arden, Jeff Chandler, Gale Gordon, Jane Morgan, Richard Crenna, Gloria McMillan.

Hallmark Playhouse (CBS); 04/10/52; episode 172, "Ben-Hur"; directed by Dee Engelbach; host, James Hilton; cast: Jeff Chandler.

Our Miss Brooks (CBS); 04/13/52; episode 158, "No Easter Vacation for Miss Brooks"; produced by Larry Berns; directed by Al Lewis; assistant director, Bob Hendricks; written by Al Lewis and Joseph Quillan; music by Wilbur Hatch; sound by Bill Gould; engineers, Lee Crager and Pat Walsh; announcer, Bob Lemond; cast: Eve Arden, Jeff Chandler, Gale Gordon, Jane Morgan, Richard Crenna, Gloria McMillan, Mary Jane Croft, Ed Begley.

Our Miss Brooks (CBS); 04/20/52; episode 159, "Stretch's Manager, Walter Denton"; produced by Larry Berns; directed by Al Lewis; assistant director, Frank Paris; written by Arthur Alsberg and Al Lewis; music by Wilbur Hatch; sound by Bill Gould; engineers, Paul McDermott and Pat Walsh; announcer, Bob Lemond; cast: Eve Arden, Jeff Chandler, Gale Gordon, Jane Morgan, Richard Crenna, Gloria McMillan, Leonard Smith, Edwin Max.

Our Miss Brooks (CBS); 04/27/52; episode 160, "Faculty Dress on Fridays"; produced by Larry Berns; directed by Al Lewis; assistant director, Frank Paris; written by Arthur Alsberg and Al Lewis; music by Wilbur Hatch; sound by Tom Hanley; engineers, Paul McDermott and Pat Walsh; announcer, Bob Lemond; cast: Eve Arden, Jeff Chandler, Gale Gordon, Jane Morgan, Richard Crenna, Gloria McMillan, Gerald Mohr.

Our Miss Brooks (CBS); 05/04/52; episode 161, "Three Gifts from Mr. Boynton"; produced by Larry Berns; directed by Al Lewis; assistant director, Frank Paris; written by Al Lewis and Joseph Quillan; music by Wilbur Hatch; sound by Tom Hanley; engineers, Lee Crager and Pat Walsh; announcer, Bob Lemond; cast: Eve Arden, Jeff Chandler, Gale Gordon, Jane Morgan, Richard Crenna, Gloria McMillan.

Our Miss Brooks (CBS); 05/11/52; episode 162, "Underground Gambling Ring"; produced by Larry Berns; directed by Al Lewis; assistant director, Frank Paris; written by Al Lewis and Joseph Quillan; music by Wilbur Hatch; sound by Tom Hanley; engineers, Paul McDermott and Pat Walsh; announcer, Bob Lemond; cast: Eve Arden, Jeff Chandler, Gale Gordon, Jane Morgan, Richard Crenna, Gloria McMillan, Edwin Max, Gerald Mohr.

Our Miss Brooks (CBS); 05/18/52; episode 163, "Late Night Radio Programs"; produced by Larry Berns; directed by Al Lewis; assistant director, Frank Paris; written by Arthur Alsberg and Al Lewis; music by Wilbur Hatch; sound by Tom Hanley; engineers, Paul McDermott and Pat Walsh; announcer, Bob Lemond; cast: Eve Arden, Jeff Chandler, Gale Gordon, Jane Morgan, Richard Crenna, Gloria McMillan.

Our Miss Brooks (CBS); 05/25/52; episode 164, "The Conklins Remarry"; produced by Larry Berns; directed by Al Lewis; assistant director, Frank Paris; written by Al Lewis and Joseph Quillan; music by Wilbur Hatch; sound by Tom Hanley; engineers, Paul McDermott and Pat Walsh; announcer, Bob Lemond; cast:

Radio

Eve Arden, Jeff Chandler, Gale Gordon, Jane Morgan, Richard Crenna, Gloria McMillan.

Club 88 Starring Peggy Lee (CBS); 05/29/52; directed by Larry Berns; music by Sonny Burke; cast: Peggy Lee, Jeff Chandler. Jeff sings "You Made Me Love You"; Peggy and Jeff sing "Walking My Baby Back Home."

Our Miss Brooks (CBS); 06/01/52; episode 165, "Miss Brooks, Girl-Taxidermist"; produced by Larry Berns; directed by Al Lewis; assistant director, Frank Jones; written by Al Lewis and Joseph Quillan; music by Wilbur Hatch; sound by Bill Gould; engineers, Art Brown and Pat Walsh; announcer, Bob Lemond; cast: Eve Arden, Gale Gordon, Jane Morgan, Richard Crenna, Gloria McMillan, Leonard Smith.

Our Miss Brooks (CBS); 06/08/52; episode 166, "An Epidemic (Named Dolores Roberts)"; produced by Larry Berns; directed by Al Lewis; assistant director, Frank Paris; written by Arthur Alsberg and Al Lewis; music by Wilbur Hatch; sound by Bill Gould; engineers, Art Brown and Pat Walsh; announcer, Bob Lemond; cast: Eve Arden, Jeff Chandler, Gale Gordon, Jane Morgan, Richard Crenna, Sandra Gould, Sarah Spencer.

Family Theater (Mut.); 06/11/52; episode 274, "Man of the House"; directed by Joseph F. Mansfield; cast: Jeff Chandler, Helen Parrish, Vic Perrin, Jeffrey Silver, Michael Hayes.

Our Miss Brooks (CBS); 06/15/52; episode 167, "Miss Brooks Tutors Stretch"; produced by Larry Berns; directed by Al Lewis; assistant director, Frank Paris; written by Arthur Alsberg and Al Lewis; music by Wilbur Hatch; sound by Bill Gould; engineers, Art Brown and Pat Walsh; announcer, Bob Lemond; cast: Eve Arden, Jeff Chandler, Gale Gordon, Jane Morgan, Richard Crenna, Gloria McMillan, Leonard Smith, Fred Clark.

Our Miss Brooks (CBS); 06/22/52; episode 168, "The Conklin House at Crystal Lake"; produced by Larry Berns; directed by Al Lewis; assistant director, Frank Paris; written by Arthur Alsberg and Al Lewis; music by Wilbur Hatch; sound by Bill Gould; engineers, Art Brown and Pat Walsh; announcer, Bob Lemond; cast: Eve Arden, Jeff Chandler, Gale Gordon, Jane Morgan, Richard Crenna, Gloria McMillan, Mary Jane Croft.

Screen Guild Theater (CBS); 06/22/52; episode 133, "Family Honeymoon"; cast: Jeff Chandler, Ann Sheridan, Charlie Smith, Gil Stratton Jr., Peter Votrian, Leif Erickson, Isa Ashdown, Benny Rubin, Arthur Q. Bryan, Ken Christy, Jane Morgan, Janet Beverly, Bob Sweeney, Larry Dobkin, Elvia Allman.

Our Miss Brooks (CBS); 06/29/52; episode 169, "June Ushers in July for Miss

Jeff Chandler

Brooks"; produced by Larry Berns; directed by Al Lewis; assistant director, Frank Paris; written by Al Lewis and Joseph Quillan; music by Wilbur Hatch; sound by Bill Gould; engineers, Art Brown and Pat Walsh; announcer, Bob Lemond; cast: Eve Arden, Jeff Chandler, Gale Gordon, Jane Morgan, Richard Crenna, Gloria McMillan, Gerald Mohr, Bob Sweeney.

Family Theater (Mut.); 07/02/52; episode 277, "We Hold These Truths"; directed by Joseph F. Mansfield; host, Col. Francis S. Gabreski; cast: Mae Clarke, Jeff Chandler, Robert Clark, Cliff Clark, Ted de Corsia, Howard Culver, Tom Holland, Stanley Waxman, Leo Cleary, Lee Millar, Roland Morris.

Club 88 Starring Peggy Lee (CBS); 07/15/52; directed by Larry Berns; music by Sonny Burke; cast: Peggy Lee, Jeff Chandler. Jeff sings "That Old Black Magic"; Peggy and Jeff sing "Accentuate the Positive."

Guest Star (Synd.); 07/20/52; episode 278, "The Woodsman"; cast: Jeff Chandler.

The Martin and Lewis Show (NBC); 09/23/52; episode 69; directed by Dick Mack; cast: Dean Martin, Jerry Lewis, Jeff Chandler.

Club 88 Starring Peggy Lee (CBS); 09/25/52; directed by Larry Berns; music by Sonny Burke; cast: Peggy Lee, Jeff Chandler. Jeff sings "That Old Black Magic"; Peggy and Jeff sing "Slumming on Park Avenue."

Frontier Town (Synd.); 09/26/52; episode 1, "The Return to Dos Rios"; directed by Paul Franklin; cast: Jeff Chandler (as "Tex Chandler"), Wade Crosby.

Frontier Town (Synd.); 10/03/52; episode 2, "His Name is John Smith"; directed by Paul Franklin; cast: Jeff Chandler (as "Tex Chandler"), Wade Crosby.

Our Miss Brooks (CBS); 10/05/52; episode 170, "The Aluminum Mouse Trap"; produced by Larry Berns; directed by Al Lewis; assistant director, Frank Paris; written by Arthur Alsberg, Al Lewis and Joseph Quillan; music by Wilbur Hatch; sound by Bill Gould; engineers, Marshall King and Pat Walsh; announcer, Bob Lemond; cast: Eve Arden, Jeff Chandler, Gale Gordon, Jane Morgan, Richard Crenna, Gloria McMillan, Hal March.

Frontier Town (Synd.); 10/10/52; episode 3, "Tod Ford"; directed by Paul Franklin; cast: Jeff Chandler (as "Tex Chandler"), Wade Crosby.

Our Miss Brooks (CBS); 10/12/52; episode 171, "Miss Brooks Buys a Cow for Mr. Boynton"; produced by Larry Berns; directed by Al Lewis; assistant director, Frank Paris; written by Al Lewis and Joseph Quillan; music by Wilbur Hatch; sound by Bill Gould; engineers, Doc Bennett and Pat Walsh; announcer, Bob Lemond;

cast: Eve Arden, Jeff Chandler, Gale Gordon, Jane Morgan, Richard Crenna, Gloria McMillan, Fred Clark, Bob Sweeney, Bill Gould.

Frontier Town (Synd.); 10/17/52; episode 4, "Marie"; directed by Paul Franklin; cast: Jeff Chandler (as "Tex Chandler"), Wade Crosby.

Our Miss Brooks (CBS); 10/19/52; episode 172, "Minerva is Missing"; produced by Larry Berns; directed by Al Lewis; assistant director, Frank Paris; written by Arthur Alsberg and Al Lewis; music by Wilbur Hatch; sound by Bill Gould; engineers, Bob Schradermier and Pat Walsh; announcer, Bob Lemond; cast: Eve Arden, Jeff Chandler, Gale Gordon, Jane Morgan, Richard Crenna, Gloria McMillan, Bill Gould.

Frontier Town (Synd.); 10/24/52; episode 5, "The Poisoned Waterhole"; directed by Paul Franklin; cast: Jeff Chandler (as "Tex Chandler"), Wade Crosby.

Our Miss Brooks (CBS); 10/26/52; episode 173, "A New Dress from Sherry's Department Store"; produced by Larry Berns; directed by Al Lewis; assistant director, Frank Paris; written by Al Lewis and Joseph Quillan; music by Wilbur Hatch; sound by Bill Gould; engineers, Bob Schradermier and Pat Walsh; announcer, Bob Lemond; cast: Eve Arden, Jeff Chandler, Gale Gordon, Jane Morgan, Richard Crenna, Gloria McMillan, Leonard Smith, Jud Conlon, Charlie Parlato, Mack Maclean.

Frontier Town (Synd.); 10/31/52; episode 6, "Dodge City in 1872"; directed by Paul Franklin; cast: Jeff Chandler (as "Tex Chandler"), Wade Crosby.

Our Miss Brooks (CBS); 11/02/52; episode 174, "Overcrowded Conditions at Madison High"; produced by Larry Berns; directed by Al Lewis; assistant director, Frank Paris; written by Al Lewis and Joseph Quillan; music by Wilbur Hatch; sound by Bill Gould; engineers, Bob Schradermier and Pat Walsh; announcer, Bob Lemond; cast: Eve Arden, Jeff Chandler, Gale Gordon, Jane Morgan, Richard Crenna, Gloria McMillan, Sammy Ogg, Stuffy Singer, Hy Averback.

Frontier Town (Synd.); 11/07/52; episode 7, "The Seminole Strip"; directed by Paul Franklin; cast: Jeff Chandler (as "Tex Chandler"), Wade Crosby.

Our Miss Brooks (CBS); 11/09/52; episode 175, "The Red, White, and Blue Pills"; produced by Larry Berns; directed by Al Lewis; assistant director, Frank Paris; written by Arthur Alsberg and Al Lewis; music by Wilbur Hatch; sound by Bill Gould; engineers, Bob Schradermier and Pat Walsh; announcer, Bob Lemond; cast: Eve Arden, Jeff Chandler, Gale Gordon, Jane Morgan, Richard Crenna, Gloria McMillan, Fred Clark.

Frontier Town (Synd.); 11/14/52; episode 8, "The Chavez Family"; directed by Paul Franklin; cast: Jeff Chandler (as "Tex Chandler"), Wade Crosby.

Jeff Chandler

Our Miss Brooks (CBS); 11/16/52; episode 176, "Walter Gets Expelled"; produced by Larry Berns; directed by Al Lewis; assistant director, Frank Paris; written by Arthur Alsberg and Al Lewis; music by Wilbur Hatch; sound by Bill Gould; engineers, Bob Schradermier and Pat Walsh; announcer, Bob Lemond; cast: Eve Arden, Jeff Chandler, Gale Gordon, Jane Morgan, Richard Crenna, Gloria McMillan, Fred Clark.

Frontier Town (Synd.); 11/21/52; episode 9, "The Opening of Tioga Reserve"; directed by Paul Franklin; cast: Jeff Chandler (as "Tex Chandler"), Wade Crosby.

Our Miss Brooks (CBS); 11/23/52; episode 177, "A Housewarming for Miss Enright"; produced by Larry Berns; directed by Al Lewis; assistant director, Frank Paris; written by Arthur Alsberg and Al Lewis; music by Wilbur Hatch; sound by Bill Gould; engineers, Bob Schradermier and Pat Walsh; announcer, Bob Lemond; cast: Eve Arden, Jeff Chandler, Gale Gordon, Jane Morgan, Richard Crenna, Gloria McMillan, Mary Jane Croft, Isabel Randolph.

Frontier Town (Synd.); 11/28/52; episode 10, "Death and Texas"; directed by Paul Franklin; cast: Jeff Chandler (as "Tex Chandler"), Wade Crosby.

Our Miss Brooks (CBS); 11/30/52; episode 178, "Up in Smoke"; produced by Larry Berns; directed by Al Lewis; assistant director, Frank Paris; written by Al Lewis and Joseph Quillan; music by Wilbur Hatch; sound by Bill Gould; engineers, Bob Schradermier and Pat Walsh; announcer, Bob Lemond; cast: Eve Arden, Jeff Chandler, Gale Gordon, Jane Morgan, Richard Crenna, Gloria McMillan, Fred Clark.

Frontier Town (Synd.); 12/05/52; episode 11, "Six-Gun Justice"; directed by Paul Franklin; cast: Jeff Chandler (as "Tex Chandler"), Wade Crosby.

Our Miss Brooks (CBS); 12/07/52; episode 179, "Mr. Conklin's New Hunting Gun"; produced by Larry Berns; directed by Al Lewis; assistant director, Frank Paris; written by Arthur Alsberg and Al Lewis; music by Wilbur Hatch; sound by Bill Gould; engineers, Bob Schradermier and Pat Walsh; announcer, Bob Lemond; cast: Eve Arden, Jeff Chandler, Gale Gordon, Jane Morgan, Richard Crenna, Gloria McMillan, Fred Clark, Jerry Hausner.

Frontier Town (Synd.); 12/12/52; episode 12, "The Return of the Badmen"; directed by Paul Franklin; cast: Jeff Chandler (as "Tex Chandler"), Wade Crosby.

The Eternal Light (NBC); 12/14/52; episode 405, "Anne Frank: The Diary of A Young Girl"; cast: Anne Whitfield, Jeff Chandler.

Our Miss Brooks (CBS); 12/14/52; episode 180, "A Jail Cell in Madison High"; produced by Larry Berns; directed by Al Lewis; assistant director, Frank Paris;

written by Arthur Alsberg and Al Lewis; music by Wilbur Hatch; sound by Bill Gould; engineers, Bob Schradermier and Pat Walsh; announcer, Bob Lemond; cast: Eve Arden, Jeff Chandler, Gale Gordon, Jane Morgan, Richard Crenna, Gloria McMillan, Fred Clark.

Frontier Town (Synd.); 12/19/52; episode 13, "The Valley of Lawless Men"; directed by Paul Franklin; cast: Jeff Chandler (as "Tex Chandler"), Wade Crosby, William (Bill) Griffis.

Our Miss Brooks (CBS); 12/21/52; episode 181, "Christmas Show"; produced by Larry Berns; directed by Al Lewis; assistant director, Frank Paris; written by Arthur Alsberg and Al Lewis; music by Wilbur Hatch; sound by Bill Gould; engineers, Bob Schradermier and Pat Walsh; announcer, Bob Lemond; cast: Eve Arden, Jeff Chandler, Gale Gordon, Jane Morgan, Richard Crenna, Gloria McMillan, Virginia Gordon, Sammy Ogg, Bill Gould.

Family Theater (Mut.); 12/24/52; episode 298, "The Nativity"; directed by Joseph F. Mansfield; hostess, June Haver; cast: Ann Blyth, Jeff Chandler.

Frontier Town (Synd.); 12/26/52; episode 14, "The Guns of Wrath"; directed by Paul Franklin; cast: Jeff Chandler (as "Tex Chandler"), Wade Crosby, William (Bill) Griffis.

Our Miss Brooks (CBS); 12/28/52; episode 182, "Christmas Week at Eagle Springs"; produced by Larry Berns; directed by Al Lewis; assistant director, Frank Paris; written by Al Lewis and Joseph Quillan; music by Wilbur Hatch; sound by Bill Gould; engineer, Pat Walsh; announcer, Bob Lemond; cast: Eve Arden, Jeff Chandler, Gale Gordon, Jane Morgan, Richard Crenna, Gloria McMillan, Patricia Iannone, Jerry Hausner.

Family Theater (Mut.); 12/31/52; episode 299, "The Presentation"; directed by Joseph F. Mansfield; host, William Lundigan; cast: Ann Blyth, Jeff Chandler.

1953

Frontier Town (Synd.); 01/02/53; episode 15, "Her Name is Bourbon Kate"; directed by Paul Franklin; cast: Jeff Chandler (as "Tex Chandler"), Wade Crosby, Ralph Moody.

Our Miss Brooks (CBS); 01/04/53; episode 183, "The Ladies Aid Society"; produced by Larry Berns; directed by Al Lewis; assistant director, Frank Paris; written by Arthur Alsberg, Al Lewis and Joseph Quillan; music by Wilbur Hatch; sound by Bill Gould; engineer, Pat Walsh; announcer, Bob Lemond; cast: Eve Arden, Jeff

Jeff Chandler

Chandler, Gale Gordon, Jane Morgan, Richard Crenna, Gloria McMillan, Virginia Gordon, Bob Sweeney.

Family Theater (Mut.); 01/07/53; episode 300, "The Finding of the Temple"; directed by Joseph F. Mansfield; hostess, Joan Evans; cast: Ann Blyth, Jeff Chandler.

Frontier Town (Synd.); 01/09/53; episode 16, "The Railroad, Dam, and the Water Works"; directed by Paul Franklin; cast: Jeff Chandler (as "Tex Chandler"), Wade Crosby.

Our Miss Brooks (CBS); 01/11/53; episode 184, "New Year's Resolutions"; produced by Larry Berns; directed by Al Lewis; assistant director, Frank Paris; written by Arthur Alsberg and Al Lewis; music by Wilbur Hatch; sound by Bill Gould; engineers, Bob Schradermier and Pat Walsh; announcer, Bob Lemond; cast: Eve Arden, Jeff Chandler, Gale Gordon, Jane Morgan, Richard Crenna, Gloria McMillan, Mary Jane Croft, Bob Sweeney, Peter Leeds.

Frontier Town (Synd.); 01/16/53; episode 17, "Land Grab"; directed by Paul Franklin; cast: Jeff Chandler (as "Tex Chandler"), Howard McNear.

Our Miss Brooks (CBS); 01/18/53; episode 185, "New Principal of Madison High"; produced by Larry Berns; directed by Al Lewis; assistant director, Frank Paris; written by Arthur Alsberg and Al Lewis; music by Wilbur Hatch; sound by Bill Gould; engineers, Harry Essman and Bob Schradermier; announcer, Bob Lemond; cast: Eve Arden, Jeff Chandler, Gale Gordon, Jane Morgan, Richard Crenna, Gloria McMillan, Mary Jane Croft, Fred Clark, Hal March.

Frontier Town (Synd.); 01/23/53; episode 18, "The Jailbird Rangers"; directed by Paul Franklin; cast: Jeff Chandler (as "Tex Chandler"), Wade Crosby.

Our Miss Brooks (CBS); 01/25/53; episode 186, "Outpost Road"; produced by Larry Berns; directed by Al Lewis; assistant director, Frank Paris; written by Al Lewis and Joseph Quillan; music by Wilbur Hatch; sound by Bill Gould; engineers, Bob Schradermier and Pat Walsh; announcer, Bob Lemond; cast: Eve Arden, Jeff Chandler, Gale Gordon, Jane Morgan, Richard Crenna, Gloria McMillan, Virginia Gordon, Isabel Randolph.

Frontier Town (Synd.); 01/30/53; episode 19, "Five Gun Final"; directed by Paul Franklin; cast: Jeff Chandler (as "Tex Chandler"), Wade Crosby.

Guest Star (Synd.); 02/01/53; episode 306, "The Great Presto"; directed by Louis Graf; cast: Jeff Chandler, Peter Leeds, Gerald Mohr, GeGe Pearson, Hy Averback.

Our Miss Brooks (CBS); 02/01/53; episode 187, "Pen Pal Project"; produced by Larry Berns; directed by Al Lewis; assistant director, Frank Paris; written by

Arthur Alsberg and Al Lewis; music by Wilbur Hatch; sound by Bill Gould; engineers, Bob Schradermier and Pat Walsh; announcer, Bob Lemond; cast: Eve Arden, Jeff Chandler, Gale Gordon, Jane Morgan, Richard Crenna, Gloria McMillan.

Frontier Town (Synd.); 02/06/53; episode 20, "Valley of the Varmints"; directed by Paul Franklin; cast: Jeff Chandler (as "Tex Chandler"), Wade Crosby.

Our Miss Brooks (CBS); 02/08/53; episode 188, "Dinner at the Ancient Mariner"; produced by Larry Berns; directed by Al Lewis; assistant director, Frank Paris; written by Arthur Alsberg and Al Lewis; music by Wilbur Hatch; sound by Bill Gould; engineers, Bob Schradermier and Pat Walsh; announcer, Bob Lemond; cast: Eve Arden, Jeff Chandler, Gale Gordon, Jane Morgan, Richard Crenna, Gloria McMillan, Virginia Gordon, Fred Clark.

Frontier Town (Synd.); 02/13/53; episode 21, "All Trails Lead to Trouble"; directed by Paul Franklin; cast: Jeff Chandler (as "Tex Chandler"), Wade Crosby.

Our Miss Brooks (CBS); 02/15/53; episode 189, "Mister … or *Miss* Carter?"; produced by Larry Berns; directed by Al Lewis; assistant director, Frank Paris; written by Arthur Alsberg and Al Lewis; music by Wilbur Hatch; sound by Bill Gould; engineers, Bob Schradermier and Pat Walsh; announcer, Bob Lemond; cast: Eve Arden, Jeff Chandler, Gale Gordon, Jane Morgan, Richard Crenna, Gloria McMillan, Hy Averback, Isabel Randolph.

Frontier Town (Synd.); 02/20/53; episode 22, "Forest Fire"; directed by Paul Franklin; cast: Jeff Chandler (as "Tex Chandler"), Wade Crosby.

Our Miss Brooks (CBS); 02/22/53; episode 190, "Apartment of the Future"; produced by Larry Berns; directed by Al Lewis; assistant director, Frank Paris; written by Arthur Alsberg and Al Lewis; music by Wilbur Hatch; sound by Ralph Cummings and Bill Gould; engineers, Jerry Dettaan and Pat Walsh; announcer, Bob Lemond; cast: Eve Arden, Jeff Chandler, Gale Gordon, Jane Morgan, Richard Crenna, Gloria McMillan.

Frontier Town (Synd.); 02/27/53; episode 23, "Thunder Over Texas"; directed by Paul Franklin; cast: Jeff Chandler (as "Tex Chandler"), Wade Crosby.

Our Miss Brooks (CBS); 03/01/53; episode 191, "Two Thousand Simoleons"; produced by Larry Berns; directed by Al Lewis; assistant director, Frank Paris; written by Al Lewis and Joseph Quillan; music by Wilbur Hatch; sound by Bill Gould; engineers, Ed Ruggles and Pat Walsh; announcer, Bob Lemond; cast: Eve Arden, Jeff Chandler, Gale Gordon, Jane Morgan, Richard Crenna, Gloria McMillan, Hy Averback.

Our Miss Brooks (CBS); 03/08/53; episode 192, "Henpecked Mr. Conklin";

Jeff Chandler

produced by Larry Berns; directed by Al Lewis; assistant director, Frank Paris; written by Al Lewis and Joseph Quillan; music by Wilbur Hatch; sound by Bill Gould; engineers, Ed Ruggles and Pat Walsh; announcer, Bob Lemond; cast: Eve Arden, Jeff Chandler, Gale Gordon, Jane Morgan, Richard Crenna, Gloria McMillan, Virginia Gordon.

Our Miss Brooks (CBS); 03/15/53; episode 193, "Baseball Rally"; produced by Larry Berns; directed by Al Lewis; assistant director, Frank Paris; written by Al Lewis and Joseph Quillan; music by Wilbur Hatch; sound by Bill Gould and Ross Murray; engineers, Ed Ruggles and Pat Walsh; announcer, Bob Lemond; cast: Eve Arden, Gale Gordon, Jane Morgan, Richard Crenna, Gloria McMillan, Leonard Smith, Hy Averback, Fred Shields.

Our Miss Brooks (CBS); 03/22/53; episode 194, "Surprise Party for Mr. Boynton"; produced by Larry Berns; directed by Al Lewis; assistant director, Frank Paris; written by Al Lewis and Joseph Quillan; music by Wilbur Hatch; sound by Ray Erlenborn and Bill Gould; engineers, Otto Remninger and Pat Walsh; announcer, Bob Lemond; cast: Eve Arden, Jeff Chandler, Gale Gordon, Jane Morgan, Richard Crenna, Gloria McMillan.

Our Miss Brooks (CBS); 03/29/53; episode 195, "Sirens of the Screen"; produced by Larry Berns; directed by Al Lewis; assistant director, Frank Paris; written by Arthur Alsberg and Al Lewis; music by Wilbur Hatch; sound by Bill Gould; engineers, Ed Ruggles and Pat Walsh; announcer, Bob Lemond; cast: Eve Arden, Jeff Chandler, Gale Gordon, Jane Morgan, Richard Crenna, Gloria McMillan, Fred Shields, Hy Averback.

Our Miss Brooks (CBS); 04/5/53; episode 196, "Free Flowers from Fleishacker's Florist"; produced by Larry Berns; directed by Al Lewis; assistant director, Frank Paris; written by Arthur Alsberg, Al Lewis and Joseph Quillan; music by Wilbur Hatch; sound by Bill Gould; engineers, Ed Ruggles and Pat Walsh; announcer, Bob Lemond; cast: Eve Arden, Jeff Chandler, Gale Gordon, Jane Morgan, Richard Crenna, Gloria McMillan, Virginia Gordon, Mary Jane Croft, Dan Tobin.

Our Miss Brooks (CBS); 04/12/53; episode 197, "Under the Oak Tree"; produced by Larry Berns; directed by Al Lewis; assistant director, Frank Paris; written by Arthur Alsberg and Al Lewis; music by Wilbur Hatch; sound by Bill Gould; engineers, Ed Ruggles and Pat Walsh; announcer, Bob Lemond; cast: Eve Arden, Jeff Chandler, Gale Gordon, Jane Morgan, Richard Crenna, Gloria McMillan, Virginia Gordon.

Our Miss Brooks (CBS); 04/19/53; episode 198, "Mr. Boynton's Daughter"; produced by Larry Berns; directed by Al Lewis; assistant director, Frank Paris; written by Arthur Alsberg and Al Lewis; music by Wilbur Hatch; sound by Bill

Gould; engineers, George Culbertson and Pat Walsh; announcer, Bob Lemond; cast: Eve Arden, Jeff Chandler, Gale Gordon, Jane Morgan, Richard Crenna, Gloria McMillan, Frank Nelson.

Our Miss Brooks (CBS); 04/26/53; episode 199, "Elmwood 6319"; produced by Larry Berns; directed by Al Lewis; assistant director, Frank Paris; written by Al Lewis and Joseph Quillan; music by Wilbur Hatch; sound by Bill Gould; engineers, George Culbertson and Pat Walsh; announcer, Bob Lemond; cast: Eve Arden, Jeff Chandler, Gale Gordon, Jane Morgan, Richard Crenna, Gloria McMillan, Mary Jane Croft, Sandra Gould, Jerry Hausner.

Our Miss Brooks (CBS); 05/03/53; episode 200, "Locked in for the Night"; produced by Larry Berns; directed by Al Lewis; assistant director, Frank Paris; written by Arthur Alsberg and Al Lewis; music by Wilbur Hatch; sound by Bill Gould; engineers, George Culbertson and Pat Walsh; announcer, Bob Lemond; cast: Eve Arden, Jeff Chandler, Gale Gordon, Jane Morgan, Richard Crenna, Gloria McMillan, Hy Averback.

Our Miss Brooks (CBS); 05/10/53; episode 201, "Blindfolded Marvel the Second"; produced by Larry Berns; directed by Al Lewis; assistant director, Frank Paris; written by Arthur Alsberg and Al Lewis; music by Wilbur Hatch; sound by Bill Gould; engineers, George Culbertson and Pat Walsh; announcer, Bob Lemond; cast: Eve Arden, Jeff Chandler, Gale Gordon, Jane Morgan, Richard Crenna, Gloria McMillan, Leonard Smith, Fred Clark, Sheldon Leonard.

Our Miss Brooks (CBS); 05/17/53; episode 202, "Mr. Stone Hires a Psychiatrist"; produced by Larry Berns; directed by Al Lewis; assistant director, Frank Paris; written by Arthur Alsberg and Al Lewis; music by Wilbur Hatch; sound by Bill Gould; engineers, George Culbertson and Pat Walsh; announcer, Bob Lemond; cast: Eve Arden, Jeff Chandler, Gale Gordon, Jane Morgan, Richard Crenna, Gloria McMillan, Bob Sweeney.

Our Miss Brooks (CBS); 05/24/53; episode 203, "Mrs. Davis' Surprise Party"; produced by Larry Berns; directed by Al Lewis; assistant director, Frank Paris; written by Al Lewis and Joseph Quillan; music by Wilbur Hatch; sound by Bill Gould; engineers, George Culbertson and Pat Walsh; announcer, Bob Lemond; cast: Eve Arden, Jeff Chandler, Gale Gordon, Jane Morgan, Richard Crenna, Gloria McMillan, Mary Jane Croft.

Our Miss Brooks (CBS); 05/31/53; episode 204, "Cosmopolitan Magazine Pictures"; produced by Larry Berns; directed by Al Lewis; assistant director, Frank Paris; written by Al Lewis and Joseph Quillan; music by Wilbur Hatch; sound by Bill Gould; engineers, George Culbertson and Pat Walsh; announcer, Bob Lemond;

Jeff Chandler

cast: Eve Arden, Jeff Chandler, Gale Gordon, Jane Morgan, Richard Crenna, Gloria McMillan, Mary Jane Croft, Dan Tobin.

The Martin and Lewis Show (NBC); 06/02/53; directed by Dick Mack; cast: Dean Martin, Jerry Lewis, Jeff Chandler.

Our Miss Brooks (CBS); 06/07/53; episode 205, "Double-Breasted Horse Blankets"; produced by Larry Berns; directed by Al Lewis; assistant director, Frank Paris; written by Arthur Alsberg and Al Lewis; music by Wilbur Hatch; sound by Bill Gould; engineers, Paul McDermott and Pat Walsh; announcer, Bob Lemond; cast: Eve Arden, Jeff Chandler, Gale Gordon, Jane Morgan, Richard Crenna, Gloria McMillan, Mary Jane Croft, Fred Clark.

Our Miss Brooks (CBS); 06/14/53; episode 206, "Square Dance Troupe"; produced by Larry Berns; directed by Al Lewis; assistant director, Frank Paris; written by Al Lewis and Joseph Quillan; music by Wilbur Hatch; sound by Bill Gould; engineers, Paul McDermott and Pat Walsh; announcer, Bob Lemond; cast: Eve Arden, Jeff Chandler, Gale Gordon, Jane Morgan, Richard Crenna, Gloria McMillan, Joseph Kearns, Herb Butterfield.

Our Miss Brooks (CBS); 06/21/53; episode 207, "Let Hawkins Guide You Through Yonkers"; produced by Larry Berns; directed by Al Lewis; assistant director, Frank Paris; written by Arthur Alsberg and Al Lewis; music by Wilbur Hatch; sound by Bill Gould; engineers, Bob McKenny and Pat Walsh; announcer, Bob Lemond; cast: Eve Arden, Jeff Chandler, Gale Gordon, Jane Morgan, Richard Crenna, Gloria McMillan, Herb Butterfield.

Our Miss Brooks (CBS); 06/28/53; episode 208, "Mr. Boynton Meets Mr. Finch"; produced by Larry Berns; directed by Al Lewis; assistant director, Frank Paris; written by Arthur Alsberg and Al Lewis; music by Wilbur Hatch; sound by Bill Gould; engineers, Bob McKenny and Pat Walsh; announcer, Bob Lemond; cast: Eve Arden, Jeff Chandler, Gale Gordon, Jane Morgan, Richard Crenna, Gloria McMillan, Jerry Hausner, Joseph Kearns.

The Phillip Morris Playhouse On Broadway (CBS); 07/01/53; episode 95, "The Web"; directed by Charles Martin; cast: Jeff Chandler.

Family Theater (Mut.); 07/15/53; episode 327, "The Flying Dutchman"; directed by Joseph F. Mansfield; hostess, Lizabeth Scott; cast: Jeff Chandler, Jay Novello, Jack Lloyd, Joy Terry, William Woodson.

Suspense (CBS); 10/19/53; episode 522, "My True Love's Hair"; directed by Elliott Lewis; cast: Jeff Chandler, Lillian Buyeff, Betty Harper, Joseph Kearns, Jack Kruschen, Clayton Post, Martha Wentworth, Paula Winslowe, Ben Wright.

Family Theater (Mut.); 10/21/53; episode 341, "East of Puntas"; directed by Lew X. Landsworth; hostess, Ruth Hussey; cast: Jeff Chandler, Theodore von Eltz, Yvonne Peattie, Ted de Corsia, John Stevenson.

The Lux Radio Theatre (CBS); 11/02/53; episode 853, "Because of You"; directed by Earl Ebi; host, Irving Cummings; cast: June Allyson, Jeff Chandler, Jeanette Nolan, Bill Johnstone, Kay Stewart, Tony Barrett, Lynn Allen, Herb Butterfield, Leonard Penn, Paul Frees, Eddie Marr, Byron Kane, Mimi Gibson, Dorothy Brown.

1954

Suspense (CBS); 02/08/54; episode 538, "Death at Skirkerud Pond"; directed by Elliott Lewis; cast: Jeff Chandler, Herb Butterfield, Herb Ellis, Byron Kane, Joseph Kearns, Jack Kruschen, Cathy Lewis, Lou Merrill, Paula Winslowe.

Family Theater (Mut.); 04/14/54; episode 366, "The Way of the Cross"; directed by Lew X. Landsworth; hostess, Maureen O'Sullivan; cast: Jeff Chandler.

Family Theater (Mut.); 06/23/54; episode 375, "Clean and Crisp and Even"; directed by John T. Kelly; host, George Murphy; cast: Jeanne Bates, Jeff Chandler, Michael Chapin, Herb Ellis, Myra Marsh.

The Lux Radio Theatre (CBS); 11/09/54; episode 896, "My Man Godfrey"; directed by Frederic MacKaye; host, Irving Cummings; cast: Jeff Chandler, Julie Adams, Virginia Gregg, Eleanor Audley, Alan Reed, Carleton Young, Yvonne Peattie, Shepard Menken, Barney Phillips, Joe Forte, George Neise, Stanley Farrar, Barbara Eiler, Eddie Marr.

The Joyful Hour (Synd.); 12/19/54; cast: Ann Blyth, Maureen O'Sullivan, Irene Dunne, Jeff Chandler, Stephen McNally, J. Carrol Nash.

1955

Red Cross Show (Synd.); 03/20/55; cast: Jane Wyman, Jeff Chandler, Donna Reed, Loretta Young, Gary Crosby, Frankie Laine, Bob Hope, Robert Armbruster.

1956

The Eternal Light (NBC); 01/08/56: episode 586, "The Human Element"; cast: Jeff Chandler.

Jeff Chandler

1957

Suspense (CBS); 03/31/57; episode 692, "A Good Neighbor"; directed by William N. Robson; cast: Virginia Gregg, Jeff Chandler.

1959

Hollywood Salutes the National Guard (Synd.); 02/02/59; directed by Artie Wayne; cast: Dinah Shore, Jack Webb, Jerry Lewis, Dale Evans, Roy Rogers, Donald O'Connor, The Four Preps, Audie Murphy, Perez Perado, Debbie Reynolds, Sammy Davis Jr., Mickey Rooney, Johnny Mathis, Jack Lemmon, Red Skelton, David Rose and His Orchestra, Jeff Chandler, Peggy Lee, Clark Gable, Frank Pollack.

Television

Entries are in chronological order

Pabst Blue Ribbon Bouts

August 15, 1951. CBS, Wednesday, 10:00 P.M.

Behind the Scenes: In their promotion of *Iron Man*, U-I arranged a special, three-state tour for Joyce Holden and Jeff as well as Frankie Van, for his experience in and out of the ring. For their personal appearances on television, the studio prepared a special three-minute clip, similar to an established five-minute short used in their television service "Movie Star Album." The latter included a biography of Jeff, twenty movie stills, and an announcer's script and recording.

The tour began in New York City with Jeff—making his television debut—interviewed between televised prize fights on *Pabst Blue Ribbon Bouts*. The tour also included a visit to the Polo Grounds, where Jeff—in front of a crowd of 25,000 that included Joe Di Maggio and Walter Winchell—went two rounds with Joe Walcott, the new, heavyweight champion of the world.[1] The next leg of the tour took the team to Pittsburgh for the movie's world premiere on August 17, 1951, followed by the Cleveland, Ohio opening. In 1947, Dorothy Fuldheim joined WEWS-TV in Cleveland and made television history by becoming the first female newscaster in the U.S. Miss Fuldheim acted as cohost for the *One O'Clock Club*, a live variety show that included book reviews, cooking and interviews. Miss Fuldheim added Jeff to a growing list of noted interviewees that included President Harry S. Truman, Adolph Hitler, Albert Einstein, Helen Keller, and actress Helen Hayes.[2]

Comments by Dorothy Fuldheim: "The late Jeff Chandler was another of my favorites, and we carried on a sort of verbal love affair on the air. He was a great guy, and I truly loved him."[3]

Comments by Jeff Chandler: "I wasn't taking any chances, though. Before I went on, I asked him [Joe Walcott] to take it easy. I'll tell you something, though. The guy doesn't have a scratch on his face. Not a single mark."[4]

Jeff Chandler

United Cerebral Palsy Telethon

June 5, 1953. ABC, KECA-TV, Channel 7, Friday, 11:00 P.M., 25 hours.

Credits: Producer, Frank La Tourette; emceed by Ben Alexander and Jack Webb.

Behind the Scenes: The star-studded Los Angeles County Cerebral Palsy Telethon featured Gracie Allen, George Burns, Sterling Hayden, Bob Hope, George Jessel, Buster Keaton, Frankie Laine, Peggy Lee, Fred MacMurray, Marilyn Maxwell, Agnes Moorehead, Margaret O'Brien, Maureen O'Sullivan and Ed Wynn; Jeff sang "That Old Black Magic."[5]

Multiple Sclerosis Telethon

August 30, 1953. CBS, KNXT-TV, Channel 2, Sunday, 12:00 P.M., 16 hours.

Credits: Hosts, Peter Potter and Jack Rourke.

Behind the Scenes: As the end of August approached, U-I coordinated with the telethon's producers, arranging for the appearances of Rock Hudson, Piper Laurie, Jeff Chandler and others. With a goal of $200,000 in support of the National and California Multiple Sclerosis Society, KNXT-TV ran the star-studded, 16-hour telethon. Guests included Celeste Holm, James Mason and Shirley Temple.[6] In the telethon's first hours, Jeff sang for the audience and helped with the telephones, staying until 4:00 A.M.[7]

Comments by Jeff Chandler: "I got a lot of encouragement from the reactions to my appearance as a singer, doing "I Believe"—that's my kind of song for sure—on that telethon recently [KNXT-TV's Multiple Sclerosis Benefit]. I didn't intend to sing there, but when it got around I was there so many watchers called in saying they would donate something extra if I would sing, well, I couldn't get out of it."[8]

Our Famous Husbands

September 15, 1953. ABC, KECA-TV, Channel 7, Tuesday, 8:00 P.M., 30 minutes.

Credits: Produced by Selig J. Seligman and Hunt Stromberg Jr.; emceed by Paul Coates; panel: Cleo (Mrs. Edward) Arnold, Elyse (Mrs. Tom) Harmon and Sheila (Mrs. Gordon) MacRae.

Behind the Scenes: Television held its own Hollywood premiere when the stars turned out for *Our Famous Husbands*. Those in attendance at the press-covered activities outside the ABC Studios on Vine Street included Edward Arnold, Gordon MacRae, Tom Harmon, Dean Martin, Jo Stafford, Paul Weston, Angela Landsbury, Ray Bolger, Fay Wray, Danny Thomas, Jeff Chandler and others.[9]

Television

Producers Selig J. Seligman and Hunt Stromberg Jr. sold *Our Famous Husbands* to ABC. The show replaced *Famous Playhouse* and drew on the popularity of its famous husbands: Edward Arnold (leading man in the 1930s; film debut, 1916), Tom Harmon (football great of the 1940s; film debut, 1941), and Gordon MacRae (musical star; film debut, 1948). The premiere episode, viewed locally, featured Jeff as its mystery guest with credit to *East of Sumatra*.[10]

Place the Face

March 11, 1954. CBS, KNXT-TV, Channel 2, Thursday, 7:30 P.M., 30 minutes.

Credits: Emceed by Bill Cullen; announcer, Jack Narz.

Behind the Scenes: Viewed coast-to-coast, the game show *Place the Face* placed contestants opposite someone from their past. The show featured celebrity guests such as Phil Harris and Xavier Cugat. With clues provided by emcee Bill Cullen, who replaced Jack Smith in January 1954, the first player to *Place the Face* won a prize of merchandise.

The March 11, 1954, show featured Jeff's song "I Should Care," with credit to the film *Yankee Pasha*. In this episode of *Place the Face*, Jeff had to identify the face of the girl who played Juliet opposite his Romeo when they played stock in New York in 1940.[11]

The Peter Potter Show

March 14, 1954. ABC, KABC-TV, Channel 7; Sunday, 9:30 P.M., 30 minutes.

Credits: Produced and emceed by Peter Potter; directed by Richard Gottlieb; guest panel.

Behind the Scenes: As 1953 eased into 1954, two television stations in Los Angeles changed their call letters (KLAC-TV, Channel 13, became KCOP-TV; KECA-TV, Channel 7, became KABC-TV) and *The Peter Potter Show* went national, replacing *Hour of Decision*.

The Peter Potter Show's format consisted of a four-man guest panel that decided on whether a record by a professional recording artist would be hit or a miss or, in the case of a tie, with the help of the studio audience. Peter Potter, professional baseball player and acting student at the Pasadena Playhouse, acted as host for television's *The Peter Potter Show* and radio's *Juke Box Jury*. The show on Sunday, March 14, 1954 featured Jeff as guest for the promotion of his song "I Should Care."[12]

The Summer Comedy Hour

July 25, 1954. NBC, KNBH-TV, Channel 4, Sunday, 8:00 P.M., 60 minutes.

Jeff Chandler

Credits: Directed by Bill Asher; emceed by Bobby Van.

Behind the Scenes: Broadcast live from Hollywood, *The Summer Comedy Hour* featured performances by singer Pearl Bailey and others. Jeff sang the song "Lamplight" with credit to Decca Records. His appearance on the variety show occurred under the stipulation that he would appear only as a "guest soloist," with no participation in any comedy or dramatic routines.[13]

What's My Line?

October 3, 1954. CBS, KNXT-TV, Channel 2; Sunday, 7:30 P.M., 30 minutes.

Credits: Produced by Mark Goodson and Bill Todman.

Behind the Scenes: Tens of millions of viewers each week watched the Emmy-award winning quiz show *What's My Line?* The show featured a panel who cross-questioned a mystery guest in order to correctly determine his or her occupation by asking questions that would result in only a "no" or a "yes" answer from their guest. The last show of January 1954 had Richard Widmark as its mystery guest; its panel of experts: columnist Dorothy Kilgallen, radio-television personality Steve Allen, actress Arlene Francis and author Bennett Cerf.

A "mystery guest" by *What's My Line?* definition: a public figure recognizable on sight by the majority of the television audience. Guests in the fall of 1954 included Alfred Hitchcock, Gina Lollobrigida, Robert Young, Dale Evans and Roy Rogers. Broadcast from New York City and sponsored by Remington Rand, the 229th episode of *What's My Line?* featured Jeff Chandler as its guest.[14]

The Colgate Comedy Hour

December 12, 1954. NBC, KNBH-TV, Channel 4; Sunday, 8:00 P.M., 60 minutes.

Credits: Produced by Bill Morrow; emceed by Gordon MacRae.

Behind the Scenes: In operation for over ten years, *Modern Screen's* annual poll surveyed the popularity of motion picture celebrities amongst its 1.5 million readers. *Modern Screen* awarded John Wayne their Silver Cup Award as the winner of the "Most Popular Male Star" for 1953. When the magazine polled its readers a year later, Rock Hudson came in first, but followed closely by Tony Curtis and Jeff Chandler, in that order. U-I set a record in the fifteen-year history of *Modern Screen's* survey with three winners in this division. As a result, *Modern Screen* made arrangements for a special award presentation to the three winners.[15]

Tentatively scheduled for broadcast over radio and television on *The Jack Benny Show*, the magazine joined U-I on television's *The Colgate Comedy Hour*. Actresses Mara Corday and Gloria de Haven presented the 1954 *Modern Screen* awards to Hudson, Curtis and Chandler on the variety show. Miss Corday and

Television

Miss de Haven, along with Tony Curtis, Gene Nelson and Paul Gilbert appeared in film clips and reenacted scenes from the soon-to-released movie musical *So This is Paris* (1955). Emcee Gordon MacRae interviewed Jeff who also sang his newly-released song "Always."[16]

The Dinah Shore Show

December 17, 1954. NBC, KNBH-TV, Channel 4, Friday.
    Behind the Scenes: Singer-actress Dinah Shore interviewed Jeff on her variety program broadcast from Hollywood and simulcast on radio.[17]

Steve Allen in Movieland

July 2, 1955. NBC, KNBH-TV, Channel 4; Saturday, 9:00 P.M., 90 minutes.
    Credits: Produced by Jack Rayel; directed by Dick McDonagh; written by Don McGuire; music directed by Buddy Bregman; emceed by Steve Allen.
    Behind the Scenes: *Steve Allen in Movieland* promoted U-I's line-up for the summer of 1955 as well as *The Benny Goodman Story* (1955), in production and starring Steve Allen. After rehearsals on July 1, Jeff sang the song "Foxfire" while backed by an orchestra. Other stars on the summer spectacular included Tony Curtis, Audie Murphy and Piper Laurie. The show also featured performances by clarinetist-bandleader Benny Goodman, drummer Gene Krupa and pianist Ted Wilson.[18]

The Perry Como Show

January 19, 1957. NBC, KNBH-TV, Channel 4; Saturday, 8:00 P.M., 30 minutes.
    Credits: Produced by Robert Finkel; executive producer, George McGarrett; directed by Grey Lockwood; written by Goodman Ace, Jay Burton, George Foster and Mort Green; musical director and orchestra conductor, Mitchell Ayres; announcer, Frank Gallop; host, Perry Como.[19]
    Behind the Scenes: Emmy-award winning singer-personality Perry Como welcomed Jeff, comedian George Gobel, the vocal group, the Mills Brothers, and orchestra leader John Scott Trotter as his guests to another "Saturday Night with Mr. C." In one segment, Como and Jeff imitated the Mills Brothers in song; in another, Jeff sang the song "There Goes My Heart."[20]

The Steve Allen Show

September 1, 1957. NBC, KNBH-TV, Channel 4; Sunday, 8:00 P.M., 60 minutes.

Credits: Music directed by Skitch Henderson; announcer, Gene Raymond; regulars, Tom Poston, Louis Nye, Don Knotts.

Behind the Scenes: With *Jeanne Eagels* and his Liberty Records' single in release and *Jeff Chandler Sings to You* just weeks away from being awarded "Album Cover of the Week" by *Billboard*, Jeff appeared as a guest on *The Steve Allen Show*. Jeff performed with singer Pearl Bailey and Allen in one sketch, paired with Allen in another, and sang the song "Hold Me."[21]

The American Jew: A Tribute to Freedom

December 7, 1958. CBS, KNXT-TV, Channel 2; Sunday, 11:30 A.M., 60 minutes.

Credits: Produced by Jack Kuney; directed by Tim Kiley; written by David Ebin; CBS Symphony Orchestra directed by Alfredo Antonini; narration by Jeff Chandler.

Behind the Scenes: The hour-long special, narrated by Jeff, featured statements, performances and conversations with representatives from the Jewish faith. Guests included Richard Tucker, Stan Freeman, Barney Balaban, Dore Schary, Al Capp and Susan Strasberg.[22]

A Call from ...

February 10, 1960. KCOP-TV, Channel 13; Wednesday, 8:30 A.M., 60 minutes.

Credits: Produced by Marsha Hunt; directed by Arthur Miller; written by Robert Presnell Jr.

Behind the Scenes: Over a dozen celebrities toasted "World Refugee Year," a United Nations' program. The stars included Steve Allen, Harry Belafonte, Richard Boone, Bing Crosby, Jeff Chandler, and Joanne Woodward. The day before, February 9, 1960, Ms. Woodward became the first star on the Hollywood Walk of Fame.[23]

Theater

The Trojan Horse

The Millpond Playhouse, 1940–41. Produced October 30, 1940. Subtitle: "A Contemporary Drama, Laid in 1185 B.C." Sixty performances: October 30, 1940 to January 11, 1941.

Credits: Produced, directed and musical arrangement by David Lowe; written by Christopher Morley; music for "A Lady Lives in Pergamus" composed by Gaylord Mason; settings designed by Edward Colin Dawson; costumes designed by Fleurette Withers.

Cast: Edward Thompson (King Piram), Ira Grossel (Hector), Peter Johnston, Victor Chapin (Dares), Otto Klemperer Jr. (Paris), Gordon MacRae (Deiphobus), Brian Gilbert (Antenor, Dr. Calchas), Edward McVitty, Peter Bayes (Aeneas), Richard Graham (Troilus), Fred Colcord (Cleon), J. Dewitt Spencer, Jack Chakrin (Fuscus), David Lowe (Ilium), John Viebrock, Gaylord Mason (Laocoon), Christopher Morley (Pandarus), Kerry Stuart, Jane Jeffreys (Cressida), Mary Jane Morrow (Antigone), Dorothy Eaton, Sheila Stephens, Marian Hartshorn (Helen), Barbara Winslow, Marjorie Hastings (Briseis, Cassandra, Creusa), Genevieve Townsend, Andrea Duncan (Andromache, Hecuba), Mary Esherick, Bertram Wood, Jess Kruger, Phillip Beaudette (Agamemnon), Brian Gilbert, Emanuel Shipow (Menelaus, Nestor), Nicholas Papalas (Achilles), Charles Kreth Jr. (Ajax), Lewis Sisk (Sarpedoni, Ulysses), Gaylord Mason, Gene Sanders, Leon Smith (Diomedes), Julia Herrick (Chryseis), Mona Francis, Shirley Lowe, Mary Ann Newman (Chippendales).

Synopsis: The city of Troy: the ancient, legendary site of the Trojan War and symbol of a beleaguered civilization. *The Trojan Horse* pointed out the similarities between the Greek-Trojan turmoil centuries ago and the Democracy-Totalitarian struggle of the late 1930s to the early 1940s.

Behind the Scenes: A founder and editor of *Saturday Review*, author Christopher Morley wrote many books, but *The Trojan Horse* held a special place in his heart.

As turmoil worldwide mounted in 1937, Morley wrote *The Trojan Horse* in book form during a summer vacation at Lake Champlain. When war erupted two years later, Morley, once again at Lake Champlain, turned his book into a play.[1]

Morley's story, told before by English poet, Geoffrey Chaucer, in *Troilus and Criseyde* (c. 1385), involves the siege of Troy in 1185 B.C. and, more specifically, of a love affair between Troilus and Cassandra; a Cassandra as contemporary to Morley's era as American journalist, Dorothy Thompson, whose radio broadcasts and widely syndicated column "On the Record" (1936–41), informed Americans of the impending threat of Nazi Germany.

Almost 9,500 theatergoers braved the Long Island winter to see *The Trojan Horse*, the fifteenth production of the 250-seat Millpond Playhouse. The play, produced in 18 scenes with 34 cast members, included musicians, soldiers, servants and priests. During its eleven-week run, a number of actors played various parts.

Under the watchful eyes of three chaperones, many of the actors received free room and board at the Roslyn Neighborhood House; pay, $5.00 a week. The House sat adjacent to the theater, so the actors often ate in costume.[2]

Christopher Morley's home, Green Escape, stood five minutes from the Playhouse in Roslyn Heights. One night, the box-office staff took ill and their usher couldn't make it; by the time the oil burner acted up, Morley came to the rescue. He sold tickets, doubled as an usher, repaired the oil burner, spoke a few words to the audience, and sold hot clam broth between acts.[3]

Comments by Christopher Morley: "We remember snowy evenings when there were more people on the stage than in the audience."[4]

Notes

Preface

1. "What Hollywood's Whispering About," *Photoplay*, December 1952.
2. "Inside Stuff," *Photoplay*, June 1953.
3. "Radio's Missing Masters," *Radio Spirits, Inc.*, 1993.

From Flatbush to Filmland

1. Fourteenth Census of the United States: 1920 Population, Los Angeles Central Library.
2. Receiving Blotter, Department of Correction, Sing Sing Prison, New York State Archives.
3. Elaine Margo to author, August 23, 2004.
4. Ibid.
5. Ibid.
6. Anne Milman Briscoe to author, October 16, 2002.
7. Anne Milman Briscoe to author, October 17, 2002.
8. Anne Milman Briscoe to author, October 16, 2002.
9. "Jeff's Other Love," *Photoplay*, January 1954.
10. Thomas E. Dewey, *Twenty Against the Underworld* (Garden City: Doubleday & Company, Inc.), p. 280.
11. "Nine Seized as Dewey Strikes at $2,000,000 Café Racket," *The New York Times*, October 21, 1936.
12. "Witness is Jailed in Racket Inquiry," *The New York Times*, October 9, 1935.
13. "Schultz Dies of Wounds without Naming Slayers; Three Aides Dead, One Dying," *The New York Times*, October 25, 1935.
14. "J.E. Hoover Shows 'Drain' of Rackets," *The New York Times*, November 18, 1935.
15. Jon Shevelew to author, October 30, 2002.
16. Rupert Hughes, *The Story of Thomas E. Dewey, Attorney for the People* (New York: Grosset & Dunlap, Publishers), p. 133.
17. "'Shakedown' Strike Used as a Weapon in the Café Racket," *The New York Times*, February 4, 1937.
18. Mary M. Stolberg, *Fighting Organized Crime—Politics, Justice, and the Legacy of Thomas E. Dewey* (Boston: Northeastern University Press), p. 186.
19. Rupert Hughes, *The Story of Thomas E. Dewey, Attorney for the People* (New York: Grosset & Dunlap, Publishers), p. 133.
20. Receiving Blotter, Department of Corrections, Sing Sing Prison, New York State Archives.
21. "No Mugs Wanted," *Movieland*, April 1951.
22. "Brooklyn Eagle," *Photoplay*, June 1951.
23. Biography of Marjorie Hoshelle, Warner Bros. Studio, Margaret Herrick Library, Academy of Motion Picture Arts and Sciences.
24. *Film Daily*, October 19, 1943.
25. Jim Bishop, *The Mark Hellinger Story: A Biography of Broadway and Hollywood* (New York: Appleton-Century-Crofts), p. 313.
26. "No Mugs Wanted," *Movieland*, April 1951.

Notes — The Films

27. *Ibid.*

28. The Hedda Hopper Collection, Margaret Herrick Library, Academy of Motion Picture Arts and Sciences.

29. The E. Jack Neuman Collection, American Radio Archives, Thousand Oaks Library.

30. Tichi Wilkerson and Marcia Borie, *Hollywood Legends: The Golden Years of The Hollywood Reporter* (Los Angeles: Tale Weaver Publishing), p. 186.

31. Burns Mantle: *Best Plays of 1945/1946* (New York: Dodd, Mead and Company), p. 401.

32. "I Walk Alone," *The Lux Radio Theatre* Collection, Margaret Herrick Library, Academy of Motion Picture Arts and Sciences.

33. Mort Fine Papers, Department of Special Collections, Young Research Library, University of California, Los Angeles.

34. William Reynolds to author, June 21, 2003.

35. Peter Graves to author, June 20, 2003.

36. Letter from Philip Gerard to David Lipton, the Universal Studios Collection, USC Cinema-Television Library.

37. Bob Rains to author, October 9, 2003.

38. Letter from Bob Rains to Rufus LeMaire, May 10, 1950, the Universal Studios Collection, USC Cinema-Television Library.

39. "Movietime USA-General 1951 Correspondence," Margaret Herrick Library, Academy of Motion Picture Arts and Sciences.

40. Letter from Bob Rains to David Lipton, the Universal Studios Collection, USC Cinema-Television Library.

41. Bob Rains to author, October 9, 2003.

42. Letter from Bob Rains to Rufus LeMaire, the Universal Studios Collection, USC Cinema-Television Library.

43. "Seven Hundred Turn Out to See Zanuck Receive Milestone Award," *Variety*, November 23, 1953.

44. "Wife Divorces Jeff Chandler, Screen Actor," *Los Angeles Times*, April 16, 1954.

45. Letter from Bob Rains to Clark Ramsay, March 5, 1955, the Universal Studios Collection, USC Cinema-Television Library.

46. Brenda Scott Royce, *Rock Hudson: A Bio-Bibliography* (Westport: Greenwood Press), p. 168.

47. Bart Andrews, *The "I Love Lucy" Book* (Garden City: Doubleday & Company, Inc.), p. 327.

48. Synopsis of *Raw Wind in Eden* from Clark Ramsay to David Lipton, the Universal Studios Collection, USC Cinema-Television Library.

49. Arline Gray to author, July 24, 2003.

50. J. J. (Joe) Cohn Oral History, USC Cinema-Television Library.

51. Arline Gray to author, July 24, 2003.

52. *Ibid.*

53. Peter Graves to author, June 20, 2003.

54. "Universal Pictures Signs Pact with Actors to Share TV Profits for Post '48 Movies," *The Wall Street Journal*, March 3, 1960.

55. "Intra-SAG Feud Fed New Fuel," *Variety*, March 3, 1960.

56. "Twenty Five Stars Buy Ad to 'Back' SAG Board," *Variety*, March 9, 1960.

57. "Arabs Ban More U.S. Films," *New York Times*, January 20, 1960.

58. "U.S. Companies Barred," *New York Times*, July 18, 1960.

59. James A. Michener, *Report of the County Chairman* (New York: Random House), p. 158.

60. Western Union Telegram from Bill Hendricks to Warner Bros., Burbank, California, April 15, 1961.

61. "Dr. N. E. Gourson, Studio's Physician," *Los Angeles Times*, February 16, 1977.

62. "Limelight Reveals Truth of Jeff Chandler's Death," *Limelight*, July 13, 1961.

63. Peter Graves to author, June 20, 2003.

64. William Reynolds to author, June 21, 2003.

65. George Jessel, *Halo Over Hollywood* (Van Nuys: Toastmaster Pub. Co.), p. 35.

66. Angela von Mizener to author, June 22, 2003.

67. "State Will Investigate Jeff Chandler's Death," *Los Angeles Times*, June 29, 1961.

68. "Actors Petition for Quiz Into Jeff Chandler's Death," *Los Angeles Times*, June 28, 1961.

69. "Actors Ask Jeff Chandler Quiz," *Los Angeles Mirror*, June 27, 1961.

70. Statement issued by the Culver City Hospital, June 28, 1961.

71. "Guild Action Unlikely On Chandler Petition," *Boxoffice*, July 3, 1961.

72. "Henaghan's Corner," *The Hollywood Reporter*, November 8, 1961.

Notes—The Films

The Films

The Invisible Wall (1947)
1. *The Hollywood Reporter*, October 10, 1947.

Johnny O'Clock (1947)
2. *Columbia News*, August 13, 1946.
3. Cobbett S. Steinberg. *Film Facts*. (New York: Facts on File, Inc.), p. 62.
4. *Columbia News*, August 30, 1946.
5. *Liberty*, March 29, 1947.
6. Tough on Reporters—But Not on Scripters," *Radio Life*, May 2, 1948.

Roses Are Red (1947)
7. *Motion Picture Exhibitor*, November 12, 1947.

Abandoned (1949)
8. Showman's Manual for *Abandoned*, the Universal Studios Collection, USC Cinema-Television Library.
9. *Motion Picture Herald*, October 8, 1949.
10. Joseph M. Newman Oral History, Margaret Herrick Library, Academy of Motion Picture Arts and Sciences.
11. Preview of *Abandoned*, July 14, 1949, Los Angeles, California, the Universal Studios Collection, USC Cinema-Television Library.

Mr. Belvedere Goes to College (1949)
12. *Motion Picture Herald*, April 9, 1949.
13. "Top-Grossers of 1949," *Variety*, January 4, 1950.

The Rugged O'Riordans (1949)
14. Showman's Manual for *The Rugged O'Riordans*, Margaret Herrick Library, Academy of Motion Picture Arts and Sciences.
15. *Boxoffice*, December 17, 1949.

Sword in the Desert (1949)
16. "By Way of Report," *The New York Times*, October 24, 1948.
17. Showman's Manual for *Sword in the Desert*, the Universal Studios Collection, USC Cinema-Television Library.
18. *Motion Picture Herald*, August 27, 1949.
19. Bob Rains to author, October 9, 2003.

Abbott and Costello in the Foreign Legion (1950)
20. *Motion Picture Herald*, July 15, 1950.
21. "Top-Grossers of 1950 (Film Rentals)," *Variety*, January 3, 1951.

Broken Arrow (1950)
22. *Motion Picture Herald*, June 17, 1950.
23. "Top-Grossers of 1950 (Film Rentals)," *Variety*, January 3, 1951.
24. Rudy Behlmer, *Memo From Darryl F. Zanuck* (New York: Grove Press), p. 186.
25. Hedda Hopper Collection, Margaret Herrick Library, Academy of Motion Picture Arts and Sciences.

Deported (1950)
26. Showman's Manual for *Deported*, the Universal Studios Collection, USC Cinema-Television Library.
27. Bob Rains to author, October 9, 2003.
28. *Motion Picture Exhibitor*, October 25, 1950.
29. The Universal Studios Collection, USC Cinema-Television Library.

Double Crossbones (1950)
30. *Motion Picture Herald*, November 25, 1950.

Two Flags West (1950)
31. *Los Angeles Times*, November 2, 1950.
32. Darryl F. Zanuck to Casey Robinson, February 24, 1950, the Universal Studios Collection, USC Cinema-Television Library.
33. Ronald L. Davis, *Hollywood Beauty: Linda Darnell and the American Dream* (Norman, Oklahoma: University of Oklahoma Press), p. 121.
34. *Saturday Evening Post*, June 29, 1951.

Bird of Paradise (1951)
35. *Hollywood Citizen-News*, March 24, 1951.
36. "Top-Grossers of 1951 (Film Rentals)," *Variety*, January 2, 1952.
37. *Man in the Shadow* Publicity files, the Universal Studios Collection, USC Cinema-Television Library.

Flame of Araby (1951)
38. *The Hollywood Reporter*, November 16, 1951.

39. "Top-Grossers of 1952 (Film Rentals)," *Variety*, January 7, 1953.

Iron Man (1951)

40. *Motion Picture Exhibitor*, July 18, 1951.
41. "Top-Grossers of 1951 (Film Rentals)," *Variety*, January 2, 1952.

Meet Danny Wilson (1951)

42. *Motion Picture Exhibitor*, January 16, 1952.
43. Tony Curtis with Barry Paris, *Tony Curtis, the Autobiography* (New York: Morrow), p. 83.
44. "The Tony Curtis I Know," *Compact*, February 1955.

Smuggler's Island (1951)

45. Robert L. Mott, *Radio Live! Television Live! Those Golden Days When Horses were Coconuts* (Jefferson, North Carolina: McFarland & Company, Inc., Publishers), p. 193.
46. Showman's Manual for *Smuggler's Island*, Margaret Herrick Library, Academy of Motion Picture Arts and Sciences.
47. *Motion Picture Herald*, April 14, 1952.
48. "Top-Grossers of 1951 (Film Rentals)," *Variety*, January 2, 1952.
49. *Chicago Tribune*, May 6, 1951.

The Battle at Apache Pass (1952)

50. "On Location with the Navajos," *Desert Magazine*, June 1952.
51. *The Hollywood Reporter*, April 5, 1952.
52. "Top-Grossers of 1952 (Film Rentals)," *Variety*, January 7, 1953.
53. William Reynolds to author, June 21, 2003.
54. "Red-Faced Redskin," *Television and Screen Guide*, November 1951.

Because of You (1952)

55. Showman's Manual for *Because of You*, Margaret Herrick Library, Academy of Motion Picture Arts and Sciences.
56. Ibid.
57. *Motion Picture Herald*, October 11, 1952.
58. "Inside Stuff," *Photoplay*, August 1952.

Red Ball Express (1952)

59. Showman's Manual for *Red Ball Express*, Margaret Herrick Library, Academy of Motion Picture Arts and Sciences.
60. "Red Ball Express Program Notes," *Photoplay*, June, 1952.
61. *Motion Picture Herald*, May 3, 1952.
62. "Top-Grossers of 1952 (Film Rentals)," *Variety*, January 7, 1953.
63. Publicity for *Red Ball Express*, November 27, 1951, the Universal Studios Collection, USC Cinema-Television Library.
64. Jeff Chandler to Viola Swisher of *Variety*, November 14, 1951, the Universal Studios Collection, USC Cinema-Television Library.

Son of Ali Baba (1952)

65. William Reynolds to author, June 21, 2003.
66. *Los Angeles Examiner*, October 2, 1952.
67. "Top-Grossers of 1952 (Film Rentals)," *Variety*, January 7, 1953.

Yankee Buccaneer (1952)

68. "News, Picture Close-Ups: On the Sets (The Stars at Work)," *Movies*, October 1952.
69. *Motion Picture Herald*, September 13, 1952.
70. "By Suzan Ball for Howard McClay," June 6, 1952, the Universal Studios Collection, USC Cinema-Television Library.

East of Sumatra (1953)

71. Meeting and Review of Producer's Picture Assignments, August 1, 1952, the Universal Studios Collection, USC Cinema-Television Library.
72. Showman's Manual for *East of Sumatra*, the Universal Studios Collection, USC Cinema-Television Library.
73. Archie Herzoff to Robert Palmer, April 1, 1953, The Universal Studios Collection, USC Cinema-Television Library.
74. *Los Angeles Examiner*, September 12, 1953.
75. Peter Graves to author, June 20, 2003.
76. Publicity for *East of Sumatra*, The Universal Studios Collection, USC Cinema-Television Library.
77. Preview of *East of Sumatra*, April 14, 1953, Long Beach, California, the Universal Studios Collection, USC Cinema-Television Library.

Notes—The Films

The Great Sioux Uprising (1953)

78. *Meeting and Review of Producer's Picture Assignments*, August 18, 1952, the Universal Studios Collection, USC Cinema-Television Library.
79. *Motion Picture Herald*, June 27, 1953.
80. "Top-Grossers of 1953 (Rentals)," *Variety*, January 13, 1954.
81. Fred Banker to Sam Israel, October 10, 1952, the Universal Studios Collection, USC Cinema-Television Library.
82. Production notes for *East of Sumatra*, the Universal Studios Collection, USC Cinema-Television Library.
83. Publicity for *The Great Sioux Uprising*, September 19, 1952, the Universal Studios Collection, USC Cinema-Television Library.

Taza, Son of Cochise (1953)

84. *Variety*, January 20, 1954.
85. "1954 Box Office Champs (Rentals)," *Variety*, January 5, 1955.
86. Publicity for *Taza, Son of Cochise*, July 21, 1953, the Universal Studios Collection, USC Cinema-Television Library.
87. Preview of *Taza, Son of Cochise*, November 6, 1953, Los Angeles, California, the Universal Studios Collection, USC Cinema-Television Library.

Sign of the Pagan (1954)

88. Showman's Manual for *Sign of the Pagan*, Margaret Herrick Library, Academy of Motion Picture Arts and Sciences.
89. *Motion Picture Herald*, November 13, 1954.
90. "1955's Top Film Grossers (Rentals)," *Variety*, January 25, 1956.
91. Rita Gam to author, June 19, 2003.
92. "Universal-International Presents a Personal Interview with Jeff Chandler, Star of *Sign of the Pagan*," Interview Record DCLA-1044.

War Arrow (1954)

93. *Motion Picture Herald*, December 12 1953
94. "1954 Box Office Champs (Rentals)," *Variety*, January 5, 1955.
95. Publicity for *War Arrow*, the Universal Studios Collection, USC Cinema-Television Library.

96. *Ibid.*
97. *Ibid.*

Yankee Pasha (1954)

98. "Daily Minutes Committee Meetings," the Universal Studios Collection, USC Cinema-Television Library.
99. *Motion Picture Herald*, March 13, 1954.
100. "1954 Box Office Champs (Rentals)," *Variety*, January 5, 1955.
101. *Mamie Van Doren's Bedtime Stories*, Mamie Van Doren Web site.

Female on the Beach (1955)

102. Bob Thomas, *Joan Crawford, A Biography* (Simon and Schuster, New York), p.197.
103. Showman's Manual for *Female on the Beach*, Margaret Herrick Library, Academy of Motion Picture Arts and Sciences.
104. *Los Angeles Examiner*, September 22, 1955.
105. "Crawford, Chandler Play 'Cave Man' Scene," *Los Angeles Examiner*, February 6, 1955.
106. Showman's Manual for *Female on the Beach*, Margaret Herrick Library, Academy of Motion Picture Arts and Sciences.
107. Preview of *Female on the Beach*, April 7, 1955, Riverside, California, the Universal Studios Collection, USC Cinema-Television Library.

Foxfire (1955)

108. Publicity for *Foxfire*, the Universal Studios Collection, USC Cinema-Television Library.
109. Jane Russell, *Jane Russell: An Autobiography* (New York: F. Watts), p. 153.
110. *Motion Picture Exhibitor*, June 15, 1955
111. "1955's Top Film Grossers (Rentals)," *Variety*, January 25, 1956.
112. "Location Lines," *Movie Spotlight*, February 1955.
113. Don Nicholl, *Jack Jackson's Record Round-Up* (London: M. Parish), p. 72.
114. Preview of *Foxfire*, November 23, 1954, Long Beach, California, the Universal Studios Collection, USC Cinema-Television Library.

The Littlest Outlaw (1955)

115. Musical Cue Sheet for *The Littlest*

Notes — The Films

Outlaw; Manager Robert Tieman to author, Walt Disney Arhives.
116. *Motion Picture Herald*, December 24, 1955.
117. "Top Film Grossers of 1956 (Rentals)," *Variety*, January 2, 1957.

The Nat "King" Cole Musical Story (1955)

118. *Motion Picture Exhibitor*, November 16, 1955.

One Desire (1955)

119. *The Hollywood Reporter*, July 5, 1955.

Six Bridges to Cross (1955)

120. Charles F. Simonelli to Milton R. Rackmil, October 6, 1954, Universal-International Publicity for *Six Bridges to Cross*, the Universal Studios Collection, USC Cinema-Television Library.
121. *The Billboard*, November 13, 1954.
122. Publicity for *Six Bridges to Cross*, the Universal Studios Collection, USC Cinema-Television Library.
123. "1955's Top Film Grossers (Rentals)," *Variety*, January 25, 1956.
124. "The Tony Curtis I Know," *Compact*, February 1955.

The Spoilers (1955)

125. "Behind the Scenes," *Screen Stories*, February 2, 1956.
126. *Motion Picture Exhibitor*, December 4, 1955.
127. "Top Film Grossers of 1956 (Rentals)," *Variety*, January 2, 1957.
128. "Behind the Scenes," *Screen Stories*, February 2, 1956.
129. *Ibid.*

Away All Boats (1956)

130. Showman's Manual for *Away All Boats*, the Universal Studios Collection, USC Cinema-Television Library.
131. *Family Weekly*, July 29, 1956.
132. "Top Film Grossers of 1956 (Rentals)," *Variety*, January 2, 1957.
133. William Reynolds to author, June 21, 2003.
134. Showman's Manual for *Away All Boats*, the Universal Studios Collection, USC Cinema-Television Library.

Brooklyn Goes to Las Vegas (1956)

135. *Motion Picture Exhibitor*, April 18, 1956.

Pillars of the Sky (1956)

136. Publicity for *Pillars of the Sky*, the Universal Studios Collection, USC Cinema-Television Library.
137. *Motion Picture Exhibitor*, August 8, 1956.
138. "Top Film Grossers of 1956 (Rentals)," *Variety*, January 2, 1957.
139. Showman's Manual for *Pillars of the Sky*, Margaret Herrick Library, Academy of Motion Picture Arts and Sciences.
140. Preview of *Pillars of the Sky*, December 21, 1955, Huntington Park, California, the Universal Studios Collection, USC Cinema-Television Library.

Toy Tiger (1956)

141. *Motion Picture Exhibitor*, May 2, 1956.
142. "Top Film Grossers of 1956 (Rentals)," *Variety*, January 2, 1957.
143. Laraine Day Oral History, Margaret Herrick Library, Academy of Motion Picture Arts and Sciences.
144. U-I Production Notes, May 16, 1956, Margaret Herrick Library, Academy of Motion Picture Arts and Sciences.
145. Preview of *Toy Tiger*, February 23, 1956, Huntington Park, California, the Universal Studios Collection, USC Cinema-Television Library.

Drango (1957)

146. Peter Graves to author, June 20, 2003.
147. *Motion Picture Exhibitor*, January 23, 1957.

Jeanne Eagels (1957)

148. Kim Novak to author, June 12, 2003.
149. *Motion Picture Herald*, July 20, 1957.
150. "Top Grossers of 1957 (Rentals)," *Variety*, January 8, 1958.
151. "Glamour Girl Circa '21!" *Los Angeles Examiner*, January 27, 1957.
152. *Ibid.*

Notes—The Films

Man in the Shadow (1957)

153. Publicity for *Man in the Shadow*, the Universal Studios Collection, USC Cinema-Television Library.
154. *Motion Picture Exhibitor*, December 11, 1957.
155. Publicity for *Man in the Shadow*, the Universal Studios Collection, USC Cinema-Television Library.
156. "A 'Hossless' Western!" *Los Angeles Examiner*, January 6, 1957.

The Tattered Dress (1957)

157. *Motion Picture Exhibitor*, March 6, 1957.
158. "Top Grossers of 1957 (Rentals)," *Variety*, January 8, 1958.
159. Publicity for *The Tattered Dress*, the Universal Studios Collection, USC Cinema-Television Library.
160. *Ibid*.

The Lady Takes a Flyer (1958)

161. *Motion Picture Exhibitor*, January 22, 1958.
162. "Top Grossers of 1958 (Rentals)," *Variety*, January 7, 1959.
163. Publicity for *The Lady Takes a Flyer*, the Universal Studios Collection, USC Cinema-Television Library.
164. *Ibid*.
165. Preview of *The Lady Takes a Flyer*, August 22, 1957, Burbank, California, the Universal Studios Collection, USC Cinema-Television Library.

Raw Wind in Eden (1958)

166. Esther Williams to author, April 15, 2003.
167. "Behind the Scenes," *Screen Stories*, September 1958.
168. *Film Daily*, July 23, 1959
169. "Top Grossers of 1958 (Rentals)," *Variety*, January 7, 1959.
170. "Behind the Scenes," *Screen Stories*, September 1958.

The Jayhawkers (1959)

171. *Motion Picture Exhibitor*, October 21, 1959.
172. "Top Grossers of 1959 (Rentals)," *Variety*, January 6, 1960.

173. *Los Angeles Times*, January 5, 1959.
174. Henry Silva to author, July 22, 2003.

The Mating Game (1959)

175. "The Mating Game Cues," by Jeff Alexander, *ASCAP* Title Code 438033059; "The Mating Game Cues," by Jeff Chandler, *ASCAP* Title Code 138006594.
176. *Motion Picture Exhibitor*, February 25, 1959.
177. "Top Grossers of 1959 (Rentals)," *Variety*, January 6, 1960.

A Stranger in My Arms (1959)

178. Peter Graves to author, June 20, 2003.
179. *Variety*, March 11, 1959.
180. Peter Graves to author, June 20, 2003.

Ten Seconds to Hell (1959)

181. *Hammer Film Productions and Seven Arts Productions*, February 26, 1958, Robert Aldrich Collection, Louis B. Mayer Library, AFI.
182. *Motion Picture Exhibitor*, July 29, 1959.
183. "Behind the Scenes," *Screen Stories*, October 1959.

Thunder in the Sun (1959)

184. *Hollywood Citizen-News*, May 5, 1959.
185. "Top Grossers of 1959 (Rentals)," *Variety*, January 6, 1960.
186. *Los Angeles Examiner*, September 7, 1958.

The Plunderers (1960)

187. *Motion Picture Herald*, November 12, 1960.
188. *Los Angeles Times*, October 27, 1999.
189. *Los Angeles Times*, October 4, 1960.

A Story of David (1960)

190. *ABC Television Network Press Release*, August 10, 1960, the Universal Studios Collection, USC Cinema-Television Library.
191. Cheryl Cagle, Editor, *Television Programming Source Books, 2002*, p. F-1285.
192. "Renewal at Allied for Jeff Chandler," *Los Angeles Times*, October 4, 1960.
193. Angela von Mizener to author, June 22, 2003.

Return to Peyton Place (1961)

194. Vital Statistics on *Return to Peyton Place*, Margaret Herrick Library, Academy of Motion Picture Arts and Sciences.
195. *Motion Picture Exhibitor*, May 3, 1961.
196. "Top Grossers of 1961 (Rentals)," *Variety*, January 10, 1962.

Merrill's Marauders (1962)

197. *New York Herald Tribune*, June 14, 1962.
198. "Big Rental Pictures of 1962," *Variety*, January 9, 1963.
199. Will Hutchins to author, July 28, 2003.
200. *Photoplay*, August 1953.

Recordings (Music and Spoken Word)

"I Should Care" / "More Than Anyone" (1954)

1. *The Billboard*, March 27, 1954.
2. *Down Beat*, December 2, 1953.

"That's All She's Waiting to Hear" / "Lamplight" (1954)

3. *The Billboard*, July 3, 1954.
4. *Jack Jackson's Record Round-Up*, (London: M. Parish), p. 70.

"Always" / "Everything Happens to Me" (1954)

5. *The Billboard*, November 27, 1954.
6. *Down Beat*, December 2, 1953.

"When Spring Comes" / "My Prayer" (1955)

7. *The Billboard*, February 12, 1955.

"Foxfire" / "Shaner Maidel" (1955)

8. *The Billboard*, June 4, 1955.

"A Little Love Can Go a Long Long Way" / "Only the Very Young" (1955)

9. *The Billboard*, July 23, 1955.
10. Don Nicholl, *Jack Jackson's Record Round-Up* (London: M. Parish), p. 70.

"Half of My Heart" / "Hold Me" (1957)

11. *The Billboard*, July 29, 1957.

Jeff Chandler Sings to You (1957)

12 *The Billboard*, September 17, 1957.

Warm and Easy (1958)

13. *The Billboard*, June 2, 1958.

"Six Bridges to Cross" (1955)

14. *The Billboard*, January 29, 1955.

"One Desire" (1955)

15. *The Billboard*, August 6, 1955.

The Adventures of Tom Sawyer (1960)

16. *The Billboard*, January 28, 1956.
17. *Audio Book Records* catalog.

Classic Tales of Adventure & Mystery (1960)

18. *Audio Book Records* catalog.

The Best of Mark Twain (1961)

19. *Audio Book Records* catalog.

Call of the Wild (1961)

20. Rear Album cover for *Audio Book Record* LP-C 312.

Television

Pabst Blue Ribbon Bouts (1951)

1. *Iron Man* Publicity files, the Universal Studios Collection, USC Cinema-Television Library.
2. Mary E. Beadle, *Indelible Images, Women of Local Television* (Ames, Iowa: Iowa State University Press), pp. 51–53.
3. Dorothy Fuldheim, *I Laughed, I Cried, I Loved, A News Analysts Love Affair with the World* (Cleveland: The World Publishing Company), p. 195.
4. *The New York Times*, August 19, 1951.

United Cerebral Palsy Telethon (1953)

5. "Star Studded Palsy Show on KECA

Tonight; Thunderbolt The Colt is New Puppet Hit," *Los Angeles Times*, June 1, 1953

Multiple Sclerosis Telethon (1953)

6. *TV Guide*, August 29 to September 4, 1953.
7. Publicity files, the Universal Studios Collection, USC Cinema-Television Library.
8. *Down Beat*, December 2, 1953, p. 5.

Our Famous Husbands (1953)

9. *Los Angeles Times*, September 15, 1953, p. 30.
10. Publicity for *East of Sumatra*, November 27, 1951, the Universal Studios Collection, USC Cinema-Television Library.

Place the Face (1954)

11. Cliff Brown to Clark Ramsay, March 9, 1954, the Universal Studios Collection, USC Cinema-Television Library.

The Peter Potter Show (1954)

12. Publicity files, the Universal Studios Collection, USC Cinema-Television Library.

The Summer Comedy Hour (1954)

13. Publicity files, the Universal Studios Collection, USC Cinema-Television Library.

What's My Line? (1954)

14. Gil Fates, *What's My Line? The Inside History of TV's Most Famous Panel Show* (Englewood Cliffs, NJ: Prentice-Hall, Inc.).

The Colgate Comedy Hour (1954)

15. Carl A. Schroeder to Sam Israel, the Universal Studios Collection, USC Cinema-Television Library.

16. *Variety Television Reviews 1946–1956*, Volume 1.

The Dinah Shore Show (1954)

17. Publicity files, the Universal Studios Collection, USC Cinema-Television Library.

Steve Allen in Movieland (1955)

18. *TV Guide*, July 2 to July 8, 1955.

The Perry Como Show (1957)

19. *Library of Congress*, Control Number 95501707.
20. *TV Guide*, January 19 to January 25, 1957.

The Steve Allen Show (1957)

21. *TV Guide*, August 31 to September 6, 1957.

The American Jew, A Tribute to Freedom (1958)

22. *Variety Television Reviews 1957–1959*, Volume 2.

A Call From... (1960)

23. *TV Guide*, February 7 to February 10, 1960.

Theater

The Trojan Horse (1940–41)

1. "Dramatist Chaucer," by Christopher Morley, *The New York Times*, October 27, 1940.
2. "The Trojan Horse," *Time*, November 25, 1940, p. 56.
3. "Of a Straw Hat in the Snow," by David Lowe, *The New York Times*, June 29, 1941.
4. Christopher Morley, *The Trojan Horse* (New York: Random House), p. ix.

Bibliography

Andrews, Bart. *The "I Love Lucy" Book*. Garden City, N.Y.: Doubleday, 1985.

Beadle, Mary E. *Indelible Images, Women of Local Television*. Ames: Iowa State University Press, 2001.

Behlmer, Rudy. *Memo from Darryl F. Zanuck*. New York: Grove, 1993.

Billips, Connie, and Arthur Pierce. *Lux Presents Hollywood: A Show-by-Show History of the Lux Radio Theatre and the Lux Video Theatre, 1934–1957*. Jefferson, N.C.: McFarland, 1995.

Bishop, Jim. *The Mark Hellinger Story: A Biography of Broadway and Hollywood*. New York: Appleton-Century-Crofts, 1952.

Bloom, Ken. *Hollywood Song: The Complete Film and Musical Companion*. New York: Facts on File, 1995.

Brady, Kathleen. *Lucille: The Life of Lucille Ball*. New York: Billboard Books, 2001.

Cagle, Cheryl. *Television Programming Source Books, 2002*. Philadelphia: North American, 2001.

Chaneles, Sol. *The Movie Makers*. Secaucus, N.J.: Derbibooks, 1974.

Ciaccia, Maria. *Dreamboats: Hollywood Hunks of the '50s*. New York: Excalibur, 1992.

Curtis, Tony, with Barry Paris. *Tony Curtis: The Autobiography*. New York: Morrow, 1993.

Daniels, William R. *The American 45 and 78 RPM Record Dating Guide, 1940–1959*. Westport, Conn.: Greenwood, 1985.

Davis, Ronald L. *Hollywood Beauty: Linda Darnell and the American Dream*. Norman: University of Oklahoma Press, 1991.

DeLong, Thomas A. *Radio Stars: An Illustrated Biographical Dictionary*. Jefferson, N.C.: McFarland, 1996.

Dewey, Thomas E. *Twenty Against the Underworld*. Garden City, N.Y.: Doubleday, 1974.

Dick, Bernard F. *City of Dreams: The Making and Remaking of Universal Pictures*. Lexington: University Press of Kentucky, 1997.

Dimmitt, Richard Bertrand. *A Title Guide to the Talkies*. New York: Scarecrow, 1965.

Dunning, John. *On the Air: The Encyclopedia of Old-Time Radio*. New York: Oxford University Press, 1998.

Fates, Gil. *What's My Line? The Inside History of TV's Most Famous Panel Show*. Englewood Cliffs, N.J.: Prentice Hall, Inc., 1978.

Fishman, Loren M., and Carol Ardman. *Back Talk: How to Diagnose and Cure Low Back Pain and Sciatica*. New York: W.W. Norton, 1997.

Kirk, Marilyn. *Jeff Chandler*. Bloomington, Ind.: 1st Books Publishing, 2003.

Fitzgerald, Michael G. *Universal Pictures: A Panoramic History in Words, Pictures, and Filmographies*. New Rochelle, N.Y.: Arlington House, 1977.

Friederich, Otto. *City of Nets: A Portrait of Hollywood in the 1940s*. New York: Harper & Row, Publishers, Inc., 1986.

Gertner, Richard. *International Motion Picture Almanac*. New York: Quigley, 1970.

Goldin, J. David. *The Golden Age of Radio*. Sandy Hook, Conn.: Yesteryear, 1998.

Grams, Martin, Jr. *Suspense: Twenty Years of Thrills and Chills*. Kearney, Neb.: Morris Publishing, 1997.

Griffith, Richard. *The Movie Stars*. Garden City, N.Y.: Doubleday, 1970.

Bibliography

Halliwell, Leslie. *Halliwell's Film Guide (Seventh Edition)*. New York: Harper & Row, 1989.

Hirschhorn, Clive. *The Universal Story: The Complete History of the Studio and its 2641 Films*. New York: Crown, 1983.

Hughes, Rupert. *The Story of Thomas E. Dewey, Attorney for the People*. New York: Grosset & Dunlap, 1944.

Jessel, George. *Halo over Hollywood*. Van Nuys, Calif.: Toastmaster, 1963.

Katz, Ephraim. *The Film Encyclopedia*. New York: HarperCollins, 1994.

Maltin, Leonard. *Leonard Maltin's 1998 Movie & Video Guide*. New York: Signet, 1997.

Mancini, Henry, with Gene Lees. *Did They Mention the Music?* Chicago: Contemporary, 1989.

Mantle, Burns. *Best Plays of 1945/1946*. New York: Dodd, Mead, 1946.

McClure, Arthur F., and Ken D. Jones. *Star Quality: The Great Actors and Actresses of Hollywood*. South Brunswick, N.J.: A.S. Barnes, 1974.

Michener, James A. *Report of the County Chairman*. New York: Random House, 1961.

Morella, Joe, and Edward Z. Epstein. *Loretta Young: an Extraordinary Life*. New York: Delacorte, 1986.

Morley, Christopher. *The Trojan Horse*. New York: Random House, 1941.

Mott, Robert L. *Radio Live! Television Live! Those Golden Days When Horses were Coconuts*. Jefferson, N.C.: McFarland, 2000.

Nash, Jay Robert, and Stanley Ralph Ross. *The Motion Picture Guide, 1927–1983*. Chicago: Cinebooks, 1985–1986.

Nicholl, Don. *Jack Jackson's Record Round-Up*. London: M. Parrish, 1955.

O'Neil, Thomas. *The Emmys: The Ultimate, Unofficial Guide to the Battle of TV's Best Shows and Greatest Stars*. New York: Berkley, 1998.

Oppenheimer, Jerry, and Jack Vitek. *Idol: Rock Hudson, the True Story of an American Hero*. New York: Villard, 1986.

Parish, James Robert. *The Hollywood Death Book*. Las Vegas, Nevada: Pioneer, 1992.

Parker, John. *Five for Hollywood*. Secaucus, N.J.: Carol, 1991.

Pickard, Roy. *The Hollywood Story*. Secaucus, N.J.: Chartwell, 1986.

Pitts, Michael R. *Radio Sound Tracks: A Reference Guide*. Metuchen, N.J.: Scarecrow, 1976.

Prouty, Howard H. *Daily Variety Television Reviews 1946–1956*. New York: Garland, 1989.

_____. *Variety Television Reviews 1954–1956*. New York: Garland, 1989.

_____. *Variety Television Reviews 1957–1959*. New York: Garland, 1989.

Quinlan, David. *Quinlan's Illustrated Directory of Film Stars*. New York: Hippocrene, 1986.

Ragan, David. *Who's Who in Hollywood, 1900–1976*. New Rochelle: Arlington House, 1976.

Rains, Bob. *Beneath the Tinsel (The Human Side of Hollywood Stars)*. Danville, Ill.: Three Lions, 1999.

Royce, Brenda Scott. *Rock Hudson: A Bio-Bibliography*. Westport, Conn.: Greenwood, 1995.

Russell, Jane. *Jane Russell: An Autobiography*. New York: Franklin Watts, 1985.

Schessler, Ken. *This Is Hollywood*. Redlands: Ken Schessler, 1998.

Schickel, Richard. *Clint Eastwood: A Biography*. New York: Knopf, 1996.

Settel, Irving. *Top TV Shows of the Year, 1954–1955*. New York: Hastings House, 1955.

Shippey, Lee. *The Los Angeles Book*. Boston, Houghton Mifflin, 1950.

Sirk, Douglas. *Sirk on Sirk: Interviews with Jon Halliday*. London: Secker, 1997.

Steinberg, Cobbett S. *Film Facts*. New York: Facts on File, 1980.

Stolberg, Mary M. *Fighting Organized Crime — Politics, Justice, and the Legacy of Thomas E. Dewey*. Boston: Northeastern University Press, 1995.

Stuart, Ray. *Immortals of the Screen*. New York: Bonanza, 1965.

Terrace, Vincent. *Encyclopedia of Television Series, Pilots and Specials 1937–1974*. New York: New York Zoetrope, 1986.

Thomas, Bob. *Joan Crawford, A Biography*. New York: Simon & Schuster, 1978.

Wilkerson, Tichi, and Marcia Borie. *Hollywood Legends: The Golden Years of* The Hollywood Reporter. Los Angeles: Tale Weaver, 1988.

Williams, Esther, with Digby Diehl. *The Million Dollar Mermaid*. New York: Simon & Schuster, 1999.

Index

Abandoned 19, 20, 42–43, 68
Abbott, Bud 47, 48, 53
Abbott and Costello in the Foreign Legion 47–48
The Abbott and Costello Show 48, 93
ABC Film Review 119
ABC *see* American Broadcasting Company
Academy Award 21, 23, 25, 44, 50, 51, 53, 54, 55, 65, 66, 68, 70, 75, 76, 81, 86, 89, 93, 98, 113, 115, 121, 128
Academy Award (radio) 14, 54, 131
Academy of Motion Picture Arts and Sciences (Beverly Hills, Calif.) 2
Academy Players Directory 12, 14, 19, 21, 23, 30, 31
"Accentuate the Positive" 180
"Accident Prevention Week" 177
Ace, Goodman 195
Ackerman, Harry S. 21, 144
Acosta, Rodolfo 68, 84
Adam, Ken 114
Adams, Gerald Drayson 56, 62, 67, 73
Adams, Julie 25, 86, 87, 91, 189
Addy, Wes 114
"The Adele Van Heusan Case" 134
Adler, Robert 49
Adventure Is Your Heritage 165
"Adventures of Baron Munchausen" 144
The Adventures of Phillip Marlowe 152
The Adventures of Red Ryder 140
The Adventures of Tom Sawyer 129–130
Aggeler, Mervyn 38

Agnello, Virginia 142
Aguglia, Mimi 51
Ahern, Lloyd 44
Aherne, Pat 135
Akins, Claude 33, 122
Albertson, Frank 147, 151
Alch, Alan 98
Aldrich, Robert 114
Aleutian Islands 12, 13
Alexander, Ben 101, 192
Alexander, Jeff 111
Alexander, Ronald 120
"All My Sons" 20, 160
"All Trails Lead to Trouble" 185
Allabough, Joe 169
Alland, William 105, 107
Allen, George W. 13, 146, 154
Allen, Gracie 192
Allen, Lynn 175, 189
Allen, Steve 194, 195, 196
Allgood, Sara 132
Allied Artists 1, 30, 35, 116, 117; *see also* Monogram
Allman, Elvia 132, 150, 179
Allman, Sheldon 38
Allyson, June 82, 112, 113, 189
Alsberg, Arthur 165, 166, 167, 168, 169, 170, 171, 172, 173, 175, 176, 177, 178, 179, 180, 181, 182, 183, 184, 185, 186, 187, 188
"The Aluminum Mouse Trap" 180
Alvin, John 21
"Always" 125–126, 195
The Amazing Mr. Malone 145
Amberg, Louis "Pretty" 9
Ambrogi, Adriano 51
American Broadcasting Company: radio 14, 134, 145, 150, 166, 171; television 119, 192, 193

The American Jew: A Tribute to Freedom 196
American Radio Archives 3
Ames, Marlene 137, 147
The Ames Brothers 125
Amfitheatrof, Daniele 55
Anatomy of a Crime 87
And Ride a Tiger 112
"And There I Stood with My Piccolo" 153
Anderson, Glenn E. 45, 64, 67, 69, 71, 72, 73, 86
Anderson, Milo 79
Anderson, Robert 95
Anderson, Roland 109
Andes, Keith 91, 94
Andrews, Dana 16, 45, 46, 140
Andrews, Edward 103
Andrews, Helen 132, 137, 160
The Andrews Sisters 50
Ankrum, Morris 64, 67, 73, 97
"Anne Frank: The Diary of A Young Girl" 182
"Annual December Dance" 174
"Annual Winter Outing" 175
Ansara, Michael 68, 75, 94
Antonini, Alfredo 196
"Apartment of the Future" 171, 185
Appel, Vick 96
"April Fool's Day" 163
The Arch 9
Arden, Eve 17, 18, 25, 143, 144, 145, 146, 147, 148, 149, 150, 151, 152, 153, 154, 155, 156, 157, 158, 159, 160, 161, 162, 163, 164, 165, 166, 167, 168, 169, 170, 171, 172, 173, 174, 175, 176, 177, 178, 179, 180, 181, 182, 183, 184, 185, 186, 187, 188
Arizona 84, 115
Arling, Arthur E. 101

Index

Arlington, Charles 138
Armbruster, Robert 189
Armendariz, Pedro 84
Armstrong, Louis 65
Arnaz, Desi 23, 25
Arnaz, Desi, Jr. 25
Arne, Peter 118
Arness, James 31, 41, 57, 58
Arnold, Cleo 192
Arnold, Danny 105
Arnold, Edward 26, 134, 192, 193
Arnold, Elliott 48
Arnold, Jack 101, 103, 105, 106
Arnt, Charles 71
Arosemena, Emita 79
Arthur, Robert 47, 48, 94
Ashdown, Isa 179
Asher, Bill 194
Astor, Mary 113, 120, 121
Atlanta (Ga.) 60
Atlantic City (NJ) 29
Atwater, Gladys 71
Audio Book Company 129, 130
Audio Books, Inc. 129
"Audition Show" 143
Audley, Eleanor 140, 143, 144, 145, 147, 148, 149, 150, 152, 189
Auerbach, Peter 11, 12
August Productions 30, 117
Aurandt, Richard 138
Austin, John 51, 52, 57, 64, 67, 86, 89, 95, 101, 103
Australia 44, 45
Austria 5, 115
Averback, Hy 144, 145, 181, 184, 185, 186, 187
Avramo, Peter 87
Away All Boats 27, 91–93, 95
Ayres, Lew 133
Ayres, Mitchell 195

"Babysitting for Three" 148
Bacall, Lauren 31
Bachmann, Lawrence P. 114
Bacigalupi, Louis 53
Backus, Jim 57, 166, 170, 171, 172
Bacon, Lloyd 71
Baer, Buddy 56
Baer, John 62
Baer, Parley 91, 97, 167, 170, 174, 177
Bailey, Bob 144, 148
Bailey, Caryl 111
Bailey, Cheryl 111
Bailey, Pearl 194, 196
Bailey, Raymond 91
Baker, Art 167
Baker, Florence 150
Baker, Virginia 114

Balaban, Barney 196
Baldridge, Frank 39, 41
Ball, Lucille 18, 21, 23, 24, 25, 27, 144
Ball, Suzan 68, 69, 71, 72, 76, 77
"Ballerina" 161
Banker, Fred 72
Bankhead, Tallulah 166
Banks, Joan 133, 140, 141, 146, 152
Banks, Terry 44
Bannon, James 76
Bannon, Jim 40
"The Barbara Dunbar Case" 138
Barbash, Bob 117
Barcroft, Roy 89
Bardette, Trevor 36, 111
"Bargain Hats for Mother's Day" 171
Barker, Lex 91, 92
"The Barney Layton Case" 144
Barr, Tony 56
Barragar, Nathan 96
Barrat, Robert 53, 67
Barrett, Bernice 134
Barrett, Rona 29
Barrett, Tony 132, 136, 139, 141, 189
Barrier, Edgar 138, 147, 152, 173
Barron, Bill 166
Barrows, Evelyn 165
Barry, Phillip, Jr. 111
Barrymore, Lionel 134
Bartell, Harry 136
Bartlett, Hall 96, 98
Barton, Charles T. 52, 53
Bartsch, Ed 93
Base, Gus 138
"Baseball Rally" 186
Basehart, Richard 70
Bates, H. E. 111
Bates, Jeanne 189
Battaglia, Rik 107
The Battle at Apache Pass 62–63, 68, 72
Bau, Gordon 122
Baxter, Anne 86, 87, 89, 90, 146
Baxter, George 57
Baxter, Les 65
Bayes, Peter 197
Baylor, Hal 91
Beach, Rex 89, 91
Beauchamp, D. D. (Bud) 47, 48
Beaudette, Phillip 197
"Beaver Lodge, Room 124" 164
Because of You 24, 63–65, 66, 83, 189

Bechi, Robo 75
Beery, Noah 54, 76
Begley, Ed 151, 154, 159, 161, 173, 176, 178
Belafonte, Harry 88, 196
Belasco, Leon 47, 67
Belgard, Arnold 39
Bell, Joseph 138
Bellah, Ross 99
Benaderet, Bea 144, 147
Bender, Dawn 135
Ben-Gurion, David 118
Ben-Hur 28, 75, 177
Bennett, Doc 180
Bennett, Marjorie 81
Bennett, Ray 72
Berest, Frederic 56
Bergerac, Jacques 115
Berkley (Calif.) 36
Berlin (Germany) 114, 115
Berlin, Irving 20
Bernard, Butch 95
Bernard, Phillip 141
Bernath, Shari Lee 109
Berneis, Peter 112
Bernerd, Jeffrey 117
Berns, Larry 18, 143, 144, 145, 146, 147, 148, 149, 150, 151, 152, 153, 154, 155, 156, 157, 158, 159, 160, 161, 162, 163, 164, 165, 166, 167, 168, 169, 170, 171, 172, 173, 174, 175, 176, 177, 178, 179, 180, 181, 182, 183, 184, 185, 186, 187, 188
Bernstein, Elmer 96, 98
Berti, Marina 51
Beshon, Irene 39, 41
The Besieged Heart 80
Best, James 62
The Best of Mark Twain 130
Bettger, Lyle 71
Beverly, Janet 179
Beverly Hills (Calif.) 2, 23, 28, 29, 32, 33, 34, 36, 37, 38, 42, 109
Bezzerides, A. I. 109
Bice, Robert 82
"The Big Clock" 148
"The Big Mistake" 152
The Big Payoff 25
"The Bill Carroll Case" 135
"The Bill Meredith Case" 139
"The Bill Worthington Case" 136
The Billboard 2, 123, 124, 125, 126, 127, 128, 129, 196
Billsbury, Rye 141
Binyon, Conrad 137
Birch, Paul 103
Bird of Paradise 1, 21, 22, 23, 55–56, 175

Index

"The Bird Rescue and the Sunken Garden" 171
"The Black Curtain" 137
Blair, Henry 140, 141, 147
Blangsted, Folmar 122
Blankfort, Michael 48, 50
Blaustein, Julian 48
Blees, Robert 86
"Blindfolded Marvel the Second" 187
"Blonde Mink" 154
Blondell, Gloria 147, 156
"Blood on the Sun" 131
Blystone, Jasper 48, 55
Blyth, Ann 46, 166, 175, 183, 184, 189
"Board of Education Visit" 158
"Body and Soul" 148
Boehm, Sydney 87
Boetticher, Oscar "Budd" 65, 66, 67, 69
Bogart, Humphrey 13, 70
Bogert, Vincent (Vin) 132, 137, 150
Bolger, John A., Jr. 89
Bolger, Ray 92
"Bon Voyage" 172
Bonanova, Fortunio 115
Bond, Ward 94, 131, 151
Bonney, Gail 151
Boone, Richard 91, 196
Borg, Veda Ann 115
Borgnine, Ernest 31
Boris, Anthony 135
Borzage, Dan 94
Boston (Mass.) 82, 87, 88, 91, 111
Botzer, Alan 133
Bouchey, Bill 139, 140, 142, 157
Bouchey, Willis 89, 94
Bourne, Neva 96
Bowers, William 42
Bowles, Phil 57, 112
Boxoffice 2, 37, 40, 41, 43, 44, 45, 47, 48, 50, 52, 53, 56, 57, 59, 60, 62, 63, 65, 68, 69, 72, 85, 86, 91, 92, 96, 100, 102, 104, 106, 116, 118, 121, 122
Boyd, Gene 87, 129
Boyd, William "Hopalong Cassidy" 23
Boyer, Charles 23
Boyle, Charles 62
Boyle, Robert 42, 57, 68, 69
Bradford, Lane 72
Bradley, Bill 121
Bradley, Truman 161
Brady, Scott 68, 69
Bramley, Raymond 49
Brand, Neville 56
Brandon, Henry 56, 76
Brasselle, Keefe 171

Braun, Judith 56, 66
Bray, David K. 55
Brayton, Margaret 177
Bregman, Buddy 195
Bren, J. Robert 71
Brennan, Walter 153
Brent, George 15, 132
Bresler, Jerry 42
Bretherton, David 120
Brewer, Theresa 125
Bricken, Jules 96
Bridges, Lloyd 31, 167
Briggs, Charles 122
British Lion 118
Britton, Barbara 89
Britton, Layne 82
Broadway (New York City) 5, 6, 8, 10, 20, 50, 59, 100
Brodney, Oscar 52, 75, 89
Broidy, Steve 35, 117
Broken Arrow 1, 20, 21, 23, 25, 48–50, 52, 68, 168, 173
Bronner, Robert 111
Bronson, Charles 30
Bronson, Lillian 82
Brooklyn (New York City) 5, 6, 8, 9, 59, 67, 93, 121
Brooklyn Goes to Las Vegas 93
Brooks, Geraldine 24
Brooks, Irene 43
Brotman, David M. 36, 37
Brown, Art 179, 180
Brown, Dorothy 189
Brown, Helen 164, 170
Brown, Hilyard 56
Brown, John 154, 157, 158
Brown, Malcolm 111
Brown, Peter 33, 122
Brown, Phil 40
Brown, Robert 118
Browne, Angela 118
Bruce, Bob 138
Bruce, Robert 132, 137, 150
Bruce, Virginia 152
Brunetti, Argentina 49
Bruzlin, Alfred 54
Bryan, Arthur Q. 152, 179
Bryan, Bill 11
Bryant, Betty 142
Brynner, Yul 27
Buchinski, Charles *see* Bronson, Charles
Buckner, Robert 45, 51
Burbank (Calif.) 19, 20
Burke, Marcella 95
Burke, Sonny 81, 87, 123, 124, 126, 127, 129, 179, 180
Burnett, W. R. 57
Burns, George 192
Burns, Tommy 44
Burr, Raymond 42, 59
Burt, A.L., Company 89

Burt, Frank C. 141, 142
Burton, James 137
Burton, Jay 195
Burton, Ken 161
Burton, Robert 73
Bushman, Francis X. 131, 161
Butler, Davis 142
Butler, Daws 138, 144, 145
Butler, Ralph 117
Butterfield, Herb 135, 136, 137, 139, 140, 141, 142, 143, 146, 147, 148, 151, 153, 157, 168, 175, 188, 189
Butts, Dale 39
Buyeff, Lillian 138, 139, 153, 175, 188

"The C. L. Tracy, M.D., Case" 135
Cabot, Susan 56, 62, 67
Cady, Frank 144
"Cafeteria Boycott" 153
Cagney, James 13, 14, 30
Cahn, Sammy 24
Calhoun, Rory 89, 91, 96
California 20, 25, 34, 35, 36, 37, 57, 58, 103, 115, 116, 121, 124, 192
A Call from … 196
Call of the Wild 130
Calleia, Joseph 68, 84
Calumet High School 11
"Camp Okeechobi" 144
Campbell, Judy 32
Canada 52
Cantor, Charlie 132, 137, 150
Cantor, Eddie 19, 150
Capitol Records 24, 65
Capp, Al 196
Carbajal, J. Carlos 84
Carey, Harry 94, 101
Carey, Leslie I. 42, 45, 47, 51, 53, 56, 57, 59, 60, 62, 64, 65, 67, 68, 69, 71, 73, 75, 76, 81, 82, 85, 86, 87, 89, 91, 94, 95, 101, 103, 106, 107, 112
Carey, Macdonald 135
Carey, Olive 94
Carli, Maria 51
Carlton, Maurice 162, 163, 164
Carnegie Hall 10
Carol, Martine 114
"The Carol Davison Case" 134
"The Carol Tracy, M. D. Case" 140
Carr, Stan 138, 144
Carreras, Michael 114
Carrington, Jack 132, 139, 142
Carroll, Bob, Jr. 18
Carroll, Jack 134
Carroll, Mary 82
Carruth, Milton 73, 86, 94, 95

Index

Carson, Charles 118
Carson, Jack 103
Carson, Ken 132
Carter, Ann 138, 140
Carter, Everett 65
Carter, Helena 53
Carter, Jack 11; *see also* Chakrin, Jack
Carter, Janis 132
Carter, Jimmy 109
Carter, John 41
Carter, Milton 47
"The Case Against Loo Doc" 175
"The Case of the Bayou Monster" 149
"The Case of the Blood-Stained Pearls" 140
"The Case of the Carnival Killer" 150
"The Case of the Constant Companion" 150
"The Case of the Crooked Wheel" 142
"The Case of the Deadly Dough" 143
"The Case of the Generous Killer" 141
"The Case of the Gray-Eyed Blonde" 141
"The Case of the High Priced Twins" 149
"The Case of the Hunted Bride" 140
"The Case of the Left-Handed Fan" 143
"The Case of the Model Murder" 141
"The Case of the Phantom Gun" 140
"The Case of the Popular Corpse" 143
"The Case of the Purloined Corpse" 142
"The Case of the Wandering Fingerprints" 142
The Casebook of Gregory Hood 14
Casey, Clark 172
Cash, Don 39, 41
Cashin, Bonnie 44
Castelli, Bertrand 115
Castle, Don 39, 41
Castle, Richard 87
Catskill Mountains 8
Caulfield, Joan 147
The Cavalcade of America 131
CBS *see* Columbia Broadcasting System
CBS Symphony Orchestra 196
Celano, Guido 51
Cerf, Bennett 194

Chadwick, Robert 176
Chakrin, Jack 11, 197; *see also* Carter, Jack
Challee, William 117
Chambers, Phil 82
Chandler, George 137, 142
Chandler, Jeff: Academy Award nomination 21; birth 5; campaigns for Senator John F. Kennedy 31; Chandlers divorce 29; Chandlers reconcile 23; Chandlers separate 21; childhood 5–7; death 35; debuts night club act 28; enters hospital 33; first daughter born 15; graduates from high school, 8; malpractice suit settled 38; meets Esther Williams 28; moves to Hollywood 13; moves to Manhattan 9; second daughter born 20; service during WWII 11–13; signs with Decca 25; signs with Universal-International 19; as "Tex Chandler" 180–185; weds Marjorie 14; work as a radio actor 13–18; works at Millpond 11; *see also* Grossel, Ira
Chandler, Marjorie Hoshelle *see* Hoshelle, Marjorie
Chandler, Tex *see* Chandler, Jeff
Chandler Music Company 30, 98, 124
Chaney, Lon, Jr. 56
Chaney, Lon, Sr. 75
Chaney, Richard 96
Chapin, Michael 166, 189
Chapin, Victor 197
Chaplin, Charlie 33, 114
Chaplin, Sydney 94
Chapman, Marguerite 132
Chapman, Pattee 162, 164
Charlotte Amalie 92
Chase, Borden 57
Chase, Frank 66
Chase, Stephen 71, 148
Chaucer, Geoffrey 198
Chauvel, Charles 44, 45
Chauvel, Elsa 44
"The Chavez Family" 181
"Cheers for Miss Bishop" 131
Chervin, Bert 115
Cheshire, Harry 39
Chicago (Ill.) 11, 25, 27, 110, 125
Christie, Howard J. 42, 52, 68, 78, 91, 92, 95
Christine, Virginia 39
"Christmas Clothing Drive" 167

"Christmas Letter Contest" 160
"The Christmas Present" 149
"Christmas Show" 174, 183
"Christmas Week at Eagle Springs" 183
Christy, Ken 145, 149, 158, 170, 173, 179
Chudnow, David 41
Ciro's Nightclub 59, 88
Clark, Al 40, 75
Clark, Carroll 86
Clark, Cliff 132, 137, 139, 142, 151, 180
Clark, Don 144, 148
Clark, Fred 111, 165, 166, 167, 170, 171, 172, 173, 174, 176, 177, 179, 181, 182, 183, 184, 185, 187, 188
Clark, James B. 55
Clark, Kendall 87, 91
Clark, Merle 150
Clark, Robert 180
"The Clark Adams Case" 142
Clark Air Force Base (Philippines) 33, 122
Clarke, Charles G. 120
Clarke, David 42
Clarke, Mae 64, 180
Classic Tales of Adventure & Mystery 130
Clatworthy, Robert 64, 80, 82, 87
Claxton, William F. 39
"Clay City Football Game" 147
"Clean and Crisp and Even" 189
"Cleanliness Is Next to Godliness" 145
Cleary, Leo 135, 137, 142, 148, 180
Cleveland (OH) 24, 191
Cloak and Dagger 14, 16, 32, 141
Clooney, Rosemary 27
Clothier, William 122
Club 88 Starring Peggy Lee, 24, 124, 179, 180
Coates, Paul 192
Cobb, Lee J. 15, 40, 78, 79, 132
Coburn, Charles 12, 113
Cochise 27, 50, 62, 63, 73, 72, 107
Coe, Peter 45
Cohen, Albert J. 63, 69, 71, 74, 75
Cohen, Arthur 93
Cohn, Harry 100
"Coincidentally" 128
Colbert, Claudette 21, 132, 161
Colcord, Fred 197
Cole, Nat "King" 85, 86, 125

214

Index

Cole, Robert 143
The Colgate Comedy Hour 88, 194–195
Colgate Variety Hour 27
Collins 114
Collins, John 85
Collins, Tom 136
Colman, Ronald 149
Colorado 31, 115
Columbia 8
Columbia Broadcasting System: radio 3, 14, 15, 18, 21, 25, 51, 72, 131, 132, 133, 134, 135, 136, 137, 138, 139, 140, 141, 142, 143, 144, 145, 146, 147, 148, 149, 150, 151, 152, 153, 154, 155, 156, 157, 158, 159, 160, 161, 162, 163, 164, 165, 166, 167, 168, 169, 170, 171, 172, 173, 174, 175, 176, 177, 178, 179, 180, 181, 182, 183, 184, 185, 186, 187, 188, 189, 190; television 25, 119, 191, 192, 193, 194, 196
Columbia Pictures 14, 15, 28, 30, 40, 41, 59, 98, 99, 100, 117
Colvig, Pinto 155
Colvig, Vance 132
Comden, Betty 8
Comer, Sam 109
Como, Perry 195
"Confession" 157
Conklin, Hal 87
"The Conklin Carelessness Code" 156
"The Conklin House at Crystal Lake" 179
"Conklin Rumors" 165
"Conklin's Anniversary" 157
"The Conklins Remarry" 178
Conlon, Jud 181
Conlon, Robert 167
Conlon, Tom, Jr. 85
Conner, Gilbert 94
Conners, Chuck 30
"Connie and the Measles" 167
"Connie Brooks, the Work Horse" 148
"Connie Is Chaperon" 160
"Connie Teaches French" 173
"Connie's Old Boyfriend" 168
Connor, Whitfield 142
Connors, Chuck 106
Conrad, Harold 63
Conrad, William 21, 133, 136, 137, 138, 140, 142, 143, 148, 149, 150, 153, 157, 165, 168, 175
Conried, Hans 139, 141, 144, 146, 150, 151
Conte, Robert 141
Contino, Dick 167

Cook, Tommy 62, 132, 137, 141, 147, 148
Cool, Gomer 140
Coolidge, Phillip 111
Coon, Gene L. 101
Cooper, Clancy 44
Cooper, Edwin 136, 137, 138
Cooper, Gary 32, 33, 34, 119, 122
Copa 92
Copelin, Campbell 46
Corbett, Lois 132, 135, 137, 150
Corday, Mara 82, 194
Corden, Henry 48
Corey, Jeff 135, 153
Corley, Cynthia 136, 166
Cornell University 9
Cornthwaite, Robert 114
Cortez, Stanley 115
"Cosmopolitan Magazine Pictures" 187
Costello, Lou 47, 48, 53
Cotten, Joseph 14, 54, 131, 137
Cotton, Joseph 14, 54, 131, 137
Coulcher, Paul N. 10
Council of Motion Picture Organizations (COMPO) 24
Courtney, Chuck 92
Cowan, Will 85
Cowling, Bruce 62
Coy, Walter 94
Crager, Lee 177, 178
Crain, Jeanne 83, 103, 104, 139
Crane, Bob 121
Craven, James 69
Crawford, Broderick 25
Crawford, Joan 1, 16, 80, 81, 82, 121, 171
Crenna, Richard 143, 144, 145, 146, 147, 148, 149, 150, 151, 152, 153, 154, 155, 156, 157, 158, 159, 160, 161, 162, 163, 164, 165, 166, 167, 168, 169, 170, 171, 172, 173, 174, 175, 176, 177, 178, 179, 180, 181, 182, 183, 184, 185, 186, 187, 188
Cripps, Henry 44
Crisp, Donald 97, 98, 132
Croft, Mary Jane 131, 148, 151, 153, 154, 155, 157, 158, 159, 160, 162, 164, 166, 167, 169, 170, 172, 173, 175, 176, 178, 179, 182, 184, 186, 187, 188
Crosby, Bing 31, 124, 128, 196
Crosby, Gary 189
Crosby, Wade 180, 181, 182, 183, 184, 185
Cross, Clive 44
Crothers, Scatman 69, 70
"Crowded School Conditions" 147
Crowe, James 40

Cugat, Xavier 193
Culbertson, George 187
Cullen, Bill 193
Culver, Howard 180
Culver City Hospital (Culver City, Calif.) 33, 36, 37, 38
Cummings, Irving 189
Cummings, Ralph 185
"Cure that Habit!" 161
Curtis, Anthony (Tony) 25, 26, 27, 29, 30, 36, 59, 60, 67, 87, 88, 167, 194, 195
Curtis, Barry 86
Curtiss, Edward 42, 65, 71, 101, 103
"Custodian of Student Funds" 151
Cutting, Richard H. 73
Czechoslovakia 115

Daheim, John 86
Dahl, Arlene 70, 83
Dailey, Dan 50, 143
Daily Cinema 119
"Daisy Kenyon" 16, 140
Dakin, Phillip 51
Dale, Michael 69
The Damon Runyon Theater 154, 157, 158
Damone, Vic 125
"The Dan Betterly Case" 137
Daniels, William H. 42, 51, 76, 82, 87, 91, 112, 113
"The Danny McNear Case" 140
Dano, Royal 56, 101
Danton, Ray 89
Danzig, Frank 165
Darby, Ken 55
The Darling Buds of May 111
Darnell, Linda 54
Darrell, Steve 42
Darvi, Bella 25
da Silva, Howard 135
Dauphin, Claude 51
Davenport, Gwen 43
Daves, Delmer 48, 55
"The David Ford Case" 135
"The David Turner Case" 138
Davidson, Jack 48
Davies, David 118
Davis, Bette 15, 31, 79, 121
Davis, Lucien 172
Davis, Robert 66
Davis, Sammy, Jr. 35, 88, 92, 129, 190
Davis, Wee Willie 47
Dawson, Edward Colin 97
Dawson, Ralph 51
Day, Dennis 135
Day, Gerry 118
Day, John 78
Day, Laraine 95, 96

215

Index

The Day the Earth Stood Still 23
"Death and Texas" 182
"Death at Skirkerud Pond" 189
Decca Records 24, 25, 65, 84, 87, 88, 113, 123, 124, 125, 126, 129, 194
de Cordoba, Pedro 115
de Cordova, Frederick 68
de Corsia, Ted 180, 189
Dee, Frances 64
Dee, Sandra 113
de Filippo, Eduardo 107
de Haven, Gloria 25, 194, 195
de Havilland, Olivia 12, 131
Dehner, John 138, 158, 160
de Kova, Frank 94, 109
Delano, Gwen 138, 139, 150
Delaplain, Warren B. 120
Delmont, Gene 40
del Valle, Jaime 158, 160, 166
Demling, Bill 150
Dempsey, Jack 10
Denning, Richard 106, 144
de Packh, Maurice 54, 127
Deported 20, 23, 50, 51–52, 70
"The Derelict and the Wandering Boy" 137
de Rose, Peter 55
de Santis, Joe 100
Desert Magazine 63
Desilu Productions 24, 27
Detroit (Mich.) 20
Dettaan, Jerry 185
DeWeese, Richard 53, 56, 59, 76
Dewey, Thomas E. 9, 36
de Wit, Jacqueline 95, 146
Dial Press 57, 75
Diamond, Anne 166
Di Maggio, Joe 191
The Dinah Shore Show 195
Dinneen, Joseph F. 87
"Dinner at the Ancient Mariner" 185
Dioguardi, Maxine 85
Disney, Walt 84, 110
Dobkin, Larry 138, 142, 157, 179
Dr. Hollywood *see* Gourson, N. Edward
"Dr. Jekyll and Mr. Hyde" 143
Dr. Paul 14
Dodd, Mead 55
Dodds, Edward 47, 57, 59, 95
"Dodge City in 1872" 181
Dodson, Kenneth M. 91, 92
"Does Clay High Want Miss Brooks?" 153
Doherty, James 106
Dolenz, George 75
Domergue, Faith 71, 72, 167

Donnelly, Ruth 89
Dorfman, Sid 132
Dorsey, Tommy 124
"Double-Breasted Horse Blankets" 188
Double Crossbones 52–53
Doud, Gil 137
Douglas, Everett 109
Douglas, Paul 111
Dover, Robert Foster 49
Dowling, Sylvia 150
Down Beat 123, 124, 126, 127, 129
Dragnet 157
Dragon, Carmen 150, 161
Drake, Charles 66, 76, 81, 99
Drake, Tom 44
Drango 96–98, 114, 117
Drapeau, Dewey 72
Drew, Ellen 40
"Driving School" 167
Dru, Joanne 96, 98, 153
Drumm, Steve 96
"Drums Along the Mohawk" 145
Dryanforth, Harold 160
Dubov, Paul 142, 143, 147, 148, 152, 168, 177
Duell, Sloane and Pearce 48
Duff, Howard 84
Duffy's Tavern 16, 132, 137, 149
Duggan, Andrew 122
Dumbrille, Douglass 47
Duncan, Andrea 197
Duncan, Rita 39
Duning, George L. 40, 99, 100
Dunlap, Scott R. 117
Dunn, George 91
Dunn, Maxwell 44
Dunne, Irene 161, 189
Dunstedter, Eddie 133, 134, 135, 136, 137, 138, 139, 140, 141, 142, 143, 144, 145, 146
Durant, Tim 121
Durante, Jimmy 135
Durbin, Deanna 48
Durocher, Leo 27
Duryea, Dan 82, 84
Duval, Jacqueline 66
"The Dynamiter" 148

Eagels, Jeanne 100
Eagle, John War 49, 71
Earle, Robert 141
Earlmar Productions 28, 97, 98, 117
"East of Puntas" 189
East of Sumatra 25, 69–71, 193
"Easter Egg Dye" 163
"Easter Outfit" 154
Easton, Robert 169, 170, 171
Eaton, Dorothy 197

Ebi, Earl 168, 175, 189
Ebin, David 196
Eckhardt, Emmy 42
Eckhardt, William 53
"Economy Drive, Dress Shop Deal" 170
"Economy Drive—Tape Recorder" 163
"Economy Wave" 151
"The Eddie Foster Case" 136
"The Edward L. Russell Case" 138
Edwards, Jack 137, 160
Edwards, James 148
Edwards, Paul 122
Edwards, Sam 147, 151, 161, 175
Egan, Richard 56, 62
The Egg and I 15, 132
Eiler, Barbara 135, 166, 189
Eiler, Virginia 160
Einstein, Albert 191
Ekwart, Walter "Whitey" 57
Elam, Jack 55, 62
Elgin (Ill.) 11
Elliott, Scott 147, 150
Ellis, Bobby 132, 137, 148, 150; *see also* Ellis, Robert
Ellis, David 139, 143, 146, 152, 158
Ellis, Georgia 21
Ellis, Herb 189
Ellis, Robert 94; *see also* Ellis, Bobby
Elman, Irving 41
"Elmer, the Great" 147
"Elmwood 6319" 187
Emerson, Ed 138, 139, 142, 146, 147, 152
Emerson, Hope 53
Emert, Oliver 56, 62, 65, 68, 73, 75, 80, 91, 94, 106
Emery, John 53
Emig, Allan 127
Emmy-Award 194, 195
Engel, Samuel G. 43, 44
Engelbach, Dee 14, 131, 145, 147, 148, 151, 152, 153, 177
"An Epidemic (Named Dolores Roberts)" 179
Erasmus Hall High School (Brooklyn, NY) 6, 8, 9
Erickson, Leif 158, 179
Erlenborn, Ray 77, 186
Escape 18, 136, 138, 152
Esherick, Mary 197
Esmond, Carl 115
Espinosa, Jose Angel "Ferrusquilla" 85
Essman, Harry 184
The Eternal Light 182, 189
Ethridge, Ella 117
Eugenia, Maria 85

Index

Europe 110
Eustrel, Anthony 69
Evans, Dale 190, 194
Evans, Douglas 85, 148
Evans, Joan 184
Evanson, Edith 97
Evelyn, Judith 81
"Everything Happens to Me" 125–126
Ewart, John 44
"Exchanging Christmas Presents" 167
The Exhibitor 45

"Faculty Cheerleader" 158
"Faculty Dance" 153
"Faculty Dress on Fridays" 178
"The Failure" 151
"Family Honeymoon" 179
Family Theater 2, 3, 23, 135, 157, 160, 166, 170, 173, 175, 179, 180, 183, 184, 188, 189
Family Weekly 92
Famous Playhouse 193
Fante, John 99
Farber, Jerry 135, 141, 144, 168
Farber, Les 135, 136
Farley, Morgan 53
The Farmer's Daughter 65, 137
Farrar, Stanley 137, 189
Farrar, Straus and Company 78
Farrell, Tommy 59
Faust, Gil 167
Favorite Story 148
Faylen, Frank 91
FBI 9
Feagin School of Dramatic Art 10, 11, 18, 41, 66
Feld, Don 120
Feld, Fritz 173
Felker, Ruby 45
Felton, Verna 173
Female on the Beach 80–82, 87, 125, 128
Fenton, Frank 109
Ferrell, Ray 117
Ferrer, Jose 103, 120, 121
Field, Norman 132, 135, 137, 138, 141, 142, 160, 175
Fielding, Lisabith 82
Fields, A. Roland 45, 60
Fierro, Paul 48
"The $50,000 Endowment" 145
Figland, Lyle 109
Fillbrandt, Laurette 138, 139, 140, 142, 145, 152
Film Daily 12, 40, 47, 48, 50, 52, 53, 54, 57, 60, 65, 66, 68, 69, 71, 73, 76, 78, 79, 85, 91, 92, 95, 98, 100, 102, 104, 106, 109, 110, 111, 114, 115, 118, 121, 122

"Find Pete Sutro" 133
"The Finding of the Temple" 184
Fine, Morton 18, 148, 149, 150, 151, 152, 153, 154, 155, 156, 160, 167
Finkel, Robert 195
Finn, H. 132
"First Show" 144
Fisher, Eddie 125
Fitch, Louise 150
Fitzgerald, Geraldine 16
"The 5:00 a.m. Burglar" 162
"Five Gun Final" 184
Fix, Paul 101, 102
Flagstaff (Ariz.) 50
Flame of Araby 56–57
Flatbush Avenue (Brooklyn, New York City) 5, 6
Flegenheimer, Arthur "Dutch Schultz" 8–9, 25
Fleming, Rhonda 70, 78, 79
"Flesh and Fantasy" 177
Flick, W. D. 55
"Flight from Home" 175
Flippen, Jay C. 54, 69, 87, 117
"The Flowers That Smelled of Murder" 148
"The Flying Dutchman" 188
Flynn, Errol 45, 68, 107
The FMB Company 167
Foch, Nina 40
Foley, Jack 61
"Foley Artist" 61
Fonda, Henry 14, 16, 131
Fontaine, Joan 19, 31, 151
Ford, Glenn 19, 30, 115, 150
Ford, John 94
Ford, Wallace 89
Forde, Eugene Francis 39
"Forest Fire" 185
"Formal Banquet" 162
Forman, Bill 157
Forrest, Sally 171
Ft. Benning (Ga.) 12
Ft. Eustis (Va.) 66
Fort Laramie (Wyo.) 116
Ft. Ord (Calif.) 12
Ft. Riley (Kans.) 11
Forte, Joe 134, 139, 143, 144, 146, 177, 189
Foster, Art 46
Foster, George 195
Foster, Phil 93
The Four Aces 125
The Four Preps 190
Four-Star Playhouse 158
Fowley, Douglas 41
Fox *see* 20th Century–Fox
Fox Film Corporation 42
Fox West Coast Theaters 42
Foxfire 27, 82–84, 111, 126, 195

"Framing Mr. Boynton" 158
France 115
"The Frances Case" 135
"The Francine Cooper Case" 141
Francis, Arlene 194
Francis, Mona 197
Frank, Fred 52
Frank, Melvin 109, 110, 115
Frank, Paul 39
Franklin, Paul 140, 180, 181, 182, 183, 184, 185
Franz, Eduard 75
"The Frederick Jerome Leech Case" 133
"Free Flowers from Fleishacker's Florist" 186
Freedman, Bill 137, 150
Freedman, Morris 137, 150
The Freedman Bros. 132
Freeman, Stan 196
Freericks, Bernard 49, 120
Frees, Paul 137, 138, 139, 140, 141, 142, 145, 146, 149, 189
French, Hugh 45
"Fresh Air, Sunshine, and Murder" 171
"Friday the 13th" 155
Friedhofer, Hugo 48, 54
Friedkin, David 18, 148, 149, 150, 151, 152, 153, 154, 155, 156, 160, 167
Friedman, David 66
Friend, Phillip 45, 60
Frings, Ketti 63, 82
Fritzell, James 169
"The Frog" 152
Frontier Fury 94
Frontier Town 180, 181, 182, 183, 184, 185
Fuchs, Daniel 99
Fuldheim, Dorothy 191
Fuller, Clem 72
Fuller, Lance 73
Fuller, Roger 75
Fuller, Samuel 121, 122
Furstenberg, Sam 8, 10

Gable, Clark 13, 14, 81, 106, 190
Gabreski, Francis S. 180
Gage, Ben 29
Gaines, Richard 39
Gallop, Frank 195
Gam, Rita 2, 70, 75, 76
Gammill, Noreen 132, 138, 143, 144, 145, 146, 147, 148, 149
Gans, Clifford R. 41
Garbo, Greta 15, 81
Garbowski, Heinz 114
Garde, Betty 86
Gardner, Ava 33
Gardner, Ed 132, 137, 150

217

Index

Garfield, John 16, 20, 89, 131, 133, 148
Garland, Judy 124
Garland, Richard 62
Garland, Stephanie 49
Garralaga, Martin 101
Garson, Greer 25
Gates, Larry 99
Gausman, Russell A. 42, 45, 47, 51, 52, 56, 57, 59, 60, 62, 64, 65, 67, 68, 69, 71, 73, 75, 76, 80, 82, 86, 87, 89, 91, 94, 95, 101, 103, 106, 107, 112
Gavaldon, Roberto 84
Geer, Will 49, 53
Gelbart, Larry 132
Gendot, Adrian 138, 139
Gene Autry's Melody Ranch 14
"Gentleman's Agreement" 89, 146
"The George Mansfield Bowman III Case" 133
Georgia 97
"The Geraldine Fairfield Case" 137
Germain, Larry 112
Germany 51, 67, 198
Gerry, Alex 137, 147
Gershenson, Joseph 47, 56, 57, 59, 60, 65, 67, 68, 69, 71, 75, 76, 78, 80, 82, 86, 87, 88, 89, 91, 93, 94, 95, 101, 103, 106, 107, 112, 123
Gerson, Betty Lou 134, 136, 137, 138, 139, 140, 141, 143, 146, 149, 150
Gerstle, Frank 150
Gertsman, Maury 53, 59, 60, 65, 67, 71, 86, 89
Gibb, Wendy 44
Gibson, Mimi 97, 189
Gielgud, Irwin 42
Giesler, Jerry 40, 103, 104
"Gifts for Mr. Boynton" 159
Gilbert, Brian 197
Gilbert, Paul 195
Gill, Frank, Jr. 69, 71
Gillis, Jackson 167
Gilman, Sam 91
Gilmore, Lowell 45
Givney, Kathryn 53
Glassburg, Irving 45, 106
Gleason, James 101
"The Glenda Barton Case" 15, 141
Glenn, Roy 166
Gobel, George 195
"The God Called Gold" 170
Goddard, Paulette 46
Goetz, William 26, 119
"Going Skiing" 169
Golden Globe 50, 81, 89

Goldman, Harold 147, 148
Goldsmith, Stanley 49
Goldstein, Leonard 52, 53, 56, 59, 62, 67, 71
Golitzen Alexander 45, 52, 60, 71, 75, 76, 80, 82, 86, 87, 89, 91, 94, 95, 101, 103, 106, 107, 112
Gomez, Thomas 40
Gonzales, Ricardo 85
Gonzalez, Gilberto 85
"A Good Neighbor" 190
Goodman, Benny 195
Goodman Theatre (Chicago, Ill.) 11
Goodson, Mark 194
Goodwin, Jimmy 114
Goosson, Stephen 40
Gordon, Billy 12, 13
Gordon, Clarke 132, 135, 137, 138, 143
Gordon, Gale 132, 133, 144, 145, 146, 147, 148, 149, 150, 151, 152, 153, 154, 155, 156, 157, 158, 159, 160, 161, 162, 163, 164, 165, 166, 167, 168, 169, 170, 171, 172, 173, 174, 175, 176, 177, 178, 179, 180, 181, 182, 183, 184, 185, 186, 187, 188
Gordon, Gloria 131, 132, 174
Gordon, Leo 75, 101, 109
Gordon, Mary 39
Gordon, Virginia 160, 165, 167, 168, 170, 174, 175, 176, 177, 183, 184, 185, 186
Gore, Chester 54
Gottlieb, Richard 193
Goude, Ingrid 103
Gould, Bill 136, 142, 147, 148, 149, 150, 151, 152, 153, 154, 155, 156, 157, 158, 159, 160, 161, 162, 163, 164, 165, 166, 167, 168, 169, 170, 171, 173, 174, 175, 176, 177, 178, 179, 180, 181, 182, 183, 184, 185, 186, 187, 188
Gould, Charles S. 99
Gould, Sandra 21, 132, 148, 159, 166, 174, 179, 187
Gourson, N. Edward 33
Grace, Henry 111
Grady, Billy J. 65
Graf, Louis 172, 184
Graham, Richard 197
Graham, Tim 132, 141, 142
Granby, Joseph 103, 136, 168, 177
Grandey, Roy 143, 144, 145, 146
Grant, Cary 1, 33, 110
Grant, John 47, 48, 52
Grant, Lou 137, 150

Grant R. Brimhall Library (Thousand Oaks, Calif.) 3
Grapperhaus, Bob 137, 150
Grauman, Sid 123
Graves, Peter 2, 20, 30, 35, 69, 70, 71, 96, 112, 113
Gray, Arline 28, 29, 30
Gray, Coleen 138
Gray, Gordon 143
Gray, Raymond 57
Great Britain 35
"Great Love Letters of History" 175
"The Great Presto" 184
The Great Sioux Uprising 71–72
Green, Eddie 132, 137, 150
Green, Howard J. 39
Green, Irving H. 37
Green, Leavis 12
Green, Marshall 91, 94
Green, Mort 195
Green, Reita 113
Green, William 175
Greene, Clarence 115
Greene, Joseph J. 101
Greenman, Alvin 44
Greenwood, Al 39, 41
Gregg, Virginia 144, 152, 189, 190
Gregory, Maya 138
Grey, Virginia 100
Griffin, Robert 49, 135, 137, 138, 139, 140, 141, 147, 148, 152, 158, 160, 168
Griffis, William (Bill) 183
Griggs, Loyal 109
Gross, Frank 47, 68, 76, 112
Grossel, Anna (mother) 5, 6, 7, 8, 9
Grossel, Dana Chandler (daughter) 20, 22, 23, 26, 29, 52
Grossel, Ira *see* Chandler, Jeff
Grossel, Jamie Chandler (daughter) 15, 22, 23, 26, 29, 34
Grossel, Maril 10
Grossel, Phillip (father) 5, 6, 8, 9, 10, 20, 30
"The Grudge Match" 154
Guard, Kit 40
Guest Star 172, 180, 184
Guffey, Burnett 40
Guilaroff, Sydney 111
Guilfoyle, Paul 41
Gulbrandsen, Synove 79
"The Guns of Wrath" 183
Gunsmoke 21
Guthrie, Carl 57, 78, 103

Hafter, Robert 133, 156
Hagen, Earle 54, 127, 128

Index

Hale, Alan, Jr. 106
Hale, Richard 94
"Half of My Heart" 100, 127
Hall, Charles R. 43
Hall, David 120
Hall, Robert 134, 136, 138, 139, 140, 141
Hall, Sherwood 127
Halliwell's Film Guide 40, 42, 43, 45, 47, 48, 51, 52, 53, 55, 56, 57, 59, 62, 63, 65, 67, 69, 71, 73, 74, 78, 80, 82, 86, 87, 89, 91, 93, 95, 96, 99, 101, 103, 105, 107, 109, 110, 112, 114, 115, 117, 120, 121
Hallmark Hall of Fame 119
Hallmark Playhouse 145, 147, 148, 151, 152, 153, 177
"Halloween" 159
Halop, Florence 137, 150
Halsey, Brett 121
Hamilton, Chuck 48, 122
Hamilton, Joseph 117
Hamilton, Murray 100
Hamilton, Sara 70
Hammerstein, Arthur 65
Hammerstein, Oscar 28
"Handsome New French Teacher" 160
Hanley, Tom 178
Hanover (Germany) 114
Hansen, Franklin, Jr. 99
Hansen, Myrna 79
"Happy New Year" 150
Hardin, Ty 32, 122
Harmon, Elyse 192
Harmon, John 89
Harmon, Tom 192, 193
"The Harold Landry Case" 143
Harper, Betty 188
Harper & Brothers, Publishers 122
Harrington, Curtis 120
Harris, Allan 118
Harris, Charles 85
Harris, Doris 52
Harris, Phil 193
Harris, Richard C. 117
Harris, Stacy 71
Harrison's Reports 45
Hart, Dolores 117
Hartshorn, Marian 197
Hartung, Joy 143
Harvey, Harry 101
Harvey, Ken 144, 146, 147, 154
Harvey, Paul 44
Harwood, Carl 147, 148, 149, 150, 151, 152, 153, 154, 156, 157
Hastings, Marjorie 197
Hatch, Wilbur 18, 138, 143, 144, 145, 146, 147, 148, 149, 150, 151, 152, 153, 154, 155, 156, 157, 158, 159, 160, 161, 162, 163, 164, 165, 166, 167, 168, 169, 170, 171, 172, 173, 174, 175, 176, 177, 178, 179, 180, 181, 182, 183, 184, 185, 186, 187, 188
"The Hate That Killed" 140
Haulani, Mylee 69
Hauser, Dwight 134
Hausner, Jerry 131, 137, 156, 159, 168, 182, 183, 187, 188
Haver, June 183
Havoc, June 141
Hawaii 21, 33, 55
Hawks, Howard 42
Hayden, Sterling 192
Haydn, Richard 95
Hayes, Allison 75
Hayes, Helen 191
Hayes, John Michael 65, 76
Hayes, Michael 175, 179
Hayes, Rosalind 79
Haymes, Dick 139
Haynes, Jack 40
Hayward, Susan 1, 6, 10, 25, 83, 115, 116, 133
Hayworth, Rita 100
Head, Edith 109
"Head English Department" 151
The Hedda Hopper Show 167
The Hedda Hopper Show: This Is Hollywood 133
Heflin, Van 31, 46
Hellinger, Mark 13
Hellstrom, Gunnar 121
Heman, Roger 44, 55
Hemingway, Ernest 13
Henderson, Skitch 196
Hendricks, Bob 177
Hendrix, Wanda 135
"Henpecked Mr. Conklin" 185
Henry, Will 94
Hepburn, Katharine 15, 135
"Her Name Is Bourbon Kate" 183
Herbert, Pitt 121
Herbert, Wilms 138, 145, 146, 148, 157, 166
Heron, Julia 59, 112
Herrick, Julia 197
Herrick Library *see* Margaret Herrick Library (Beverly Hills, Calif.)
Hersholt, Jean 167
Herzbrun, Bernard 42, 47, 51, 52, 56, 57, 59, 60, 62, 64, 65, 67, 68, 69, 73, 76, 78
Heston, Charlton 21, 28
Hibbs, Jesse 71, 89
Hicks, Chuck 36, 122
Hiecke, Carl 40
Hiestand, John (Bud) 144
Higgins, Charles "Vannie" 9
Hill, James 115
Hill, Ramsey 131, 132, 143, 144, 169
Hill, Robert 80
Hillside Memorial Park 36
Hilton, James 145, 147, 148, 151, 152, 153, 177
"Hired Wife" 170
"His Name Is John Smith" 180
Hitchcock, Alfred 14, 166, 194
Hite, Kathleen 135
Hitler, Adolph 191
Hoch, Winton C. 55
Hoey, Dennis 158
Hoffman, Charles 89
Hoffman, Joseph 78
Hogan, Pat 75, 94
Hogsett, Albert 48, 55
Hokom, Lillian 54
"Hold Me" 127, 196
Holden, Joyce 57, 58, 191
Holland, Bill 60
Holland, Tom 180
Holland, William 42, 62
Holliman, Earl 69
Hollywood (Calif.) 1, 2, 3, 10, 11, 12, 13, 14, 18, 19, 20, 21, 24, 25, 26, 27, 28, 30, 31, 32, 33, 34, 35, 36, 38, 39, 40, 42, 45, 47, 50, 51, 52, 54, 55, 58, 59, 61, 63, 66, 67, 68, 72, 75, 77, 79, 81, 98, 106, 107, 109, 110, 114, 115, 117, 121, 122, 123, 124, 127, 192, 194, 195, 196
Hollywood Citizen-News 56, 65, 68, 69, 73, 88, 109, 113, 115
The Hollywood Reporter 2, 39, 41, 42, 43, 44, 47, 48, 50, 52, 53, 54, 56, 57, 59, 60, 62, 63, 65, 66, 68, 69, 71, 72, 73, 76, 78, 79, 81, 84, 85, 87, 89, 90, 92, 94, 96, 98, 100, 101, 104, 106, 109, 110, 111, 114, 116, 118, 121, 122
Hollywood Salutes the National Guard 190
Hollywood Secrets 29
Hollywood Sound Stage 175
Hollywood Star Playhouse 111, 170
Hollywood Star Theater 158
Holm, Celeste 192
Holmby Hills 34
Holmes, Elsie 148
Holmes, Milton 40
Holmes, Taylor 44
"The Homestretch" 141
Honolulu (HI) 32

Index

Hoover, J. Edgar 9
Hope, Bob 31, 44, 110, 147, 189, 192
Hopper, Hedda 21, 133, 167
Hopper, Jerry 86, 95
Hopper, William 86
Horning, William A. 111
Horvath, Charles 73, 75, 91, 94, 97, 101
Hoshell, Leah 11
Hoshell, Marjorie Leah see Hoshelle, Marjorie
Hoshell, Norman 11
Hoshelle, Marjorie (wife) 11, 12, 13, 14, 15, 19, 21, 22, 23, 24, 25, 26, 28, 29, 32, 37, 52, 92, 117, 141, 145
"Hot Weather at Summer School" 157
Houghton Mifflin Company 82
"A Housewarming for Miss Enright" 182
Hovey, Tim 95
"How Green Was My Valley" 132
"How High the Moon" 170
Howard, Fred 138
Howard, Leslie 98
Howard, Ronald 97, 98
Howe, James Wong 96, 98
Hoy, Robert 73, 86, 92
Hoyt, John 122
Hoyt, Waite 8
Huber, Harold 93
Hubert, Rene 49
Hudson, John 62, 66
Hudson, Rock 21, 25, 26, 27, 28, 57, 58, 63, 73, 86, 192, 194
Hughes, Howard 72
Hughes, Kathleen 44
"The Human Element" 189
Hunnicutt, Arthur 49, 54
Hunt, Helen 99
Hunt, Jimmy 150
Hunt, Marsha 117, 118, 196
Hunter, Gloria 160
Hunter, Jeffrey 119
Hunter, Ross 56, 62, 67, 73, 86, 89, 91, 112, 113
Huntington Hartford Agency 19
Hussey, Ruth 189
Hutchins, Will 2, 33, 122
Hutchinson, Max M. 39

"I Believe" 192
I Love Lucy 24, 25, 27
"I Should Care" 123–124, 193
I Walk Alone 16, 36, 142
"I Wished on the Moon" 127, 128
Iannone, Patricia 183

Ibanez, Alicia 79
Ibbetson, Arthur 118
Idaho 31
Iglesias, Eugene 69, 73
"I'll String Along with You" 127
Illinois 31
"The Ilse Case" 136
"I'm Not Cochise Anymore" 27
"Indian Burial Ground" 166
Indiana 52
Indianapolis (Ind.) 31
Inescort, Frieda 82
Iness, Sim 75
Ingram, Jack 62, 72
International Pictures 60
"Intrigue" 141
The Invisible Wall 39–40
Ireland 77
"Irish Eyes Are Smiling" 139
Iron Man 57–59, 191
Irvine, Richard 43
"The Irving Richards Case" 135
Irwin, Ruby 150
"Is Football Canceled at Madison High?" 173
"Is Martha Conklin Going to Have a Baby?" 168
"Is Miss Brooks Engaged?" 173
Israel 23, 31, 118, 119
"It Could Happen to You" 128
Italy 20, 28, 51, 52, 70, 107
Ito, Kinuko 79
"It's Been So Long" 128
"I've Got a Crush on You" 59
"I've Got My Love to Keep Me Warm" 128

J. Messner 120
Jackman, Bob 85
Jackson, Brad 73, 76
Jackson, Howard 122
Jackson, Simon 127
Jacobs, John 138
Jacobson, Arthur 43
"A Jail Cell in Madison High" 182
"The Jailbird Rangers" 184
"Jailbreak" 172
"The Janice Manning Case" 133
Janiss, Vivi 155, 157, 159
Janssen, David 68, 91, 95
Japan 11, 12
Jarman, Claude, Jr. 138, 148
"The Jason King Case" 138
Javor, Paul 57
Jay, Lester 145, 146
The Jayhawkers 109–110
Jeanne Eagels 28, 98–100, 196
Jeff Chandler Sings 125
Jeff Chandler Sings to You 127–128, 196

Jeff Regan, Investigator 145, 146
Jeffers, Ray 47
Jeffrey, Howard 132
Jeffreys, Jane 197
Jellison, Bob 155, 157, 159, 172
"The Jen Cather Case" 135
Jenkins, George 124
Jenkins, Gordon 123
"The Jennifer Carr Case" 144
Jennings, Al 111
Jerome, Edwin 103
Jessel, George 35, 192
"The Jessica Lehr Case" 145
"The Jessica McKee Case" 134
"The Joan Carter Case" 136
"The Joe Carney Case" 142
"The Joe Haydn Case" 146
Johansen, Al 132, 137
"The John Christopher Case" 139
"The John Ellbridge Cleaver Case" 134
"John Quincy Adams" 134
"The Johnnie McCall Case" 134
Johnny Modero: Pier 23 133
Johnny O'Clock 14, 15, 40–41, 132
"The Johnny Rizzo Case" 134
Johnson, Bubber 66
Johnson, Tor 47
Johnson, Van 14, 23, 26, 27
Johnston, Peter 197
Johnstone, Bill 132, 133, 134, 135, 136, 137, 138, 139, 140, 141, 142, 143, 146, 147, 148, 150, 151, 153, 162, 165, 168, 175, 189
Johnstone, Jack 161, 170
Jones, Frank 179
Jones, Harmon 44, 55
Jones, Kenneth V. 114, 118
Jones, Ralph 154, 155, 156, 157, 158, 159, 160, 161, 162, 163, 164, 165, 166, 167, 168, 169, 170, 171, 172, 173, 174, 175, 176
Jones, Shirley 27
Jory, Victor 67
"The Joseph Coursey Case" 15, 133
Jourdan, Louis 55, 175
Jowett, Corson 62, 75, 95, 106
The Joyful Hour 189
"The Judas Face" 173
Juke Box Jury 125, 193
"July 4th Weekend" 156
"June Bride" 148, 156
"June Ushers in July for Miss Brooks" 179
Juran, Nathan 51, 59
"Juvenile Delinquency at Madison High" 145

Index

KaDell, Carlton 139, 141, 142, 148
Kalili, Maiola 55, 69
Kallen, Kitty 125
Kane, Byron 36, 131, 134, 143, 157, 173, 175, 189
Kapetansky, Seymour 150
Karath, Frances 64
Karn, Bill 160, 161, 166, 170, 172
Katcher, Aram 69
Katz, Lehman 40
Kautner, Helmut 112
Kaye, Danny 29, 31, 44, 110, 119
Kayser, Carl 44
Keane, Edward 39, 41
Kearney, Mark 147
Kearns, Joseph 137, 147, 150, 151, 156, 159, 168, 169, 170, 175, 188, 189
Keaton, Buster 192
Keefer, Don 87, 91
Keel, Howard 167
Keighley, William 16, 132, 133, 134, 135, 136, 137, 138, 139, 140, 141, 142, 143, 146, 147, 148, 150, 151, 153, 168, 175
Kellaway, Cecil 81, 95
Keller, Helen 191
Kelley, Alice 67
Kellogg, John 40
Kelly, Barry 44
Kelly, Jack 66, 143
Kelly, John T. 189
Kelly, Orry 51
Kemper, Ray 71, 172
Kendall, Cy 151
Kennedy, John F. 32
Kennedy, John Milton 16
Kennison, Lois 132
Kenny, Joseph E. 78
Kent, Ted J. 56, 60, 62, 82, 91
Kentucky 31
Kenworthy, Wayne 167
Kenyon, Curtis 53
Kerr, Deborah 147
"Key to the School" 155
Keyes, Evelyn 40, 41, 57, 60, 61, 62, 150
"The Kiddy Story" 173
Kieffer, Phillip 94
Kiernan, William 99
Kiley, Tim 196
Kilgallen, Dorothy 8, 194
The Killers 13, 14, 51
Kine Weekly 119
King, Marshall 180
Kirkpatrick, Jess 150
Kish, Joseph 69, 71, 76, 117
"Kiss of Death" 138
Kissel, William 121

Kitt, Eartha 31
Klauber, Marcel 65
Klein, Adelaide 21
Klemperer, Otto, Jr. 197
Kline, Benjamin 39, 41
Knight, David 118
Knight, Patricia 41
Knopf publishers 86
Knotts, Don 196
Knudsen, Peggy 41
Knudson, Barbara 67
Koessler, Walter 39, 41
Kohner, Frederick 95
Korbin, Marvin A. 33, 34, 38
Koski, Mario 157
Kramer, Glen 94
Krams, Arthur 111
Krantz, Sam 10
Kreth, Charles, Jr. 197
Kroeger, Berry 142, 145, 152
Krompler, Martin "Marty" 9
Kronman, Harry 175
Kruger, Jess 197
Kruger, Otto 160
Krugman, Lou 152, 153, 158
Krupa, Gene 195
Kruschen, Jack 132, 135, 137, 145, 146, 148, 150, 152, 171, 175, 188, 189
Kuhn, Mickey 49
Kuluva, Will 42
Kuney, Jack 196

Ladd, Alan 67, 135
"The Ladies Aid Society" 183
"Ladies Good Deed Club Drive" 172
Lady Esther Screen Guild Players 177
The Lady Takes a Flyer 28, 105–106
Laemmle, Carl, Jr. 67
La Frano, Tony 133
Laine, Frankie 189, 192
Lake Arrowhead (Calif.) 24
Lake Champlain (NY) 198
Lally, William 138, 161
Lamarr, Hedy 12, 13
Lamas, Fernando 32
Lamington National Park 45
Lamm, Mario 69
Lamont, Charles 47, 48, 56
Lamont, Martin 45
Lamont, Syl 66
Lamour, Dorothy 146
L'Amour, Louis 69
"Lamplight" 124–125, 194
Lancaster, Burt 16, 17, 18, 20, 28, 36, 142, 168
"Land Grab" 184
Landis, Jessie Royce 44
Landrith, Hoby 36

Landsbury, Angela 192
Landsworth, Lew X. 189
Lane, Ben 99
Lane, Charles 41, 111
Lane, Priscilla 10
Lang, Charles B. 81
Lang, Harry 134, 144
Lani, Prince Lei 55
Lansburgh, Larry 84
Lansing, Mary 133, 134, 135, 136, 137, 138, 139, 140, 141, 142, 143, 144, 145, 146, 157, 160
Lapis, Joe 42, 51, 57, 65, 68, 87, 91, 101
"Larceny" 147
Larch, John 101
Larkin, William 170
Las Vegas (Nev.) 27, 41, 88, 92, 93
Lasco, Lou 132
Lasky, Jesse L. 26
Lasky, Jesse, Jr. 24
Laszlo, Ernest 114
"Late Night Radio Programs" 178
LaTorre, Charles 141
La Tourette, Frank 192
Launders, Perc 42
Laurie, Piper 21, 67, 127, 192, 195
Lauter, Harry 78
Lava, William 1, 84, 85, 124
LaVigne, Emile 42, 45, 52, 117
Lawrence, Barbara 101
Lawrence, Charlotte 147, 148, 150, 151
Lawrence, Jerome 149
Lawrence, Marc 47
Lawrence, Viola 99
Lawrence, William (Bill) 166, 171
Layman, Beth 144
Lean, David 25
Lee, Earl 132, 135, 137, 142
Lee, Jack 49
Lee, Leonard 60
Lee, Nancy 114
Lee, Palmer 62, 66
Lee, Peggy 24, 179, 180, 190, 192
Lee, Senor 85
Leeds, Carole Sue 138
Leeds, Peter 21, 133, 140, 143, 144, 146, 156, 172, 184
Leigh, Janet 27, 29, 30, 35
Le Maire, Charles 44, 49, 55, 115
Lemmon, Jack 190
Lemond, Bob 144, 145, 146, 147, 148, 149, 150, 151, 152, 153, 154, 155, 156, 157, 158,

Index

159, 160, 161, 162, 163, 164, 165, 166, 167, 168, 169, 170, 171, 172, 173, 174, 175, 176, 177, 178, 179, 180, 181, 182, 183, 184, 185, 186, 187, 188
Lenard, Grace 82
Leonard, Harry M. 49, 54
Leonard, Sheldon 149, 166, 187
"The Leonard Hazelton Case" 15, 133
Leonard Maltin's Movie and Video Guide 40, 42, 43, 45, 47, 48, 51, 52, 53, 55, 56, 57, 59, 60, 62, 63, 65, 67, 68, 69, 71, 73, 74, 76, 78, 80, 82, 84, 86, 87, 89, 91, 93, 95, 96, 99, 101, 103, 105, 107, 109, 110, 112, 114, 115, 117, 120, 121
"Leopard's Spots" 154
LeRoy, Mervyn 12
Let George Do It 144, 148
"Let Hawkins Guide You Through Yonkers" 172, 188
"Let's Get Lost" 127, 128
"A Letter from Mr. Boynton" 174
Leven, Boris 115
Leverett, Winston 109
Levien, Sonya 99
Levitt, Ruby R. 42, 82, 87
Levy, Annabell 43
Levy, Melvin 71
Lewis, Al 18, 35, 143, 144, 145, 146, 147, 148, 149, 150, 151, 152, 153, 154, 155, 156, 157, 158, 159, 160, 161, 162, 163, 164, 165, 166, 167, 168, 169, 170, 171, 172, 173, 174, 175, 176, 177, 178, 179, 180, 181, 182, 183, 184, 185, 186, 187, 188
Lewis, Cathy 131, 171, 189
Lewis, Elliott 138, 171, 173, 175, 188, 189
Lewis, Forrest 89, 101
Lewis, Harry 152
Lewis, Jerry 28, 180, 188, 190
Lewis, Joe E. 93
Lewis, Sam 124
Lewis, Warren 158
Libbott, Robert 141, 142
Liberace 27
Liberty 41
Liberty Records 98, 100, 127, 128, 196
Life 11
Life with Luigi 21
"Lifeboat" 166
Light, David 156, 166
"The Linda Andrews Case" 15, 140
Lipstein, Harold 94

Lipton, David A. 35
Little, Brown 91, 111
Little, Thomas 43, 49, 54, 55
"A Little Love Can Go a Long Long Way" 87, 126–127
The Littlest Outlaw 84–85
Livadary, John 99
"The Liza Zernig Case" 144
Lloyd, Jack 188
Locher, Felix 115
"Locked In for the Night" 187
Lockhart, Gene 100
Lockwood, Alexander 103
Lockwood, Grey 195
Loeb, Lee 144
Loeffler, Louis 54
Logan, Stanley 45, 53
Lollobrigida, Gina 194
London 35, 114, 119
London, Jack 130
London, Julie 97, 98
"The Lonesome Reunion" 152
Long Beach (Calif.) 25
Long Branch (NJ) 9
Long Island (NY) 198
Lontoc, Leon 60
Look Magazine 26
Loos, Mary 43
Lorimer, Louise 132
Los Angeles (Calif.) 13, 19, 20, 27, 29, 32, 34, 35, 36, 37, 43, 50, 57, 79, 86, 92, 98, 103, 121, 192, 193
Los Angeles Daily News 52, 58
Los Angeles Examiner 33, 43, 56, 57, 61, 67, 69, 70, 73, 78, 81, 84, 85, 92, 94, 98, 101, 109
Los Angeles Mirror 53
Los Angeles Mirror-News 88
Los Angeles Times 41, 44, 48, 50, 52, 54, 56, 59, 60, 62, 63, 65, 68, 69, 71, 72, 73, 76, 78, 79, 81, 84, 87, 91, 92, 95, 96, 98, 102, 104, 106, 109, 110, 111, 113, 114, 116, 118, 121, 122
Losby, Donald 111
"Lost Angel" 131
Louie, Ducky 60
Louis, Jean 40, 99
"Love Is Just Around the Corner" 128
"The Love Pact" 146
Lovejoy, Frank 133, 140, 142, 145, 167
"Lovely to Look At" 128
"A Lovely Way to Spend an Evening" 127, 128
Lovsky, Celia 82
Low, Warren 40
Lowe, David 197
Lowe, Shirley 197
Loy, Myrna 31

Luboff, Norman 150
Lucarelli, Rosanna 51
Luciano, Charles "Lucky" 9, 10, 20
"The Lucy Brown Case" 145
Ludwig, Edward 60, 61
Ludwig, Otto 45
Lukather, Lee 96
Lukather, Paul 97
Lummis, Dayton 89
Luna, Margarito 85
Lund, Charles 158
Lund, John 62
Lundberg, Dan 107
Lundigan, William 183
Lung, Charlie 139, 141, 142
Lupino, Ida 16, 140, 147
Lupton, John 96
"The Luscious Louie Case" 141
The Lux Radio Theatre 2, 14, 15, 16, 18, 19, 36, 43, 50, 54, 65, 77, 89, 98, 103, 132, 133, 134, 135, 136, 137, 138, 139, 140, 141, 142, 143, 146, 147, 148, 150, 151, 153, 168, 175, 189
Lydia Bailey 23
"The Lyle Madden, M. D. Case" 138
Lyndon, Barre 75
Lynley, Carol 120, 121
Lynn, Rita 158
Lynn, Robert 85

"Ma Chere, Miss Brooks" 159
MacDonald, Edmund 141
MacDonald, Ian 73
MacDonald, Kenneth 121
MacDonald, Margaret 153
Macdonnell, Norman 21, 138, 152
MacGregor, C. P. 164
Mack, Dick 180, 188
MacKaye, Frederic 17, 132, 133, 134, 135, 136, 137, 138, 139, 140, 141, 142, 143, 146, 147, 148, 150, 151, 153, 189
MacKenzie, Joyce 49
MacLane, Barton 82
Maclean, Fred 120
Maclean, Mack 181
MacMurray, Fred 15, 132, 142, 192
MacRae, Gordon 11, 27, 150, 192, 193, 194, 195, 197
MacRae, Sheila 11, 192, 197
"Madison High Auction" 162
"Madison Summer Athletic Festival" 157
"Madison's Birthday Ceremonies for Washington" 176
"Madison's Post-Season Game" 167

Index

Magalona, Pancho 122
Magginetti, William 122
"Magic Christmas Tree" 150, 160, 167
Magic Town 16, 136
Magnificent Obsession 113, 133
"The Maharaja of Shish Kebab" 146
Maher, Wally 84, 131, 137, 144, 148, 160
Mahoney, Jock 91
Maine 121
Major Bowes' Original Amateur Hour 14
"Malcolm the Rabbit" 149
Maley, Laila 85
Malneck, Matty 132, 137, 150
Malone, Dorothy 94
Mammoth Lakes (Calif.) 32
The Man Called X 14
Man in the Shadow 100–102
"Man of the House" 179
"The Man Who Lived Forever" 139
"The Man Who Was Murdered Twice" 144
"The Man Without a Country" 143
Mancini, Henry 1, 84, 87, 88
Mango, Alec 118
Manhattan (New York City) 8, 9, 10
Manila (Philippines) 32, 33
Mansfield, Joseph F. 170, 173, 175, 179, 180, 183, 184, 188
Maple, Terence 118
March, Hal 78, 149, 150, 151, 155, 158, 159, 160, 163, 180, 184
Marcus, Larry 140
Marden, Adrienne 86
Margaret Herrick Library (Beverly Hills, Calif.) 2
Margo, Elaine Shapiro 5, 6, 7
Margolis, Herb 60, 133
"Marie" 181
Marin, Jesus 84
Marion, Paul 45
Markheim, Lou 133
Markle, Fletcher 24
Marr, Eddie 132, 135, 136, 137, 138, 139, 140, 141, 142, 143, 146, 147, 148, 150, 151, 153, 168, 189
Marrener, Edythe *see* Hayward, Susan
Marsh, Myra 155, 189
Marshall, E. G. 17
Marshall, Edison 78, 79
Marshall, George 94, 111
Marshall, Herbert 131
Marshall, Joan 168
Marshall, Zena 118
Marson, Truda 139, 140, 148
Martel, Christiane 79
Martell, Gregg 53
Martin, Andra 106
Martin, Charles 188
Martin, Dean 27, 32, 180, 188, 192
Martin, Dewey 56
Martin, Jules 10
Martin, Nora 141, 148
Martin, Steve 57
Marvin, Lee 30, 94
The Martin and Lewis Show 180, 188
Marx, Groucho 5
Marx, Harpo 27
Marx, Sam 27
"Mask for Kinsella" 154
Mason, Gaylord 197
Mason, James 62, 84, 192
Masterson, Gerard 92
Mastin, Will 88
Mathews, George 68
Mathis, Johnny 190
"The Matilda Fogarty Case" 136
The Mating Game 36, 110–111
"The Mating of Millie" 150
Mature, Victor 16, 138
Maugham, Somerset 100
Maurey, Nicole 109, 110
Max, Edwin 132, 136, 138, 142, 151, 152, 153, 174, 178
Maxwell, Charles 84
Maxwell, Marilyn 25, 69, 70, 71, 93, 192
Mayer, Louis B. 26
"Mayor Rides by Madison High" 163
Mazurki, Mike 42
MCA 113
MCA Artists 12
McAdoo, Tom 117
McCall, Mary, Jr. 43
McCambridge, Mercedes 172
McCook, Phillip J. 10
McCrea, Joel 132
McDermott, Paul 178, 188
McDonagh, Dick 195
McDowall, Roddy 23
McDowell, Virginia 143
McGarrett, George 195
McGovern, Johnny 132, 140, 146, 150, 168
McGraw, Charles 41, 53, 91, 139, 143, 146, 150
McGrew, Stephanie 82
McGuire, Don 59, 195
McGuire, Dorothy 89, 166
McGuire, Paul 89
McIntire, John 76, 77, 78, 89, 91, 151, 161
McKenny, Bob 188
McMillan, Gloria 132, 144, 145, 146, 147, 148, 149, 150, 151, 152, 153, 154, 155, 156, 157, 158, 159, 160, 161, 162, 163, 164, 165, 166, 167, 168, 169, 170, 171, 172, 173, 174, 175, 176, 177, 178, 179, 180, 181, 182, 183, 184, 185, 186, 187, 188
McNally, Stephen 45, 46, 57, 189
McNaught, Herbert (Bob) 118, 119
McNear, Howard 139, 141, 142, 143, 146, 148, 152, 156, 170, 177, 184
McSweeney, John, Jr. 111
McVey, Paul 154, 170
McVey, Tyler 132, 134, 135, 136, 137, 138, 139, 141, 152, 157, 168
McVitty, Edward 97
"Measles" 165
"Medford Reform School at Madison" 170
Medina, Patricia 47
Meet Danny Wilson 24, 59–60, 66
Megowan, Don 109
"The Melody Windsor Case" 140
Menacker, Sam 47
Menken, Shepard 158, 189
Mercer, Johnny 125
Meredith, Burgess 46
Meredith, Lucille 159
Meriman, Randy 25
Merkel, Una 111
Merlin, Jan 87
Merrill, Lou 139, 150, 171, 176, 177, 189
Merrill's Marauders 1, 32, 33, 36, 38, 121–122
Meston, John 21
Metalious, Grace 120
Metropolitan Restaurant and Cafeteria Owners Association 8, 9, 10
Metty, Russell 56, 64, 68, 73, 75
MGM (Metro-Goldwyn-Mayer) 15, 25, 28, 30, 81, 95, 106, 107, 110, 113
MGM Records 111
Michener, James 31, 32
Michigan 31
Milestone, Lewis 40, 114
Millan, Lynn 86
Milland, Ray 115, 148
Millar, Lee 180
Miller, Arthur 196

223

Index

Miller, Colleen 101, 102
Miller, Marvin 60, 130, 146, 147, 150
Miller, Sidney 137, 173
Millpond Playhouse (Roslyn, NY) 11, 18, 197, 198
Mills, Ingrid 79
Mills, Mort 101
The Mills Brothers 195
Milner, Martin 94
Milo, George 96
Milton, David 117
Minciotti, Silvio 51
Mineo, Sal 87
Miners, Howard 147
"Minerva Is Missing" 181
"Minerva's Husband" 177
"Miracle in Manhattan: A Christmas Story" 16, 132, 137, 149
"The Miracle of the Bells" 142
Les Miserables 23, 147
Mishkin, Meyer 18, 19, 20, 21, 24, 28, 30, 31, 35, 36, 96, 97
Mishkin Agency 21, 28
"Miss Brooks Buys a Cow for Mr. Boynton" 180
"Miss Brooks Follows Mr. Boynton to Eagle Springs" 176
"Miss Brooks, Girl-Taxidermist" 179
"Miss Brooks Gives Up on Mr. Boynton" 177
"Miss Brooks, Head of the English Department?" 174
"Miss Brooks Makes a Costume for Mr. Boynton" 174
"Miss Brooks Might Lose All Her Furniture" 176
"Miss Brooks Needs a Winter Coat" 174
"Miss Brooks' Oil Buy for Martha Conklin" 169
"Miss Brooks Plans for a Barbecue" 164
"Miss Brooks, Second Delegate?" 177
"Miss Brooks Takes Over Miss Enright's First Aid Class" 172
"Miss Brooks Tutors Stretch" 179
"Miss Enright's Birthday Party" 169
"Mister ... or *Miss* Carter?" 185
Mr. Belvedere Goes to College 43–44
"Mr. Boynton and Miss Enright" 162
"Mr. Boynton, Head of the Biology Department?" 176
"Mr. Boynton Interviews for State University" 161
"Mr. Boynton Meets Mr. Finch" 188
"Mr. Boynton Returns" 174
"Mr. Boynton to Leave Madison?" 168
"Mr. Boynton's Daughter" 186
"Mr. Boynton's Fire Rescue Practice" 165
"Mr. Boynton's Uncle Visits" 173
"Mr. Conklin Fires the Football Coach" 165
"Mr. Conklin, the Greatest Show on Earth" 176
"Mr. Conklin's Induction Notice" 170
"Mr. Conklin's New Hunting Gun" 182
"Mr. Conklin's Talent Party" 153
"Mr. Conklin's Wake-up Plan" 154
Mr. President 134
"Mr. Stone Hires a Psychiatrist" 187
Mitchum, Robert 16, 31, 107
Mix, Tom 40
"Mix-up Over an Elephant" 159
Mladova, Milada 67
Mockridge, Cyril 115
Modern Screen 26, 194
Moffitt, Jack 111
Mohr, Gerald 14, 36, 67, 138, 139, 140, 141, 142, 147, 149, 150, 151, 152, 153, 156, 159, 172, 173, 178, 180, 184
"Money Management" 146
Monogram 12, 117; *see also* Allied Artists
Monroe, Marilyn 1
Monsarrat, Sam 55
Monterey (Calif.) 19
Montgomery, Robert 46, 131, 137
Monthly Film Bulletin 42, 43, 45, 47, 48, 50, 52, 53, 54, 56, 57, 59, 60, 62, 63, 65, 66, 68, 69, 71, 72, 73, 76, 78, 79, 81, 84, 85, 87, 89, 91, 95, 96, 98, 100, 102, 104, 109, 110, 111, 113, 114, 116, 118, 119, 121, 122
Montoya, Julia 71
Montrose, Dave 40
Moody, Ralph 166, 183
Moore, Constance 132
Moore, Terry 26, 158
Moorehead, Agnes 99, 100, 192
Moran, Betty 144
"The More I See You" 127, 128
"More Than Anyone" 123–124
Morelli, Ernesto 48
Morey, Edward, Jr. 117
Morgan, Boyd "Red" 72
Morgan, Dennis 133
Morgan, Jane 144, 145, 146, 147, 148, 149, 150, 151, 152, 153, 154, 155, 156, 157, 158, 159, 160, 161, 162, 163, 164, 165, 166, 167, 168, 169, 170, 171, 172, 173, 174, 175, 176, 177, 178, 179, 180, 181, 182, 183, 184, 185, 186, 187, 188
Morgan, Maxine 79
Morheim, Louis 60
Morin, Alberto 94
Morley, Christopher 11, 197, 198
Morley, Fay 86
Morley, Jay A., Jr. 73, 87, 103
Moross, Jerome 109
Morris, Carol 103
Morris, John 150
Morris, Roland 180
Morris, William 31
Morrison, Anne 135, 136, 143
Morrison, Donald 135, 143
Morrow, Bill 194
Morrow, Brad 95
Morrow, Jeff 75
Morrow, Mary Jane 197
Morton, Arthur 99
Mosier, Wilbur 112
"Mother Didn't Tell Me" 166
"Mother's Day" 154
"Mother's Day Presents" 164
Motion Picture 21, 26
Motion Picture Exhibitor 41, 42, 43, 44, 47, 48, 50, 52, 53, 54, 56, 57, 58, 59, 62, 63, 65, 66, 68, 69, 71, 72, 73, 78, 79, 81, 84, 85, 86, 87, 89, 90, 92, 93, 94, 96, 98, 100, 101, 102, 103, 106, 109, 110, 111, 114, 116, 118, 121, 122
The Motion Picture Guide 39, 40, 41, 42, 43, 44, 45, 47, 48, 51, 52, 53, 55, 56, 57, 59, 60, 62, 63, 65, 67, 68, 69, 71, 73, 74, 76, 78, 80, 82, 84, 86, 87, 89, 91, 93, 95, 96, 99, 101, 103, 105, 107, 109, 110, 112, 114, 115, 117, 118, 120, 121
Motion Picture Herald 40, 41, 42, 43, 44, 45, 47, 48, 50, 52, 53, 54, 56, 57, 59, 60, 61, 63, 65, 66, 68, 71, 72, 73, 75, 78, 79, 81, 84, 85, 86, 87, 89, 91, 92, 93, 95, 96, 98, 100, 102, 104, 106, 109, 110, 111, 114, 116, 117, 118, 121, 122
Movie Life 2, 21, 26

Index

Movie Spotlight 26
Movieland 26, 125
Movieland and TV Time 31
Moyles, Jack 173
"Mrs. Davis May Lose Her House" 169
"Mrs. Davis' Surprise Party" 187
"The Mrs. Margaret Barnstack Case" 143
Mueller, Charles 40
Muhl, Edward 26, 35
Multiple Sclerosis Telethon 192
Murphy, Audie 21, 26, 190, 195
Murphy, George 189
Murphy, Horace 137, 140, 142
Murphy, William 87
Murray, Forbes 79
Murray, Rickey 111
Murray, Ross 177, 186
Musial, Stan 31
Mutual Network 133, 135, 137, 144, 148, 157, 160, 166, 170, 173, 175, 179, 180, 183, 184, 188, 189
My Favorite Husband 18, 24, 144
"My Friend Flicka" 148
"My Man Godfrey" 189
"My Prayer" 126
"My Reputation" 15, 132
"My True Love's Hair" 188
Myerson, Bess 25

Nadel, Robert 36
Nader, George 26, 87, 91, 92
Nagel, Conrad 113
"The Nameless Patient Case" 143
Napier, Alan 53
Naples (Italy) 51
Narz, Jack 193
Nash, J. Carrol 189
The Nat "King" Cole Musical Story 85–86
Nathaniel, Violet 55
National Broadcasting Company: radio 2, 3, 14, 131, 132, 137, 146, 149, 150, 157, 158, 160, 161, 166, 167, 170, 172, 173, 180, 182, 188, 189; television 27, 88, 119, 193, 194, 195
"National Clean-Up" 162
National Police Gazette 29
"The Nativity" 183
Natteford, Jack 69
NBC *see* National Broadcasting Company
Nealis, Edward G. 40
Nebraska 31
Needs, James 114
Negley, Harrison 145

Negley, Jack 168
Neise, George 135, 137, 138, 142, 143, 151, 189
Nelson, Frank 146, 147, 148, 151, 152, 153, 155, 156, 158, 161, 163, 165, 187
Nelson, Gene 195
Nelson, Terry 91, 95, 107
Neuman, E. Jack 15, 133, 134
Neumann, Kurt 67
Nevada 115
The New Adventures of Michael Shayne 16, 19, 139, 140, 141, 142, 143, 149, 150
"New Bus Line" 168
"A New Dress from Sherry's Department Store" 181
New Mexico 115
"New Principal of Madison High" 184
"The New School Television Set" 170
"New Year's Eve" 161
"New Year's Resolutions" 184
New York 48, 55, 57, 78, 86, 87, 89, 112, 120, 122
New York (city) 5, 6, 8, 9, 18, 20, 25, 27, 50, 191, 194
New York (state) 5, 9, 12, 14, 17, 19, 27, 28, 29, 36, 40, 52, 75, 92, 93, 115, 124, 193
New York Daily News 40, 42, 43, 45, 47, 48, 51, 52, 53, 55, 56, 57, 59, 60, 62, 63, 65, 67, 68, 71, 73, 74, 78, 80, 82, 86, 87, 89, 91, 93, 95, 96, 99, 101, 103, 105, 107, 109, 110, 112, 114, 115, 117, 120, 121
New York Herald Tribune 122
The New York Times 40, 41, 42, 43, 44, 47, 48, 50, 52, 53, 54, 56, 57, 59, 60, 62, 63, 65, 66, 68, 72, 75, 78, 79, 81, 84, 85, 87, 89, 91, 92, 95, 96, 100, 102, 104, 106, 109, 111, 113, 114, 116, 121, 122
Newark (NJ) 8, 9
Newberry, Bill 94, 103
Newman, Alfred 43, 48, 54, 127
Newman, Joseph M. 42, 43
Newman, Mary Ann 197
Newport News (Virg.) 66
Nicholas, Bert 44
Nicholson, Emrich 67, 73, 75
Nicol, Alex 59, 64, 66
Nilsson, Norma Jean 138, 141, 144, 158, 175
Niven, David 30, 132
Nixon, Richard M. 32
"No Easter Vacation for Miss Brooks" 177

Nobody Lives Forever 16, 136
Nogales (Ariz.) 77
Nolan, Jeanette 42, 189
Nolan, Lloyd 151
Noriego, Felix 94
Norman, Charles 132, 137, 150
North, Edmund H. 106
North, Robert 170
Northern Music Company 84, 87
"A Note from Mr. LeBlanc" 158
Novak, Kim 2, 35, 98, 99, 100
Novello, Jay 131, 132, 139, 141, 142, 145, 147, 152, 153, 188
Nugent, Elliott 43, 44
Nugent, Frank S. 53
Nurney, Fred 47, 75
Nusser, James 173
Nye, Ben 44, 49, 54, 55, 120
Nye, Louis 196

Ober, Phillip 111
O'Brian, Hugh 62, 66, 67
O'Brien, Edmund 115
O'Brien, Margaret 131, 134, 158, 192
O'Brien, Marissa 131
O'Brien, Sheila 80
"An Occurrence At Owl Creek Bridge" 136
O'Connor, Donald 48, 53, 190
O'Connor, Rod 137
Odell, Cary 40
Odell, Rosemary 67, 78, 94, 95
O'Flynn, Damian 97
Ogburn, Charlton, Jr. 122
Ogg, James 132, 138, 141, 153, 168
Ogg, Sammy 181, 183
O'Hara 173
O'Hara, Maureen 56, 76, 77, 78, 103, 141
O'Herlihy, Dan 147, 158
O'Keefe, Dennis 42, 43, 139
Olivier, Laurence 62
Olsen, Moroni 75
O'Malley, John 44
One Desire 86–87, 123, 129
"One More Tomorrow" 133
"One, Two, Button Your Shoe" 128
O'Neill, Eugene 10
"Only the Very Young" 87, 126–127
"Only Yesterday" 172
"Opening Baseball Game with Clay City" 163
"The Opening of Tioga Reserve" 182
Oppenheimer, Jess 18
Orbom, Eric 47, 78, 85
Oregon 94

225

Index

Orschel, Marina 103
Ortigoza, Carlos 85
Ortiz, Pepe 84
Osborne, Ted 158
O'Shea, Michael 131
O'Sullivan, Maureen 132, 148, 189, 192
O'Sullivan, Richard 118
"The Other Wise Man" 160
"Oui" 173
Our Famous Husbands 192–193
Our Miss Brooks 1, 3, 17, 18, 19, 20, 21, 24, 25, 50, 51, 52, 54, 55, 63, 72, 143, 144, 145, 146, 147, 148, 149, 150, 151, 152, 153, 154, 155, 156, 157, 158, 159, 160, 161, 162, 163, 164, 165, 166, 167, 168, 169, 170, 171, 172, 173, 174, 175, 176, 177, 178, 179, 180, 181, 182, 183, 184, 185, 186, 187, 188
"Outpost Road" 184
"Overcrowded Conditions at Madison High" 181
Owen, Tudor 78
Oxford 8

P. S. 181 6, 114–115
Pa, Solomon 55
Pabst Blue Ribbon Bouts 191
Pacific Pioneer Broadcasters 3
Page, William 42
Paget, Debra 49, 50, 55, 168, 173, 175
Paige, Mabel 40
Paiva, Nestor 106, 173, 174
Palance, Jack 75, 76, 114
"Palm Beach Santa Claus" 158
Palm Springs (Calif.) 27, 38, 114
Palmer, Ernest 49, 50
Palmer, Gregg 67, 73
Palmer, Lilli 141
Paluzzi, Luciana 121
Panama, Norman 109, 110, 115
Papalas, Nicholas 197
"Paradise, U.S.A." 158
Paramount Pictures 16, 22, 30, 53, 62, 109, 110, 115, 116, 128
Paris, Frank 176, 177, 178, 179, 180, 181, 182, 183, 184, 185, 186, 187, 188
Paris, Gloria 7
Paris, Jerry 106, 173
Paris, Joseph 7
Paris, Leonard 7
Paris, Lillian Shapiro (aunt) 5, 7
"Paris, Anyone?" 169
Parker, Eleanor 120
Parker, Fess 109, 110
Parker, Franklin 132, 137, 150

Parker, Warren 121
Parlato, Charlie 181
Parnell, James 68
Parrish, Helen 179
"Party Line" 159
Pasadena Playhouse (Pasadena, Calif.) 193
Pataky, Veronica 142
Pate, Michael 44
Patrick, Gail 139
Patten, Bob 44
Patterson, Ken 117
Patton, George 66
"The Paul Dennison Case" 142
"The Paul Melville Case" 139
Payne, John 147
"Peanuts, the Great Dane" 155
Pearl Harbor (Haw.) 11
Pearson, GeGe 184
Peattie, Yvonne 189
Peck, Charles K., Jr. 68
Peck, Gregory 16, 30, 110, 138, 146
"Pen Pal Project" 184
Pendleton (Ore.) 72
Penn, Leonard 189
"Pensacola Popovers" 156, 175
Perado, Perez 190
Pereira, Hal 109
Perrin, Vic 179
Perrott, Ruth 138, 144
Perry, Bob 40
The Perry Como Show 195
The Peter Potter Show 193
"The Peter Scarbo Case" 134
Peters, Hans 120
Peters, Ken 131, 132, 137, 150
Petracca, Joseph 109
Petrie, Howard 66, 75
Petruzzi, Jack 138, 139, 141
Pevney, Joseph 57, 59, 63, 78, 80, 82, 83, 87, 91, 117
Peyton, Father Patrick 23
The Phoenix 114
Philippines 32, 33, 122
"The Phillip Martell Case" 144
The Phillip Morris Playhouse On Broadway 188
Phillips, Alex 84
Phillips, Barney 97, 138, 189
Phillips, Bernard 153
Phoenix (Ariz.) 27, 106
"Photo Finish" 131
Photoplay 2, 21, 26, 29, 31, 32
Pichel, Irving 161
Picistrelli, Umberto 107
Pickard, John 66, 91
Pickford, Mary 29
Pidgeon, Walter 147
The Pied Pipers 124
Pillars of the Sky 93–95, 111
"Pin-up Pictures" 171

Pitcher, George 118, 119
Pittsburgh (Penn.) 191
Place the Face 193
Planck, Robert 99
Platt, Edward C. 103
"Please Make a Pass at My Heart" 128
Pleasence, Donald 118
Pleis, Jack 24, 125, 126
The Plunderers 116–118
Podesta, Rossana 107
Poe, Edgar Allan 130
"Poetry Mix-up" 153
"The Poisoned Waterhole" 181
Poitier, Sidney 66
"Police Academy" 157
Polito, Eugene 117
Pollack, Frank 190
Pollock, Dee 117
Pondosa (Ore.) 94
"The Portrait" 144
Portrait of Jennie 54
Post, Clayton 171, 188
Poston, Tom 196
Potter, Peter 192, 193
Poule, Ezelle 144
Powell, Addison 111
Powell, Dick 14, 15, 18, 40, 41, 110, 128, 132
Powell, Edward 43, 48, 55
Powell, William 146
Powers, Mala 167
Pratt, Judson 95
"The Presentation" 183
Presnell, Robert, Jr. 196
Price, Jack 147
Pritchard, Robert 47, 60, 81, 82, 103, 112
The Private Practice of Dr. Dana 1, 3, 15, 16, 133, 134, 135, 136, 137, 138, 139, 140, 141, 142, 143, 144, 145, 146
"A Problem in Murder" 149
"Problem Over Clothes" 154
"The Promise" 170
"Promise of Murder" 158
The Prudential Family Hour of Stars 161
"Psycho-Drama" 175
Pugh, Madelyn 13, 18
"Puppy Love, Mr. Barlow, and Miss Davis" 168
"The Pursuit of Death" 141
Putnam 112

Qualen, John 21
Quigley Publications 40
Quillan, Ed 147
Quillan, Joseph 145, 153, 154, 155, 156, 157, 158, 159, 160, 161, 162, 163, 164, 165, 167, 168, 169, 170, 171, 172, 173,

Index

175, 176, 177, 178, 179, 180, 181, 182, 183, 184, 185, 186, 187, 188
Quinn, Anthony (Tony) 69, 70, 71

Raaf, Vici 82, 86
Rackmil, Milton R. 26, 88
Rader, Alan 145, 146, 147, 148, 149, 151
Radio Life 3, 16
Radio Spirits 3
Raft, George 141
Ragan, Kirk 142
Ragaway, Martin 47
"The Railroad, Dam, and the Water Works" 184
The Railroad Hour 150
"Rain" 100
Rains, Bob 20, 24, 47, 52
The Ralph Brewster Singers 124
Rambeau, Marjorie 42
Rameau, Emil 46
Rand, Jess 36, 117
Randall, Meg 20, 42
Randall, Tony 111
Randolph, Isabel 182, 184, 185
"The Randolph Grey Case" 143
Random House 11
"Rare Black Orchid" 164
Raw Wind in Eden 28, 29, 32, 33, 107–109
Rawlinson, Herbert 136, 137, 142, 143, 146
Ray, Johnnie 125
"The Ray Wardell Case" 139
Rayel, Jack 195
Raymond, Gene 196
Raymond, Jack 48
The Razor's Edge 89, 147
Reagan, Ronald 12, 16, 30, 31, 136, 141
Red Ball Express 25, 65–67, 119
Red Cross Show 189
Red River 19, 153
"The Red, White, and Blue Pills" 181
"Red Wine" 152
Redmond, Liam 45
Reed, Alan 137, 138, 139, 140, 153, 158, 189
Reed, Donna 50, 143, 189
Reed, Gayle 64
Reed, Maxwell 56
Reed, Phillip 103
Reeves, Richard 85
Reeves, Theodore 16
Reid, Carl Benton 86, 89
Reilly, Betty 64
Reineck, William 115
Reis, Irving 20, 160

"Relentless" 142
Remington Rand 194
Remninger, Otto 186
Republic 125
"The Return of the Badmen" 182
"The Return to Dos Rios" 180
Return to Peyton Place 32, 120–121
Revue 36
Reynolds, Debbie 21, 30, 111, 190
Reynolds, William 2, 19, 35, 62, 63, 67, 91, 92
Rhine, Larry 137, 150
Rhodes, Ted 174, 175, 176
The Rhythmaires 126
Richards, Frank 142
Richardson, Henry 114
Richmond, Ted 60
Richter, Conrad 86
Riddle, Nelson 85
Ridgway, Suzanne 69
Ridout, Arthur 118
Riedel, Richard H. 62, 65, 91, 95, 106, 112
Rigney, Bill 34, 36
Riss, Dan 168
"The Rita Rowan Case" 136
Ritz, Al 93
Ritz, Harry 93
Ritz, Jimmy 93
The Ritz Brothers 93
"Rival Football" 158
Riviera (Las Vegas, Nev.) 27, 92
Rizzo, Carlo 51
RKO (Radio-Keith-Orpheum) 21, 25, 95, 125
RKO Pantages Theatre 23
"Roar of the River" 140
Robbins, Charles 7
Robbins, Laura Shapiro (aunt) 5, 7
The Robe 1, 12
Rober, Richard 51
Roberson, Chuck 75, 122
Roberts, Bart 73, 78
Roberts, Dorothy 144
Roberts, Kenny 87
Roberts, Lynne 64
Roberts, William 111
Robertson, Dale 54
Robinson, Casey 53
Robinson, Edward G. 20, 31, 35, 160
Robinson, Frances 132, 133, 135, 136, 137, 139, 140, 141, 144, 146, 147, 148, 154
Robinson, George 47, 85, 95
Robinson, Thelma 64
Robisa, Jane 55

Robson, William N. 136, 190
Rockwell, Robert 25
Rode, Fred J. 49, 54, 55
Rodgers, Richard 28
Rodriguez, Orlando 94
Rogers, Ginger 1, 15
Rogers, Jeanne 133
Rogers, John W. 57, 76
Rogers, Roy 190, 194
Rogers, Ted 138, 155
Rogue's Gallery 14, 41
Roland, Henry 166
Rolfe, Eric 137
Rolfe, Sam 94
Roman, Larry 86, 134, 140, 141, 142, 143, 144, 145
Romance 21
"Romantic Warfare" 172
Rome (Italy) 51, 108, 109
Rondell, Ronnie 51, 82, 87
Rooney, Mickey 35, 190
Rorke, Hayden 45, 53, 113
Rosa, Malia 55
Rose, David 24, 190
Rose, Edward M. 36, 37
Rose, Helen 111
Rose, Ralph 143, 144, 147
Rosen, Milton 65, 93
Rosenberg, Aaron 57, 65, 82, 87
Rosenman, Leonard 117
Roses Are Red 41–42
Roslyn (NY) 11, 198
Ross, Earle 135, 154
Rossen, Robert 40
Rourke, Jack 192
Rouse, Russell 115
Rousseau, William P. 139, 140, 141, 142, 143, 145, 149, 150, 157
Route 66 88
Roy, Billy 132, 135, 137
"The Roy St. John Case" 139
Rubin, Benny 78, 179
Rudley, Herbert 109
The Rugged O'Riordans 44–45
Ruggles, Ed 185, 186
Rush, Barbara 73
Russ-Field Corporation 83
Russell, Gail 103
Russell, Jane 82, 83, 84
Russell, Rosalind 158, 170
Ruysdael, Basil 49
Ryf, Robert 133, 134, 135, 136, 137, 138, 139, 140, 143

"Safety School Advisor" 159
St. Francisville (La.) 98
St. George, Charlie 40
St. Oegger, Joan 42, 45, 47, 51, 52, 56, 57, 59, 60, 64, 65, 67, 69, 71, 73, 75, 80, 82, 86, 87, 89, 91, 94, 95

Index

Sale, Richard 43
Salkow Agency 12, 14, 19
Salt Lake City (Ut.) 116
Salter, Hans J. 62, 75, 101, 107
Salvation Army 43
"The Sam Farnsworth Case" 136
"The Samuel Jessup Case" 133
San Bernadino (Calif.) 88
San Diego (Calif.) 20, 36, 47
Sande, Walter 71, 97
Sanders, Gene 197
Sanders, George 23
Sanderson, Ruth 42
Sands, John 54
"The Sandy Bartlett Case" 136
Santa Barbara (Calif.) 13
Santa Fe (New Mexico) 54
Santa Maria (Calif.) 69
Santa Monica Public Library (Santa Monica, Calif.) 2
Santos, Edmundo 85
Sanville, Richard 154, 157, 158
Saturday Review 197
Saunders, Bob 117
Savage, Carlos 84
Savo, Jimmy 10
Sawyer, Hal 147
Sawyer, Joe 41, 73
Saxon, John 117
Scalzo, Ralph 92
Scannell, Frank 103
Schaefer, George 119
Schaeffer, Chester W. 115
Schafer, Natalie 81
Schallert, William 101, 103
Scharf, Walter 42, 51
Schary, Dore 28, 196
Schelling, Charles 117
Schildkraut, Kitty Paris 7
Schiller, Bob 137, 150
Schindell, Cy 40
Schlesinger, Arthur, Jr. 31
Schneider, Joe 101
Schoengarth, Russell 53, 57, 81, 87, 107
"School on Saturday" 161
"The School Telephone Bill" 165
Schradermier, Bob 181, 182, 183, 184, 185
Schrager, Rudy 41
Schultz, Dutch *see* Flegenheimer, Arthur "Dutch Schultz"
Schwartz, Maurice 55
Schweiger, Joe 136
Scott, Dorothy 131
Scott, Janet 132, 134, 135, 137, 141, 146, 148
Scott, Lizabeth 16, 142, 188
Scott, Morton 39

Scott, Thelma 44, 45
Scott, Walter M. 120
Scourby, Alexander 64, 75
Screen Actors Guild (S.A.G.) 2, 16, 30, 31, 36, 37, 117, 121
Screen Album 26
The Screen Directors' Playhouse 20, 21, 160, 161, 166, 170, 172, 173
Screen Gems 119
Screen Guild Players 166, 171
Screen Guild Theater 179
Screen Producers Guild 26
Screenland 21
Scribner 87
Sealtest Variety Theater 146
Seattle (Wash.) 29
The Secret Heart 81, 147, 171
The Secret of Convict Lake 23
Sedan, Rolfe 142, 147
Seel, Charles 132, 133, 135, 157
Seiter, William A. 170
Selby, Sarah 166
Seligman, Selig J. 192, 193
"The Seminole Strip" 181
Sennett, Mack 48
Serafin, Enzo 107
Seton, Anya 82, 84
Shack, Sammy 40
Shadow of a Doubt 14, 131, 175
Shakespeare, William 11
Shamroy, Leon 54
Shane, Sara 75
"Shaner Maidel" 126
Shannon, Harry 39
Shapiro, Charles (uncle) 5, 7
Shapiro, George (uncle) 5, 6, 7
Shapiro, Laura *see* Robbins, Laura Shapiro
Shapiro, Lillian *see* Paris, Lillian Shapiro
Shapiro, Lionel S. B. 51, 52
Shapiro, Max (grandfather) 5, 6, 7, 8
Shapiro, Paul 6, 7
Shapiro, Sarah (grandmother) 5, 7
Shapiro, Shirley (aunt) 6, 7
Shapiro, Sophie (aunt) 5, 6, 7
Sharp, Phil 137, 150
Sharpe, Don W. 18, 19, 20, 21, 24
Sharpe, Norah 117
Shaw, Frank 45, 59, 63, 76, 89, 95
Shaw, Martha 175
Shaw, Reta 106
Shaw, Tom 51, 69, 73, 86, 91
Shearer, Harry 174
Sheehan, Howard J., Jr. 39, 41, 42
"The Shelby Withers Jr. Case" 134

Shelley, Barbara 118
Sherdeman, Ted 91, 95
Sheridan, Ann 22, 23, 79, 179
Sherin, Leo 132
Sherman, George 45, 62, 76
Sherman, Teddi 114
Sherwood, John 57, 75, 80
"Sh-h-h!" 177
Shields, Fred 186
Shipow, Emanuel 197
Shore, Dinah 190, 195
Shore, Lillian 96
"Should I" 128
Showalter, Max 121
Shrevelew, Max 9
Shutta, Jack 48
Sidney, George 99, 100
Siena (Italy) 51
Sierra Nevada 32
Sign of the Pagan 74–76
Siletti, Mario 101
Silva, Henry 2, 109, 110
Silver, David 101, 103, 105
Silver, Jeffrey 148, 160, 161, 177, 179
Silvera, Darrell 109
Silverheels, Jay 49, 62, 68, 76
Simmons, Floyd 91, 94
Simmons, Richard Alan 80
Simms, Eddie 57
Simon, Robert F. 82
Simonelli, Charles F. 88
Sinatra, Frank 24, 59, 60, 124, 128, 129, 142
Sinatra, Ray 27
Sincere, Jean 11, 12
Sing Sing 10, 18, 20
Singer, Stuffy 181
Singleton, Doris 157, 166
Siodmak, Robert 51
"Sirens of the Screen" 186
Sirk, Douglas 73, 74, 76
Sisenby, Dave 140
Sisk, Lewis 197
Six Bridges to Cross 26, 27, 87–89, 111, 123, 129
"Six-Gun Justice" 182
Skelton, Red 90
Skinner, Frank 45, 51, 52, 64, 65, 73, 75, 82, 86, 91
"The Skipper's Pants" 165
Sklover, Carl 59
Skouros, Spyros 35
Slezak, Walter 47
Sloane, Everett 55
"Slumming on Park Avenue" 180
"Smart Girl" 157
Smith, Alexis 72, 133
Smith, Bill 111
Smith, Charlie 179
Smith, Earl 135

Index

Smith, Jack 193
Smith, Jack Martin 120
Smith, Kent 16
Smith, Leonard 152, 153, 154, 155, 156, 157, 158, 159, 161, 162, 163, 164, 165, 166, 167, 170, 172, 173, 174, 178, 179, 181, 186, 187, 197
Smith, Paul 62, 94
Smith, Verne 146, 147, 148, 149, 150, 151, 152, 153, 154, 155, 156, 157, 158, 159, 160, 161, 162, 163, 164, 165, 166, 167, 168, 169, 170, 171, 172, 173
"Smoky" 132
Smuggler's Island 60–62
"Snake Doctor" 138
"Snodgrass Barbecue" 157
"The Snowball Dance" 176
Snowden, Eric 131
Snyder, Allan 54
Snyder, Howard 149
"So Big" 152
"Social Butterfly" 147
"Social Error" 157
"Somebody Loves Me" 128
Somlyo, E. T. 18
Son of Ali Baba 67–68
Song Hits 124, 125
"The Song of Roland" 157
"The Sophia Howard Case" 3, 137
Sorel, George 135
Space, Arthur 39, 78, 82, 91
Spain 115, 119
Spalla, Ermino 51
Spencer, Alfred E. 99
Spencer, Herbert 127, 128
Spencer, J. Dewitt 197
Spencer, Sarah 179
The Spencer-Hagen Orchestra 127
Sperling, Milton 32, 121, 122
Spire, William 131, 137
The Spoilers 89–91
Spring, Helen 150, 151
"Square Dance Troupe" 188
Stafford, Jo 192
"The Stag Party" 166
Stahl, Francis M. 122
Stallings, Charles 51
Stanford, Antony 132, 137, 150
Stanwyck, Barbara 15, 33, 132
"A Star Is Born" 167
Star of Tomorrow 41, 53, 59, 70, 75, 77, 84, 89, 93, 95, 100, 103, 111, 117
"The State Highway Patrolman Case" 145
"Stay as Sweet as You Are" 128
"Steel River Prison Break" 173
Stein, Herman 67, 106

Stein, Lotte 44
Stephens, Harvey 117
Stephens, Sheila Margo *see* MacRae, Sheila
Sterling, Jan 81, 167
Sterling, Robert 120
Stern, Leonard 47
Stern, Stewart 115
Steve Allen in Movieland 195
The Steve Allen Show 195–196
"The Steve Dana Case" 16, 146
Stevens, Leith 131
Stevens, Mark 147, 151
Stevenson, Bob 143, 144
Stevenson, Edward 54, 76
Stevenson, John 189
Stewart, Elaine 103
Stewart, James "Jimmy" 1, 14, 16, 49, 50, 98, 136, 151, 173
Stewart, Kay 189
Stine, Clifford 69
"Stolen Symphony" 166
Stollery, David 97
Stoloff, M. W. 40, 99
Stone, Anne 135, 173
Stone, Lewis 134
Storm, Gale 20, 42, 43
A Story of David 31, 118–119
"The Story of the Gambler and the Lady" 146
"The Story of the Man Who Liked the Mountains" 145
Strange, Glenn 53, 71
A Stranger in My Arms 29, 111–113
Strasberg, Susan 196
Stratton, Gil, Jr. 137, 139, 143, 151, 179
"The Street with No Name" 151
"Stretch Has a Problem" 152
"Stretch Is Ineligible for Basketball Team" 152
"Stretch Snodgrass is in Love" 166
"Stretch Wins Yodar Kritch Award for English" 171
"Stretch's Manager, Walter Denton" 178
Strickland, Amzie 97
Stricklyn, Ray 117
"Strictly Amateurs" 135
Stromberg, Hunt 12
Stromberg, Hunt, Jr. 192, 193
Stuart, Gilchrist 46
Stuart, Kerry 197
Stuart, Randall 81
"Student Government Day" 151
Studio City (Calif.) 25
Suarez, Rafael 84
Sullivan, Barry 167
Sully, Frank 89

The Summer Comedy Hour 193–194
"Sunnydale Finishing School" 149
"Surprise Party for Mr. Boynton" 186
"The Surprise Party" 147
"The Surprise Wedding Anniversary" 146
Surrey, Berne 134
Suspense 18, 25, 131, 137, 171, 173, 175, 188, 189, 190
Sutton, John 69
Sweeney, Alfred 71, 89, 101
Sweeney, Bob 162, 179, 180, 181, 184, 187
Swift, Dave 169
"The Swiss Chrono-Mono-Thing" 145
Sword in the Desert 19, 20, 23, 33, 43, 45–47, 52, 118
Sydney, Basil 118
Syndicated 133, 134, 135, 136, 137, 138, 139, 140, 141, 142, 143, 144, 145, 146, 148, 149, 150, 154, 157, 158, 164, 165, 172, 180, 181, 182, 183, 184, 185, 189, 190

"T-Men" 139
Tacey Cromwell 86
"Tall, Dark and French" 149
The Tattered Dress 103–105
"Taxidermy" 155
Taylor, Elizabeth 31, 83
Taylor, George 173
Taylor, Glenhall 146
Taylor, Robert 31, 135
Taylor, Ross 152
Taylor, Vaughn 59, 117
Taza, Son of Cochise 72–74
Tcherina, Ludmilla 74, 75, 76
"Tea Leaves" 163
Tedrow, Irene 160
"Telegram for Mrs. Davis" 156
Tell It Again 143, 144, 147
"Tell Me" 127
Tello, Luis Sanchez 84
Temple, Alvina 132, 143
Temple, Brooke 140
Temple, Isaiah 35
Temple, Shirley 26, 39, 44, 192
Ten Seconds to Hell 113–115
Tennessee Jed 14
Terry, Joy 188
"Tex Barton, Basketball Star" 169
Texas 118
"Thanksgiving Mix-up" 160
"That Old Black Magic" 59, 180, 192
That's a Good Idea 13

229

Index

"That's All She's Waiting to Hear" 124–125
"Theodore Roosevelt" 134
"There Goes My Heart" 195
Thomas, Bill 56, 57, 59, 60, 64, 68, 69, 71, 75, 82, 86, 89, 101, 106, 112
Thomas, Danny 192
Thomas, Gilbert 173
Thompson, Carlos 107
Thompson, D. J. 168
Thompson, Dee J. 106
Thompson, Dorothy 198
Thompson, Edward 97
Thompson, Glenn 75
Thoms, Jerome 99
Thorne, Conway (Tex) *see* Chandler, Jeff
Thorsness, Cliff 163, 164
Thousand Oaks (Calif.) 3
"Three Gifts from Mr. Boynton" 178
"Three Wise Fools" 134
Thunder in the Sun 29, 115–116
"Thunder Over Texas" 185
Tinling, James 41, 42
"To You" 127
Tobias, George 16, 103
Tobin, Dan 165, 186, 188
"Tod Ford" 180
Todd, Sherman 106
Todman, Bill 194
Tom and Jerry 137
Tomack, Sid 42
Tomlinson, Everett 173
Tomlinson, Tommy 15
Tomorrow Is Forever 21, 161
"The Tony Garabaldi Case" 145
Toomey, Regis 62 170
Topete, Manuel 84
Tor, Michail 51
Toren, Marta 20, 21, 23, 45, 46, 51, 52, 84
Torme, Mel 127
Torrey, Roger 117
Torvay, Jose 85
Totter, Audrey 170, 177
Townsend, Genevieve 197
Toy Tiger 95–96
Tracy, Spencer 31
Tracy, Sterling 15, 133, 134, 135, 136, 137, 138, 139, 140, 141, 142, 143, 144, 145, 146, 157, 173
"Traffic Ticket" 164
Traubner, Ed 35, 36
Travilla 55
Trevor, Claire 142
The Trojan Horse 11, 197–198
Trosper, Guy 115
Trotter, John Scott 195

"Trouble with Miss Enright" 166
Trout, Dink 144, 146
Truman, Harry S 191
Tsiang, H. T. 60
Tucker, Richard 196
Tully, Richard Walton 55
Tully, Tom 168
"Turkey Dinner" 166
Turner, Lana 1, 83, 105, 106
Turpin, Helen 120
Tuttle, Lurene 131, 148
Tuttle, William 111
TV Guide 2
Twain, Mark 130
20th Century–Fox 1, 13, 16, 22, 23, 30, 35, 39, 41, 43, 44, 48, 49, 50, 53, 54, 55, 117, 120, 127
Two Flags West 1, 23, 53–55, 127
"Two Thousand Simoleons" 185
"Two-Way Doublecross" 133
"Two Years Before the Mast" 135
Tyler, Beverly 62
Tyne, George 45

U-A *see* United Artists
UCLA 34
U-I *see* Universal-International
"Uncle Ben's Widow" 146
"Under the Oak Tree" 186
Undercurrent 15, 135
"Underground Gambling Ring" 178
Unicombe, John 44
United Artists 1, 96, 97, 113, 114
United Cerebral Palsy Telethon 192
United Nations 31, 196
United Service Organizations (USO) 12, 92
Universal City (Calif.) 88
Universal-International 1, 13, 15, 19, 20, 21, 22, 23, 24, 25, 26, 27, 28, 30, 33, 35, 42, 43, 44, 46, 47, 48, 50, 51, 52, 53, 55, 56, 57, 58, 59, 60, 61, 62, 63, 64, 65, 66, 67, 68, 69, 70, 71, 72, 73, 74, 75, 76, 77, 78, 79, 80, 81, 82, 83, 84, 85, 86, 87, 88, 89, 90, 91, 92, 93, 95, 96, 97, 100, 101, 102, 103, 104, 105, 106, 107, 108, 110, 111, 112, 113, 118, 124, 125, 127, 191, 192, 194, 195
Universal Pictures 45, 48, 67, 94
"Up in Smoke" 182

USO *see* United Service Organizations
Utah 31, 62, 73

Vaccarino, Maurice 41
"Valentine's Day Show" 162
"The Valerie Carter Case" 139
"The Valley of Lawless Men" 183
"Valley of the Varmints" 185
Valli, Alida 142
Van, Bobby 194
Van, Frankie 58, 191
Van Antwerp, Albert 140
Vander Pyl, Jean 141
Van Doren, Mamie 25, 78, 79
Van Eyssen, John 118
Van Horn, James 73
Van Marter, George 96
Van Nostrand, Jack 158
Van Rooten, Luis 135, 136
Van Zandt, Phillip 67
Vargas, Pedrito 85
Variety 1, 2, 22, 30, 31, 40, 41, 42, 43, 44, 45, 47, 48, 50, 52, 53, 54, 56, 57, 59, 60, 62, 63, 65, 66, 68, 69, 71, 72, 73, 75, 78, 79, 81, 84, 85, 87, 89, 91, 92, 95, 96, 98, 100, 102, 104, 106, 109, 110, 111, 113, 114, 116, 118, 119, 121, 122, 125, 126, 127, 128, 129
Velazquez, Andres 84
Venice (Calif.) 23
Ventura, Mary Ann 55
Verdera, Claire 132
Vernon, Glen 170
Victor, David 167
Victor, Jarl 91
Viebrock, John 197
Vigran, Herb 132, 147, 151, 166, 171
Vilna (Russia) 5
Vincent, June 131
Vincent, Romo 81
Virgin Islands 27, 92
Vitale, Joseph 68
Vogel, Virgil W. 59, 64, 67, 69, 78
Volkie, Ralph 40
von Eltz, Theodore 146, 189
von Mizener, Angela 35
Von Zell, Harry 54
Vonn, Veda 145
Votrian, Peter 179
Votrian, Ralph 94
The Voyage of the Scarlet Queen 137

Wagner, Karel 87, 129
Wagner, Murray 133, 134
Walburn, Raymond 89

Index

Walcott, Joe 191
Wald, Jerry 120, 121
Waldis, Otto 55, 175
Waldo, Janet 149
Walker, Clint 36
Walker, Ray 85
"Walking My Baby Back Home" 179
Wallace, Helen 97
Wallace, Regina 141, 147, 151
Wallach, Eli 8
Waller, Eddy C. 82
Wallington, James 132
Walsh, Bill 84
Walsh, Pat 147, 148, 149, 150, 151, 152, 153, 154, 155, 156, 157, 158, 159, 160, 161, 162, 163, 164, 165, 166, 167, 168, 169, 170, 171, 172, 173, 174, 175, 176, 177, 178, 179, 180, 181, 182, 183, 184, 185, 186, 187, 188
Walt Disney Productions 30
"Walter Denton's Editorial" 161
"Walter Gets Expelled" 182
Walters, Marie 44
"Walter's Wonderful Radio" 165
War Arrow 33, 76–78
Warburton, John 69
Ward, E. Clayton 44
Warm and Easy 128–129
Warner, Jack L. 26
Warner, Les 59
Warner Bros. 2, 11, 12, 13, 15, 16, 22, 25, 30, 33, 36, 38, 40, 94, 121, 122, 125
Warren, Earl 32
Warren, Katherine 67
Washington, D.C. 32
Washington, Ned 100
Waterman, Willard 151, 153, 163, 164
Wattis, Richard 114
Waxman, Franz 120
Waxman, Stanley 133, 143, 180
"The Way of the Cross" 189
Wayne, Artie 190
Wayne, Billy 64, 85
Wayne, David 167
Wayne, John 19, 30, 33, 70, 94, 153, 194
Wayne, Ken 44
"We Hold These Truths" 180
Weatherwax, Paul 89
Weaver, Dennis 76
"The Web" 188
Webb, Clifton 26, 44
Webb, J. Watson, Jr. 49
Webb, Jack 133, 140, 141, 142, 143, 145, 146, 149, 150, 157, 190, 192

Webb, Jane 151
Webber, Peggy 136
Wedlock, Hugh 149
Weems, Ted 93
"Weenie-Roast Chaperone" 144
Weil, Jeri 64
Weinberg, Roger 117
Weintraub, Murray 14
Welch, Jim 91
"Welcome Stranger" 127
Weld, Tuesday 121
Welles, Orson 1, 21, 101, 102, 107
Wentworth, Martha 131, 188
Wescoatt, Rusty 75
Westbrook, Nancy 69
Westerfield, James 91, 117
Westmore, Bud 42, 45, 47, 51, 53, 56, 57, 59, 60, 64, 65, 67, 68, 69, 71, 73, 75, 76, 80, 82, 86, 87, 89, 91, 94, 95, 101, 103, 106, 107, 112
Weston, Paul 24, 192
What's My Line? 26, 194
Wheeler, Lyle 43, 48, 54, 55
"When Spring Comes" 126
"Where Am I" 127
The Whistler 146, 154, 157
White, Byron "Whizzer" 31, 32
White, Jimmy 44
White, Lester 148, 149, 151, 152, 153, 154, 155, 156, 157, 158, 159, 160, 161, 162, 163, 164
Whitfield, Anne 144, 182
Whitfield, Smoki 86
Whitley, June 132, 135, 137, 138, 141, 147, 171
Whitney, Peter 71
"Whoopee" 150
Who's Who in Hollywood 21, 38
"Why Is Everybody Arguing?" 155
Widmark, Richard 16, 27, 110, 138, 151, 194
Widom, Bud 132, 137
Wilde, Cornel 27, 54, 141
Wilder, Robert 111, 112
Wilkerson, Billy 49
Wilkerson, Guy 82
Wilkinson, Dudley 65
Wilkinson, Frank H. 94
"Will Connie Resign?" 156
Williams, Esther 2, 14, 28, 29, 31, 32, 33, 35, 107, 108, 109
Williams, Grant 91
Williams, Jack C. 122
Williams, Rhoda 147
Williams, Rod 91
Willock, Dave 114
Wills, Henry 92
Wilson, Eileen 50
Wilson, Elizabeth 107

Wilson, Frank 131
Wilson, Harry 48
Wilson, Meredith 153
Wilson, Ralph 176, 177
Wilson, Richard 107
Wilson, Sam 122
Wilson, Ted 195
Wilson, Terry 94
Winchell, Walter 191
Windsor, Marie 137, 138, 141, 148
"The Winifred Whitehead Case" 138
Winslow, Barbara 197
Winslowe, Paula 188, 189
Winston, Irene 139, 140
"Winter Carnival at Crystal Lake" 162
Winters, Shelley 21, 31, 35, 59, 84, 147
Wise, Robert 53
"The Wishing Well School Dance" 155
"With Cradle and Clock" 131
"With My Eyes Wide Open I'm Dreaming" 127
Withers, Fleurette 197
Wolfe, David 46
Wolff, Nat 133, 158
Wood, Bertram 197
Wood, Natalie 86
Wood, Yvonne 42, 53
Woods, Donald 150
"The Woodsman" 180
Woodson, William 188
Woodward, Joanne 196
Woolf, Charles 137
"Working in the Stockroom" 152
World Series 26
World War II 5, 11, 12, 106, 114, 122
Worlock, Frederic 132
Worth, Frank 167
Wray, Fay 192
Wright, Ben 141, 188
Wright, Will 170
Writers Guild of America 50, 121
Wurtzel, Paul 39
Wurtzel, Sam 54
Wurtzel, Sol M. 39, 41
Wyatt, Jane 173
Wyldeck, Martin 118
Wyler, William 28, 29
Wyman, Jane 12, 16, 79, 133, 136, 138, 148, 189
Wyman, Steve 76
Wynters, Charlotte 82

Yale 8
Yale, Frankie 9

Index

Yankee Buccaneer 68–69
Yankee Pasha 25, 33, 78–79, 193
Yarborough, Barton 157, 173
Ybarra, Alfred 107
"The Yearling" 138
"You and I" 127
"You Gotta Stay Happy" 151
"You Made Me Love You" 179
You Were Meant for Me 50, 143
Young, Alan 44, 146
Young, Bob 137
Young, Carleton 189

Young, Clifton 42
Young, David 135
Young, Lee 85
Young, Loretta 1, 16, 23, 64, 65, 137, 161, 189
Young, Robert 142, 194
Young, Victor 24, 81, 87, 123, 124, 128
"Young Mr. Lincoln" 131
"You're a Sweet Little Headache" 128
Yurka, Blanche 115

The Zane Grey Show 14
Zanuck, Darryl F. 26, 50, 54
Zazueta, Enriqueta 85
Zeisler, Alfred 55
Zimbalist, Sam 28
Zimmerman, Harry 133
Zoller, Jack 131
Zuckerman, George 57, 73, 103
Zugsmith, Albert 80, 101, 103

www.ingramcontent.com/pod-product-compliance
Ingram Content Group UK Ltd.
Pitfield, Milton Keynes, MK11 3LW, UK
UKHW050532150426
5217IPUK00026B/1898